PRECARIOUS DEMOCRACY

PRECARIOUS DEMOCRACY

Ethnographies of Hope, Despair, and Resistance in Brazil

EDITED BY
BENJAMIN JUNGE, SEAN T. MITCHELL,
ALVARO JARRÍN, AND LUCIA CANTERO

Rutgers University Press
New Brunswick, Camden, and Newark, New Jersey, and London

Library of Congress Cataloging-in-Publication Data

Names: Junge, Benjamin, editor. | Mitchell, Sean T., editor. | Jarrín, Alvaro, 1980– editor. | Cantero, Lucia, editor.
Title: Precarious democracy : ethnographies of hope, despair, and resistance in Brazil / edited by Benjamin Junge, Sean T. Mitchell, Alvaro Jarrín, and Lucia Cantero.
Description: New Brunswick : Rutgers University Press, [2021] | Includes bibliographical references and index.
Identifiers: LCCN 2020053254 | ISBN 9781978825666 (cloth) | ISBN 9781978825659 (paperback) | ISBN 9781978825673 (epub) | ISBN 9781978825697 (pdf)
Subjects: LCSH: Social movements—Brazil—History—21st century. | Ethnology—Brazil. | Brazil—Social conditions—1985– | Brazil—Politics and government—2003–
Classification: LCC HN283.5 .P734 2021 | DDC 306.0981—dc23
LC record available at https://lccn.loc.gov/2020053254

A British Cataloging-in-Publication record for this book is available from the British Library.

This collection copyright © 2021 by Rutgers, The State University of New Jersey
Individual chapters copyright © 2021 in the names of their authors
All rights reserved
No part of this book may be reproduced or utilized in any form or by any means, electronic or mechanical, or by any information storage and retrieval system, without written permission from the publisher. Please contact Rutgers University Press, 106 Somerset Street, New Brunswick, NJ 08901. The only exception to this prohibition is "fair use" as defined by U.S. copyright law.

∞ The paper used in this publication meets the requirements of the American National Standard for Information Sciences—Permanence of Paper for Printed Library Materials, ANSI Z39.48-1992.

www.rutgersuniversitypress.org

Manufactured in the United States of America

References to internet websites (URLs) were accurate at the time of writing. Neither the author nor Rutgers University Press is responsible for URLs that may have expired or changed since the manuscript was prepared.

For John Burdick (1959–2020), who showed us what collaborative, antiracist, and feminist ethnography looks like, in Brazil and beyond

CONTENTS

List of Acronyms — ix

Introduction: Ethnographies of the Brazilian Unraveling — 1
BENJAMIN JUNGE, ALVARO JARRÍN, LUCIA CANTERO, AND SEAN T. MITCHELL

Critical Overview: A Plan for a Country Still Looking for Democracy — 13
LILIA MORITZ SCHWARCZ

PART I: THE INTIMACY OF POWER

1 "Family Is Everything": Generational Tensions as a Working-Class Household from Recife, Brazil, Contemplates the 2018 Presidential Elections — 25
BENJAMIN JUNGE

2 Among Mothers and Daughters: Economic Mobility and Political Identity in a Northeastern *Periferia* — 38
JESSICA JEROME

3 Dreaming with Guns: Performing Masculinity and Imagining Consumption in Bolsonaro's Brazil — 50
ISABELA KALIL, ROSANA PINHEIRO-MACHADO, AND LUCIA MURY SCALCO

4 Whiteness Has Come Out of the Closet and Intensified Brazil's Reactionary Wave — 62
PATRICIA DE SANTANA PINHO

PART II: CORRUPTION AND CRIME

5 Cruel Pessimism: The Affect of Anticorruption and the End of the New Brazilian Middle Class — 79
SEAN T. MITCHELL

6 The Effects of Some Religious Affects: Revolutions in Crime — 91
KARINA BIONDI

7 "Look at That": Cures, Poisons, and Shifting Rationalities in the Backlands That Have Become a Sea (of Money) — 103
JOHN F. COLLINS

8   "The Oil Is Ours": Petro-Affect and the Scandalization of Politics   116
    LUCIA CANTERO

    PART III: INFRASTRUCTURES OF HOPE

9   Despairing Hopes (and Hopeful Despair) in Amazonia   129
    DAVID ROJAS, ALEXANDRE DE AZEVEDO OLIVAL,
    AND ANDREZZA ALVES SPEXOTO OLIVAL

10 Tempered Hopes: (Re)producing the Middle Class in Recife's
    Alternative Music Scene   142
    FALINA ENRIQUEZ

11 Withering Dreams: Material Hope and Apathy
    among Brazil's Once-Rising Poor   155
    MOISÉS KOPPER

12 Bolsonaro Wins Japan: Support for the Far Right
    among Japanese Brazilian Overseas Labor Migrants   169
    SARAH LEBARON VON BAEYER

    PART IV: OLD CHALLENGES, NEW ACTIVISM

13 Holding the Wave: Black LGBTI+ Feminist Resilience
    amid the Reactionary Turn in Rio de Janeiro   183
    LASHANDRA SULLIVAN

14 LGBTTI Elders in Brazil: Subjectivation and Narratives
    about Resilience, Resistance, and Vulnerability   195
    CARLOS EDUARDO HENNING

15 Disgust and Defiance: The Visceral Politics of Trans and
    Travesti Activism amid a Heteronormative Backlash   206
    ALVARO JARRÍN

16 "Barbie e Ken Cidadãos de Bem": Memes and Political
    Participation among College Students in Brazil   218
    MELANIE A. MEDEIROS, PATRICK MCCORMICK,
    ERIKA SCHMITT, AND JAMES KALE

    Acknowledgments   233
    Notes on Contributors   235
    Index   239

ACRONYMS

BBB	*Bala, Boi e Bíblia.* Bullets, Bulls, and Bibles (a conservative voting bloc in the Brazilian Congress)
BOVESPA	*Bolsa de Valores de São Paulo.* São Paulo's stock market
BRICS	Brazil, Russia, India, China, and South Africa (five major emerging national economies)
DEM	*Partido Democratas.* Democrats party
FIES	*Fundo de Financiamento ao Estudante do Ensino Superior.* Fellowship Fund for Students within Higher Education
IBGE	*Instituto Brasileiro de Geografia e Estatística.* Brazilian Institute of Geography and Statistics
IBRAT	*Instituto Brasileiro de Transmasculinidades.* Brazilian Institute of Transmasculinities
IMF	International Monetary Fund
IOV	*Instituto Ouro Verde.* Ouro Verde Institute, a sustainable development NGO
IPO	Initial public offering
LARP	Live-action role-playing game
LGBTTI	*Lésbica, gay, bissexual, travesti, trans e intersexual.* Lesbian, gay, bisexual, travesti, trans, and intersex
LpT	*Luz para Todos.* Light for Everyone (government electrification program)
MCMV	*Minha Casa Minha Vida.* My House, My Life (government housing program)
MDB	See PMDB
MEI	*Microempreendedor Individual.* Individual Microentrepreneur
MPF	*Ministério Público Federal.* Public Prosecutor's Office
MST	*Movimento dos Trabalhadores Rurais Sem Terra.* Landless Rural Workers' Movement
MTST	*Movimento dos Trabalhadores Sem Teto.* Homeless Workers' Movement
NGO	Nongovernmental organization
PAC	*Programa de Aceleração do Crescimento.* Growth Acceleration Program
PCB	*Partido Comunista Brasileiro.* Brazilian Communist Party
PCC	*Primeiro Comando da Capital.* First Command of the Capital (a criminal cartel)
PMBA	*Polícia Militar da Bahia.* Bahia's military police
PMDB	*Partido do Movimento Democrático Brasileiro.* Party of the Brazilian Democratic Movement (1965–1979 and again, since 2017, the acronym MDB is used)
PRONAF	*Programa Nacional de Fortalecimento da Agricultura Familiar.* National Program for Strengthening Family Agriculture
PROUNI	*Programa Universidade Para Todos.* University for Everyone program
PSL	*Partido Social Liberal.* Social Liberal Party
PSOL	*Partido Socialismo e Liberdade.* Socialism and Liberty Party
PT	*Partido dos Trabalhadores.* Workers' Party
RENFA	*Rede Nacional de Feministas Anti-Prohibicionistas.* National Feminist Network against the War on Drugs
SBT	*Sistema Brasileiro de Televisão.* Brazilian System of Television (Brazilian TV network)

SIC	*Sistema de Incentivo à Cultura.* System of Cultural Incentives
STF	*Supremo Tribunal Federal.* Supreme Federal Court
SUS	*Sistema Único de Saúde.* Unified Health System (Brazil's publicly funded health care system)
UCSC	University of California, Santa Cruz
UOL	*Universo Online.* Online Universe (Brazilian internet content provider)

PRECARIOUS DEMOCRACY

INTRODUCTION
Ethnographies of the Brazilian Unraveling

BENJAMIN JUNGE, ALVARO JARRÍN, LUCIA CANTERO,
AND SEAN T. MITCHELL

Writing in mid-2021, with Brazil in the grips of the devastating COVID-19 pandemic,[1] it is difficult to find words to depict—let alone account for—the extraordinary transformations to the country's political, economic, and affective landscapes that characterize the past decade. Even before the virus emerged and began ravaging Brazil, those transformations were devastatingly manifest. Circa 2010, Brazil seemed poised to become a global economic and political power, and the country was hailed worldwide as an example of successful progressive governance. During the two-term presidency of Luiz Inácio Lula da Silva (hereafter, "Lula") of the leftist Workers' Party (Partido dos Trabalhadores; PT), from 2003 to 2010, some thirty million people had exited poverty (Neri 2014), as the poor and working classes saw an enormous expansion of opportunities for educational, economic, and geographic mobility. When Lula completed his second term in office in 2010, he had an 87 percent approval rating and was widely credited for having steered the country around the global economic crisis. On these laurels, many pundits assumed that the next decade would bring continued reduction of poverty and inequality and a deepening of progressive governance to this brutally unequal nation. And indeed, the overall economic trends characterizing the Lula years continued during the first term of Lula's PT successor, Dilma Rousseff (2010–2014).

Brazil rose to become the world's sixth-largest economy in 2012 (Inman 2012), and the nation's rising international status seemed cemented when Brazil was confirmed to host two sporting mega events: the 2014 World Cup and the 2016 Summer Olympics. In the summer of 2009, when Rio de Janeiro was awarded the bid to host the 2016 Summer Olympics, Mayor Eduardo Paes erected a gargantuan diamond screen on Copacabana Beach so that Cariocas (Rio residents) could follow the results of the International Olympic Committee's deliberations live. When the announcement came—with Brazil beating out Chicago, Madrid, and Tokyo—more than one hundred thousand attendees, clad in yellow-and-green "Brasil" T-shirts, erupted in ecstatic jubilation. The owner of a nearby beauty salon, Ana Paula, expressed her elation as follows, "I can't even tell you how happy I am! When I heard the news about the win, that the judges in Copenhagen are going to give us, the Third World, a chance to put on a good show, everyone at the salon began to celebrate! And if we finally show the world how great Brazil, and this 'marvelous city' is, then we will finally be a modern nation. I'm ready to enter the First World, and I hope all of Rio's ugliness gets the chance for a makeover" (Cantero 2015). Note the anticipatory elation and the strong optimism for the future embodied in Paula's statement—almost unthinkable a decade later. What we were witnessing in 2009 was the affective engagement of individuals within a community of feeling mediated by forms of mass communication, which allowed them to share in an outpouring of optimism for the nation.

While Brazil's successes at the time were real, a range of then-submerged social antagonisms have now become devastatingly apparent. The rising fortunes of the poor and working classes under PT governance threatened the established position and prestige for elites and middle classes in the established class hierarchy. Simultaneously, the rising profile of LGBTQ+, feminist, Black, and Indigenous movements increasingly provoked sometimes vicious forms of conservative backlash. Additionally, the waning of the commodities boom that was fueled by Chinese demand (Lyons and Kiernan 2015) revealed certain structural limits of the PT-era growth model, precipitating economic crisis and emboldening opponents of the PT. Meanwhile, even in the midst of poverty reduction, long-standing problems of crime, political corruption, deficient public services, and environmental destruction fueled popular discontent. All this created opportunities for conservative political and religious actors that had been organizing, growing, and cementing international alliances during the long period of left-wing governance.

Precarious Democracy examines how Brazilians from diverse walks of life have experienced and responded to economic precarity, political crisis, and diminishing hopes for the future from 2013 to 2019—a pivotal period in Brazilian history, bookended by the explosion of massive protests across the country in 2013 and the first year in office of hard-right president Jair Bolsonaro (2019). As our chapters show, these were years of not only deepening cynicism about institutional politics but also new forms of hope and resistance with transformative promise for the future.

More than a decade after the optimism of 2009, Brazil looks radically different. Even before the COVID-19 pandemic, many of the social gains of the previous decade had been dismantled. Brazil's economy had sunk to ninth place globally in terms of gross domestic product (GDP; IMF 2019), and 4.5 million people fell into extreme poverty (IBGE 2019). Moreover, in 2019, Brazil became the democratic country with the world's highest concentration of income among the top 1 percent (Canzian and Mena 2019). Few now view Brazil as a formidable emerging international power, despite its planetary environmental significance. Between April 2018 and November 2019, Lula was imprisoned under politically motivated charges to remove him from running in the presidential election for which he was leading the polls, as leaked chats among the presiding judge and prosecutor reveal (Greenwald and Pougy 2019a). And crucially, riven by violent political polarization, Brazil has seen the rise of a vast far-right movement—capable of marshaling massive political and electoral support, somewhat paradoxically, even among those populations who most benefited under PT governments (Kalil 2018).

Let's juxtapose Ana Paula's 2009 expression of elation—typical of that bygone optimistic era—with the 2018 sentiments of an Uber driver from Recife, Clodoaldo. His words are exemplary of the sentiments that dominate the era in which we publish this book. Reflecting on the rapidly approaching presidential elections, which would pit PT candidate Fernando Haddad against Jair Bolsonaro, Clodoaldo exclaimed, "Our country no longer needs democracy, it needs order. Then you'll say 'Who would you vote for?' Man, I'd vote for the crazy Bolsonaro. I think that the military regime isn't like we're thinking it's going to be. I think there's going to be order. It's a matter of respect, man. Respect the teachers, respect everything and everyone" (Junge and Prado 2020). Here optimism is replaced with a strong desire for law, order, and traditional hierarchies, expressed as an aspirational nostalgia for Brazil's 1964–1985 military regime. Of course, such conservative nostalgia was hardly new in the Brazil of 2009. But what had been a somewhat marginal, even stigmatized point of view in 2009 became a pervasive national mood less than a decade later.

There has been a remarkable shift not only in Brazilian politics but also in how Brazilians feel about their nation, with many fearing it is imperiled and pining for an imagined past that was more orderly. In 2009, during what seemed to be an increasingly successful democratization process that followed the dictatorship, few of us could have imagined that by 2018, the fantasy of returning to that period of authoritarianism and political torture would make such a potent comeback (Atencio 2014; Cowan 2016a). Without oversimplifying the diversity of sentiment that is always present in such a vast, diverse, and unequal country as Brazil, this volume seeks to trace ethnographically how overwhelming national optimism for so much of Brazil's population was so dramatically supplanted by darker cultural moods.

BRAZIL'S REVERSAL OF FORTUNE

This book provides ethnographic perspectives on a pivotal period in Brazilian history (2013–2019), yet one that does not easily fit into simple binary narratives about the period (e.g., Frazão 2018). From the massive nationwide protests that broke out in 2013—under PT president Dilma Rousseff—to the post-Rousseff-impeachment presidency of Michel Temer (2016–2018), this period is sometimes subsumed under a reductive narrative of an epochal pendulum swing from the left-wing governance of the PT to the far-right governance of Bolsonaro. But the forces that made Bolsonaro's presidency possible were gathered in the much more ideologically ambiguous period that this book explores.

It may be useful to the reader to map out some key elements in this historical progression. The global economic crisis of 2007–2008 seemed not to touch Brazil, in part due to the Lula administration's effective reliance on Keynesian countercyclical spending. The first indication to many national and international observers that something might be amiss was the explosion of protests across Brazil in June 2013. Those protests began with grassroots demands for free bus fares and for public services on par with those being produced for upcoming sporting mega events, but the mobilizations were pushed by elite media and political institutions to increasingly conservative ends (Mitchell 2014).

A severe economic crisis finally hit shortly before the 2014 elections, and as corruption scandals and right-wing political movements were featured prominently in the media, many of the country's elites abandoned the PT and began to look for alternatives that would protect their interests (Souza 2017). Still, bolstered by the continuing support of Brazil's poor and by voters in the northeast region, incumbent PT president Dilma Rousseff won a tight reelection in 2014. The losing center-right challenger, Aécio Neves, denied the validity of the election results. He and other conservative actors—particularly the dominant conservative media conglomerate Rede Globo—availed themselves of those protest movements to challenge the legitimacy of the reelected PT president. Massive counterprotests in favor of Rousseff also took off, and the country became increasingly polarized between PT supporters and detractors. The chapters in this volume explore the chaos, political uncertainty, and economic precarity that seemed to deepen each month during this tense period.

As the economy was faltering, a vast corruption scheme involving Brazil's political parties and its major corporations came to light, and a sprawling "anticorruption" case, Lava Jato (Operation Car Wash), was used to take down the PT government. It has been made clear from leaks reported on by the *Intercept Brasil* and *Agência pública* that corruption investigations in Brazil at the time were principally aimed at the PT and that the U.S. government was covertly but deeply involved in this process—with further echoes of 1964 (Viana and Neves 2020). And it is far from certain that the PT was more culpable than other parties for corruption. In fact, those leaks have shown the case's chief prosecutor, Deltan Dallagnol, and chief judge, Sergio Moro, to have illegally conspired to protect former president Fernando Henrique Cardoso because he was an important political ally

(Martins et al. 2019). Still, this conjuncture led to the soft-coup impeachment of Dilma Rousseff, to the two-year presidency of the ideologically ambiguous and opportunistic career politician Michel Temer, and to the imprisonment of 2018 presidential front-runner Lula, facilitating the election of Bolsonaro. Moro was appointed minister of justice in the incoming Bolsonaro administration, a position he would leave after breaking with the Bolsonaro government a year and a half later.

Bolsonaro emerged as a figure of national political significance under Temer's presidency. Yet the Temer period doesn't easily fit prevailing narratives: He was Rousseff's vice president, brought in because the PT needed the support of his (then) massive Party of the Brazilian Democratic Movement (Partido do Movimento Democrático Brasileiro; PMDB), in order to pass legislation. So for defenders of the PT, Temer's presence signals the sordid nature of these politics. For defenders of Bolsonaro's purifying right-wing politics, on the other hand, the Temer period muddies the easy moralistic narrative of victory over leftist depravity.

Temer was Dilma's vice president, but he was ideologically closer to his presidential successor than to his predecessor. Indeed, Temer has said that he voted for Bolsonaro, and his policies of austerity, privatization, and realignment of Brazil with the United States and away from the so-called BRICS nations (Russia, India, South Africa, and China) were much more consonant with those of Bolsonaro than with anything that was part of the PT platform.

The chapters in this book chronicle a period of increasing democratic and economic precarity, and the defeat of progressive governance, and yet it was also a period of renewed activism, resistance, and hope—and of forms of violence that sought to silence those voices. This period saw the largest general strike in Brazilian history, mobilized against Temer's government (Perrin 2017). And this period also witnessed the assassination of the Afro-Brazilian, bisexual, socialist, city councilwoman from Rio de Janeiro, Marielle Franco. But that very assassination was the result of her influential critique of police violence and of the police's alliances with paramilitaries. At the same time, it was during this period that Franco became a potent symbol of resistance for Black, feminist, and LGBTQ+ activist groups seeking to reorganize themselves in the face of the conservative backlash and find new forms of activism (see chapters by Jarrín and Sullivan, this volume).

This is a brief outline of Brazil's unraveling in the past decade, sketched here to give some wide-angle context for the rich ethnographic accounts in the pages that follow. At a still wider angle, we note the commonalities of Brazil's recent political-economic trajectory with that of many other Latin American countries during this period. Brazil's period of left-leaning governance and export-led growth was coincident with similar trends across the region, as are its more recent economic decline and turn to the right. After long Cold War and post–Cold War periods in which much national policy making in Latin America was dominated by the imperatives of Washington, the twenty-first century saw the rise of leftist governments across the region, from Argentina to Honduras, a process often referred to as the "pink tide." Benefiting from commodity-fueled economic growth—and perhaps from Washington's focus on its disastrous Middle East wars—these governments experimented with novel forms of redistribution and geopolitical independence. As we write this introduction, however, Latin American economic growth has stalled, leftist projects swell in some nations but ebb in others, and the right is resurgent across the region, signaling a possible new political realignment.

BEYOND "TRUMP OF THE TROPICS"

While this volume's ethnographic panorama extends far beyond voting and elections, it will likely be looked to for insight into the rise of Jair Bolsonaro and the global spread in recent years of what is often referred to as "right-wing populism." But while many of the individuals in these chapters voted for Bolsonaro, many did not—and many who did voted out of disillusionment and disdain with politics in general, with the PT, or with the hypocrisy of anticorruption politics itself (see Mitchell, this volume) rather than out of ideological affinity with the right-wing candidate. And while some people in these ethnographic accounts are politically active, many are not. If there is a political sentiment most often expressed in these pages, it is less frequently one of right-wing ideological affinity than one of *ambivalence and disenchantment*.

By giving privileged ethnographic attention to the deep disillusionment with politics and democracy during the years leading up to Bolsonaro's election in 2018, the chapters comprising this volume inevitably lead us to the conceptual doorstep of populism—or, more precisely, the category of populism so often used by scholars and pundits to describe a certain style of politics. Within the social sciences, conceptualizations of populism have tended to focus on discourses, movements, and styles of leadership that pit some notion of "the people" against elites and cultural Others who threaten popular sovereignty, prosperity, or some other conception of popular well-being. In left-wing versions of populism, this frequently involves threats to some conception of justice, and for right-wing versions, to some conception of in-group purity or continuity. The backdrop for the rise of this style of politics tends to be the invocation of crisis, frequently regarding the economy, popular sovereignty, security, or morality. Certainly, many of our chapters show how amid a generalized sense of crisis, disillusionment with politics, and fears of crime, the violent narrative of an authoritarian "cleansing" of Bolsonaro's campaign came to seem like an avenue of possible salvation to many. (See, for example, chapters by Junge; Mitchell; and Kalil, Pinheiro-Machado and Scalco, this volume.)

Explicit anthropological interest in populism—as both theoretical construct and empirical phenomenon—has intensified notably against the post-2016 backdrop of Donald Trump and Brexit.[2] While the experiences depicted in our case studies are certainly ripe for comparison with other global contexts undergoing rightward political and cultural shifts, we see significant limitations in the "global spread of populist conservativism" theoretical trope accounting for the ethnographic complexity and reality of what led Brazil to Bolsonaro. Without doubt, Bolsonaro's rise would seem to index many often-identified traits associated with populist leadership and appeal, including his status as an outsider in Brazil's mainstream sociopolitical order, his military background, his use of "the ground of public resentment as [his] field of play" (Webb 2018, 5), and his heavy reliance on cultural nostalgia for an era (chiefly, Brazil's 1964–1985 military dictatorship) when life is imagined to have been more moral, more prosperous, and safer (see Schwarcz 2019; Gusterson 2017, 210). And yet imposing populism as a metaconcept to analyze Bolsonaro's rise detracts from the specificity of Brazilian political, economic, and cultural conditions of recent years—and the concomitant, emergent political subjectivities we seek to bring into relief in this volume, in all their complexities, contradictions, and states of unfinishedness (Biehl and Locke 2017).

As we have noted, at the level of formal, institutional politics, Brazil's trajectory from 2013 to 2019 bears some resemblance to that of other rightward-turning nations in "post–pink tide" Latin America, not to mention a similarity of Bolsonaro's rhetorical style to that of far-right, heavily tweeting, media-disparaging leaders elected elsewhere in the world during the second decade of the twentieth century. Our volume, however, is not about Bolsonaro; it is about Brazilian citizens, communities, and movements living through the years leading up to Bolsonaro's election. Hence the notion of Bolsonaro as the "Trump of the Tropics"—the latest in a wave of populist demagogues (Davis 2018)—holds little appeal for us, since it oversimplifies both the motivations of the electorate and the appeal of the man for whom enough of the electorate voted to secure victory. We also note the analytic weaknesses of a political concept that is capacious enough to be applied to both far-right authoritarian figures such as Bolsonaro and his democratic socialist foil and nemesis, Lula. Moreover, applied to the pre-Bolsonaro years, the populism trope also tends to strip ordinary citizens of agency, rendering them as merely "duped" subjects—duped by the media, duped by neoliberal capitalism, duped by fake news, duped by corrupt politicians, and so on—and seeing their emergent affective states as inherently "bad for democracy."[3] To be clear, these and other forms of deception were undeniable factors of the 2018 election outcome, and this volume's editors and contributors share a deep concern that, roughly since PT president Dilma Rousseff was reelected for a second term in 2014, the roots of Brazil's young democracy have weakened.

THE AFFECTIVE POLITICS OF PRECARIOUS DEMOCRACY

Contemporary forms of mass disenchantment and disaffection have been described by social scientists using a range of conceptual vocabularies.[4] The overall complex of attitudes and affects, however, tends to resonate with a deep sense that "real-existing democracies are either dysfunctional, corrupt, or hollowed-out," leading to "a significant demographic of people—liberal and illiberal—who feel betrayed by the very institutions that profess to serve them" (Gagnon et al. 2018, vii).[5] The chapters in this volume reveal a complex panorama of sentiments driven as much by cultural tensions around race, gender, kinship and family, sexuality, religion, and generation as by material conditions of everyday life and struggles for survival. Our intent is to show how these dimensions of identity and experience come together—in both clear and murky intersections—to shape political consciousness and behaviors (including, but by no means limited to, voting).

Affect is a useful analytic to consider the momentous political shift in Brazil because it helps account for how ambivalent feelings of disaffection, disillusionment, and anger can spread across a body politic rapidly, building like a snowball and turning into an avalanche that disrupts previous social and political structures. These forms of affect experienced by individuals are not merely a by-product of a nation's economic, social, and political conditions. Rather, they co-constitute those conditions and shape them in very particular ways. We understand affect not to be an individual emotion but, rather, to be a description of collective capacities to feel and generate feelings in others, as affect is being constantly transmitted between bodies (Gregg and Seigworth 2010). Affect is characterized by preconscious, prelinguistic, and visceral responses to stimuli that can crystallize into certain dispositions or habits but are also volatile and have the potential to rapidly capture and transform the collective mood (Massumi 2002). Mass media is particularly adept at shaping and provoking these shifts in mood, particularly with the aim of selling a product or a political project.

Anthropologists, moreover, have begun to locate affect as instrumental to legal and technocratic procedures, as "pre-social" emotional practices figure prominently in arbitration and juridical decision-making (Clarke 2019). We saw this play out, ultimately, in the legal procedures against Dilma Rousseff, which often took on a morally self-righteous collective affect, where she became the iconic scapegoat for all that must be cleansed of governance—and thus PT leadership (Ansell 2018). For Mazzarella (2019, 46), "whipping public affect into a state of normalized crisis is an elementary form of statecraft." When enough members of a society become disillusioned or disenchanted, for example, these feelings become embodied in ways that can lead to unpredictable transformations of political subjectivities and actions.

As ethnographers, the contributors to this volume bring into relief not only expressions of manifest anger, resentment, and disillusionment but also feelings of hope and profound ambivalence—the coexistence of conflicting feelings and opinions (Webb 2018)—that have spread through the hearts and minds of Brazilians during these tumultuous times. Indeed, ethnography is particularly suited for capturing nuance in contemporary affective moments, akin to how scholars have sought relevant "structures of feelings" in literature and other cultural work (Williams 1977). Theorists like Brian Massumi (2015, 55) argue that affect is always already political because it is a "collective event" that is "distributed across . . . bodies" and primes those bodies to act in unison. This insight helps us analyze the form through which (Brazilian) democracy operates and to consider how affective transformations have contributed to the precarity of democracy. Ethnography helps us catalog different types of affective politics and the mechanics that produce consent or apathy among a large proportion of the population in the face of contemporary reactionary politics.

As the lines between liberal democracy and fascism once again blur—in Brazil and elsewhere—it is urgent to show how, in people's everyday lives, democracy has become precarious. We must examine the deployment of mass digital communicative technologies and infrastructures that open up novel forms of mass propaganda (e.g., through WhatsApp groups in the chapter by Medeiros et al.) and the increased circulation of internet memes and other modalities that prime the public for forms of mass politics—mass politics that are both democratic and nondemocratic. As Lucia Cantero (2015) has argued elsewhere, mass communication has the cunning ability to produce a public through affect, interpellating people at an intuitive, visceral level. The primacy of the image becomes exceedingly real in the face of "fake" news, such as the false articles spreading the idea that the PT enabled the gay indoctrination of children, which circulated uncontrollably during the 2018 election (see Jarrín, this volume). These shifts in the mass mediation of politics helped bring together the politics of affect with the politics of truth such that feeling became a recurrent default that people revert to when facts fail—truth as what *feels* right.

The PT endeavored to cultivate positive forms of affect among its base, winning four consecutive elections built on national optimism, redistributive economic policies, the initial enthusiasm around sporting mega events, and new citizenship claims based around race, gender, and LGBTQ+ identities. Yet these affective forms of hope, joy, and optimism that were so important to the PT's successes were also instrumentalized in the party's takedown. First, this messaging was easily co-opted by neoliberal discourses that interpellated Brazilians as consumers rather than citizens (see Jerome, this volume). Second, even many Brazilians who believed in the political project of the PT remained skeptical of the government's promises (Junge 2018), having been betrayed by politicians in the past.

The mass protests in 2013 signaled an entrenched disenchantment with the way in which "the design" of development mapped onto everyday forms of precarity experienced by Brazilians. Many people felt duped—a sentiment that was deftly seized upon by actors seeking to dismantle the apparatus of social mobility built up under the PT. Precarity, Anne Allison (2014) argues, is characterized by contemporary economic conditions that weaken the safety net and render workers chronically vulnerable to flexible labor regimes, but it also registers, quite literally, onto the body politic as a diverse array of affects, such as feelings of hopelessness, anger, or estrangement from others. As the economy slowed down and the contradictions of global sporting events became obvious, these negative affects took hold of protesters, and some among the base that had elected the Workers' Party and benefited from its policies began to turn their backs on it (see Kopper; Mitchell; and Rojas, Olival, and Spexoto Olival, this volume).

Affects like optimism and pessimism are the opposite sides of the same coin because affect has no predetermined, teleological outcome (Massumi 2002). Additionally, affect is always surprising us in its multiplicity and stickiness, attaching and deattaching itself to objects and bodies with ease (Ahmed 2013). Thus once the positive form of an affect collapses, it is fairly easy to give in to its negative underside, and these forms of affect are highly contagious, moving through crowds and communities mimetically[6] and becoming amplified by forms of mass media (Mazzarella 2009). Traditional parties quickly lost control over how these crowds behaved, and powerful media outlets like Rede Globo increasingly portrayed not only the PT but *all* political parties as inherently corrupt—thus undermining the democratic system as a whole, according to authors like Jessé Souza (2016). The 2014 Petrobras scandal, for instance—buoyed by highly politicized corruption investigations aimed at the PT (Fishman et al. 2019)—tarnished a public institution that until then had been a symbol of Brazil's promise (see Cantero, this volume), and transformed the nation's optimism for the future into visceral anger at the traditional political class.

We note that, independently of each other and while covering different Brazilian regions, a number of the volume's authors who addressed these tensions developed similar affective terms for the analysis of their ethnographic material: "despairing hope" (Rojas, Olival, and Spexoto Olival), "negative hope" (Kopper), and "cruel pessimism" (Mitchell). In each of these ethnographic cases, the authors identified local manifestations of the national political-affective shift that we describe here.

It was this volatile shift in sentiments that gave rise to the nation's political polarization (Borba 2019) and to increasingly authoritarian social movements, made up of mostly middle- and upper-class Brazilians (Ansell 2018), who literally draped themselves in the national flag and began to wax nostalgic for the dictatorship and the order it supposedly provided to society. By then the memory of the dictatorship had been affectively reconfigured by the political right as a symbol of order, patriotism, and traditional family values, which meant forgetting all the atrocities it enabled or embracing them as necessary. In fact, in the eyes of the new right, one of Dilma Rousseff's greatest sins had been her effort to establish a National Truth Commission in 2011 to review the dictatorship's human rights violations, which had been subject to various forms of "institutional forgetting" since the 1979 Amnesty Law (Atencio 2014). Thanks to this 1979 law, the military regime retained significant political power during the democratization period, despite relinquishing formal control of the government (Zaverucha 2005). The National Truth Commission failed to change public perception about the dictatorship's abuses, in part because Rousseff herself had been a victim of torture during the dictatorship as a member of an underground resistance group, which made it easier for the political right to mount a sharp counteroffensive that portrayed her as bent on "revenge" against the military forces (Dias 2013) and as a sexually suspect "communist subversive" in disguise (Sosa 2019). The sexual moralism that had characterized the dictatorship's response to subversion (Cowan 2016a) returned in force during the impeachment trial as conservative members of Congress began to embrace authoritarianism as the only solution to the country's perceived immorality and chaos (Cowan 2016b).

The significant parallels between the dictatorship and the new right demonstrate that both political formations tapped into similar anxieties to gain traction. First, the sentiments of today's Brazilian right draw directly on the militarism, patriarchal traditionalism, anticommunism, and U.S. alignment of the dictatorship years (Snider 2018). Second, they also draw on the forms of transnational right-wing organization that were honed in those years (Cowan 2018), including the transnational moral panic surrounding feminism and LGBTQ+ rights that describes them as insidious forms of "gender ideology" (Corrêa 2018). The main advantage the new right had in relation to the dictatorship was that its political ideology took hold of average Brazilians as it spread like wildfire over social media such as WhatsApp, entering routine public discourse and even intimate family circles (see Junge, this volume). People began to enthusiastically adhere to this newfound conservative patriotism, as became evident in the joyous group dances (heavily featuring national symbols) that people choreographed in favor of Bolsonaro. Even old fascist slogans like "God, Nation, and Family" resurfaced as centerpieces of the Bolsonaro regime (Singer et al. 2020).

It seems that democracy itself has been rendered precarious in Brazil by the politics that emerge from hopelessness, disenchantment, and anger. Democratic institutions in Brazil have been delegitimized, and the party system is in disarray. And Bolsonaro himself clamors to dissolve the Congress and the Supreme Court in a Fujimori-style auto-coup (Barros 2020; Brum 2020)—something unthinkable just a few years prior. The "fantasy-work of national identity" (Berlant 1991, 2), which previously constructed the nation as united in its difference through myths like racial democracy, has been seriously fractured, perhaps irreparably, and some Brazilians are struggling to redefine their national community in ways that do not violently exclude certain members of society. Afro-Brazilians, LGBTQ+ Brazilians, and Indigenous Brazilians are making claims to the nation that are simply incompatible with the far-right principles embraced by Bolsonaro, and their resistance is organizing against Bolsonaro in innovative ways, responding with affective appeals of their own. Additional conflicts, political assassinations, and democratic instability seem more likely in the short term than a return to normal political elections; but a radically different future spurred by progressive activism may also be in the cards.

OVERVIEW OF THE VOLUME

Twenty-first-century Brazil clearly presents one of the most vertiginous and puzzling sociopolitical about-faces in the contemporary world. And yet we—the editors and chapter authors—do not always share the same explanations for the origins and implications of Brazil's "unraveling." Rather than downplaying these divergences, we embrace them as generative and indicative of the different methodological and theoretical affinities we each bring to this undertaking, exposed as we were to very different Brazilian populations during our ethnographic fieldwork.

We have organized chapters into four subsections, meant to help the reader think through different themes that defined the period between 2013 and 2019. First, we tackle "The Intimacy of Power," with four chapters that describe the gendered, classed, and racialized shifts occurring within intimate spheres such as the family but that also had a wider political impact because they generated intergenerational tensions and disrupted how upward mobility, masculinity, guns, and whiteness were perceived by political actors. The second section, "Corruption and Crime," delves into the ways in which criminality within and outside the government came to be associated with particular (im)moral projects, and destabilized national symbols, trust in government, and forms of reciprocity important to particular national communities. The third section, entitled "Infrastructures of Hope," is centered on the forms of hopeful affect expressed by different populations that once directly benefited from government programs started by the PT but have become disillusioned with those programs or whose precarious situations have pushed them to put hope in Bolsonaro instead. The final section, "Old Challenges, New Activism," chronicles forms of resistance emerging in response to the rise of far-right politics across Brazil, particularly among Afro-Brazilian, LGBTQ+, and student activists. For a more detailed discussion of each chapter, please read the critical overview, written by Lilia Moritz Schwarcz, after this chapter.

BEYOND THE UNRAVELING

It is hard to see what the future holds for Brazil, but this volume attempts to understand crucial transitional years for the nation and add ethnographic depth to our understanding of the major shifts that Brazil has undergone during this period. With democracy itself rendered precarious, grand narratives to describe these radical national shifts seem to fail. Any claim made about the present is like an attempt to hold steady a constantly changing object, making academic analysis feel impossible. But by paying close ethnographic attention to how different communities in Brazil lived through the country's momentous transformations of the past decade, this book attempts to account for the multiplicity of experiences that have structured the current moment. One of the most powerful attributes of ethnography is its ability to show us how different people engage in meaning making during crises and social transformations and can experience the same event differently according to perspective—whether that perspective is shaped by race, gender, class, region, or any of the many other vertices along with the social experiences, harms, and benefits that may be distributed. This volume avoids the "danger of a single story" (Adichie 2009) by highlighting how diverse populations from various regions of the country experienced the Brazilian unraveling of the second half of this century's second decade and how every sphere of life was impacted by this remarkable shift—from family dynamics and individual aspirations to political allegiances and collective forms of mobilization.

We complete final revisions on this introduction amid a COVID-19 pandemic that seems both a symptom and an accelerant of an environmental and political unraveling that is global in scale. But to understand such large-scale transformations, it is also important to scale down in order to understand how historical processes are lived and understood in particular times and places. This ethnographic focus on the intimate and local can also help us understand how people try to constitute new orders out of what has been unraveled. This volume provides no definite answers to why and how Brazil shifted as it did (although we develop several hypotheses), nor do we claim we can predict what the future holds. Rather, through a close examination of the experiences, narratives, affects, and actions of people from many perspectives who lived through this period of unexpected sociopolitical change, *Precarious Democracy* aspires to be an enduring account of life under conditions of political and economic precarity and unpredictable political change.

REFERENCES

Adichie, Chimamanda Ngozi. 2009. "The Danger of a Single Story." TED Talk video. Accessed March 5, 2020. https://www.ted.com/talks/chimamanda_ngozi_adichie_the_danger_of_a_single_story?language=en.
Ahmed, Sara. 2013. *The Cultural Politics of Emotion*. New York: Routledge.
Allison, Anne. 2014. *Precarious Japan*. Durham, N.C.: Duke University Press.
Ansell, Aaron. 2018. "Impeaching Dilma Rousseff: The Double Life of Corruption Allegations on Brazil's Political Right." *Culture, Theory and Critique* 59 (4): 312–331.
Appadurai, Arjun. 2017. "Democracy Fatigue." In *The Great Regression*, edited by Heinrich Geiselberger, 1–12. Cambridge, UK: Polity.
Atencio, Rebecca J. 2014. *Memory's Turn: Reckoning with Dictatorship in Brazil*. Madison: University of Wisconsin Press.
Barros, Celso Rocha de. 2020. "O golpismo tem que custar caro." *Folha de São Paulo*, March 1, 2020, sec. Celso Rocha de Barros. https://www1.folha.uol.com.br/colunas/celso-rocha-de-barros/2020/03/golpismo-tem-que-custar-caro.shtml.
Berlant, Lauren. 1991. *The Anatomy of National Fantasy: Hawthorne, Utopia, and Everyday Life*. Chicago: University of Chicago Press.
Biehl, João, and Peter Locke. 2017. *Unfinished: The Anthropology of Becoming*. Durham, N.C.: Duke University Press.
Borba, Rodrigo. 2019. "Injurious Signs: The Geopolitics of Hate and Hope in the Linguistic Landscape of a Political Crisis." In *Making Sense of People and Place in Linguistic Landscapes*, edited by Amiena Peck, Christopher Stroud, and Quentin Williams, 161–181. New York: Bloomsbury.
Boswell, John, Jack Corbett, Kate Dommett, Will Jennings, Matthew Flinders, R. A. W. Rhodes, and Matthew Wood. 2019. "State of the Field: What Can Political Ethnography Tell Us about Anti-politics and Democratic Disaffection?" *European Journal of Political Research* 58 (1): 56–71.
Brum, Eliane. 2020. "O golpe de bolsonaro está em curso." *El País Brasil*, February 26, 2020. https://brasil.elpais.com/opiniao/2020-02-26/o-golpe-de-bolsonaro-esta-em-curso.html.
Cantero, Lucia Esther. 2015. "Specters of the Market: Consumer-Citizenship and the Visual Politics of Race and Inequality in Brazil." PhD diss., Yale University.
Canzian, Fernando, and Fernanda Mena. 2019. "Brazil's Super-rich Lead Global Income Concentration." *Folha de São Paulo*, August 19, 2019.

Chow, Rey. 2010. "The Elusive Material: What the Dog Doesn't Understand." In *New Materialisms: Ontology, Agency and Politics*, edited by Diana Coole and Samantha Frost, 221–233. Durham, N.C.: Duke University Press.

Clarke, Kamari M. 2019. *Affective Justice: The International Criminal Court and the Pan-Africanist Pushback*. Durham, N.C.: Duke University Press.

Corrêa, Sonia. 2018. "A 'política de gênero': Um comentário genealógico." *Cadernos pagu* 53. https://www.scielo.br/scielo.php?script=sci_arttext&pid=S0104-83332018000200401&lng=pt&tlng=pt.

Cowan, Benjamin A. 2016a. *Securing Sex: Morality and Repression in the Making of Cold War Brazil*. Chapel Hill: University of North Carolina Press.

———. 2016b. "Holy Ghosts of Brazil's Past." *NACLA Report on the Americas* 48 (4): 346–352.

———. 2018. "A Hemispheric Moral Majority: Brazil and the Transnational Construction of the New Right." *Revista brasileira de política internacional* 61 (2). https://www.scielo.br/scielo.php?script=sci_arttext&pid=S0034-73292018000200209.

Davis, Donagh. 2018. "A 'Populist' Revolt of Elites against the People." *Morning Star*, October 31, 2018. https://morningstaronline.co.uk/article/brazil-populist-revolt-elites-against-people.

Dias, Reginaldo Benedito. 2013. "A Comissão Nacional da Verdade: A disputa de memória sobre o período da ditadura e o tempo presente." *Patrimônio e memória* 9 (1): 71–95.

Fishman, Andrew, Rafael Moro Martins, Leandro Demori, Alexandre de Santi, and Glenn Greenwald. 2019. "Breach of Ethics: Exclusive: Leaked Chats between Brazilian Judge and Prosecutor Who Imprisoned Lula Reveal Prohibited Collaboration and Doubts over Evidence." *Intercept*, June 9, 2019. https://theintercept.com/2019/06/09/brazil-lula-operation-car-wash-sergio-moro/.

Frazão, Heliana. 2018. "'Após 16 anos de comando do país, o PT vai ser derrotado', diz ACM Neto." *UOL Notícias*, UOL Eleições 2018. https://noticias.uol.com.br/politica/eleicoes/2018/noticias/agencia-estado/2018/10/28/para-acm-neto-nao-ha-clima-de-virada.htm.

Gagnon, Jean-Paul, Emily Beausoleil, Kyong-Min Son, Cleve Arguelles, Pierrick Chalaye, and Callum N. Johnston. 2018. "What Is Populism? Who Is the Populist? A State of the Field Review (2008–2018)." *Democratic Theory* 5 (2): vi–xxvi.

Gledhill, John. 2019. "The Brazilian Crisis and the Ghosts of Populism." In *Democracy's Paradox: Populism and Its Contemporary Crisis*, edited by Dimitrios Theodossopoulos and Bruce Kapferer, 55–73. New York: Berghahn.

Greenwald, Glenn, and Victor Pougy. 2019a. "Hidden Plot: Exclusive: Brazil's Top Prosecutors Who Indicted Lula Schemed in Secret Messages to Prevent His Party from Winning 2018 Election." *Intercept*, June 9, 2019. https://theintercept.com/2019/06/09/brazil-car-wash-prosecutors-workers-party-lula/.

———. 2019b. "'E agora, José?': Deltan Dallagnol, em chats secretos, sugeriu que Sergio Moro protegeria Flávio Bolsonaro para não desagradar ao presidente e não perder indicação ao STF." *Intercept Brasil*, As mensagens secretas da Lava Jato, Parte 11, July 21, 2019. https://theintercept.com/2019/07/21/deltan-dallagnol-sergio-moro-flavio-bolsonaro-queiroz.

Gregg, Melissa, and Gregory J. Seigworth, eds. 2010. *The Affect Theory Reader*. Durham, N.C.: Duke University Press.

Gusterson, Hugh. 2017. "From Brexit to Trump: Anthropology and the Rise of Nationalist Populism." *American Ethnologist* 44 (2): 209–214.

IBGE. 2019. *Síntese de indicadores sociais: Uma análise das condições de vida da população brasileira: 2019*. Estudos e pesquisas: Informação demográfica e socioeconômica, no. 40. Rio de Janeiro: IBGE.

Inman, Phillip. 2012. "Brazil's Economy Overtakes UK to Become World's Sixth Largest." *Guardian*, Business, March 6, 2012. https://www.theguardian.com/business/2012/mar/06/brazil-economy-worlds-sixth-largest.

International Monetary Fund. 2019. *World Economic Outlook: Global Manufacturing Downturn, Rising Trade Barriers*. Washington, D.C.: IMF, October 2019.

Junge, Benjamin. 2018. *Cynical Citizenship: Gender, Regionalism, and Political Subjectivity in Porto Alegre, Brazil*. Albuquerque: University of New Mexico Press.

Kalil, Isabela Oliveira. 2018. "Quem são e no que acreditam os eleitores de Jair Bolsonaro." Fundação Escola de Sociologia e Política de São Paulo. https://www.fespsp.org.br/upload/usersfiles/2018/Relat%C3%B3rio%20para%20Site%20FESPSP.pdf.

Lyons, John, and Paul Kiernan. 2015. "How Brazil's China-Driven Commodities Boom Went Bust." *Wall Street Journal*, August 28, 2015.

Markoff, John. 2011. "A Moving Target: Democracy." *European Journal of Sociology/Archives européennes de sociologie* 52 (2): 239–276.

Martins, Rafael Moro, Amanda Audi, Leandro Demori, Glenn Greenwald, and Tatiana Dias. 2019. "Lava Jato fingiu investigar FHC apenas para criar percepção pública de 'imparcialidade', mas Moro repreendeu: 'Melindra alguém cujo apoio é importante.'" *Intercept Brasil*, As mensagens secretas da Lava Jato, Parte 7, June 18, 2019.

Maskovsky, Jeff, and Sophie Bjork-James, eds. 2020. *Beyond Populism: Angry Politics and the Twilight of Neoliberalism*. Morgantown: West Virginia University Press.

Massumi, Brian. 2002. *Parables for the Virtual: Movement, Affect, Sensation*. Durham, N.C.: Duke University Press.

———. 2015. *Politics of Affect*. Malden, Mass.: John Wiley & Sons.

Mazzarella, William. 2009. "Affect: What Is It Good For?" In *Enchantments of Modernity: Empire, Nation, Globalization*, edited by Saraubh Dub, 309–327. London: Routledge.

———. 2019. "The Anthropology of Populism: Beyond the Liberal Settlement." *Annual Review of Anthropology* 48:45–60.

Mitchell, Sean T. 2014. "The Politics of Violence and Brazil's World Cup." *Anthropoliteia* (blog), June 30, 2014. https://anthropoliteia.net/2014/06/30/the-politics-of-violence-and-brazils-world-cup/.

Neri, Marcelo Côrtes. 2014. "Poverty Reduction and Well-Being: Lula's Real." In *Brazil under the Workers' Party*, edited by Fábio de Castro, Kees Koonings, and Marianne Wiesebron, 102–125. London: Palgrave Macmillan.

Perrin, Fernanda. 2017. "Greve é a maior da história, dizem sindicalistas." *Folha de São Paulo*, April 24, 2017. https://www1.folha.uol.com.br/mercado/2017/04/1879539-greve-e-a-maior-da-historia-dizem-sindicalistas.shtml.

Samet, Robert. 2019. "The Subject of Wrongs: Crime, Populism, and Venezuela's Punitive Turn." *Cultural Anthropology* 34 (2): 272–298.

Schwarcz, Lilia Moritz. 2019. *Sobre o autoritarismo Brasileiro*. São Paulo: Companhia das Letras.

Singer, Andre, et al. 2020. "Por que assistimos uma volta do fascismo à brasileira." *Folha de São Paulo*, June 9, 2020.

Snider, Colin M. 2018. "'The Perfection of Democracy Cannot Dispense with Dealing with the Past:' Dictatorship, Memory, and the Politics of the Present in Brazil." *Latin Americanist* 62 (1): 55–79.

Sosa, Joseph Jay. 2019. "Subversive, Mother, Killjoy: Sexism against Dilma Rousseff and the Social Imaginary of Brazil's Rightward Turn." *Signs* 44 (3): 717–741.

Souza, Jessé. 2016. *A radiografia do golpe: Entenda como e por que você foi enganado*. São Paulo: Editora LeYa.

———. 2017. *A elite do atraso: Da escravidão à Lava Jato*. Rio de Janeiro: Leya.

Theodossopoulos, Dimitrios, and Bruce Kapferer. 2019. "Introduction: Populism and Its Paradox." In *Democracy's Paradox: Populism and Its Contemporary Crisis*, 1–34. New York: Berghahn.

Viana, Natalia, and Rafael Neves. 2020. "Como o FBI influenciou procuradores da Lava Jato." *Agência pública* (blog), July 1, 2020. https://apublica.org/2020/07/o-fbi-e-a-lava-jato/.

Webb, Adele. 2018. "In Praise of Democratic Ambivalence." *Democratic Theory* 5 (2): 17–36.

Williams, Raymond. 1977. *Marxism and Literature*. Oxford: Oxford University Press.

Zaverucha, Jorge. 2005. *FHC, forças armadas e polícia: Entre o autoritarismo e a democracia, 1999–2002*. Rio de Janeiro: Editora Record.

NOTES

1. As of this writing, Brazil has registered more than 4.1 million cases of COVID-19 and more than 125,000 deaths from the disease.
2. See Maskovsky and Bjork-James (2020); Mazzarella (2019); Samet (2019); Gledhill (2019); and Gusterson (2017).
3. As Samet (2019) has argued, for example, populism is not necessarily antidemocratic, not necessarily reducible to charismatic leadership, and not necessarily aligned with a particular economic paradigm or political ideology.
4. These include descriptions such as "subaltern resentment towards global cosmopolitics" (Theodossopoulos and Kapferer 2019, 16); "anti-politics and democratic disaffection" (Boswell et al. 2019); "public ambivalence toward democracy" (Webb 2018); "disenchantment with existing democracy" (Markoff 2011, 257); and "democracy fatigue" (Appadurai 2017).
5. Notions of "anger" (Maskovsky and Bjork-James 2020) and "resentment" (Cramer 2016) also figure prominently in contemporary ethnographic research of populism. See also Guderjan (2018).
6. The literature on affect remarks on the contagiousness of sentiments, as people become keyed into communal ways of feeling through mimesis, particularly within crowds. Rey Chow (2010), for example, expands on René Girard to argue that desire itself is mimetic, because we tend to crave what others see as desirable.

CRITICAL OVERVIEW
A Plan for a Country Still Looking for Democracy

LILIA MORITZ SCHWARCZ

Precarious Democracy is much more than a mere collection of chapters. From various angles—many unexpected and novel—this volume confronts and analyzes the period between 2013 and 2019, a time during which, after a long moment of democratic stability, Brazil experienced a clear reversal of expectations marked by economic recession, unemployment, and scarcity. Written by anthropologists, this volume shows how every crisis is multifaceted and how different groups mobilize distinct strategies to confront adversity. The collection also presents avenues to understand how an apparent consolidation of democracy can give way to unimagined outcomes such as the election of Jair Bolsonaro in October 2018, which signaled a shift toward a radical right-wing project and the rescinding of hard-won rights achieved after the ratification of Brazil's Citizen Constitution in 1988. In other words, after years of institutional stability and clear economic growth, where Brazil was seen as a "model for the world," the country had to face the persistent character of its inequality. Genuine conditions of religious, gender, and racial intolerance were laid bare with the election of a politician known to be a reactionary, averse to dialogue, and uninspired by the idea of democracy.

Precarious Democracy responds to this turnaround, and to profound economic, political, and cultural changes, with sixteen ethnographic chapters that focus on the daily lives of Brazilians. This volume shows how "God is in the details" and how it is possible and desirable to paint smaller portraits as a means to understand the larger picture. To this aim, the collection draws from seemingly niche ethnographic case studies in order to understand a nation's broader political and cultural landscape. The result is an edited volume that, through anthropology, engages wide-ranging but crucial subjects for contemporary Brazil. These themes include discourse analysis, social markers of difference such as gender, sexuality, and race, and the analysis of social movements. The authors share the common objective of describing the political subjectivities of individuals who both reflect and react to moments of crisis, translating them in terms of their particular experiences.

The richness of themes and realities is such that it is worth briefly summarizing the different chapters, in order to show how, as a whole, they portray the fragilization of democracy experienced by Brazilians, who have witnessed a sometimes astonishing reversal of civil and social rights. Let us consider the different contributions that, collectively, compel us to reflect on the "past of the present": how the Brazil of yore sometimes explains—but sometimes belies—the country of today.

Benjamin Junge's opening chapter focuses on the capital city of Recife in the northeastern state of Pernambuco. Junge focuses on social and institutional transformations that appear unique to this particular moment in Brazil's history. Centered on the reaction of the Pereira family to the

2018 election, the chapter maps the educational achievements of the family's grandchildren and their entrance into a public university. This is one of the great dreams of ascension in a country historically marked by a perverse educational process: where elites attend the best private elementary and high schools and, consequently, monopolize places in highly prestigious and free public universities. The lower classes, on the other hand, often reach higher education only in the form of expensive private schools that have limited prestige in the national academic imagination.

Junge's analysis draws from conversations he had with his interlocutors as well as from online material, with special attention to social media tools used widely and innovatively in the 2018 elections. As he shows, social media platforms such as Facebook and WhatsApp proved to be a catalyst for interfamilial hostilities. Junge reflects on how the concept of *family* became an "idiom" to navigate the political crisis that erupted at the ballots in 2018. The notion of family also became a powerful way to understand the crisis of masculinity and a broader dispute over the public sphere. In the end, we are left with a "certainty" that we can expect an "uncertain" future for Brazil.

The chapter by Jessica Jerome deals with a parallel scenario in the neighboring state of Ceará, focusing on that state's capital city of Fortaleza. Jerome's work brings into relief the existence of major regional divides in Brazil: While the states of Brazil's Northeast consistently voted for the Workers' Party (Partido dos Trabalhadores; PT) following the 2002 election of Luiz Inácio Lula da Silva, voters in the South moved increasingly to the right. This political shift is best illustrated in the broad support for Jair Bolsonaro, a federal deputy who served in Congress for twenty-eight years without developing major projects and without significant participation in congressional committees or policy working groups. Jerome focuses on a group of six women and their extended families, in a period spanning from 1988 to 2018, to understand how the political construction of various forms of identity emerged through the unfolding electoral reality of 2018. While much of the literature analyzes how the Workers' Party failed to reflect upon and react to the formation of new consumer groups, which the party itself had helped create, Jerome details a certain generational shock, with the older generations remaining loyal to the Workers' Party while the younger generations disengaged from it or embraced a kind of nostalgia for a distant past lost during childhood that, in fact, never existed.

Jerome's research shows how regional and generational markers intersect with markers of class and consumption. These intersections have demarcated the noteworthy rise of a "new middle class" in Lula's Brazil based on a model of inclusionary market consumerism. The result is an ethnographic portrait that allows us to think not only of the PT's successes in this region, even in the 2018 elections, but also of the failure of older generations to create not only economic ascension but also *equity*, and to provide for a new consumer group impacted by the gains of democracy.

The chapter by Isabela Kalil, Rosana Pinheiro-Machado, and Lucia Mury Scalco analyzes the symbolism of firearms in two different Brazilian cities. In Porto Alegre's favelas, firearms have recently become desirable beyond criminal groups, and even young men who seek more respectable careers want to possess guns to protect themselves and their families from crime. The authors analyze this desire for firearms as a way for these men to shore up their own masculinity, which aligned them politically with Bolsonaro and made them more likely to vote for him. Bolsonaro's embrace of guns was also politically beneficial in São Paulo, where his supporters widely adopted his famous firearm gestures during political demonstrations and used car and gun ownership as a way to divide good citizens from criminals or "communists." Interestingly, women also took a central role in these demonstrations, demanding these weapons become accessible to protect good Christian families. Guns and cars, the authors conclude, become fetishized as signs of class distinction, power, and moral superiority during an economic crisis that threatens everyone's social position.

The theme of *branquitude* (whiteness) structures the next chapter by Patricia de Santana Pinho. The chapter differs slightly from the others in this volume in terms of form, in that Pinho's writing reads more like a theoretical essay than an ethnographic chapter. In the expression "coming out," she identifies a series of reactionary values that have always existed in Brazilian society but that until recently were closed and contained. She shows how, "without realizing it," social groups perpetuate structures of privilege while reproducing entrenched structures of racism, sexism, and class inequality. She brings additional sophistication to her analysis, focusing attention on the intersections of social classes with racial groups. Only in this way is it possible to understand how 45 percent of "Blacks" (using the IBGE [Brazilian census bureau] term) and 65 percent of families receiving two to five minimum salaries voted for Jair Bolsonaro.

Pinho explores how the concept of "whiteness" represents a tacit admission of the universal model of humanity on which it is based and enables a normative identity that operates invisibly through the privileges and special treatments from which it benefits. There is no whiteness without the devaluation of blackness. These are polar yet related concepts that are promoted as social values and whose preservation is naturalized. Representations of whiteness and blackness function as expressions of identity but also as mechanisms that reproduce racism through other social markers of difference such as gender, sex, and social class. The main objective of the chapter is thus to help remove the opaque veil of blindness—to remove whiteness as a privileged position of silence and supposed neutrality. By challenging whiteness as a privileged position, Pinho shows how, in the last elections, the rise of the *senzala* (slave quarters) to a position of proximity to the *casa grande* (master's home) generated class hatred but also of race hatred expressed by those who believed they were losing their places because others were usurping them. Ignorance and silence are epistemologically privileged positions that can help explain the phenomenon of middle-class resentment that grew during the 2018 election. Whiteness, on the other hand, is an invisible concept because it is only maintained through the constraint of a socially imposed "consensus."

The chapter by Sean T. Mitchell focuses on corruption, exploring the topic through the so-called "new middle class"—thirty-five to forty million Brazilians who left poverty between 2003 and 2014. This economic ascension, which was highly touted by the PT governments, changed shape from 2016 onward and collapsed completely in 2018. According to Mitchell, the end of a rising wave of social mobility, the impeachment of Dilma Rousseff, and the arrest of Luiz Inácio Lula da Silva all contributed to the growth of a "cruel pessimism," a condition of possibility for the election of a candidate like Jair Bolsonaro and the radical right turn in Brazilian politics.

Mitchell conducted his research in the North Zone of Rio de Janeiro, more specifically in a condominium in Rio Comprido. Mitchell is particularly interested in a family he met during a period of prosperity and euphoria. This period of observation was followed by a dizzying fall and a return to poverty. Mitchell's goal is to show how this despair and pessimism led to a period of widespread loss of hope and of distrust in the very institutions, parties, and people that once enabled people to glimpse another and new reality. This is, therefore, a "chronicle of decline."

In her chapter, Karina Biondi presents her ethnography of Brazilian prisons and explores, in a very original way, the unusual confluence of the Evangelical Christian movement and the criminal organization Primeiro Comando da Capital (First Command of the Capital; PCC). Her chapter notes how the biblical discourses underpinning Bolsonaro's political narratives also circulate intensively on São Paulo's periphery, stimulating a variety of forms of affect. She shows how these affects produce different effects in distinct social contexts: in some cases, resulting in "revolutionaries in crime" and, in others, sustaining the conservative "revolution" advocated by Bolsonaro.

A changing community in the North of the state of Bahia, on the border between Pernambuco and Sergipe, is the scene of an ethnography carried out by John F. Collins. Given the pseudonym

Riacho Seco (dry stream) by Collins, the population of the small town remained, during the Lula governments, concerned with their retirement pensions, the lack of doctors, and the provision of entertainment for the *Festas Juninas* (June festivals) and for carnival parties. It was at those times that political candidates sought to gain the public's attention, especially during the election period. Their initiatives, moreover, were understood as "favors" rather than as citizens' rights. Gains such as the arrival of running water, electricity, school buses, and (conditional cash transfer program) Bolsa Família were treated as if they were personal, rather than public, resources and even as private gifts from candidates. These values changed with more recent electoral disputes and the entry of concepts such as "rationality," "modernity," and "capitalism" into local lexicons, showing how political changes and discursive formulations can lead to pragmatic changes and the end of traditional forms of reciprocity. The introduction of new forms of consumption brought significant changes to the old rules internal to local politics. It is not, then, a question of believing that the *sertão* (the desert region encompassed by Collins's ethnography) became a liberal regime. Nor does Collins argue that violence took over a peaceful region from one day to the next. Rather, violence may have become exacerbated in this period and entered new places. As the anthropologist provokes, "The *sertão* became a sea [of money]" and thus survived. But the "sea did not become the *sertão*."

Lucia Cantero's chapter explores the behind-the-scenes contexts of Brazil's largest oil company, Petrobras. During the Lula government, Petrobras was considered a highly successful public industry and experienced its most profitable years, opening a period of euphoria with regards to Brazil's oil industry. The story turned quickly, however, with the company going from utopia to dystopia after a series of corruption scandals dominated the media. One of the most interesting components of Cantero's work explores the various symbolic meanings that the company has acquired over time: from a past of extreme national pride to a more recent history of profound disgrace. Cantero traces this history from the time of Monteiro Lobato[1] and Getúlio Vargas to the 2016 corruption scandals, revealing what she calls the "social life of oil" in Brazil and the weakened sense of national pride associated with Petrobras. These events destabilized the government of Dilma Rousseff and led to her eventual impeachment. Cantero makes clear the importance of the symbolic dimension of political power and how Petrobras risked much more than the image of a company. Petrobras was a business that carried with it a certain Brazilian identity along with its name, which was then lost during the political scandal.

David Rojas, Alexandre de Azevedo Olival, and Andrezza Alves Spexoto Olival turn the discussion toward the Amazon region, with the objective of defining what they call "despairing hopes" or "hopeful despair." The assumption is similar to that presented in other chapters, in which the general picture is of a profound hopelessness, especially when compared to the democratic period experienced by the country in the previous thirty years. The fundamental reference points are the federally provisioned arrival of electricity, the strengthening of family farming (through the federal agency National Program for the Strengthening of Family Farming [PRONAF]), and other improvements designed to help Brazil's rural poor. But even though these investments benefited millions of people in the southern Amazon, the Workers' Party failed to establish a more solid foundation and the population continued to feel abandoned and exploited by powerful local forces. Focusing on *assentados* (residents of rural settlements), the anthropologists show how, despite the substantial investments made by PT governments, the fall in the PT's perceived credibility during the years of crisis was immense, and many voted for a political project with a clearly authoritarian profile.

Falina Enriquez's chapter discusses the middle-class musical scene in the city of Recife, Pernambuco, particularly how alternative groups challenged mainstream music and occupied a significant part of Recife's local scene. Enriquez, who carried out her initial observations in 2011, found a different music scene when she returned to Brazil in 2015. In a moment of economic and political crisis, Recife's environment had shifted. Before, a succession of new music groups was able to gain clear prominence on the national music scene, but during the crisis period, they were thrust into austerity. According to the author, it was in that year that the state of Pernambuco experienced its most severe economic decline in twenty years, followed by a drop in quality-of-life indicators in the country as a whole. This period of stagnation was still reigning and in force when the researcher returned in 2018. The chapter is thus about change—but also about the professional strategies of musicians and entrepreneurs involved in cultural work who, in their own way, had been part of the so-called rising new middle class. As the reader will see, in Brazil, the "middle class" does not go to "paradise."[2]

Moisés Kopper had a similar experience in Porto Alegre. In his chapter, Kopper describes the move of 160 families to the Condominium Bento Gonçalves as part of the national housing program known as Minha Casa Minha Vida (My House, My Life). Minha Casa Minha Vida was created by the Workers' Party in 2009 and was the largest housing program ever seen in Brazil. The author and his team had already visited the site in 2014 and found happy families, eager to comment and boast about their new material and symbolic status. But the context had changed in 2017, and Kopper too tries his hand at explaining the results of Brazil's elections the following year. Analyzing the subjectivities of these populations and their contradictions, as well as the effects of the rapid political-economic changes between 2003 and 2014, Kopper shows how the hopes and fears of locals shifted, rendering them skeptical when not simply negative.

Kopper is also attentive to the rapid growth of Evangelical Christianity in Porto Alegre, a phenomenon that mixed religion and politics, with the church "forcing" parishioners to vote for their own candidates. If the research team had already noted a significant amount of apathy and limited satisfaction with the PT's national policies in 2015, the apathy and dissatisfaction were much greater in 2018. The research shows a change in the perception of respondents and new understandings of what constituted domestic and private interactions. Ultimately, Kopper's interlocutors felt increasing levels of insecurity and, with it, distrust toward institutions and politicians in general. The wager made on the "new" (which has turned out to be so "old"), and the acceptance of a model of "private democracies," with private notions of well-being shaping local disputes, seemed to demonstrate a new local sensibility. The research showed how, in this way, changes in politics and in the economy were accompanied by clear changes in the behavior and subjectivity of the investigated population.

Sarah LeBaron von Baeyer's chapter explores the ambiguity that exists between, on the one hand, the stereotyped view that Jair Bolsonaro holds of the Japanese—for example, making frequent jokes about the supposed size of Japanese men's genitalia—and, on the other hand, the paradoxical popularity of the president among Japanese Brazilians currently living in Japan. While this dynamic was already made manifest in previous elections, in which the Japanese Brazilian electorate showed itself to be averse to the PT, the 2018 elections only amplified it. However, the author ventures a hypothesis. In von Baeyer's opinion, given the precariousness these populations suffer in Japan, their conservative votes expressed their desire to find stability in their country.

So working with transnational migrants in the Brazil-Japan axis, von Baeyer seeks to uncover generational aspirations influenced by religion, work, and education. Given that her informants receive significantly higher salaries in Japan than what they would earn in Brazil, the possibility that they might be able to return to Brazil and enter the national labor market there is increasingly reduced. This motivated them to vote en masse for Jair Bolsonaro. Von Baeyer also shows us how this type of support for Bolsonaro is not an isolated phenomenon, since Brazilian immigrants living in countries such as the United States, Italy, Portugal, and the United Kingdom also favored candidates from Bolsonaro's conservative party, the PSL. However, in Japan the phenomenon is especially pronounced, with 90 percent of votes going to Bolsonaro. Von Baeyer refines the analysis and shows that the reason for this overwhelming victory was voters' hope that the new government would bring stability and comfort. For those who live outside Brazil, social immobility and marginality remain central concerns, and they would like to find, as the author explains, a place to call home within Brazil.

LaShandra Sullivan's chapter analyzes feminist and LGBT activism in the city of Rio de Janeiro. In contrast to the chapters that demonstrate a certain pessimism directly resulting from a succession of financial, political, and moral crises, the chapter by Sullivan highlights the ability of these activists to stand firm despite a highly adverse context. Examining the concept of *se segurar* (to hold on), and understanding it as a social practice, Sullivan shows how it is possible to overcome racism, class, and heteronormative patriarchy. The chapter explores metaphors and emic categories from the researcher's fieldwork and finds, in the concepts *se segurar* and *segurar a onda* (to catch a wave), a collective attempt to avoid pessimism and skepticism growing in Brazilian society. The author discusses lesbian and Black feminists from 1990 until 2018. In March of that year, Marielle Franco was murdered and became a symbol of a more generous and inclusive Brazil. This article focuses most specifically on the Black LGBT movement, ethnographically describing its events and spaces such as "Batekoo," "Afro-Bafo," and "Bicha Preta" parties. But "holding" means not just "holding on"; it also represents a way of taking the lead and keeping the pace through dancing and fighting. "Holding" represents a response to the financial crisis and crisis of values sweeping across the country and also a purposeful way out, created and developed over a long period of time by people long made invisible.

In June 2018, Carlos Eduardo Henning participated in the XV National LGBT Workshop, funded by progressive sectors of the National Congress in Brasília. At that time, he presented his research on older lesbian, gay, bisexual, transgender, and intersex (LGBTI) people, among other subjects. Henning did not know, but his investigation of a nongovernmental organization (NGO) in São Paulo—an NGO focused on aging and elderly LGBTI individuals—would change a lot with Brazil's recent political polarization. If, during Henning's first phase of research carried out from 2009 to 2013, the informants were more concentrated in a certain economic elite that resides in São Paulo, in the most recent phase, it was possible to add markers such as race, class, gender, and sexuality. This time, many of the informants were of the lower-middle and working classes, living in precarious conditions. In short, the same research topic now included many distinct social groups. But what is particularly interesting in Henning's research is how, unlike in the other ethnographies presented in this volume, many of the people described still speak of resilience based, above all, on past victories. If most of them show concern in the face of the financial crisis and the homophobic wave of the current government, the participants do not seem ready to simply give up their battles and subjectivities. In this case, they prefer to fight.

Alvaro Jarrín's chapter deals with a neighboring theme, so to speak, analyzing the role of transgender and *travesti* activism in the midst of a regressive heteronormative politics in Brazil growing out of the 2018 election. The author analyzes Transclandestina 3020, part of a scene of "artivism," which uses and mixes artistic expressions that include fashion, art, music, theater, and social media. These are new forms of expression, using performance and theater as ways to comment on and criticize the perceptible loss of democratic freedoms. In this specific case, the direct confrontation of transphobia and oppressive gender norms is celebrated as political art. The article concludes by showing how this nonconformist activism ended up producing a visceral reaction in its audience, acting as a force capable of destabilizing previously established models.

All this artistic expression goes very much against the grain, given that homophobia and transphobia are central policies in Jair Bolsonaro's government. According to the author, the visibility of the LGBT community was on the rise when Bolsonaro won the election, and the LGBT community became an easy scapegoat and ideal enemy for him, with the executive investing heavily against policies he calls "gender ideology." This led to a rise in "transfemicide," a term introduced and taken on by trans and travesti groups, referring to the high numbers of deaths among these populations. In this case, transfemicide is entirely intersectional and becoming increasingly visible despite the conservative shift experienced in the country. It is also important to note that, according to Jarrín, despite recent setbacks, the LGBT community has maintained not only its ability to challenge realities that are exceedingly heteronormative but also its hope for a more plural and inclusive Brazil.

The chapter written by Melanie A. Medeiros, Patrick McCormick, Erika Schmitt, and James Kale shows how the creation of "political memes" represents a new form of participation in Brazil's political arena. The authors carried out their ethnographies in different Brazilian universities, with the aim of showing how, in some universities, the use of memes, featuring figures like Barbie and Ken dolls, grew exponentially in 2018 and represented a way to oppose Bolsonaro and his discriminatory rhetoric. These memes also became a way to create political participation specific to these generations. According to the authors, such memes ended up producing an unexpected political subjectivity focused on sexism, racism, inequality, meritocracy, homophobia, power, and privilege.

As one can see, ethnography is a powerful tool *to identify the symptom and thus confront the underlying causes*. Conversations, presentations, and brief questionnaires also have the potential to produce a vigorous body of knowledge. Such methods reveal that, after a period of stability and the rise of a so-called new middle class, this same group lives today in a state of despondency, which helps explain the conservative turn that occurred in Brazil and the bet on highly authoritarian governments. What's more, it represents a bet on a country that is undemocratic and that is making its institutions even more fragile.

Not by chance, the current Brazilian government, like others around the world, has resorted to a series of common strategies: emphasizing a mythical and glorious past; creating a base anti-intellectualism; returning to a patriarchal logic; emphasizing concepts of hierarchy and order; and promoting a veritable sexual hysteria that accuses women, gays, *travestis*, and other minorities of being responsible for social degeneration. This call to victimization beckons the population to react to the supposed tormentors of old, providing an incentive to polarize the nation because it divides the population between "us" and "them," as if "we" were the doers and "they," the usurpers. This all goes hand in hand with an extensive use of propaganda that does not value reality but appears to invent a new one by naturalizing certain national groups and consequently turning immigrants into strangers. We can also see a "nostalgic" return to a past that never existed and certain imaginary values regarding the land and traditions, as if these feelings were simply pure and good.

In Brazil's current political hour, nostalgic history lessons often become cure-alls and easy excuses. This book accounts for these bent and warped histories. Remade pasts and altered narratives are typical phenomena in these moments of crisis and are given to quick turns. If I had been invited to write an article in this collection and not simply an opening commentary, I might find an opportune case study in the southern state of Santa Catarina, located in a municipality called Treze de Maio (May 13). This small city's name, coat of arms, and anthem celebrate the abolition of slavery in Brazil. However, although the town had a *quilombo* (escaped slave settlement) on its outskirts that was legally recognized as such in 2015 and land was returned to the descendants of former slaves who had lived in the area, in recent years, the town has increasingly come to understand its origins as exclusively white and Italian. In the last census, a mere 0.8 percent of the local population declared themselves to be Black (*preto*), while those who considered themselves to be white reached more than 97 percent. The city also voted en masse for Jair Bolsonaro in the 2018 presidential elections. Bolsonaro had 83.89 percent of votes in the first round of the election—one of the largest percentages for a Brazilian municipality—and 89.24 percent in the second election. Not surprisingly, in this rural town of 7,070 inhabitants, most people are proud to be armed and believe that the president is there to help the agribusiness that sustains local economies.

It does not seem accidental, then, that one of the greatest local controversies revolves around the statue of a Black man in chains. According to local legend, the statue was removed from the town and replaced by a statue of the same character only without chains (figure 0.1). There are also those who say that the artwork was, at a certain moment, painted white—reflecting the mania for social whitening that many Brazilians still have. What is certain is that the statue today lives unpretentiously in front of a local church. In fact, today it seems a little pointless because the statue's arms, which once broke chains, now look very artificial as if something is missing. And in fact, they *are* missing.

These days, at the entrance to town, there is a monument that honors Italian immigrants who arrived in 1877, coming up the Tubarão River. As nothing in this world is just a coincidence, it is precisely these families that now dominate the region and seek to "forget" a regional history of slavery, to forget the Black populations that lived in the region, and to forget the Black communities that still live there. These are examples of how memories are built on the basis of particular emphases but also from the blurring and erasing of certain narratives.

But if what I describe in Treze de Maio sounds like strategies of denial and retreat, this book also highlights examples of groups that were strengthened by the crisis, "held onto" it, and invented new agendas. This is how *Precarious Democracy* explores different angles that cross social markers such as race, ethnicity, generation, region, gender, sex, and class. In this sense, a specific chapter on the phenomenon of the religious growth of Evangelicals is perhaps missing in this volume—even though the phenomenon is mentioned in some of its ethnographies. But it is difficult to deny that the crises have unfolded in synchronicity with the Evangelical explosion and its chain of influences. I also believe this volume leaves space for an ethnography of elites, to help understand how they have behaved during these decisive years in Brazilian history.

But as it stands, this book already promises and delivers a great deal. Above all, it helps to reflect on what "went wrong" in the last thirty years of democracy in Brazil. How could it be that after institutions were strengthened, new social agents appeared, and education improved, we have come to live a moment of regression in our rights as citizens? *Precarious Democracy* revisits this movie, selects different scenes than those usually considered, and opens up a critical and necessary perspective on this long process—and also on what we effectively failed to accomplish. It is easy to mythologize the recent past; it is difficult to try to make a sincere assessment of what has failed. Inequality, for example, is a problem that Brazilians still have to face, both in cities and in the countryside. Brazil is the ninth-most unequal country in the world (among those with reliable data) and rises to the fifth-most unequal if the criterion is income inequality in the countryside.

This collection of texts also allows us to think about how the PSDB and PT[3] governments that sought to cement their power following Brazil's 1989 redemocratization neglected another urgent and thorny issue on Brazil's agenda: the violence and insecurity that continue to plague the country. In this way, those governments left open a space for a retrograde government to assume power, one that presents a critical opposition to the defense of ecological and environmental rights, Black and LGBTQ activism, and human rights.

FIGURE 0.1. Statue of a now freed, formerly enslaved Black man in Treze de Maio, Santa Catarina, left behind after its bound counterpart was removed
Photo by Giovanni Bello

For these and other reasons, this is a volume that is not afraid to gaze into the crisis. On the contrary, these chapters frequently *dive* into the crisis. Etymologically, the word *crisis* means "decision"; this seems to be the angle presented by this set of chapters—the decision to move your group forward and not give up and, in contrast, the decision to retreat.

This is also a book about the anthropological "way of listening," which as such does not favor a political party, a given message, or a specific destiny. So while some of the ethnographers in the collection have an affinity with the groups of people or topics they cover, other authors appear to discuss settings that are far from their own political ideals.

Athenians wrote of *dēmokratia*, a word that combines two nouns. *Kratos* means "strength, solidity, the ability to assert oneself." The term *kratos* also serves to describe sovereign power—that is, the power attributed to those who determine the choices of the community. *Demos* generically designates "people." This represents the first challenge of democracy: knowing who the people are and who is part of them. Democracy is a type of government and a type of society that makes the political equality of people with different interests and goals its great engine for transformation. For this reason, democracy is rooted in normative ideals of citizenship that emphasize the right to participate in political life. Importantly, these definitions do not hinge on the status of participants. This type of enfranchisement is guided by a set of inclusive criteria that extend citizenship to all members of society, indicating that each citizen has the same weight in political decisions regardless of their personal merits.

That is why, however paradoxical the phrase *Precarious Democracy* may seem at first, it is fitting for what is in the end a paradoxical book—it gives voice and listens to groups with whom we agree but also others with whom we do not; it embraces different perspectives, rather than selecting among them. On the other hand, we know that, by definition, democracy is an unfinished project; it is *precarious*. Every democracy is imperfect and, in that way, complete. After all, social and civil rights are never definitively won or "lived happily ever after." They need always to be reclaimed and won, each day anew.

NOTES

1. Lobato was one of Brazil's most noted authors and proponents of petro-nationalism.
2. The film *A Classe Operária Vai ao Paraíso* (*The Working Class Goes to Paradise*) was released in 2009.
3. Editors' note: The PSDB (Brazilian Social Democracy Party) and PT (Workers' Party) are the political parties that dominated presidential elections for much of the democratic period that followed military rule in Brazil. The two parties held the presidency from 1995 until 2016, competing from the center right and center left, respectively, and for shifting alliances with large opportunistic political parties such as the PMDB (Party of the Brazilian Democratic Movement).

PART I THE INTIMACY OF POWER

1 · "FAMILY IS EVERYTHING"

Generational Tensions as a Working-Class Household from Recife, Brazil, Contemplates the 2018 Presidential Elections

BENJAMIN JUNGE

> I have one thing that I see very strongly, and that is unity and respect. Because thanks to God, my family is here … my house, you know, which is, as they say, "My house, my life."
> —Luzimar, July 9, 2018

> My God, when this election is finished … I'm already going to schedule an appointment with a psychiatrist, because from October 8 onward, someone in the family is going to need it.
> —Dona Helena, October 3, 2018

"A LITTLE CROSS-EYED" (MONDAY, SEPTEMBER 17, 2018)

For a large family like the Pereiras, birthdays are frequent, and they come with the expectation of a *party*. So despite it being a busy weeknight, the extended family,[1] a handful of neighborhood friends, and I—the hybrid observer-friend—have assembled to commemorate Luzimar's fifty-seventh birthday. Her son, Carlinhos, shares some warm remarks about his mother: "We decided to make this simple tribute to reciprocate the attention that Luzimar has for each one of us. Anyone close to her knows how sweet she is, how special she is, how dedicated, how hardworking she is." Luzimar is the daughter-in-law of the Pereiras' matriarch, a sixty-three-year-old widow named Helena, who seems content as she sits on the sofa and listens to Carlinhos speak. Dona Helena has two sons and two daughters, all of them married adults in their thirties or forties. Her sons—Gabriel and Ednilson (Luzimar's husband)—are here tonight with their families; her two daughters, Sônia and Katia, are not. Sônia lives with her husband and daughter in the nearby city of João Pessoa (though she will send along her birthday greetings to Luzimar via WhatsApp before the evening is over); Katia lives in Switzerland where, a few years back, she married a Portuguese man and has recently had a daughter.

The party foods—an enormous chocolate cake surrounded by platters of *empadas* with their savory aromas wafting through the room—are proving a distraction, and Carlinhos soon wraps up the homage to his mother: "We wish you good energies, health, protection … positive thoughts. We want you to enjoy every moment of your life, with those who love you, and respect you, and cherish you … people who are part of your life, each one present here." Someone launches into "Happy Birthday to You,"[2] and everyone sings and claps enthusiastically. Soon after, cake is served, and people sit around for the next hour or so, chatting and snapping photos and videos to post on Facebook or send on WhatsApp. The photo Dona Helena posts—which I took at her request—shows the whole family flanking Luzimar. I wasn't the only photographer in this moment, so the photo captures family members gazing in slightly different directions, leading one of Helena's Facebook friends to comment, "A família tá vesguinha visse kkk" (The family is a little cross-eyed you know LOL).

Despite the usual intergenerational tensions, sibling rivalries, and frictions with in-laws, the Pereiras—like most working-class Brazilian families—manifest a powerful solidarity, supporting each other when times are tough and celebrating milestones such as birthdays, weddings, baptisms, and graduations. Still, there was palpable tension in the air on this particular night, as Luzimar's birthday fell just three weeks before the date set for Brazil's first-round presidential election (October 7), and anticipation of the election had introduced new anxieties into everyday life for the Pereiras. On this night, family members were *indeed* gazing in different directions—different directions for their own lives and for Brazil. These were the elections that saw the extraordinary rise and eventual triumph of hard-right candidate Jair Bolsonaro, a former army captain and seven-term congressman from Rio de Janeiro. Relying heavily on social media, Bolsonaro took a tough stance on crime and defended "traditional family values." He promised austerity measures and cuts in government spending and vowed to stamp out crime and violence by providing greater access to firearms for ordinary citizens. After Workers' Party (Partido dos Trabalhadores; PT) candidate and former president Luiz Inácio Lula da Silva was arrested in April 2018 in a highly politicized process, Bolsonaro became the front-runner. Though finishing in first place in the first-round election (with 46 percent of the popular vote), he failed to win 50 percent of valid votes outright and so proceeded to the second-round election on October 28, when he faced PT candidate Fernando Haddad.

The one family member openly supporting Bolsonaro—Helena's oldest son, Gabriel—had, in recent weeks, increasingly used his own Facebook page and the family's private WhatsApp group to praise his candidate and to argue the need to demolish the entire political establishment in Brazil. If asked about his support for Bolsonaro, Gabriel would likely mention at least one of the following themes: (a) the need for a president who "owes nothing to anybody" and would thus be singularly capable of bulldozing an irredeemably corrupt political system based on bribes; (b) the problem of violence in public, urban spaces and the promising solution of making gun ownership easier for the citizenry; (c) the critique of human rights discourses, which exacerbate violence by giving undue respect and legal protection to undeserving criminals; (d) the urgent need to reintroduce discipline, respect, and morality through a more structured vision of education; and (e) the need to keep the PT from *ever* assuming power again in Brazil.

In this chapter, I present a reflexive ethnographic account of daily life for the Pereiras during the final weeks of Brazil's 2018 election season, with special attention to Helena, her son Gabriel, and her grandson Ewerton. As in all election seasons, these weeks were characterized by the "acceleration, intensity, [and] greater visibility of politics" in daily life (Rubim 2002, 329) and a disruption of routinized perceptions of political process and actors (Palmeira 1990, 6), during which ordinary citizens are prompted through traditional and social media[3] (as well as through the legal requirement to vote) to consider possible futures for their nation and for other groups they might care about (Junge 2018, 48–49; also see Cesarino 2019).

After providing additional background on the Pereiras, I present a series of ethnographic narratives based on fieldnotes, informal and structured conversations, and observations (both face-to-face and online), followed by post facto analysis and reflections.[4] With special attention to

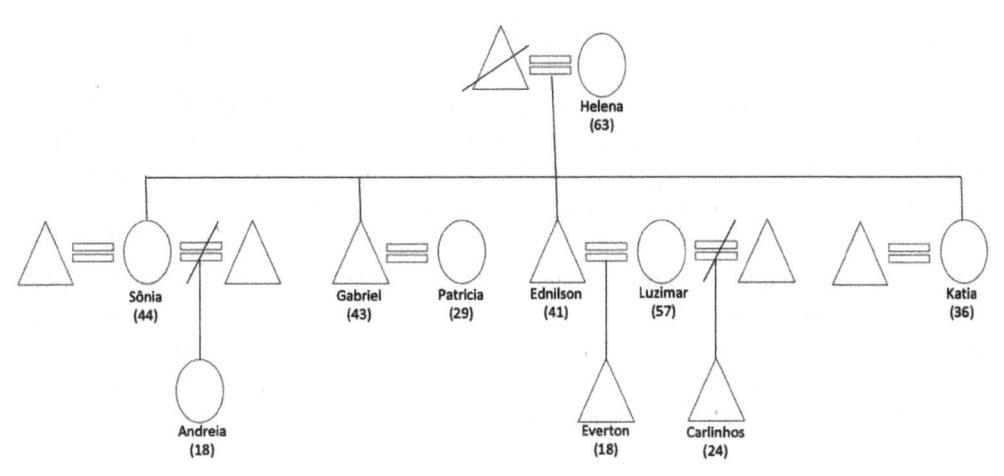

FIGURE 1.1. Dona Helena's family
Diagram by author.

anxieties arising from squabbles on Facebook and WhatsApp, I argue that assertions of "family" became an idiom for navigating interpersonal tensions against the backdrop of crises alternately perceived as political, economic, and moral. More specifically, "family" was frequently evoked and conceived as a corrective to the fracturing effect of politics. I contend, moreover, that reassertions of family evince a crisis of masculinity, disputes over moral disintegration in the public sphere, and a blurring of public and private experience brought on by online social media. I will argue that this blurring of public and private has destabilized conventional meanings of "family," rendering it "strange" for the Pereiras and across Brazil. While sexuality, social media, and cultural memory will all appear as important, intersecting domains for the elaboration of political sentiment, this chapter above all explores a parallel between the kind of family and the kind of society working-class Brazilians like the Pereiras might desire. Instead of a theoretical discussion with ethnographic detours, I aim here for an evocative ethnographic account leading inductively to a series of provisional theoretical claims.

THE PEREIRAS: INROADS AND EXPERIENCES OF MOBILITY

I first met the Pereiras in 2017 when I was introduced to Dona Helena through a mutual friend from her neighborhood who had worked for me the previous year on a citywide survey for a three-year anthropological investigation of the lifeways and political subjectivities of Brazil's "once-rising poor."[5] I rented a room from Helena for three months that year and, in 2018, when I returned to Recife for seven months to teach at the local university and complete project fieldwork, I regularly visited the Pereiras to catch up on the family's comings and goings. Like many working-class Brazilian families, the Pereira family has thrived in recent years. Over the past two decades, their house—once a precarious hillside dwelling—has been fortified into a safe and stable residence in which Helena and the families of her children occupy separate households connected by mazelike hallways. The house sits on the main thoroughfare in a peripheral neighborhood I refer to as "Morro Doce" (Sweet Hill).[6] The Pereiras' overall economic situation has also improved: After years below the poverty line, by 2018, the family's per-capita household income had risen to the category economists typically refer to as "lower middle class" (or "lower C class").[7] This stability comes in large part due to gainful employment for most of Helena's children. Her oldest son, Gabriel, is a sergeant in the Brazilian army, giving him a robust salary that provides financial security for the family and has enabled the purchase of a humble country house a couple hours from Recife.

Perhaps the strongest symbol of socioeconomic mobility for the Pereiras has been the grandchildren's educational achievements: Just a month before Luzimar's party, her son Carlinhos completed his undergraduate degree in social sciences at one of Recife's two prestigious federal universities. Earlier in the year, both Carlinhos's younger brother, Ewerton, and his cousin, Andreia, had passed their college entrance examinations on the first attempt and were now a semester into their courses of study (graphic design and economic sciences, respectively). Both had succeeded through a federal affirmative action program that prioritizes nonwhite and poor applicants, initiated during the years Brazil was governed by the leftist PT, 2003 to 2016 (a period when the Pereiras routinely voted for PT candidates in presidential elections).[8] Finally, Gabriel's wife, Patricia, had just completed her doctorate in agricultural sciences—an achievement without precedent for the family. With these triumphs, Helena was overflowing with pride and hope for her family.

FACING THE ELECTIONS: GROWING TENSIONS FOR THE PEREIRAS

Particularly uncomfortable with Gabriel's support for Bolsonaro was his nephew Ewerton (Helena's grandson and Luzimar's son). Ewerton is gay, though at the time of the elections, he was not out to his family. In private, however, the family regularly speculated about the sexuality of this beloved grandson. Gabriel, who at the time of the elections had no children of his own, was particularly anxious about the sexuality of his nephew—an anxiety that resonated with his concerns about the breakdown of morality and respect in Brazilian society and his ever-intensifying conviction—consonant with social media–fueled shifts in opinion across Brazil—that the lion's share of blame for this lay with Lula and the PT. At the time of his mother's birthday party, Ewerton was several months into his first-ever relationship (with a classmate from his program at the university), and he felt a growing sense of disconnect between his "out life" (*vida assumida*) on campus and the secrecy at home. I myself identify as gay and, by the elections, most of the family was aware of this and, perhaps offset by my status as an American with academic credentials, seemed to have little issue. Nonetheless, background tension grew as Ewerton became increasingly frustrated with his uncle's postings on Facebook and WhatsApp about the moral menace of homosexuality. For his part, Gabriel grappled with the growing disconnect between the longstanding affection between him and his nephew and their intensifying discord online—a disconnect that Gabriel, perhaps, linked to my own friendship with the family. There was some basis for this, as I enjoyed a strong friendship with his mother (Helena), with his wife (Patricia), and with Ewerton, whom I tried to support as he moved forward in constructing a new sexual subjectivity. Indeed, the day before Luzimar's birthday party, Recife's 2018 LGBTQ pride festival had taken place, and I had posted on Facebook a few photos of myself with friends riding on top of a large float (*trio-elétrico*); Helena and Ewerton had both "loved" the photos, and Ewerton had expressed to me his frustration that he couldn't be there.

For other family members, anxiety around the elections was less about Bolsonaro than about a perceived destabilization of a more unified and more *social* family dynamic. Helena, for her part, had grown irate with the politicization of the family's WhatsApp group, as did Luzimar, who considers voting a personal and private matter. Carlinhos identifies ideologically as on the left but is nonconfrontational by disposition and, perhaps more than anyone in the family short of his grandmother, prioritizes the maintenance of social harmony over arguing political positions with friends and family—and he too had become weary of the growing rancor.

With these background anxieties manifest at Luzimar's party, then, Carlinhos's speech was as much a call or plea for family as a celebration of it. It was a performance of a particular vision of togetherness rooted in the notion of "family" as a social unit, which is, at its core, nonconfrontational and apolitical.

"I DON'T LIKE TO SEE MY FAMILY DISCUSSING POLITICS" (SEPTEMBER 3, 2018)

In the early hours of a Monday morning, two weeks prior to Luzimar's birthday party, Dona Helena shares a YouTube video on her Facebook page in which Bolsonaro gives a speech promising that as president he will preserve family values and devotion to God and homeland, and that he will protect Brazil from "gender ideology"[9] and "communism." (As of October 1, 2018, the clip had more than forty million views.) There's no accompanying commentary, but Helena's post quickly elicits a handful of "likes" (including from her oldest son, Gabriel) and, within an hour, a comment from a distant friend, Hamilton. "How great that you changed your vote, Helena," he writes. "Congratulations!" Helena quickly responds, "I didn't change, nor did I decide if I will vote. [Politicians] all make promises and do nothing. The government with its gang of thieves are sinking our country. When Jair [Bolsonaro] makes his explanations there [in the video clip], really what I think is that no one will change anything, unfortunately. I don't believe it and don't like to see my family discussing politics or religion." A longtime neighborhood friend named Joanna responds, encouraging Helena to pick a candidate who "has a clean record"—a thinly veiled pitch for Bolsonaro—to which Helena responds, "I'm looking for one . . . LOL." Soon after, another neighborhood friend, Sandra, comments, "I've already decided and I justify my vote with pleasure, my friend," which I later learned was also a nod to Bolsonaro. This elicits a more thoughtful response from Helena:

> I'm thinking the same thing. On certain points I agree with Jair. Except that he is being very radical on other points. I don't accept fighting violence with violence. Despite what people are saying about Lula, he was the only president who really cared about the people and there will be no other who will do the same, unfortunately. I respect the choices of other people, but I don't believe in politics. I only had one president and he is gone but still lives in my heart as a person who solved the problem of hunger for many. "Lula always Lula."

That evening, Helena's grandson Ewerton chimes in with a single word—"Misericórdia!"—a northeastern colloquialism that can loosely be translated as, "Good lord!" Hamilton (who Ewerton doesn't know personally) responds to this with a variation on a widely circulated Bolsonaro campaign slogan, "É bom Jair se acostumando" (You'd better start getting used to Jair).[10] For the next hour or two, Ewerton and Hamilton respond to each other's posts with growing antagonism. Ewerton chides Hamilton for thinking a candidate with so few accomplishments in his twenty-eight-year political career could do anything as president. Hamilton is initially playful in his rebukes to Ewerton—asserting that governing the country requires different qualifications than being a congressman—but eventually calls him "uninformed and unpoliticized" and tells him to stop posting "bobagens" (nonsense). At this, Ewerton responds, "Typical of Bolsonaro voters, they can't manage to dialogue without offending others. If you vote for someone who thinks arming the population will work in Brazil, who has no clue on women's rights, is extremely racist and homophobic among other ABSURDITIES, well for sure I am unpoliticized. I'm not going to stay here on the internet dialoguing with you because my thinking isn't going to change and neither is yours. Next time, don't respond to commentaries that have nothing to do with you." Hamilton quickly responds, "And cursing at Bolsonaro with those adjectives isn't offensive? CMON. You think you've got it all figured out, kid." Hamilton adds a colloquial expression with a possible sexual reading: "Vá tomar seu gagau, vá!" which could be read either as an admonishment to a testy child or as a directive to give someone a blowjob. Helena's follow-up is directed at her grandson: "Dear, don't discuss it [with this person]. You are beginning now, you'll have a lot of time to understand how everything works, my grandson. Kisses." Ewerton acquiesces to his grandmother's request, stating, "Ok, I'm gonna call it quits here. Patience for adults that should have a DROP of conscience. Good night."

The next day, Ewerton's cousin Andreia chimes in with her own "Misericórdia!" to which Hamilton responds (again) with "You'd better start getting used to Jair" followed by a series of happy-face emojis. Soon after, a neighborhood friend—a twenty-six-year-old leftist activist named Pedro—offers his own "Misericórdia!" followed with an apology for intruding and a series of reflections about the need for Brazilians to vote based on who can best promote employment and economic growth rather than "hate": "Bolsonaro only represents the hatred of those who have hatred of politics and hatred of the PT, and he gives them an irrational proposal to ignite more fires, that are about to become civil war. Anyway, I think we need to unite Brazil, pacify the spirits, and this is not done with weapons, this is done with jobs and income or rather, with a well-structured national development plan." Helena's oldest daughter, Sônia, now chimes in: "I don't understand how people lose their principles and manners because of their political candidates. Respect is good and I like it, especially if it's with my mother." Here a longtime neighborhood friend of Helena's (and public PT supporter), Bethe, enters the conversation as follows: "[Bolsonaro] is a fool. I don't call him an animal because that would be offensive to other species. He is a disgusting person who apologizes to torturers, homophobes, racists, and so on. I am and will always be for the PT, Lula and Haddad. [Lula was] the best president of all time." Now Helena's other daughter, Katia (who lives in Switzerland), responds to Bethe's post with, "That's right. With all of the mistakes and successes [of the PT], they were the best for us, in my opinion"—a comment that Helena, Ewerton, and Gabriel's wife, Patricia, promptly "like."

Reflections: Not long after she shared the provocative Bolsonaro clip, I had asked Helena what her motivations had been. "I thought it was interesting, that's it," she had responded. Hence there was some indeterminacy to Helena's motivations and, in her political views, a certain moving-away from the impulse to arrive at a coherent position or candidate in favor of circulation through a series of provocations. By the same token, many of Helena's contributions to the discussion that followed her initial post do seem to indicate that she was using Facebook to *work through* her thoughts about Bolsonaro (including her discomfort with his proposal to make gun ownership easier for ordinary citizens) and about Lula (who for Helena had been a great president, despite the allegations of corruption contributing to her empty expectations of politics and the state). In this discussion stream, there is also a form of interaction reminiscent of some form of deliberative public (Habermas 1989). However, the "public" is far from the Habermasian ideal, as reason is not held as the guiding discursive principle and little attempt is made to bracket status differences. Rather than deliberation, for Helena, the guiding discursive principle was something closer to *family solidarity*, which she perceived at the time to be in a vulnerable state of disarray. Further, because this particular Facebook public isn't limited to "face-to-face" friends, it is both strange and volatile. Such a public elicits incongruous stances from Helena toward her grandson—one protective, the other chiding. Helena wants not to "see

[her] family discussing . . . politics," but on Facebook "family" is reconstituted as what I conceptualize as a "strange public" in which usual principles of privacy, solidarity, and nonconfrontation are troubled.

By asking Hamilton to exit a conversation that "has nothing to do" with him, Ewerton also makes overtures toward a notion of family that is untenable on Facebook. Different from his grandmother, however, Ewerton uses Facebook as a platform on which to cultivate his own political voice—although the effort turns cynical to the extent that he feels his main interlocutor, Hamilton (and even his grandmother) is attempting to shut him down (which he understands in explicitly generational terms). His explicit mention of homophobia in the stream of comments is an experiment of sorts—a provisional assertion prioritizing a particular form of injustice to which he *might* have a personal connection. The lukewarm response Ewerton gets from his grandmother, the heavy frequency of "like" emojis Gabriel posts on Hamilton's posts, and the absence of participation from his parents or brother (whether through text or emojis) heighten his feelings of alienation. Increasingly, virtual space would come into conflict with the experience of "family" in face-to-face interactions during the election.

"YOU'RE A TEENAGER. . . . YOU DON'T KNOW ANYTHING" (WEDNESDAY, OCTOBER 3, 2018)

Helena invites me over for afternoon coffee and snacks, and when I stop by on the way home from teaching, I see she's dressed up and has bought fresh rolls and cheese. I'm aware—as Helena knows—that since Luzimar's birthday party a couple of weeks ago, familial frustrations and arguments linked to the elections have been intensifying. A few days after her party, for example, Luzimar—at Gabriel's suggestion—modified her Facebook profile photo to indicate support for the Bolsonaro campaign, using a template that was circulating widely at the time.[11] She had taken immediate heat for the post (receiving "sad" emojis from Ewerton and Andreia and a lighthearted comment from Helena that she'd lost first-place status in Luzimar's heart to Gabriel). A day later, she removed the campaign template from her profile photo without commentary. Ewerton had shared with me how disturbing he found this, though he blamed his uncle, not his mother. Ewerton had aired frustration about his grandmother as well: "She has a very conservative way of thinking. For her there is no such thing as left and right, for her it's all the same. She supports some things that Bolsonaro says, but she supports Lula." For her part, Helena had continued using Facebook to occasionally share pro-Bolsonaro content, including a video of a father complaining about a textbook that represents a family led by two homosexual men as natural. As usual, though, Helena rarely posted her own framing comments with these clips, apparently preferring to see how others responded.

With a much fancier coffee-and-snacks setup than I'm accustomed to, I have the sense that Helena is trying to perform some sense of normalcy and, indeed, as we start catching up, she focuses on conspicuously nonpolitical themes such as her infant granddaughter in Switzerland (she has new photos to show me) and a massive cake she is planning to bake for a party at the military officers club her son Gabriel manages. The vibe is disrupted, however, soon after Ewerton comes down from his family's household and joins the conversation. While he's telling us about a new desk his father got him, the TV news playing in the background turns to Bolsonaro, at which point Helena turns down the volume and blurts out, "My God, I can't take it anymore, Bolsonaro here, Bolsonaro there! But it doesn't change, does it, Ewerton? Today, the whole day [the family] discussed [Bolsonaro] in the [WhatsApp] group. Everyone has a point of view on Bozo, right. But my dear for God's sake! This week I went to sleep and woke up at one-thirty in the morning—almost two o'clock—and they were still in the group debating." It comes as little surprise to learn that the recent arguments have pitted Ewerton and his cousin Andreia against their uncle, Gabriel. This has in turn frustrated Luzimar with her son. ("She hates me these days," Ewerton says, laughing a bit.) I'm surprised, however, to learn that Gabriel's wife, Patricia, has increasingly challenged her husband in the family WhatsApp group of late (something she's never done explicitly on Facebook).

Helena brings up the Facebook fiasco involving Hamilton ("His politics are sick," Helena says) but now accuses her grandson of having been too confrontational:

HELENA: [Hamilton] wasn't being mean.
EWERTON: Yes, he was, c'mon! He was bashing me there, said I was immature.
HELENA: [But] isn't that right?
EWERTON: But why am I immature to you?
HELENA: You're a teenager, you only got interested recently, you have no knowledge of politics, you don't know anything.
EWERTON: Why don't I know?
HELENA: How are you going to debate something? Do you see me debating? I don't debate, why? Because I don't understand politics.
EWERTON: But you're not a teenager, you're full of experience, why don't you debate?
HELENA: Because you have things, opinions, things that for us are private.
EWERTON: Just like I have opinions that are mine.
HELENA: Listen . . . that's exactly why you're immature, you won't even vote, but you have to confront people, which is a lack of respect.
EWERTON: You expect me to be a mature teenager, but you don't expect maturity from a person who's more than forty years old, like Uncle Gabriel.
HELENA: That's his problem.
EWERTON: It's my problem too.

Later in the conversation, Helena reiterates her general dismissal of politics in Brazil. "For me, no candidate is any good," she tells me. She's frustrated with Lula and the PT but is also frustrated with those who blame all of Brazil's problems on the PT, as when she says, "Lula helped—He didn't *only* rob. But they blame all of the ills of the world on the PT." Helena says she hasn't decided who she'll vote for but is thinking it should be a "protest vote."

Elsewhere in the conversation, with Luzimar now present, there's a delicate moment when Ewerton implies Helena allowed Gabriel to take over her thinking on the elections. She responds defensively but with a provocation of her own: "No, he didn't convince me! If he had, I'd vote for Bolsonaro. I don't accept it, you can be a homosexual, you can be a thief, you can be a married man, you can be whatever, but you have to have dignity, respect for others." That Helena begins her statement with an affirmation of the rights of homosexuals is powerful for the awareness and acceptance it implies of her grandson's homosexuality. And yet soon after, she starts complaining about the "gender ideology" promoted by the PT and proceeds to show me on her cell phone a video of a "gay hunky-Jesus contest" consisting of several scantily clad male contestants on a stage competing in a highly sexualized manner under the campy judgment of drag queens.[12] (Gabriel himself posts this video a few days later with the caption "BOLSONARO WILL PUT AN END TO THIS.") When Helena exclaims, "I can't support this!," Luzimar quickly interjects, "It's fake, Helena! These days it's all fake." To this, Helena responds, "Still, I think it's a lack of respect." At this point, Ewerton is rolling his eyes, says "I have to study," and excuses himself.

Reflections: The exchange recounted above started off playfully enough, but Ewerton ended up challenging his grandmother at every turn, in a manner I had never seen before—and Helena became palpably frustrated. She became especially upset at her grandson's challenge to her statement that she "doesn't understand politics"—to which she responded with an assertion that political opinions are best kept private. To Helena, Ewerton's attempts to "debate" (on Facebook, in the family's WhatsApp group, and in our conversation) violated a sense of "respect" rooted (alternately) in acceding to elders and not pushing people to discuss "private" matters. For his part, Ewerton was confounded that his grandmother, who has rich life experience, doesn't join family discussions of matters he feels to be of personal and national importance; he was also, I think, vexed and somewhat hurt that Helena didn't support his attempts to cultivate an adult political consciousness and hadn't defended him when he was attacked (by Hamilton) in a public forum. I also note that, for Helena, "respect" has congealed into a "real" phenomenon, challenges to which she can *observe* in YouTube clips and in the context of interactions with her grandson (both in person and on social media). In this conversation and more generally, the "lack of respect" that discomfits Helena often pertains to off-putting expressions of nonnormative masculinity.

"THE GIANT HAS AWAKENED" (OCTOBER 7–28, 2018)

Late morning, I message Helena on WhatsApp: "Dona Helena, good vibes for the whole family today!" To this, she quickly responds, "A day of peace and light for you! Today is a day of much expectation, may God lead us through it." Just a few minutes later, Gabriel posts on his Facebook page: "I bump into my mother and my brother-in-law and hear that they'll vote Bolsonaro 17, priceless!" To this, Helena responds, "Your mother loves you whoever your candidate is." An hour later, Gabriel draws an apparent parallel between his own family and Brazil as it prepares to vote, posting, "In my family, counting my wife, my mother, my brothers and in-laws, the result is: Bolsonaro 8 votes, another candidate 1 vote, undeclared 2 votes. Here in the house Bolsonaro will win in the first-round election, and I didn't even need to see about the other relatives. I believe in a better and more just country." Patricia—almost certainly the person who Gabriel counted as voting for "another candidate"—quickly responds to her husband's post with a crying-while-laughing emoji.

Mid-afternoon as voting returns are pointing toward a possible Bolsonaro sweep, a close friend of Ewerton, who is the son of one of Gabriel's military colleagues, posts, "The giant has awakened, and he's racist, LGBT-phobic, sexist, misogynist, hateful to poor people even though he is one, and has zero value for the people around him." To this, Patricia replies, "And yet many voted [for Bolsonaro] just out of wanting to be on the winning team." Ewerton responds to Patricia's post with a sad-face emoji and comments, "Embarrassing that this man leads the country's elections! [We in the] northeast [have] serious back pain from carrying the country in every election."[13] Among the dozen or so who "like" Ewerton's post is his older half-brother, Carlinhos, breaking out of his usual stealth mode of Facebook participation.

For the Pereiras, the three weeks between the first- and second-round elections are turbulent and disorienting. Gabriel steps up the frequency of pro-Bolsonaro and anti-PT posts on Facebook, averaging three or four per day. Among the themes addressed in his posts, homosexuality emerges as central, typical examples being the threat to traditional family values posed by the PT's promotion of the so-called Gay Kit;[14] gay Brazilians who proudly support Bolsonaro; and homophobic violence under the PT's watch. Also prominent in his posts are rebuffs to youth and PT supporters speaking ill of the dictatorship, as in the two memes he shared: "My 80-year-old grandparents don't complain about the 1964 military regime. But my 20-year-old friends are traumatized!" "For a generation without limits, following rules is a DICTATORSHIP." In the midst of a particularly intense flurry of Facebook activity, Gabriel posts a photo of himself and his wife, Patricia, hugging each other and both looking happy. Among the dozen or so praising remarks, Dona Helena has responded with a provocation to his childless son and daughter-in-law: "You look beautiful, but where are my grandchildren. I'm waiting, you hear?"

Other than chance encounters at the house entrance, Ewerton hasn't seen much of his uncle lately and, other than adding frown emojis on some of Gabriel's postings, has scaled down his own Facebook activity since the first-round election. While Ewerton's mother, Luzimar, has ceased posting much of anything on Facebook, his father, Ednilson, has been posting on politics more frequently, alternating between comic images of Bolsonaro's most eccentric public statements and behaviors and apparently serious posts expressing nostalgia for the Lula era and indignation at the prospect of "militarizing" education in Brazil (both varieties of posting "liked" by his son Ewerton).

It is also during this period that my own online posture shifts to more explicitly engage my Brazilian Facebook friends. On October 8, I post a five-hundred-word text in Portuguese summarizing Bolsonaro's odious statements about LGBTQ people and ending with a challenge:

> To my friends and acquaintances who are considering whether or not to vote for Jair Bolsonaro on October 28: Do you have a daughter or son, niece or nephew, granddaughter or grandson, mother or father, aunt or uncle, grandmother or grandfather who is lesbian or gay? If you love your LGBT relative—whether they are "out" or not—I ask you to consider the message a Bolsonaro vote would send them—a message that you agree with Bolsonaro when he publicly stated that he would prefer a gay child to "die in an accident." How can we not see this as a message of hatred? How can you look your LGBT relative in the face after voting for a man who feels that way?

My motivations for the post were both therapeutic and political—my attempt to channel growing anxiety around the elections in the form of a targeted intervention that explicitly contemplated my Recife-based LGBTQ contacts and their families. Certainly, I hoped (and assumed) the Pereiras would see and consider my post, though I was aware that, given Ewerton's closetedness, I was walking a fine line. (I showed him the text beforehand and he was surprisingly comfortable with me posting it.) The post gets "likes" and "loves" from several of my Morro Doce friends, including Patricia and Ewerton (though not Helena); there are no negative responses. A few days later, at lunch with Dona Helena's gay half-brother, Jorginho, he tells me he appreciated my post and has been feeling frustrated and mystified about Gabriel's online tirades about homosexuality: "We grew up together, you know, we're the same age, and [when I was a kid] he was one of my protectors when other kids teased me." Jorginho is optimistic, however, about the fate of "the family" after the election, telling me, "I think this moment will pass, everything will return to normal. In December, everyone's gonna be more united."

On October 18, I post a somewhat more polemical, seven-hundred-word text interrogating the recent portrayal by U.S.-based astrologer and Bolsonaro-mentor Olavo de Carvalho of the social climate in the United States as harmonious and conflict-free following the election of Donald Trump.[15] After taking Carvalho to task for his downplaying the deepening cultural polarization characterizing the Trump era, I end—as in the earlier post—with a provocation focused specifically on the fears of what a Bolsonaro victory might mean for LGBTQ Brazilians. This post garners "likes" from Luzimar, Carlinhos, and Jorginho, and "loves" from Patricia and Ewerton. Helena later tells me she thought it was an "academic text" and so hadn't read it carefully.

"MY PERCEPTION OF PEOPLE CLOSE TO ME" (OCTOBER 29–DECEMBER 1, 2018)

The day after the elections, Dona Helena shares on Facebook her responses to a series of questions about her essential characteristics as a person: "What 7 things are totally true about you?" The answer: "She has a lot of faith in God. Her soul is enlightened. She loves to travel. She protects those she loves. She doesn't give up easily. She does everything for her family. She does good without self-interest." That same day, she sends me the following note on WhatsApp: "I'm so happy! I'm so tired of my family bickering. But now things can get back to normal. For me, family is everything and I'm glad now I can get back to normal." And indeed, in posts like the one above, she seems to be reasserting the social, harmonious view of family she had felt to be slipping away these past few months.

Gabriel, meanwhile, divides his still-frequent Facebook posting between expressions of excitement and hope for the return of order and respect to Brazil, frustration at Brazilians (including both his nephew and his niece) who have modified their profile photos to integrate the anti-Bolsonaro slogan "I will be the resistance," and declarations of pride and love for his wife. Patricia, meanwhile, is on Facebook very little but does reshare a short text about what led Lucifer to be expelled from heaven—rather than behaviors such as prostitution, homosexuality, or drug use, it was his pride in thinking he was right to judge others. This thinly veiled condemnation of the sentiment behind Bolsonaro's campaign slogan "Brazil above everything, God above everyone" is "liked" almost immediately by Ewerton.

Late in the day on October 28, Ewerton texts me, "These elections have forever changed my perception of people close to me."

FINAL CONSIDERATIONS: "STRANGE PUBLICS"

In the age of social media, the Pereiras—like all Brazilians—struggle to reconcile divergences between virtual and face-to-face interactions and histories. During the months leading up to the 2018 elections, these divergences intensified and prompted various anxieties about the status of "family" within the household—and in Brazilian society. For Helena, the "family" under threat is a harmonious, hierarchical social unit in which children (even adult children) do not question their elders and do not discuss private matters with outsiders. For Gabriel, the notion of "family" crystalizes a patriarchal vision of order and respect founded upon a man's ability to provide for his kin—a normative masculinity that was undermined with the expansion of public discourse around the rights of LGBT Brazilians emblematic of the PT years, as well as material transformations in the form of increased value of traditionally feminized forms of work and decreased value of industrial/manual labor.[16] Whereas, however, Helena and Gabriel (each in their own way) seek to restore a "family" understood to be under threat, the 2018 elections have led Ewerton to deep ambivalence regarding his interactions with and obligations to kin. Unlike his uncle and grandmother—for whom "family" is the *solution*—for Ewerton, "family" has become, irrevocably, a *problem*. For all the Pereiras, the possibility of a shared vision of "family" has been contaminated by the blurring of lines between public and private experience (and between social and political communication) brought on by online social media. In the anxious, interactive flux of election-season disputes, "family" for the Pereiras has become what I have referred to as "strange public"—a strangeness fully manifest at Luzimar's birthday party.

It is perhaps fitting to end this account with news that Dona Helena gleefully conveyed to me via WhatsApp months after the elections: "Gabriel is going to be a father! It's a girl!" After expressing my congratulations, I asked Helena how far along Patricia was in the pregnancy. Doing the math, it was easy enough to work out that this child had been conceived in early October of 2018—a moment of extreme familial tension among the Pereiras and of more or less incessant Facebook postings by Gabriel about the breakdown of family values in Brazil. The newest addition to a family whose members diverge so profoundly about what constitutes a "good family" in a historical moment characterized by economic precarity and political polarizations, Patricia and Gabriel's infant daughter faces a profoundly uncertain future.

REFERENCES

Burns, Nick. 2019. "The New Brazilian Right." *American Affairs Journal* 3, no. 3 (Fall 2019): 97–122.
Cesarino, Leticia. 2019. "On Digital Populism in Brazil." *PoLAR: Political and Legal Anthropology Review* (blog), April 15, 2019. https://polarjournal.org/2019/04/15/on-jair-bolsonaros-digital-populism/.
Habermas, Jürgen. 1989. *The Structural Transformation of the Public Sphere: An Inquiry into a Category of Bourgeois Society.* Translated by Thomas Burger. Cambridge, Mass.: MIT Press.
Junge, Benjamin. 2018. *Cynical Citizenship: Gender, Regionalism, and Political Subjectivity in Porto Alegre, Brazil.* Albuquerque: University of New Mexico Press.
———. 2019. "'Our Brazil Has Become a Mess': Nostalgic Narratives of Disorder and Disinterest as a 'Once-Rising Poor' Family from Recife, Brazil, Anticipates the 2018 Elections." *Journal of Latin American and Caribbean Anthropology* 24 (4): 914–931.
Klein, Charles H., Sean T. Mitchell, and Benjamin Junge. 2018. "Naming Brazil's Previously Poor: 'New Middle Class' as an Economic, Political, and Experiential Category." *Economic Anthropology* 5 (1): 83–95.
McCallum, Cecilia. 2005. "Racialized Bodies, Naturalized Classes: Moving through the City of Salvador da Bahia." *American Ethnologist* 32 (1): 100–117.
Miskolci, Richard. 2018. "Exorcising a Ghost: The Interest behind the War on 'Gender Ideology.'" *Cadernos pagu*, no. 53. E-book.
Palmeira, Moacir. 1990. *Concepções de política e ação sindical.* Rio de Janeiro: Mimeo.
Penha-Lopes, Vânia. 2017. *Confronting Affirmative Action in Brazil: University Quota Students and the Quest for Racial Justice.* Lanham, Md.: Lexington.
Pinheiro-Machado, Rosana. 2019. *Amanhã vai ser maior: O que aconteceu com o Brasil e possíveis rotas de fuga para a crise atual.* São Paulo: Planeta.
Priante, Anna, Michel L. Ehrenhard, Tijs van den Broek, and Ariana Need. 2018. "Identity and Collective Action via Computer-Mediated Communication: A Review and Agenda for Future Research." *New Media and Society* 20 (7): 2647–2669.
Reiter, Bernd, and Gladys L. Mitchell, eds. 2009. *Brazil's New Racial Politics.* Boulder, Colo.: Lynne Rienner.
Rubim, Antonio Albino Canelas. 2002. "Visibilidades e estratégias nas eleições presidenciais de 2002 no Brasil Política, mídia e cultura." *Civitas—Revista de ciências sociais* 2 (2): 327.

NOTES

1. See figure 1.1 for a simplified kinship diagram of the Pereiras.
2. For a detailed ethnographic analysis of the birthday as a cultural formation in Brazil, see McCallum 2005.
3. In Brazil, candidates and parties receive free television and radio airtime to make their appeals to voters, effectively flooding mainstream media networks with campaign advertisements. (See Junge 2018, 50–51.)
4. In an earlier publication (Junge 2019), I examine apparent nostalgia for Brazil's 1964–1985 dictatorship among the Pereiras during the eighteen months leading up to the first-round elections on October 7, 2018.
5. See Klein, Mitchell, and Junge (2018) for more information about the broader study (funding source: National Science Foundation, Division of Behavioral and Cognitive Sciences, Cultural Anthropology Program, grant no. 1534606). Additional support for analysis and writing provided by the Brazil Institute at the Woodrow Wilson Center for International Scholars, the Fulbright Commission of Brazil, the School for Advanced Research, and the State University of New York at New Paltz.
6. All names for neighborhoods and people in this text (other than the names of cities and politicians) are pseudonyms.

7. Per-capita income for the Pereiras in 2017 was R$650 (approximately US$200, at the 2017 exchange rate), placing them in the "C3" (lower middle class) category, according to the income-based classificatory system devised by the federal government's Secretária de Assuntos Estratégicos.
8. For detailed sociological analyses of the origins, implementation, and cultural effects of affirmative action initiatives in Brazil, see Reiter and Mitchell (2009) and Penha-Lopes (2017).
9. For historical and cultural analysis of the discourse of "gender ideology" in contemporary Brazil, see Miskolci (2018).
10. This slogan relies on wordplay, since *Jair* can reference either Bolsonaro's first name or, as a grammatical formulation, the prospect of becoming familiar with someone ("já ir se acostumar").
11. For a detailed review of contemporary scholarship on the influence of social media on identity and collective action, see Priante et al. (2018).
12. This clip is available at https://www.youtube.com/watch?v=H8ke-kSUE1w.
13. In both the first- and second-round elections, the national voting pattern (i.e., heavy support for Bolsonaro) was inverted. For example, in the second-round election, nearly 70 percent of northeastern voters chose the PT candidate Haddad over Bolsonaro.
14. "Gay Kit" is the pejorative name given to a textbook, entitled *School without Homophobia*, developed in 2010 by various LGBTQ organizations in partnership with the Ministry of Education. The textbook provided guidance to teachers for addressing homophobia among students. See chapters by Henning, Jarrín, and Pinho, this volume.
15. For astute cultural and historical analysis of Olavo de Carvalho and his influence on political climate during the 2018 elections, see Burns (2019).
16. In this sense, the turn toward Bolsonaro can be seen as a move to restore a gender order that fell into disarray during Brazil's "pink tide" period (Pinheiro-Machado 2019).

2 · AMONG MOTHERS AND DAUGHTERS

Economic Mobility and Political Identity in a Northeastern *Periferia*

JESSICA JEROME

Dinner plates had been cleared at the open-air restaurant in which I was sitting with a group of friends on a hot night in June of 2016 in Barra do Ceará, one of Fortaleza's[1] oldest peripheral neighborhoods. B., the older brother of a close friend, continued a wide-ranging diatribe about the current state of the country. He had started by recounting how his maid was mad at then-president Dilma Rousseff for getting caught up in the Petrobras scandal.

"It's not the ethics that bother her. All she cares about is her Bolsa Família stipend. She's worried she won't get it unless the Workers' Party [Partido dos Trabalhadores; PT] is reelected. Can't she understand that the PT has done so much more than this [the Petrobras scandal]? It's just like the mayor of my town—he's a good guy, I like him, but he pockets everything over and over again. What crooks! We need order—we need someone who will think of our safety, and our families. Even the dictatorship was better than what we have today!"

The son of a policeman in Barra, B. now worked for a large, multinational construction company in Juazeiro do Norte, the largest city in the interior of Ceará. His ascent epitomized the economic mobility I had observed in the neighborhood as a whole, and I assumed he was still a PT supporter.

Arriving back at N.'s home where I would be staying for the next month of fieldwork, I asked her cautiously, "You think he's right?"

"About what? Dilma, and the PT?" she asked. "Lula with his pickup truck, driving south from the poor northeast—you love that story don't you?" She continued laughing, "American academics—your Left, they just love the romance of Lula. The truth is always more complicated. Go to sleep, Jessica" (field notes, June 6, 2016).

The northeast of Brazil has been portrayed as a Workers' Party stronghold since 2002 when Luiz Inácio Lula da Silva was first elected president and continuing through the most recent election in 2018 when the Northeast was the only region to back PT candidate Fernando Haddad instead of the election's eventual victor, Jair Bolsonaro. In the state of Ceará, national electoral politics shifted leftward four years earlier; in 1998, the majority of its citizens voted for their former governor, Ciro Gomes (majorities in every other Brazilian state voted for the centrist candidate, Fernando Henrique Cardoso). Neighborhood-level presidential election data for the city of Fortaleza, however, reveal pockets of opposition even in areas thought to be solidly pro-PT. Starting in 2006, the percentages voting for the opposition candidate to the PT in Barra do Ceará have slowly risen. In 2018, more than 40 percent of Barra's residents voted against the PT, despite it being one of the neighborhoods that had gained the most from the party's expansion of social benefits and opportunities.

This chapter examines this paradox by charting the upward economic trajectories and shifting political identities among a group of eight women and their extended families between the years of 1998 and 2018. Like other contributors to this volume, I seek to broaden the range of narratives that have been used to explain Brazil's shift from left- to right-wing governance and to look more closely at the origins of what became for some citizens a deep disenchantment with democracy itself.

A number of scholars (Anderson 2019; Klein, Mitchell, and Junge 2018; Singer 2018) have cited the failure of the PT to establish a citizen consciousness among an emerging middle class of consumers—a consciousness that would connect their personal transformations to specific policy paradigms rather than to their own individual discipline and efforts. As I describe in the sections below, my data support this argument, but I also found a distinct generational split in Barra residents' political engagement and civic consciousness. Older residents that I knew in Barra had maintained a staunch loyalty to the PT since its elevation to national politics in 2002. These residents, whose birth cohort ranged from 1950 to 1965, shared the defining experience of having been born in the interior of the state and migrating to Fortaleza as adolescents or young adults. They were also more likely than their children to be members of community associations or local councils and to depend more regularly on welfare programs and services. In contrast, the younger residents I came to know well in Barra typically started out as enthusiasts of the PT and other leftist candidates but were more likely to have become vocal critics of the PT by 2018. They also became less engaged in neighborhood-level associations and more disillusioned with public services. These residents, whose birth cohort ranged from 1980 to 1989, were born in the city of Fortaleza and, unlike their parents, would occasionally express a deep nostalgia for their childhoods.

The chapter is based on data collected during research trips I took to Barra do Ceará starting in 1998 and concluding in 2017. The longitudinal dimension of this data is important because it captures a shift in the political views among a younger cohort of residents that occurred alongside a transformation in their material circumstances. I first lived in this neighborhood from October of 1998 to August of 1999 while conducting dissertation research about Brazil's public health care system. I returned to the area seven times over the next two decades to conduct research on a variety of related topics.

Throughout this period, I was fortunate to sustain close contact with a group of women with whom I had formed friendships during my first year of research. My data and conclusions are drawn from lengthy periods of participant observation, extensive conversations, and informal interviews with this group of women, their friends, and their immediate and extended families. I have also included public national and local-level election data from the six election cycles (1998 through 2018) that occurred during the timespan of my field visits.[2]

THE SUBPROLETARIAT: 1998–2000

In early October of 2000, I was walking with I. and her daughter J. toward an election site in Barra do Ceará. The mayor of Fortaleza, Juraci Magalhães, a stalwart of the Brazilian Democratic Movement Party (Partido do Movimento Democrático Brasileiro; PMDB), was up for reelection, and his strongest contender was Inácio Nunes Arruda, a member of the Brazilian Communist Party

(Partido Comunista Brasileiro; PCB). Mother and daughter were deep in an argument over who was the better candidate.

"Inácio is for the poor, Mãe—he's the only one who understands us, who will bring us more services, put more schools here."

"Juraci me entendeu, me reconhece" [Juraci understands me, sees me], replied her mother.

"Of course you think this—he was your *patrão* [boss]."

"No, not because of this, I'm saying this because he's a good mayor."

"He's old, Mãe."

"Old?! Deus is old, isn't he *minha filha* [my daughter]? Deus is the oldest man in the world—and yet?! You misunderstand *filha*—Juraci has done so much for our city. He's fixed the roads, made the bus terminals much easier for us to access, he rebuilt the Hospital José Frota—this used to be an embarrassment, and now it's a hospital of the *Primeiro Mundo* [first world]! Maybe he hasn't done everything for the poor, but the poor are God's problem, only God can truly transform them" (field notes, October 3, 2000).

I was on a return field trip to Barra, and although the election was not the topic of my research, I had been observing and participating in conversations like the one above since landing in Fortaleza in mid-September. All three candidates—Juraci, Inácio, and Patrícia Aguiar (of the PT)—made visits to Barra do Ceará to plead their cases. As the race headed for a runoff in late October, a series of virulent TV advertisements were aired that played directly to the fears of Fortaleza's white elite by accusing Inácio of being a "*diabo negro*" (black devil), with an untrustworthy past.

Though the snippet of conversation transcribed above revolves around a local election, it illustrates more general patterns I observed during my first two fieldwork stays in Barra (1998–1999 and 2000). First, members of both older and younger generational cohorts that I knew in Barra understood *os pobres* (the poor) as a political category, to which they belonged and which was in direct contrast to *os ricos* (the rich). Second, both cohorts understood the poor as a category that was amenable to structural improvements introduced by the government. Here the daughter focuses on the introduction of additional schools that Inácio had promised in peripheral neighborhoods around the city, while her mother identifies Juraci's transformation of the public bus system, which allowed riders to transfer buses throughout the day on one fare (a crucial improvement for many residents who required three and sometimes four bus transfers to reach their jobs) as a concrete improvement that set him apart from other candidates. As the mother's closing comment suggests, some older residents also saw the poor as an otherworldly category, in which poverty was to be addressed ultimately by God alone.

The daughter in this conversation, J., was born in 1985. During her early childhood, she had watched her mother take part in protests and collective actions to transform their neighborhood from a collection of cardboard shacks at the edge of the Atlantic Ocean to solid cinderblock homes with a smattering of city services. J. was among the members of this generation that I was growing closer to by the end of my first year of fieldwork in 1999. Having survived the first several months of research, I was lonely and discouraged by how difficult it was turning out to be. One Saturday morning late in 1998, I was "discovered" by a group of young women, close friends themselves who had been combing the neighborhood looking for something to do and were dumbfounded to find an American living in their midst. Though I was nearly a decade older than these women who became close friends over the ensuing years, our life stages made us rough contemporaries: unmarried, childless, working or in school, with small disposal incomes.

I luxuriated in their company, feeling more at ease than I had been since starting fieldwork in the fall of 1998. "*Nos somos pobres* [We are poor], but we know how to have fun" was a common refrain. As their respective histories unfolded over the ensuing months, I tried to interpret the nuanced differences in their lives: L. lived with seventeen older brothers and sisters in a three-room house and had been adopted late in her parents' lives. Her conservative father had strongly discouraged her from finishing high school and forbade his wife from working outside the home. And next door to her, in an even smaller house that had dirt floors, a wood-burning stove, and an outdoor toilet, lived N. Her father had left for the Amazon in 1984 when she was four years old and returned only once since then. Her mother, who had finished primary school in the interior and was illiterate, began taking in wash from the neighbors in order to feed her four children and still made a small income this way. One of N.'s older brothers worked at a nearby meatpacking factory, the other at a shoe factory, and neither had finished high school. J.'s father had been a fisherman until his alcoholism overcame him. Now he spent his days watching television and occasionally mending fishing nets, strewn out on his living room floor. Her mother was now the family's breadwinner. She worked six days a week, eleven months out of the year, cleaning the rooms of a nearby motel and, in her off hours, caring for her six children and various grandchildren that were beginning to arrive.

L. S.'s mother died when she was nine, and after her father left home, she was sent to live with an aunt. None of her seven older brothers had finished high school, and the oldest one had been diagnosed with AIDS just several months prior. While still in high school, L. S. started working as a cashier at Lojas Americanas, Brazil's ubiquitous retail chain, where she met G. I initially considered G. and her sister to be the group's most sophisticated and upwardly mobile members. Their father had a job in the coveted civil service as a policeman and contributed regularly to the household income, despite having left their mother years ago and being responsible for what were now two additional families. The inside of the sisters' small house was covered in a glassy-green tile and had an upstairs that had been converted into a separate apartment their older brothers use. Though their mother suffered from a mental illness that prevented her from leaving the house, the sisters took turns watching her so they could finish high school and start jobs of their own.

These young women were all between the ages of eighteen and twenty when I met them in the waning days of 1998, and though they described themselves and their families as *bem pobre* (very poor), they were in fact part of a generation who would soon become identified as "Brazil's expanding middle class" (*Economist* 2012), "Brazil's 'C' class" (Marinheiro 2015), and the "previously poor" (Klein, Mitchell, and Junge 2018). In a magisterial analysis of Lula's denouement, André Singer argues that "mobilizing the category of the poor" is fundamental for understanding how Lulismo was torn apart (Singer 2018, 44). This insight encouraged me to examine shifts in the political identity among these young women first in relationship to the category of the poor from which this putative middle class emerged.

In his piece, Singer goes on to explain that although support for Lula was "forged in the organized fraction of the working class" (2018, 44), it primarily addressed itself to "the poor" and that the PT thus relinquished the advantages of class identification, settling instead for an antagonism derived between "the rich" and "the poor." Crucial for Singer is the distinction between what in Marxist terms would be defined as the proletariat (the working class) and the subproletariat (the poor). Unlike the proletariat, whose involvement in wage labor produced class consciousness, the subproletariat typically lacked formal employment as well as its accompanying class consciousness and thus was easily exploited by reactionary or counterrevolutionary forces (Marx and Engels [1848] 2002). It was Lula's eventual decision to focus his rhetoric and socioeconomic interventions on the idealization of *os pobres* rather than the working class, which Singer argues precipitated the PT's downfall.

My fieldwork notes from 1998 through 2000 reveal that during this period, both younger and older generations in Barra do Ceará conceptualized their city as being composed of two groups:

the rich (a small but increasingly visible segment of the population) and the poor (a much larger and somewhat more fluid category). The older generation tended to emphasize that it was their relatively recent arrival from the interior that set them apart from *os ricos*, who lived in the wealthy neighborhoods just east of the city center, as well as the organized social movements they had participated in to attain city services and recognition.

When I asked members of the younger generation, who were in their late teens and early twenties in 1999 or 2000, why they classified themselves as poor, they often cited their parents' illiteracy, their parents or their own informal or intermittent employment, and the emphasis the city's major universities placed on a single entrance exam, making it nearly impossible for students to be admitted unless they had studied at a private secondary school. Neither younger nor older residents tended to mention the lack of material goods as a defining characteristic of their poverty. In 1998, almost all households in Barra owned a television, but personal computers were not yet ubiquitous even among the very wealthy in Fortaleza, and cell phones were still nearly a decade away. Occasionally conversations would drift toward the desire for a larger television or a newer refrigerator, but in general consumption habits were not a frequently used index for identifying social class. Throughout all my notes from this period, the category of "middle class" is conspicuously absent; neither generational cohort used the term when describing the composition of their city or when identifying existing social antagonisms.

What is also striking about my field notes from this period is that both younger and older residents frequently cited government aid and interventions such as increased bus service, improvements to school buildings, and additional social security benefits as being essential to constructing a better life. For older residents, this belief was often stated in reference to past government actions that their activism helped precipitate. While residents in their late teens and early twenties tended to advance future-oriented statements, such as their hope that the government would expand *concursos* (exams) so that they too would have a chance at the table, they associated civil service jobs with the rich. Occasionally a younger resident would reference even larger structural forces such as the International Monetary Fund (IMF), the relatively recently implemented *Plano Real*, or globalization as contributing to their community's impoverishment, and their expectation that with the right political candidate, these forces might shift in their favor.

None of the women I knew in Barra were old enough to have voted in the 1998 presidential election, but local election results demonstrate that eligible residents had already plainly identified the Workers' Party as aligned with their interests: though Fernando Henrique Cardoso won the 1998 national presidential election handily, in Barra do Ceará, 53 percent of the eligible voters voted for Luiz Inácio Lula da Silva, and 33 percent for Ceará's former governor, Ciro Gomes. Only 11 percent voted for the centrist candidate, Fernando Henrique Cardoso.

Walking along the beach with G. soon after my return to Fortaleza in 2000, I spotted a series of new shanty homes that had been built close to the water's edge.

"It's because of the road the government says it's going to build," explained G. "They want to make a road starting from here and connect it to the Beira Mar [a highly popular pedestrian path along Fortaleza's most central beach]. So people put up houses, thinking the government will pay them to move when they build the road."

"Will the government follow through?" I asked.

"Maybe. Things are changing, in Fortaleza," replied G. "And we have to keep moving too. We [referencing her group of friends] need to go to college, become educated—I'm not going to work as a cashier at Lojas forever!"

A BRAZILIAN RAG-AND-BONE SHOP: 2007–2009

In May of 2007, I was sitting at a popular pizzeria that surrounds a small manmade lake, near the Fortaleza airport. Six of the eight women I knew well were there, as were a few of their friends. My last trip had been nearly two years earlier, and everyone was eager to tell me their best news. They started with the completion of the pedestrian path the government had promised back in 2000. "You won't believe it!" I'm told. "It's full of families now, and on Saturday evenings it turns into a fair with food and games."

Now in their late twenties and early thirties, the changes in my friends' lives had begun to accelerate. Three of the women had started postsecondary training at the private technical colleges that have sprung up around Fortaleza. Both L. and N. were studying physical therapy; G. was at a different school for accounting. In contrast to media accounts I'd read that often depicted the new colleges as overpriced and predatory, L. told me, "They're amazing. These colleges have a lot of evening classes, and the loans are so cheap." N. chimed in that she'd been working on the beaches south of the city, giving massages to tourists. The group of masseuses she belonged to had recently unionized, so she was eligible for the same benefits as salaried workers. "Five-day work weeks," she cheered.

"I still have to work a half day on Saturdays," lamented J. A., who was still in a cashier's job at a small boutique for party favors. "But my brother's got his own business—he's started a print shop upstairs in our house; he'll take any document you give him and get you as many copies as you need."

L. S. reported on a recent trip she took to Portugal as part of the new church she'd joined, *Assembleia de Deus*. It was her first time on an airplane, and she recounted the journey in minute detail. Only later does G. confide in me that the group is worried about the role the church is playing in the lives of both L. S. and N. "They're *crentes* [believers] now—nothing but God," she says rolling her eyes.

As the night wound down, I heard sadder tales as well. L.'s father had died the previous winter and her family buried him in one of the large public graveyards to the west of the Fortaleza. Everyone shuddered at this. "That's how you know you haven't escaped the favela for the *classe média*," J. A. offered, "when you lie for eternity in the *Cemitério Público*." A chorus of laughter followed.

As we packed up to go, I remember J. A. checking her cell phone. The phones were another new addition to these women's lives, though they used prepaid cards, carefully logging their minutes and tracking their texts. The most remarked-upon development was that G. now had her driver's license and had borrowed her father's car for the occasion. Not everyone fit, so half of the group took the bus home. But still, the car was understood as a portent. "Soon we'll all be driving," G. reported confidently.

Here we have the emerging lower middle class that André Singer described as "increasingly fragmented and difficult to classify. A rag and bone shop made up of . . . trade unions of contract laborers, a precariat with access to the university and poor entrepreneurs" (Singer 2018, 46). However difficult this group was for analysts to classify, the women I knew increasingly saw themselves as middle class. And as other ethnographers of this emerging class have observed (Braga 2015; Yaccoub 2011), consumption practices appeared to be their primary instrument for asserting middle-class identity. During my 2005, 2007, and 2009 fieldwork visits, I witnessed countless displays of aspirational consumption, from changes in daily habits such as more frequent and more expensive meals out, casual *cafezinhos* at the mall, perfumes, branded clothing, and weekly mani-pedis to more monumental changes such as extensively remodeled homes, private health care plans, and foreign travel.

Among my group of friends and others like them, consumption had also become a potent way to differentiate themselves from poorer residents in Barra do Ceará. Sometimes these distinctions were made with respect to generations (Jerome 2015); for example, many of the women complained that their mothers preferred the wood-burning stoves of the interior to gas cooktops. At other times, the gulf between siblings' or neighbors' consumption habits was elaborated as when a friend commented, "Of course I buy bottled water now, but my brother still takes it from the tap." Or the raucous laughter that followed a neighbor's question about which bus I was going to take back to the United States.

Again, in keeping with prior scholarship (O'Dougherty 2002; Pinheiro-Machado and Scalco 2020), I found that claims of moral superiority almost always accompanied these evaluations. L., for example, delighted in explaining the difference between herself and her brother as follows: She was employed in the formal sector, halfway through her college degree, and sleeping soundly in a wooden bed on the second floor of her parents' house that she had recently paid to have renovated; her brother was unemployed, an alcoholic, and routinely passed out in a worn, threadbare hammock he'd strung across their patio. Even parts of Barra were becoming classified as *a favela verdade* (the true favela) and juxtaposed with the better-kept areas that the women I knew tended to live in. "I never come down here anymore," said N. as we were walking to Associação dos Moradores, a community housing association deep in Barra, where narrow dirt roads, naked children, and faulty sewers were still the norm. "People like this, they're going to waste their whole lives right here."

Despite uneven development, by 2006, Lula's social policies had significantly reduced rural and urban poverty, and there was a growing mass of people, including those subsisting in the informal economy, who recognized Lula's achievements and identified them with their own success (Anderson 2019, 8). Local election results from 2002 and 2006 were emphatic: 89 percent of Barra do Ceará's residents voted for Lula in 2002, and nearly as many (86 percent) voted to reelect him in 2006. In a stunning victory for the PT, the rest of the nation joined with the Northeast during these election cycles to win Lula the presidency.

While the media, academics, and politicians insisted on referring to this swath of Lula supporters as "the new middle class," in fact, as Anderson has pointed out, the socioeconomic gains of this new group were decidedly more modest (higher minimum wage and technical degrees rather than structural changes to the ruling class) and thus fundamentally precarious (2019, 8). The intricate barriers to car and home ownership in Barra, two of the most coveted consumer items among the women I knew, reveal precisely the kind of precarity alluded to by Anderson.

Even after assembling the money required to purchase a car, one of the major challenges of car ownership in Barra was where to store it. Many of the neighborhood's streets are too narrow, still cobblestoned, dusty, or unsafe to park a car on, and even larger homes seldom had garages. But one feature many houses had was a front-facing enclosed interior courtyard. In the late 1990s and early 2000s, I noticed that these small courtyards often contained gardens, wash lines, and plastic chairs for socializing. By 2007, some families had transformed these courtyards into full-time garages for existing or anticipated vehicles. C., for example, had paid to have an interior courtyard built in 2006 for the car she hoped one day to buy. But when I complimented her on the small garden currently growing there, she laughed and said I had missed the interval in which one of her neighbors had "temporarily" housed his car in the space. When I raised an eyebrow in disbelief, she told me the following story.

Nine months prior, a middle-aged man who lived across the street from the two-room home C. lived in with her mother, two brothers, and (intermittently) her nephew approached her mother to ask if he could store his car in what was then an open courtyard. Her mother agreed, assuming he only intended to keep it there for a couple of days. C. arrived home that night to find his car in her courtyard and an added wall of bricks made by the neighbor to further protect his car, which significantly narrowed the entryway to their home. Incensed, she asked her neighbor to remove his car. He refused, and none of the neighbors would intervene on her behalf. Every other week, the man would bring her mother a tin of sardines, as a "thank you" for the parking space, but no other payment was forthcoming. When I asked why she hadn't called the police, C. laughed, "What would they do? No one's coming to this neighborhood to settle a dispute like this." Eventually she paid a friend to knock down the brick structure and told the man that if he didn't move his car, it would be next. Shortly thereafter, the neighbor returned his car to his side of the street.

Unlike the more established middle class of 1990s Brazil (O'Dougherty 2002) that was already embedded in infrastructures that enabled and supported their acquisitions (i.e., clean, safe streets, attached garages, and police protection), the emerging middle class of the *periferia* had to cobble together this infrastructure after the fact, often with unsatisfactory results. C.'s foray into car ownership generated personal animosity toward her neighbor and increased disgust with city officials, neither of which brought her closer to her goal of purchasing a car.

Home ownership posed even greater structural barriers. Of the eight women I knew well, seven of them were living in homes owned outright by their parents. The homes' titles, however, were in dispute for all but one of them. N.'s story is exemplary. Though technically her mother owned the house she lived in, N. had spent approximately eleven years attempting to obtain its title. She explained how when her parents first moved to Barra in the mid-1980s, there was nothing but sand on her road and a few cardboard houses. One family, who still lived nearby, began to make small improvements to the area, including putting in a well. N.'s father bought a small piece of land from them and slowly put up a house on it. He paid the family in small increments, with the understanding that whatever home he built would eventually be his. When he left (permanently it turned out) for the Amazon in 1984, N.'s mother used money from washing clothes to complete the payments. In a common oversight, the title itself was never formalized and was still registered with the city in the other family's name.

Starting in 2007, N. began making trips to the city housing department in Fortaleza to try to get the title reversed to her family's name. She recounted the copious amounts of paperwork, photographs, witness testimonies, and signed affidavits she'd left at the office, as well as her extreme frustration at having to take time off from work to resolve the issue. A long-standing community association in Barra that provided free legal help to residents had recently closed, and she could never have paid for a private lawyer. Instead, she continued to make the monthly trips with mounting disgust, always being told that "soon the title would appear."

Contrast this story in which N. worked on her own with mounting antipathy to try to rectify the title dispute to what anthropologist James Holston (2008, 204) recounts of his experiences with the generational cohort senior to N.: "Residential illegality generates an insurgence of political and civil rights among the urban poor, who learn to use law to legitimate their land claims . . . and to create a new kind of participatory citizenship that demands full inclusion." Note that for the older cohort of residents that Holston writes about, residential illegality produced social activism, rights claims, and eventually a new and expanded experience of citizenship. For N., however, what residential illegality generated most profoundly was disgust and distrust of state bureaucracy. It is precisely this type of experience and its interpretation among the younger cohort of residents as a cause for disillusionment rather than activism that helps explain their growing impatience with the PT during the latter half of the 2010s and their willingness to consider other political candidates.

THE "C CLASS": 2015, 2016, AND 2017

On an early August evening in 2015, I was talking to a nursing professor and her husband on an outdoor patio in an upscale Fortaleza neighborhood, when suddenly our conversation was interrupted by a cacophony of metal clanking. The sound rose and fell, appearing to come from the windows of the residential apartment buildings that surrounded us. "It's the anti-Dilma protestors," my hosts explained. "As soon as she comes on TV, people in this neighborhood start banging their pots." The din lasted another five minutes or so, and then slowly ebbed.

Back in Barra do Ceará, I ask J., with whom I was staying on this trip, if she had heard a similar racket. "Of course not! This is the neighborhood that voted Dilma into office. You'd never get a protest like that here!" The scorn in her voice matched the sour political mood that enveloped many of my friends on this trip. Since my arrival, I'd heard nothing but complaints about the corruption endemic to the PT, the cutback in services in Fortaleza, and the uncertain economic future of Brazil.

Election results during the two presidential cycles I'd missed in 2010 and 2014 echoed this pessimism at the national level: Dilma won the presidency with 56 percent of the national vote in 2010 and was narrowly reelected in 2014 with 51 percent of the vote. Even in Barra, confidence in the PT had started to wane: almost 25 percent of Barra's residents voted against the PT in 2010 and 2014.

My experiences doing fieldwork in the years 2015, 2016, and 2017 suggested the emergence of a deepening generational divide between the voters in Barra do Ceará. While the older cohort of residents I knew, most of whom were now in their late fifties and early sixties, continued to express their staunch support for Dilma and the PT more generally, their children, now in their mid- to late thirties, were much more critical of the political climate. For example, I remember watching TV one afternoon with M. J., the mother of two sisters I knew well, when news about Dilma's connection to the Petrobras scandal appeared.

"She was in the president's office, how was she supposed to know what was going on at Petrobras?" M. J. scoffed as she took down the wash from the nearby line. "You don't think she was involved?" I asked. "No! She's been a very good president—look at all the benefits she's kept, Bolsa Família, Minha Casa Minha Vida, everything!"

When I got home, I related these comments to J., curious to know what she thought.

"Dilma didn't know? Right. Of course that's what she's going to say. She doesn't know any better. But you just have to open your eyes to see all of this corruption. And it's not just the politicians; it's in our neighborhood. You remember how I told you that our neighbor lied about the number of children she had to get extra Bolsa benefits? That type of thing happens all the time; our system tolerates it."

"Or," she continued, "what about my mother's social security benefits that have stopped coming?" Here she was referring to a problem she'd been having getting her mother's pension payments restarted. They had stopped nine months ago when someone misreported the household's income, a mistake she said was also very common. Scholars have argued that it was through a series of these little failures that the "C class" most commonly experienced the state (Ansell 2013). And although the women I knew were sometimes able to circumvent state failures with the purchase of private health care plans or consistent garbage removal in their neighborhood, it was at enormous cost to their savings and time.

Even the government benefits that this cohort did see positively impacting their lives weren't necessarily attributed to the PT. For example, I received several explanations about the origins of the FIES student loans from friends in Barra who had received them, and both of them emphasized that the favorable loans upon which they depended were not the direct result of Lula. As G. explained to me, "That's what the PT wants you to think—that everything good is because of them! But here in Ceará, we had these loans years before. All Lula did was to expand them."

Meanwhile, this group's experiences with the private sector were steadily increasing. N., for example, had begun working as a receptionist and medical assistant in a private gynecologist's office downtown. Not only had her take-home wages tripled from her prior job, but she now worked in the upper-class business district of Fortaleza and lunched with professionals on a regular basis. Another friend, L. S., was working in a small accounting firm in the same part of town and was considering law school, and G. worked as an assistant in a textile import business.

While exposure to the professional, globalized elite of Fortaleza had increased their incomes and expanded their aspirations, it was striking that not one of these women attributed their rise to government assistance or intervention. Instead, they emphasized the moral character of their bosses, as well as their own ferocious work ethics. N., for example, explained that her boss (a doctor) was a saint who had "assumed a huge risk by hiring her, an unknown with only a secondary degree from Barra." And L. S. explained, "We're *guerreiras* [warriors]. You have to be to live in Barra and put yourself to school by working like we do." As these sentiments reveal, moralistic and meritocratic discursive frameworks rather than social and political frameworks were most often invoked to explain socioeconomic mobility. (For similar findings, see Klein, Mitchell, and Junge 2018; and Junge, this volume.)

These types of explanations were in direct contrast to those that I saw their mothers advance for what they had achieved in their lives. Here, for example, is Dona C. reflecting on the ongoing renovations to her home:

> When we first got here, you couldn't eat without putting sand in your mouth, you would sit here and eat, and the mounds of sand were so high that your feet would sink into them—up to your knees, and the sand would fall from the ceiling and from the wind into your food. *Nao tinham nada aqui. Nao tinham nada, luz, electricidade, ou aqua. O governo ajuda muito.* (There was nothing here, not light, electricity, or water. The government helps a lot.) It was the government that gave us bricks to build with, and then when we marched, they finally got us electricity out here.

Note that instead of identifying only her own hard work, as her daughter's generation tended to do, Dona C. emphasizes the government's intervention, seeing the transformations in her home as a sign of a strong work ethic *and* expanded resources from city officials.

The younger generation of residents that I knew were more likely to channel their energy into personal and individual development than projects that required community collaboration. By 2015, my research had shifted to examine the local health councils that were a requirement of every *posto de saude* (health clinic) in Barra. These councils were an integral part of the 1988 Citizen's Constitution that Brazilians had worked so hard to establish in an array of government departments. But none of the younger generation of residents I knew had even considered joining a health council. "Why would we waste our time?" they asked. "Our futures are out there," one friend said, pointing to *Leste Oeste*, the now massive boulevard that brought residents of Barra swiftly into Fortaleza.

The only counterexample to this pattern was L. By 2015, L., now in her late thirties, had finished her BA in physical education and was beginning work at a technical high school up the coast from Fortaleza as a teacher of massage therapy. After finishing their degrees, high school students would fill positions at local hotels or hospitals, which validated alternative treatments such as massage. L. explained that the technical high school model was started by the governor of Ceará in 2008 and continued to receive strong support from the PT. Unlike the other women, L. connected many of the improvements she saw in her own and her students' lives to programs implemented by the PT (at either the state or federal levels of government). She regularly attended protests in the city against Dilma's impeachment and Lula's imprisonment, and she had developed strong friendships with fellow civil service workers, rather than the corporate professionals with whom the rest of the group had begun to associate.

On my last morning in Barra in November of 2017, everyone had gathered at N.'s house for breakfast. The topic of the conversation that morning was the deterioration of security in the neighborhood. Several instances of armed muggings had occurred in the past month, and only last week there had been an attempted robbery at one of the restaurants that flanked Barra's pedestrian path. Businesses were struggling to generate income due to the falloff in foot traffic.

It didn't take long for the conversation to turn to politics and the upcoming presidential race of 2018. N., G., and L. S. said they were considering Jair Bolsonaro, who at that point was still a little-known federal deputy. "He's a dictator!" shouted L. in response.

"Let me tell you something," retorted G. "During the military dictatorship, at least we had security, and families could walk together on the street without fear of criminals. Now you know what happens? Brazil pays criminals in prisons more per day than they do to people making minimum wage!"

L. contended that she would vote for the PT candidate, whoever it was, including Lula if he were allowed to stand for election. The group shook their heads in disgust, and the conversation shifted to other subjects.

CONCLUSION

In October of 2018, Brazil narrowly elected Jair Bolsonaro to the presidency. Ceará's premier newspaper reported that Bolsonaro had earned the majority of the votes in Fortaleza's six wealthiest neighborhoods (*Tribuna do Ceará* 2018). It did not add that even in peripheral neighborhoods of Fortaleza, Bolsonaro had won substantial support. In Barra do Ceará, 42 percent of eligible residents voted for Bolsonaro, almost double the number of voters who chose the opposition candidate in 2014, and four times as many as those who voted against Lula in 2002.

This shift away from the PT in Barra occurred despite the fact that the economic fortunes and future aspirations of many of its residents, particularly those residents who were roughly between the ages of thirty and forty-five in 2018, had increased substantially. These were the residents who in my observation managed to capitalize on the expanded educational opportunities and higher minimum wages that the PT delivered, without also being encouraged by the party to see their personal transformation as even partly a product of government intervention.

My data demonstrate that the unwillingness to attribute personal betterment to structural change was not a forgone conclusion; indeed, from 1998 to 2000, I witnessed many of these same residents, then in their late teens and early twenties, articulate strong support of communist and PT political figures and connect their socioeconomic betterment to government intervention. The chapters in part IV of this volume also reveal that political activism throughout the 2010s was propelled by passionate young Brazilians, so the cases I examine here cannot be seen as exemplary.

Nonetheless, for the younger generation of residents I knew in Barra do Ceará, class mobility during the 2010s became closely tied to opportunities in the privatized corporate sphere and individual self-discipline. During the same time period, their desired futures became grounded in individual consumption, civic disengagement. and an idealized past. Voting for Bolsonaro expressed their deep discontent with what they perceived as a corrupt state and a strong confirmation of their self-made status. They had become a class in, but not *for*, itself (Singer 2018, 44).

REFERENCES

Anderson, Perry. 2019. "Bolsonaro's Brazil." *London Review of Books* 41 (3): 11–22.

Ansell, Aaron. 2013. "The Vinegar Revolts and the Diverse Faces of Democracy in Brazil." Fieldsights—Hot Spots, *Cultural Anthropology* (online), December 20, 2013. http://www.culanth.org/fieldsights/429-the-vinegar-revolts-and-the-diverse-faces-of-democracy-in-brazil.

Braga, Robson da Silva. 2015. "Eu era feio, agora tenho carro: Encenações e práticas de consumo em clubes de forró de Fortaleza." PhD diss., Universidade Federal do Rio Grande do Sul, Porto Alegre, Brazil. http://www.lume.ufrgs.br/handle/10183/109704.

Economist. 2012. "The Expanding Middle; Class in Latin America." November 10, 2012.

Holston, James. 2008. *Insurgent Citizenship: Disjunctions of Democracy and Modernity in Brazil*. Princeton, N.J.: Princeton University Press.

Jerome, Jessica. 2015. *A Right to Healthy: Medicine, Marginality, and Health Care Reform in Northeastern Brazil*. Austin: University of Texas Press.

Klein, Charles H., Sean T. Mitchell, and Benjamin Junge. 2018. "Naming Brazil's Previously Poor: 'New Middle Class' as an Economic, Political, and Experiential Category." *Economic Anthropology* 5 (1): 83–95.

Marinheiro, Vaguinaldo. 2015. "Todos querem tirar a nova classe média para dançar." *Folha de São Paulo*. 15 June, 2015.

Marx, Karl, and Friedrich Engels. (1848) 2002. *The Communist Manifesto*. London: Penguin Classics.

Miles, Tshombe. 2019. "The Afro-Brazilian Struggle for Visibility in Ceará." *NACLA Report on the Americas* 51 (4): 394–400.

O'Dougherty, Maureen. 2002. *Consumption Intensified: The Politics of Middle-Class Daily Life in Brazil*. Durham, N.C.: Duke University Press.

Pinheiro-Machado, Rosana, and Lucia Mury Scalco. 2020. "From Hope to Hate: The Rise of Conservative Subjectivity in Brazil." *HAU: Journal of Ethnographic Theory* 10 (1): 21–31.

Singer, André. 2018. "Do sonho rooseveltiano ao pesadelo golpista." *Revista piauí*, no. 140: 42–48.

Tribuna do Ceará. 2018. "Bolsonaro foi o mais votado em 6 dos bairros mais ricos de Fortaleza." October 28, 2018. https://tribunadoceara.com.br/noticias/eleicoes-2018/bolsonaro-foi-o-mais-votado-em-6-dos-bairros-mais-ricos-de-fortaleza-ja-haddad-nao-venceu-em-nenhum/.

Yaccoub, Hilaine. 2011. "A chamada 'nova classe média': Cultura material, inclusão e distinção social." *Horizontes antropológicos* 17 (36): 197–231.

NOTES

1. Fortaleza is the capital of the northeastern state of Ceará. During the eighteenth and nineteenth centuries, the state relied predominately on Indigenous and free agricultural workers rather than enslaved Africans. This practice skewed its population whiter than other northeastern states, leading Afro-Brazilians to struggle for visibility and recognition in Ceará (Miles 2019). Despite entrenched poverty, a condition it shares with the whole of the Northeast, the state earned national and international recognition in the 1990s under the government of Ciro Gomes, for enacting a series of political and socially oriented reforms.

2. National and local election data are available at http://www.tse.jus.br/eleicoes/estatisticas/repositorio-de-dados-eleitorais-1/repositorio-de-dados-eleitorais. For local election data before 2006, I had to rely on the aggregate for zone 114 in Fortaleza, which encompasses Barra do Ceará but is roughly three times bigger. Raw election totals were converted to percentages for all the local elections.

3 · DREAMING WITH GUNS
Performing Masculinity and Imagining Consumption in Bolsonaro's Brazil

ISABELA KALIL, ROSANA PINHEIRO-MACHADO, AND LUCIA MURY SCALCO

In the 2018 presidential elections, one of hard-right candidate Jair Bolsonaro's main electoral promises was to legalize both the possession of firearms and the ability to carry them concealed. This promise addressed and galvanized popular anxieties during a period of economic, democratic, and urban security crises in Brazil. Furthermore, Bolsonaro's signature "pistol-hand gesture" was central to the candidate's brand and the main icon of his campaign, most likely inspired by Donald Trump, who used the gesture as host of *The Apprentice*. Bolsonaro and his sons frequently appeared in the media, sometimes making the shooting gesture, and sometimes shooting machine guns. On social media, Bolsonaro's admirers adopted firearm-toting profile pictures. While progressive sectors of the electorate widely repudiated the association with firearms and interpreted it as a symbol of death threats to minorities, Bolsonaro supporters perceived the pistol-hand gesture as a humorous performance representing life, family, and property. For Bolsonaro, this bodily symbol was assigned to his persona as a former army captain who would be uncompromising against *vagabundos*[1] (criminals) or *communists* (used as a loose definition to categorize any political opponent). As Hall, Goldstein, and Ingram (2016) have shown, this hand gesture conveys "sovereign power and commanding force" but in an ambiguous and playful manner.

By looking at two different ethnographic settings, Porto Alegre (Pinheiro-Machado and Scalco 2020) and São Paulo (Kalil 2018), this chapter analyzes the role of firearms in the 2018 race among Bolsonaro-supporting male voters. We take firearms as both a material artifact that protects or kills living beings and an immaterial symbol of social distinction and gendered power over life and death. Weapons have both material and semiotic qualities based on myth consolidation, reifying identity, propaganda staging, and advertising threats (Saramifar 2018).

"Masculinity" was a frequently unspoken electoral theme in 2018, but it is worth noting that masculinity is not a static category but varies based on local/regional configurations—an intersectional category that allows us to explore other dimensions of social life, such as gender, class, race, and generation (Kimmel 1987; Beasley 2008; Connell and Messerschmidt 2005).

Analyzing the two ethnographic settings side by side, we examine the narratives, aspirations, and expectations engendered when male voters expressed desires for firearms. We argue that disparate modes of masculinities, anxieties, and perceptions of urban security are produced through these different imagined forms of access and uses of firearms and that they vary according to class, race, and age among low-income groups (Porto Alegre) and lower-middle-class groups (São Paulo). Although the meanings of firearms were multifaceted, discussing and demonstrating desire for and mastery of firearms had significance independent of the firearms themselves. Such discussions provided an experience in which the public demonstration of desire and knowledge about weapons didn't require the possession of the object.

As Campbell's (1987) work on consumption suggests, the imaginative hedonism (of guns) originates from a romanticized projection about the object and, ultimately, its supreme power over life and death. In stories we present here, guns represent a bridge between a frustrating present and the aspiration of a better future imagined in individual and meritocratic terms. Following Appadurai's (1996) work on the articulation of commodities, media, and class imagination, we argue that the images of guns that circulated on social media during Bolsonaro's campaign met male frustrations about the economic, political, and social context, facilitating the emergence of new subjectivities and dreams for those men. Through the symbolism of guns, our interlocutors could complain about the present and envision a heroic, powerful, and virile, fairer, and safer future.

The chapter is based on deep longitudinal participant observation in Porto Alegre, by Pinheiro-Machado and Scalco (2009–2018), and São Paulo, by Kalil and her team (2013–2020). In both cases, we give particular focus to the data from the election year of 2018.

The Porto Alegre ethnography was divided into two phases. The first part was conducted from 2009 to 2014, during peak Brazilian economic growth. We investigated the impact of Lula's financial inclusion and politics of consumption among low-income groups in Morro da Cruz favela. The second part began at the end of 2016, when we returned for a follow-up visit amid an economic crisis. During 2017, we regularly visited the same interlocutors and places we had previously studied, and in 2018, in order to understand political motivations, we intensified our fieldwork, conducting seventeen focus groups of Bolsonaro voters who were engaged in online discussion groups.

The São Paulo fieldwork had three phases. The first phase (2013–2015) investigated the participation of extreme-right groups within public protests and demonstrations. Data collection took place during mass protests starting in 2013 and amid the emergence of new right-wing groups. The second phase (2016–2017) began with demonstrations both against and in favor of Dilma Rousseff's impeachment. It was in this context that Jair Bolsonaro's candidacy began to consolidate. The third phase (2017–2020) analyzed the presidential campaign and the government of Bolsonaro, based on the analysis and categorization of sixteen voter-profile types collected from more than one thousand interviews, mainly from public demonstrations and monitoring internet groups.[2]

The comparison of the two ethnographies highlights nuances that show similarities between the desire for weapons on the part of low-income young men (Porto Alegre) and lower-middle-class young men (São Paulo) as related class anxieties within aspirational social mobility projects. Such a comparison, moreover, enables us to understand how the desire for weapons operates by articulating distinct moralities based on *masculinity* and on the *aspiration to become a consumer*. In Porto Alegre, we observe the desire of men to be different from a *vida bandida* (criminal life) in favelas. In São Paulo, we notice the interlocutors' desire to be *cidadãos de bem* (good citizens [upstanding citizens]).

GUNS, BRANDS, AND HARD WORK IN PORTO ALEGRE

Significant anthropological literature about Brazilian favelas has shown that firearms play a key role in the local imaginary and in ordinary life, especially among men (Fonseca 2000; Soares

2004; Zaluar 2010). In Morro da Cruz, firearms were a pervasive object in many of our interlocutors' narratives of everyday life. We routinely witnessed events in which guns appeared in the socialization and communication of children. When a six-year-old boy wanted to thank one of us for a 2014 visit to a local nursery school, he gave her a drawing of a pistol. The teacher added that this object was one of the most frequently drawn objects in her class.

Beco das Águas is a small alley in Morro da Cruz marked by extreme poverty. Because of the direct influence of drug trafficking in this area, many children grow up playing with toy guns. A video made by our key interlocutor, Maroba (aged fifty-one in 2020), for example, shows his son his friends acting as though they were executing people in a drug dispute. Their pistols were small pieces of pipe, but Maroba added the sound and fire effects while he edited the video. A child played the role of a drug dealer who demanded payment of a debt from another dealer, who then reacted by shooting at the head of the child. A third dealer appeared in the scene and shot the leg of the aggressor, who limped and ran away to hide himself. Mimicking classic movie images of gun confrontations, the children hid in the walls of the alley and shot at each other until one of them was hit. The injured body fell on the floor with seventeen lethal shots. The three boys played as criminals (not as the police). These children regularly attend school, and their parents have no connections to drug trafficking. However, guns are images of power and respect in a large part of the community.

As in numerous favelas dominated by drug trafficking, many men join the drug trafficking path during childhood, and their life expectancies are extremely low. As an interlocutor said, "They join the factions when they are twelve and die before twenty-two." These particular children mimicking gunfire may not join drug factions, but it is impossible to predict who will and who won't. Over ten years of fieldwork, we witnessed a large part of our male teenagers joining criminal gangs for practical and symbolic reasons. On one hand, they were trying to help their families financially. On the other hand, they were fascinated by what Fonseca (2000) called the *vida bandida*. *Vida bandida* is the adventurous, brave, and heroic ethos of the hypermasculine figure who possesses status-branded goods and guns. Most of the youngsters who followed this path are now in jail or dead.

This chapter focuses on those men who do not take on drug trafficking careers. These men tend to consider themselves survivors who evaded the lure of luxury and power, which shortens the life span of drug traffickers but allows them to be surrounded by cars, famous brands, and the attention of women. Those who followed this path emphasize that they made the choice to be honest instead of becoming criminals. They say that such a choice (to remain honest) demanded great effort, since most encouragement for male youths in their context is focused on crime. The typical story of these self-labeled "honest men" is one where they started working when they were teenagers and became fathers in their early twenties. In their effort to overcome the crossroads offered to them, they develop a fierce opposition to the criminal lifestyle and also an identity in which they pride themselves on being hard workers or simply *trabalhadores* (workers) in contrast with the criminals, who are supposedly lazy and acquire goods and prestige with "easy money."

The opposing identities of "workers" versus "criminals" have appeared in several ethnographic settings in Brazilian favelas (see Perlman 2010; Zaluar 2010). However, as Zaluar (2010) has highlighted, such a divide is not rigid or absolute at the level of concrete social relationships; it is a complex and ambiguous phenomenon. Indeed, the actual possession of a firearm or its aspirational ownership constitutes a commoditized common ground between these two identities. The children playacting a gun confrontation mentioned earlier, which was filmed and posted on Facebook by a *trabalhador*, is a good example of a combination of a male ethos and an aspirational mobility project through which many people in the community dream of having firearms, regardless of their professional status. As Pinheiro-Machado and Scalco (2020) have noted, Morro da Cruz's men do not have many educational and professional opportunities. Various people who escape crime in the community try to join the army or police force. This job is only an option for a few of these young adults, so working as a security guard may be a third career alternative that allows one to have a place in the hierarchical structure, to embody a career that symbolizes power, and to carry and display a gun.

WHEN BOLSONARO MET MORRO DA CRUZ

In Morro da Cruz, a deep economic recession unleashed a crisis among men who were unable to fulfill their traditional roles as workers and breadwinners. For such men, Bolsonaro's campaign—with its imagery and iconography permeated by violence and guns—resonated heavily. The hypermasculine figure of Bolsonaro inspired various interlocutors who described the alternative as becoming a man who is an *otário* (fool), who dresses as a *ninguém* (nobody), and who possesses nothing. For these men, the desire to possess guns and talk about them was a way to avoid "being victimized by armed peers and gain respect and status" (Zaluar 2010, 17). Ultimately, our male interlocutors were enchanted by then-candidate Bolsonaro and the possibility of having guns to gain power and respect.

Firearms didn't mean the same thing to all male Bolsonaro voters whom we interviewed. For the youngsters attending secondary technical school, talk of the guns was similar to talk of luxury brands. Since 2009, we have studied the important influence of brands, like Nike and Adidas, on youth sociability. In our 2018 focus groups, we were intrigued as to the way in which male students were talking less about specific brands in comparison with recent past years and more about guns and Bolsonaro. In times of economic recession, urban security crisis, and a diminished capacity to consume goods, both the artifact of a gun and the candidate who defended them became the new icons of power for these men.

Both Bolsonaro and the young voters we interviewed shared a strong narrative against *vagabundos* (criminals, drug dealers). In Morro da Cruz, the *vagabundos* were the drug dealers. Yet these young Bolsonaro voters were experiencing a liminal life phase. Many of them were still going to *baile funk* parties and listening to MC Felipinho, a local artist who sings about AK-47 pistols, luxury cars, and armed assaults. At the same time, they were technical school students, around eighteen years old preparing themselves to work in "respectable" professions, such as bakers and assistants in radiology, but they were also at life's crossroads because they were witnessing their close friends quickly obtaining desired things through drug trafficking, such as brands, money, cars, and girls—or being arrested and dying for taking that path. For these students, Bolsonaro made sense and became an icon toward the path of honesty they were pursuing. The iconography of the candidate was a means to reconcile the possibility of being a worker and a transgressive youngster instead of a fool or a *ninguém* (nobody).

Their political views were exposed to many progressive demands. Most of them said that they supported feminist struggles, and some youngsters were actually in favor of legalizing abortion. Some declared themselves to be against the impeachment of Dilma Rousseff. Yet beyond that surface narrative, everyday negotiations and tensions occurred in practice. Many times, we heard these youngsters calling female peers *vagabundas* (sluts) and *maconheiras* (literally, marijuana users, meaning girls adrift in life). In focus groups with both male and female voters to discuss *bolsonarismo*, female students controlled the political discussion by talking about gender, race, sexuality, and national politics, while their male counterparts became intimidated by the debate. Men mostly talked about the importance of legalizing firearms to protect themselves.

Yet beyond urban security, it seems there was an underlying generational and existential anxiety in their yearnings for guns. First, young men were vulnerable to everyday violent muggings threatening their lives, and also their masculinity—since these mugging events were highly humiliating. Armed young thieves often ritualized violence, demanding a servile attitude from the victim. Second, these men were becoming adults without great professional prospects in a country that was facing a profound economic crisis. Third, they were becoming adults and were witnessing a new feminist wave that had reached low-income groups in Brazil. Now their female peers were not only talking about politics but also controlling the debates. Firearms had a pragmatic use in the belief they could protect their lives, but it was also a virile and aspirational totem pole that protected their anxieties in a changing world in which they could not envision a future for themselves based on their life choices to become a worker.

Among the male adults we interviewed, especially men in the age range of approximately twenty to thirty-five years old, both the worker identity and the conservative narrative were more delineated. Now they were working as security guards, construction workers, moto-deliverers, or Uber drivers. Becoming a father was a turning point in their lives as they were forced to become breadwinners. At this point in their lives, they despised funk and said that the problem of Brazilian society was that people were lazy, immoral, corrupt, and deviant. They admired Bolsonaro for declaring the need for guns to protect both their property and their family morality.

As we have discussed elsewhere (Pinheiro-Machado and Scalco 2020), in the interlocutors' "them-against-us" view of the world, there was an easy life for lazy people and a hard one for hard workers. Thus life was interpreted as profoundly unjust for those who made a great effort to work "in an honest way." They saw themselves in a position of disadvantage, losing the few things they had acquired to the people who supposedly looked for shortcuts. They often mentioned that they felt punished by the government and that the Workers' Party helped only criminals and not honest workers. Our male interlocutors often told us detailed stories about relatives or close friends who had a "great life" and "luxurious life" in prison. They said that being a criminal is good business because the family of the incarcerated person receives social benefits. It was felt that human rights activists just supported rapists, while nobody came to help them (honest people) when they were violently mugged. The "honest workers" saw a world of impunity and the way to address this injustice was to support the strong punitive worldview endorsed by Bolsonaro, in which the police should be allowed to kill criminals and the death sentence should be reinstated.

By possessing guns, they believed they would be able to achieve several aims: (1) impose fear on the *vagabundos*; (2) return shots at thieves; and (3) protect their properties and families, especially their female children from rapists. If the youngsters demonstrated an existential generational anxiety by dreaming about guns, the adults' desire to be armed suggests a kind of class anxiety. Even facing hardships, these men considered themselves to be economically better off than their neighbors in the community. They stressed that they were workers and possessed a car or even a house. They unanimously despised those who received social benefits or affirmative action. It was not a coincidence that all of them narrated stories in which they failed to receive some benefits because they were white, or in the case of Black interlocutors, slightly above the income range required to access certain benefits. By failing to qualify for social benefits, such as the cash transfer program Bolsa Família or higher education program loans, this group of workers immediately affirmed that the process was unjust because "richer people" received it. At the same time, in an ambivalent narrative, they were proud to say they had failed to qualify for these programs precisely because they were "richer."

One of the ways these men conveyed that they were "richer" than their neighbors was through talking about firearms, stressing that they would be able to pay for a gun. At a dinner we had with some interlocutors, both the waiter of the local pizzeria and our friends started talking about the price of a Taurus (Brazilian brand gun). They were aware of different models of revolvers and pistols. Mario (a twenty-six-year-old handyman) said that he would be able to buy a ".38 revolver" with R$2,000 in Bolsonaro's administration (while the current price was nearly double). The waiter said he would buy a 0.38 pistol with R$2,000 and would make money with it by informally renting it on a daily basis to those who wanted to use it for a short period of time (gun rental is a common practice in local drug trafficking). This conversation engaged the men for a full forty minutes while their wives distracted themselves by checking social networks on cell phones.

Finally, both the youngsters and the adults strongly shared the frustration that "the criminal is armed, the worker isn't," which was generally considered unfair. It was felt that "criminals" had a monopoly on power and prestige, and they were the only ones who were feared. Legalizing firearms would intimidate the *vagabundos*. As our interlocutors said, *vagabundos* were confident that the "foolish" worker is disarmed. In the Bolsonaro administration, this inequality certainly would change. Moreover, interlocutors from both generational groups believed that being legally armed would be a privilege and that just mentally stable workers would be entitled to purchase a firearm simply by passing a psychological test. Nobody ever mentioned the possibility of failing these supposed tests. In the end, possessing a legal gun was the crowning moment of their efforts, a compensation for past humiliations and a means through which to break up the monopoly on this key symbol of prestige, protection, and masculinity.

ON MACHINE GUNS AND ENGINES IN SÃO PAULO

In March 2018, just over six months before the presidential election, Jair Bolsonaro was in second place in the polls among 20 percent of interviewed voters. The former president, Luiz Inácio Lula da Silva, topped the polls, almost doubling Bolsonaro's numbers. Additionally, polls showed that among every ten likely Bolsonaro voters, there were eight men for every two women. At that time, the figure of Bolsonaro capitalized on the desires of young men for firearms (especially those between sixteen and thirty-four years old). However, Bolsonaro's candidacy faced the challenge of gaining women's sympathy and trust in a scenario of strong rejection by the female electorate.

Several elements pointed to the discrepancy between women and men. Among other issues, the countless misogynous statements made by the candidate were important. Mobilizing the promise of expanding gun ownership and possession as one of the pillars of his campaign strengthened his base of male voters but caused rejection by female voters. The issue of weapons, in this sense, was one of the key elements in understanding the growing support of the electorate for Bolsonaro's candidacy and, ultimately, his victory.

For Porto Alegre, we described the ethnography more broadly; for São Paulo we will focus on a particular situation that took place in March 2018. This situation was emblematic of a trend that started during the Bolsonaro campaign and grew in frequency over the months leading up to the election.

It all began with Carreata Bolsonaro (Bolsonaro's motorcade). From an ethnographic point of view, this situation provided three important analytic elements for the understanding of the issue of weapons among Bolsonaro's voters: (1) the relationship between guns and entertainment; (2) the overlap between guns and other commodities, like cars; and (3) the ways in which weapons are mobilized with the logic of protecting the Christian family, women, and children. These elements help us understand an intriguing moment of inflection in Bolsonaro's campaign, in which the rhetoric of the cult of weapons (previously more restricted to the male universe) expanded to include a female audience, and by extension, mobilized a female constituency.

Although we present a description of a single event, the analysis is based on the collection of longitudinal data drawing on more extensive fieldwork research of groups and movements on the internet and in public spaces. We decided to select a specific situation as an example of a trend that started at the beginning of Jair Bolsonaro's campaign and that would be repeated in the following months throughout the presidential race. The rally was organized by one of the most active Bolsonarista groups that we have researched over the last four years (2016–2020). In our ethnography, we followed the most important events organized by them. For this event, we monitored, for a few weeks, the preparation of the rally on different discussion groups on Facebook and WhatsApp. We followed the rally in a sport utility vehicle (SUV) during the entire route described here, and we participated in the dispersion of the event that took place at a historic landmark in the city.

PISTOLS AND MACHINE GUN GESTURES: WEAPONS AS ENTERTAINMENT

"Better get used to it!" was one of the slogans spoken during the Jair Bolsonaro support rally on Saturday, March 24, 2018, in the state capital. For more than three hours, around fifty people gathered in a square near Paraíso subway and then toured important points of the city, including Paulista Avenue, Roosevelt and Sé Squares, and City Hall, and then dispersed in Ibirapuera Park. To participate in the rally, protesters who did not possess a car took a ride with other motorized protesters.

In all, about ten motorcycles, followed by fifteen cars, left the meeting point. The motorcade began to travel the streets waving Brazilian flags and blowing horns. Many participants wore Bolsonaro T-shirts on which the politician was depicted as the Don Corleone character in Francis Ford Coppola's film *The Godfather*. Although the motorcade was small, it received support from observers throughout its course. Supporters included firefighters, ambulance drivers, military police, homeless people, metropolitan police guards, families walking with their children, and young skaters and cyclists.

Some observers greeted the motorcade while inside their cars, on motorbikes and bicycles, on foot, or from inside stores and houses. Along the way, gestures simulating the carrying of firearms marked the communication and interaction between people amid the blaring horns, which made it difficult to hear much else. Some of the observers made arm gestures to show support for the motorcade and its candidate, and rally participants returned the same gesture or variations of it as a way of thanking them for their support.

A particularly iconic scene during the rally included a long, loud greeting that an ambulance gave to the convoy, which in turn responded when two participants in the front-line car reenacted the two-handed gestures symbolizing a machine gun firing into the air. Along the way, two gestures were used as a form of self-identification and recognition. The first, which was more contained, was made with one hand just simulating the possession of a pistol. The second, which was more mocking and daring, involved both hands and arms simulating possession of a rifle or machine gun.

The greetings were repeated by men, women, and children in an atmosphere of humor, parody, and entertainment, as if the participants and their accomplices were playing a movie or a video game. Thus "weapon play" assumed different forms and meanings for different people. For a few, a serious claim existed among those who actually awaited possession of a weapon concretely or already had their own. For many, especially the younger ones, the gesture was an invitation to a Saturday playdate with friends wearing T-shirts depicting a Mafia movie, amid the roar of car engines, providing an almost LARP-like opportunity to act out the roles of heroes and villains from the

Fast and Furious franchise films. For just over an hour, these young people visibly enjoyed themselves, running red lights with police permission, and stopping traffic to be the temporary center of attention on one of the most important streets in South America's largest city.

The mobilization of humor and entertainment was not an isolated case. Bolsonaro's campaign was based on the construction of his cartoonish caricature; in this sense, he became known to the general public for his humorous and entertaining time on TV programs. However, as Piaia and Nunes (2018) pointed out, unlike Trump, who used the same resource as the host of the reality show *The Apprentice*, Bolsonaro has become a continuing character in lowbrow broadcast programs, becoming the target of parodies and humorous pictures in various situations. His campaign was able to take advantage of these appearances and publicize their participation even when the references to the candidate were used as a resource to make the audience laugh. These continual appearances on Brazilian TV have gone on for more than a decade, since 2010.

SUVS AND THE MILITARIZATION OF CITY LIFE

Bolsonaro was elected not only on the promise of expanding access to weapons but also on introducing a range of more permissive legislation for drivers, such as the removal of mobile speed cameras, increasing the maximum permitted road speed, exemption from the use of safety devices (such as child seats), and tax breaks for cars. The measures mainly serve the middle classes, who have access to these kinds of goods. The relationship of guns in this case sometimes merges and overlaps with the purpose of defending against general theft and, in particular, the theft of automotive vehicles. On a recurring basis, the discourse in favor of releasing weapons to the population is justified as a way of defending one's own life, family, and property, whether it be the residence or the car itself.

There is an overlap, therefore, between the reverence for weapons and cars present in our ethnographic research in São Paulo, which reveals elements about the tactics and purpose of this manifestation of the motorcade. Choosing the modality of a motorcade offered the possibility of a quick mobilization over the duration of the act itself. Discounting concentration and dispersion, the displacement lasted a little over one hour, with the possibility of mobilizing and convening with scarce resources, and without requiring much time or organization. In Facebook discussions and WhatsApp groups, the sharing of rides created both close ties between unfamiliar protesters who would share the same car and reinforced the obligation to participate in the act by those who had confirmed their presence in social media.

If not enough motorized participants showed up to the event, despite confirming their presence online, there was a risk of nonparticipation for those who depended on their rides. On the other hand, a motorized vehicle could easily compensate for the absence of a potential participant without a car. In addition, ownership of the car itself was a sign of distinction from those who had no vehicles, drawing a kind of dividing line between "good citizens" (the entrepreneurs and workers who managed to become life's winners, evinced by car ownership), and the *vagabundos* and "communists," on the other, who did not achieve the same material success as the "good citizens."

The motorcade, besides being a quick event, also responded to safety concerns among Bolsonaro's supporters. They "protested" while being protected from the inside of their cars, shielded from possible negative crowd reactions. These (mostly male) bodies were guarded by motorcycles and cars—machines that compensated for the noise and space they occupied on the streets—and the presence of a small number of people at the demonstration (especially for a country like Brazil, where thousands of protesters are routinely mobilized). Thus a group of fifty people traveled through strategic spaces and places of São Paulo without any issues. The freedom to travel greater distances also allowed cars to travel around meeting places or among crowds that showed either their affection or their disaffection, such as passing in front of a fire station to greet them or passing in front of a public school teachers' strike manifestation at City Hall in order to provoke them.

Even though the motorcade itself gathered only a small number of participants, its model of action was significant, especially as it reflects the militarization of everyday life experienced phenomenologically, especially in urban areas. Scholarly work has previously examined this phenomenon, exemplified by Stephen Graham's (2011) report concerning the use of military technologies, such as the use of SUVs in major cities, especially after the September 11, 2001, terrorist attacks. In this sense, cars are increasingly privileged technologies of the "new military urbanism" in the world's largest cities.

According to Graham (2011), cars are akin to safety "capsules," capable of protecting and isolating drivers against the dangers of the city and urban violence, through machines and military intelligence such as cameras, global positioning systems (GPS), security signals, internet, armor, phones, and of course, guns. In Brazil, this isolation would create driver perceptions of being safe from populations deemed undesirable, dangerous, or insurgent, including people from the urban periphery, the Black population, poor people, *vagabundos*, or *nóias* (crack drug users living on the streets) in São Paulo.

FIREARMS FOR THE PROTECTION OF WOMEN, CHILDREN, AND THE CHRISTIAN FAMILY

As mentioned earlier, Bolsonaro's motorcade is exemplary in that it signifies a change in the way in which pro-gun groups operate in São Paulo. Until 2013, public pro-arms demonstrations by right and extreme-right groups in São Paulo had majority male participation, based on the mobilization of masculinity models that claimed a gun could help a "manly man" defend his property and his own life, especially against other men. Such a strategy, as already mentioned, proved to be successful in expanding Bolsonaro's support base among men but was initially unsuccessful among women (Kalil 2018).

From that moment on in the campaign, the pro-weapon demonstrations were also aimed at women, especially older women, mothers of young people, and younger women with or without children. In this context, the mobilization of family protection became paramount. It was no longer about the speech of manly men expressing the desire to rival other men by showing strength or protecting themselves and their properties or belongings. The discourse mobilized in this arena started to place the protection of the family as its central theme (Kalil 2020). In Carreata Bolsonaro's own inner circle, a woman played a leading role in the event by discussing the death of her son, who had been murdered by a "criminal" when he tried to rob the family car. This woman spoke publicly about the need to release weapons for the population for addressing these types of situations.

This resource used two distinct but complementary strategies. The first was the approximation of the pro-weapons campaign to the defense of religious discourse, focusing on older women, mothers, and grandparents. Thus the weapons would represent protection of the family (especially women and children) but not any family, specifically the Christian family of the "citizen of good." In this way, weapons would be at the service of life and against a culture of death. The second strategy dealt with the approximation of the pro-weapons campaign undertaken by Bolsonaro support groups aimed at young women so that they could defend themselves against sexual violence. In this way, young women started to show images of women in sexy dresses, high heels, red lipstick, and pistols in hand on their social media profiles. The weapon started to be mobilized as a form of "female empowerment" with the protection of virile men who protected families.

As Sayan-Cengiz and Tekin (2019) point out, considering the cases of France and Germany, gender perspectives are fundamental for understanding the rise of the radical populist right in Europe because of the way in which parties instrumentalize women's rights, often in contradictory terms. Similarly, authors like Nancy Fraser (2006) and Wendy Brown (2006) have demonstrated how the supposed protection of women, the family, and religious values have been exploited by conservatives in the United States in favor of austerity and neoliberal policies. In the Brazilian case, as our research points out, speeches regarding the protection of women by Brazilian populist leaders have also been instrumentalized, above all, mobilizing the accusation of "gender ideology" (Kalil 2019), which, in the case of Latin America, takes on specific meanings (Corrêa and Kalil 2020).

FURTHER NOTES

The effort to analyze two long-term ethnographies carried out side by side in different contexts is justified by the attempt to contribute to the debate regarding the rise of Jair Bolsonaro as a far-right populist leader and to examine part of the social processes that resulted in his victory in the elections. Yet from a methodological point of view, this choice poses the challenge of how to present and compare two different contexts with research carried out by different teams. The selection of the data itself and the snapshot of the object of analysis deal with different perspectives and realities. This chapter, therefore, did not provide a conclusive or comprehensive comparison between the two settings but, we hope, that it nonetheless opens new grounds for future dialogue, insights, and research.

First, we highlight the fact that the locations we studied are not static. Rather than trying to account for these nuances over a decade, we opted to present data that portrayed events in 2018—the period preceding Jair Bolsonaro's election. We chose to discuss the changes and specificities of local contexts, with special attention to the intersection of gender, race, class, and age, since the focus was on the performance of men in the research. In addition, the reflections presented here are part of a study in which the issue of weapons and masculinity are multidimensional and can only be understood in relation to other factors, such as neoliberalism, urban violence, public security, and representations of the Brazilian state. A reflection on how our research subjects see themselves in relation to the state, especially in relation to repressive forces, such as the military police, for example, is crucial and demands more comparative efforts, which are beyond the scope of this chapter.

In terms of differences between both contexts, our male interlocutors represent two distinct figures from the point of view of race, class, generation, and territory. In the case of Porto Alegre, we engaged with low-income white and nonwhite young people from a favela. They aspired to be "workers" and to differentiate themselves from *vagabundos* and their *vida bandida*. They are proud to have obtained a few goods through their own merit and effort and not through theft or robbery. They wanted to protect the few things they have. In São Paulo, however, the lower-middle-class men do not frame themselves as hard workers but rather as entrepreneurs. They face financial troubles, have little economic capital, but do not live in favelas. Yet they also differ from *vagabundos*, and perceive themselves not only as *trabalhadores* (workers), like in Porto Alegre, but as *cidadãos de bem* (good citizens).

In both research settings, firearms represented a way to balance a sense of injustice in which "the other" (the internal enemy) is armed but our interlocutors are not. This fact differs from stereotypes about weapons in Brazil, which link them to low-income groups and favela residents, where social actors are supposedly immersed in the world of crime and transgression. Different from such imagery that associates the universe of weapons in Brazil with the world of crime and violence (strongly present in landmark Brazilian movies, such as *City of God* and *Tropa de Elite*), our male interlocutors claimed that legal possession of weapons would differentiate them from the *vagabundos*, who have access to weapons illegally and without formal state mediation. For this very reason, these men deal differently with guns as an object. Weapons, indeed, were not visible or shown in São Paulo. Even in situations where the men were armed in São Paulo, it was very discreet. Yet, although not physically present, guns were always verbally and gesturally omnipresent as icons that positively emphasized aspirational categories of entrepreneurship or hard work.

Another highlighted aspect is the meaning and stake of firearms in both contexts. While most progressive sectors that opposed Bolsonaro's administration perceived guns through their most obvious and immediate goal (to kill people) his voters in urban areas tended to interpret the object positively, as a symbol of life—that is, a resource to prevent death and disempower those armed bandits who seek to mug, kill, and rape. From this point of view, we can understand why our male informants were continually making the hand pistol gesture to express their political engagement. In a playful manner, they are indicating in their terms that since the state fails to provide security, they wish to obtain the right to individually protect their properties, women, and families.

In both cases, guns are symbols that materialize the struggle of "good against evil," the struggle of a superior and noble side of humanity that is devoted to the family and getting items through individual merit. Our interlocutors believed that the other side of this coin rose to prominence under the Workers' Party administrations, embodied in the figure of Lula, considered to be "lazy," "drunk," and "corrupt" by Bolsonaro voters.

Despite economic and geographic differences, these men would have financial difficulties in acquiring weapons, which are expensive in Brazil. They expected a significant price reduction under the Bolsonaro government. The dream of acquiring these objects expresses a kind of class anxiety of those who search for class distinction, power, and comfort when acquiring cars, brands, cell phones, houses, and other items they fear losing. Bolsonaro's campaign emphasized "the talk of the crime" that segregates Brazilian cities (Caldeira 2000), and these men were trying to situate themselves on the supposedly morally and economically superior side of such a divide. Compared to their peers and neighbors, many of these men are proud to have climbed the socioeconomic ladder and to have paid for certain commodities. In this sense, the desire for guns cannot be dissociated from other commodities; guns are part of the commoditized and performed male anxiety regarding social class, urban security, and moral conditions.

Finally, in this chapter, we tried to analyze the desire for firearms from our interlocutors' political perspective to shed light on the rationale behind the abrupt rise of authoritarian rule in Brazil and its fall as a democratic global power. The election of Bolsonaro is one of the most intriguing political phenomena in twenty-first-century Latin America, demanding scholarly efforts to make sense of it. We tried to cover one among many possible perspectives to address the subject. We focused on the most iconographic symbol that bonded the former captain Bolsonaro with his male voters in a campaign marked by the candidate's many misogynic public declarations. After the impeachment of the first female president in the country's history, and the rise of a giant feminist wave in recent years, we cannot forget that firearms are totems that affirm masculinity: the male figure that protects material and immaterial things and ultimately has supreme power over political life.

REFERENCES

Appadurai, Arjun. 1996. *Modernity at Large: Cultural Dimensions of Globalization*. Minneapolis: University of Minnesota Press.

Beasley, Christine. 2008. "Rethinking Hegemonic Masculinity in a Globalizing World." *Men and Masculinities* 11 (1): 86–103.

Brown, Wendy. 2006 "American Nightmare: Neoliberalism, Neoconservatism, and De-democratization." *Political Theory* 34 (6): 690–714.

Caldeira, Teresa P. 2000. *City of Walls: Crime, Segregation, and Citizenship in São Paulo*. Berkeley: University of California Press.

Campbell, Colin. 1987. *The Romantic Ethic and the Spirit of Modern Consumerism*. Oxford: Blackwell.

Connell, Robert, and James Messerschmidt. 2005. "Hegemonic Masculinity: Rethinking the Concept." *Gender and Society* 19, no. 6 (December 2005): 829–859.

Corrêa, Sonia, and Isabela Kalil. 2020. *Políticas antigénero en América Latina: Brasil—¿La catástrofe perfecta?* Rio de Janeiro: ABIA/SPW.

Fonseca, Claudia. 2000. *Família, fofoca e honra: Etnografia de relações de gênero e violência em grupos populares*. Porto Alegre, Brazil: Editora da Universidade.

Fraser, Nancy. 2006. "Mapping the Feminist Imagination: From Redistribution to Recognition to Representation." In *Die Neuverhandlung sozialer Gerechtigkeit*, 37–51. VS Verlag für Sozialwissenschaften.

Graham, Stephen. 2011. *Cities under Siege: The New Military Urbanism*. London: Verso.

Hall, Kira, Donna M. Goldstein, and Matthew Bruce Ingram. 2016. "The Hands of Donald Trump: Entertainment, Gesture, Spectacle." *HAU: Journal of Ethnographic Theory* 6 (2): 71–100.

Kalil, Isabela. 2018. "Who Are Jair's Bolsonaro Voters and What They Believe." *SPW* Report on Brazil's 2018 Presidential Elections. https://sxpolitics.org/who-are-jair-bolsonaros-voters-and-what-they-believe/19224.

———. 2019. "'Gender Ideology' Incursions in Education." *Sur* 16 (29): 115–123. https://sur.conectas.org/en/gender-ideology-incursions-in-education/.

———. 2020. "Políticas antiderechos en Brasil: neoliberalismo y neoconservadurismo en el gobierno de Bolsonaro." In *Derechos en riesgo en América Latina: 11 estudios sobre grupos neoconservadores*, edited by Ailynn Torres Santana. Bogotá, Fundación Rosa Luxemburg. https://sxpolitics.org/es/wp-content/uploads/sites/3/2020/12/DerechosenRiesgoenAmericaLatina.pdf.

Kimmel, Michael. 1987. "Rethinking 'Masculinity': New Directions in Research." In *Changing Men: New Directions in Research on Men and Masculinity*, edited by M. S. Kimmel, 9–24. Newbury Park, Calif.: SAGE.

Perlman, Janice. 2010. *Favela: Four Decades of Living on the Edge in Rio de Janeiro*. Oxford: Oxford University Press.

Piaia, Victor, and Raul Nunes. 2018. "Política, entretenimento e polêmica: Bolsonaro nos programas de auditório." IESP nas Eleições. http://iespnaseleicoes.com.br/politica-entretenimento-e-polemica-bolsonaro-nos-programas-de-auditorio/. No longer extant.

Pinheiro-Machado, Rosana, and L. M. Scalco. 2020. "From Hope to Hate: The Rise of Conservative Subjectivity in Brazil." *HAU: Journal of Ethnographic Theory* 10 (1): 21–31.

Saramifar, Younes. 2018. "Enchanted by the AK-47: Contingency of Body and the Weapon among Hezbollah Militants." *Journal of Material Culture* 23 (1): 83–99.

Sayan-Cengiz, Feida, and Caner Tekin. 2019. "The 'Gender Turn' of the Populist Radical Right." *Open Democracy*. https://www.opendemocracy.net/en/rethinking-populism/the-gender-turn-of-the-populist-radical-right/.

Soares, Luiz Eduardo. 2004. "Juventude e violência no Brasil contemporâneo." In *Juventude e sociedade: Trabalho, educação, cultura e participação*, edited by R. Novaes and P. Vannuchi, 130–159. São Paulo: Fundação Perseu Abramo.

Zaluar, Alba. 2010. "Youth, Drug Traffic and Hypermasculinity in Rio de Janeiro." *Vibrant—Virtual Brazilian Anthropology* 7 (2): 7–27.

NOTES

1. The term *vagabundo* (vagabond) is a frequently racialized term that connotes a person who does not work hard, and who is also a cheater and a criminal.

2. Phases 2 and 3 were carried out with the research team of the Center for Urban Ethnography (NEU) at São Paulo School of Sociology and Political Science.

4 · WHITENESS HAS COME OUT OF THE CLOSET AND INTENSIFIED BRAZIL'S REACTIONARY WAVE

PATRICIA DE SANTANA PINHO

In the lead-up to the second round of the 2018 Brazilian presidential elections, Regina Duarte, one of the country's most famous actresses, explained her support for Jair Bolsonaro as a "coming out" process: "I was in the closet, and my youngest son started questioning me. Since I had always been a democratic, open, and fair person, how could I simply accept the idea that Bolsonaro is brute, rough, ignorant, violent? . . . When I met Bolsonaro in person, I encountered a sweet guy, a man from the 1950s, like my dad, and who makes homophobic jokes, but which is just for show, [and with] a masculine way of being, like that of Monteiro Lobato, who used to call Brazilians lazy and say that the place of Blacks is the kitchen" (Brasil 2018).

Long before these words were publicly uttered and published in a major Brazilian newspaper, leftist and antiracist activists were already employing the "coming out" metaphor to critically refer to the newfound ease with which many middle- and upper-class Brazilians had begun to make openly reactionary remarks.[1] This trend became increasingly common throughout the presidencies of the center-left Workers' Party (Partido dos Trabalhadores; PT, 2003–2016), but it peaked during four particularly shocking events that revealed the precariousness of Brazilian democracy: the parliamentary coup that ousted Dilma Rousseff, the country's first female president, in August 2016; the ordered assassination of the socialist, queer, Afro-Brazilian councilwoman Marielle Franco in March 2018; the imprisonment of former president Luiz Inácio Lula da Silva on unfounded charges in April 2018; and the election, in October 2018, of the far-right and explicitly racist, sexist, and homophobic Jair Bolsonaro. While each of these tragic events has its own specificities, they are also profoundly interconnected in the endorsement that they received from a growing reactionary wave that has been engulfing Brazilian culture, politics, and society.

Most of the analyses of the current juncture have highlighted class prejudice, racism, sexism, homophobia, and religious fundamentalism as the major propellers for the rise of the far-right in Brazil (Souza 2016; Pinheiro-Machado and Scalco 2018; *Yahoo! Notícias* 2019; Santos 2018; Braga 2019; among others). My contribution seeks to add to these important studies an investigation of the significance of whiteness in informing and inciting Brazil's reactionary wave and the election of Bolsonaro. I argue that the examination of whiteness not only makes possible a deeper understanding of each of these propellers; it also reveals how they intersect with and mutually support one another. As we can hear in Regina Duarte's comment, homophobia, sexism, and racism are explicitly intertwined, but what is left unstated is the whiteness of the speaker as well as that of her father, of Monteiro Lobato, and the president she helped elect. This concealed and thus "neutral" whiteness is, however, the very position of power from where these absurdities can be nonchalantly enunciated and rendered acceptable.

As Valeria Ribeiro Corossacz aptly explains, "not knowing" their own whiteness allows whites to continuously reproduce their structurally privileged position. It is therefore crucial to unveil whiteness, not to reify it, but to understand "the mechanisms that mutually reproduce racism, sexism, and class inequalities in Brazilian society" (Ribeiro Corossacz 2018, xii). At the same time, because it operates discursively, whiteness is not restricted to the groups that most directly benefit from it. In fact, although I initially thought that this analysis would focus exclusively on the middle-class backlash against the PT's pro-poor and pro-Black policies, I realized that only a more nuanced study of whiteness that encompasses its appeal across social classes and racial groups may help explain the paradox in which 45 percent of Black Brazilians (Datafolha 2018a) and 64 percent of Brazilians whose families receive between two and five minimum wages voted for Bolsonaro (Datafolha 2018b).

This chapter is divided into four parts. First, I briefly discuss what has been identified as the major propellers of the reactionary wave. The second section is an overview of the definitions of whiteness in the Brazilian studies of *branquitude* that have been flourishing since the early 2000s. In the third and fourth parts, I explain, respectively, two specific concepts that I have developed to account for the significance of whiteness in Brazil's current reactionary wave: "injured whiteness" and "aspirational whiteness." I draw on the findings of several recent ethnographies of everyday life in Brazil (Alves 2018; Maia 2017; Mitchell 2017; Pinheiro-Machado and Scalco 2018; Pinho 2015; Ribeiro Corossacz 2018; Roth-Gordon 2016) to show how whiteness has been a central factor in Brazil's current juncture. The major goal of this study is to offer a conceptual contribution that may serve to remove whiteness from its privileged "default" position.

PROPELLERS OF THE REACTIONARY WAVE

Similar to other Latin American pink tide governments, the PT administrations took advantage of the global commodities boom to strengthen the country's economy and promote its welfare state. The hallmarks of the PT era included crucially important income distribution programs, such as Bolsa Família,[2] minimum wage valorization policies, and the expansion of the job market, all of which enabled lower-class Brazilians to engage broadly in consumption and take on new employment opportunities beyond the typical manual and undervalued jobs to which they had been previously restricted. In addition to that, the expansion of affirmative action in higher education resulted in a noticeable shift in the demographics of the student body, increasing the number of nonwhite and first-generation college students. These important social transformations generated a strident reaction among the so-called traditional middle class, who saw, in the upward mobility of the poor, a threat to its existence.[3] Several analyses, therefore, identified class prejudice as one of the major propellers of Brazil's reactionary wave (Souza 2016; Miguel 2018; among others).

For scholars working on racial politics, racism is what really lies at the heart of bolsonarismo and Brazil's overall turn to the far right. In an article published before the second round of the presidential elections, longtime Black activist and economics professor Hélio Santos (2018) warned Afro-Brazilians not to vote for Bolsonaro given his explicitly racist discourse and unapologetic position against policies intended to tackle racial inequality, such as affirmative action in higher education and land titling for quilombo and Indigenous communities. Santos pleaded with Black and antiracist Brazilians to prevent the election of a man who denies the historical debt of the country to the descendants of slaves. In the perspective of legal scholar Ana Flauzina (2019), instead of representing the rupture of Brazilian democracy, bolsonarismo expresses much more the continuation of a racist history of dehumanization that naturalizes Black pain and promotes the genocide of Brazil's Black population.[4]

The rise of the far right and the subsequent election of Bolsonaro has also been explained as a backlash against a new generation of young feminists, whose vigor and robustness are unprecedented in Brazil, as shown in Rosana Pinheiro-Machado and Lucia Mury Scalco's decade-long ethnography among impoverished youth in Rio Grande do Sul (2018). Their research found cases of husbands who voted for Bolsonaro in order to punish their wives who were becoming "too empowered." In this view, sexism and misogyny are the central propellers of Brazil's reactionary wave.

For the socialist and openly gay politician Jean Wyllys, who had to renounce his term as reelected congressman to go into exile following terrifying threats to his life and family, Bolsonaro's election is due, above all, to homophobia. Alongside the bombardment of fake news to deliberately mobilize specific types of fear within particular sectors of Brazilian society, the widespread hatred for the LGBTQ community was the force that ultimately shifted Brazil to the far right. For Wyllys, Bolsonaro's campaign propagated homophobia in order to tap into the unfounded yet ingrained fear of gay people as a threat to the heteronormative Brazilian family ideal (*Yahoo! Notícias* 2019).

Another important assessment of the rise of the far right has focused on the surge of religious fundamentalism among neo-Pentecostals, and their fanatic war against the bizarrely named gender ideology, to explain the heightening of the moral conservatism that was, in this view, what ultimately elected Bolsonaro. The significance of neo-Pentecostalism has been central even in analyses of class, labor, and precarity. Sociologist Ruy Braga, for instance, argues that Evangelical churches have replaced the trade unions as the primary site of working-class organizations, and this helps explain why "in a country as unequal as Brazil, a substantial part of the working class chose a candidate clearly opposed to a redistributive agenda and who promised to attack social security and labor rights" (2019).

All of these assessments are crucially important to understanding Brazil's reactionary wave. It would not make sense to critique them for having highlighted one factor over another since all analyses are necessarily incomplete. By scrutinizing the significance of whiteness in informing this juncture, I do not seek to simply add another ingredient to the mix, but to examine how whiteness operates in and through each of these propellers, sometimes silently and in other cases evermore vociferously.

DEFINING WHITENESS

The pioneers of the studies of *branquitude* in Brazil have defined whiteness as the "social identity of whites" (Bento 2002), the "silent condition of the white subject" that is conceived of and conceives of itself as the universal model of humanity (Bento 2002), and the dominant identity that is considered normative, invisible, and worthy of preferential treatment (Piza 2000). For Piza (2000, 108), "to be white [in Brazil] is to live without noticing oneself racially." Bento emphasizes that white neutrality, and thus dominance, only makes sense vis-à-vis the existence of its visible, marked, opposite—that is, blackness. Along the same lines, Sovik (2009) explains that, as the attribute of those who are at the top of the social pyramid, whiteness is a social practice that requires the devaluation of blackness.

Agreeing with all these definitions, I propose that, in addition to understanding whiteness as a social identity, a social condition, and a social practice, we conceive of whiteness also as an ideal, promoted discursively as a major social value to be preserved, by those who already possess it, or acquired, by those who do not. In the specific context of Brazil, the ideal of whiteness must be understood in light of a long history of slavery (1532–1888) that profoundly shaped Brazilian society, culture, and politics. Slavery was widely disseminated across social strata, and one did not need to be wealthy to be a slave owner, a characteristic that brought together priests, small property owners, merchants, and even former slaves. The legacy of slavery continues to inform a far-reaching racial hierarchy that encompasses the belief in white superiority and Black inferiority, the association between blackness and manual labor, the notion that Black (and poor) people should "know their place," both physically and symbolically, the authoritarianism of everyday life, and an overall fear of blackness and desire for whiteness that have crucial effects over identities, discourses, and representations.

If identity is produced in and through discourse, greater attention must be placed on the representations that these discourses entail and the fears and desires that they incite. Focusing on whiteness as a discursive configuration and affective cultural politics does not take attention away from whiteness as embodied and lived experience. Rather, it helps understand the intricate ways in which whiteness functions simultaneously as an expression and a mechanism of reproduction of racism and other forms of social discrimination. As the editors of this volume argue, the affective engagement of individuals into a community of feeling played a crucial role both in the initial support for the PT as well as in its subsequent takedown.

Attentive to the importance of discursive practices, more recent studies of whiteness in Brazil have shown that, given the national narrative of racial democracy, it is necessary to identify how whiteness operates through registers that are not always explicitly racial, such as sexuality and intimacy (Ribeiro Corossacz 2018), morality and respectability (Maia 2017),[5] upward mobility (Mitchell 2017), discipline and worthiness (Miskolci 2012), and even linguistic performance (Roth-Gordon 2016). It is crucial, therefore, to examine the intersections of whiteness with discourses that are more obviously about: gender and sexuality, such as the depiction of certain kinds of contemporary Brazilian music and dance as immoral (Maia 2017); class, such as support for meritocracy in discourses that attack redistribution policies (Santos et al. 2008); consumption, such as the search for brands that promise the reification of class boundaries; and hygiene, such as the concern with preserving the physical and symbolic boundaries between maids' bodies and their employers' families (Pinho 2015). These multiple registers allow whiteness to operate in different although interconnected ways among distinct social classes.

Richard Miskolci's (2012) definition of Brazilian whiteness as an ideal created by the elites in the late nineteenth century through political, medical, and literary discourses is very productive in explaining how, functioning discursively, the appeal of whiteness spills over and across class cleavages. Whiteness lies at the heart of what Miskolci aptly defined as *o desejo da nação* (the desire of/for the nation), the ideal that would fill the spaces of the bodies, the cities, and the cultural values. The rejection, despise, and fear of the elites regarding the "masses" have ever since sustained the authoritarian character of Brazil's national project, fueling a biopolitical order that imposes upon the poor and nonwhite population a moralizing discipline meant to whiten Brazilian culture and society.

The material consequences of whiteness easily explain its adherence among the elites, but it is its discursive functioning that makes whiteness appealing to those it most directly hurts, materially and otherwise. My argument here is not that there are different types of whiteness in different social classes—although I do contend that there are various gradations of whiteness in Brazil (Pinho 2009)—but rather that whiteness operates differently for the Brazilian middle and upper classes (i.e., those who recognize themselves and are recognized by others as white or as accessing whiteness) and the Brazilian lower classes (i.e., those who either are not seen as white by themselves and others or do not easily access the privileges of whiteness). This means that, although whiteness is accessed differently, in fact, unequally, by members of the different social classes, the imaginary around the meanings of whiteness is shared across classes and, to a great extent, also across racial groups. Thus while *injured whiteness* refers to the traditional Brazilian middle class and *aspirational whiteness* refers to the Brazilian lower class, these two phenomena support one another, and they reveal the interclass complicity necessary to sustain the power of whiteness.

INJURED WHITENESS

The vociferous response of Brazil's traditional middle class to the social ascension of the poor during the PT era produced what many analysts have defined as a "class resentment" (e.g., Souza 2016; Miguel 2018). I argue that this backlash cannot be understood exclusively on the basis of class. Racism and attachment to the long-established valued position of whiteness played a significant role in informing the anti-PT sentiment and the rise of the reactionary wave, which were, to a great extent, a reaction against the social transformations whereby approximately forty million Brazilians, the majority of whom are Black, were lifted out of poverty and began to access spaces that had been the exclusive purview of middle- and upper-class Brazilians, the majority of whom are white.[6] Thus the resentment that is so often discussed as a class reaction should also be characterized as the response of an *injured whiteness*.

Similar to the concept of injured masculinity, injured whiteness results from a crisis of a dominant model due to a change in the status quo and a real or perceived loss of power and privilege of the dominant group. The challenge to the long-standing premise that poor and Black people should "know their place," both physically and symbolically, deeply mobilized the already existing fear of otherness, no longer because the Other meant an external threat to the Self, but because the Other was threatening to "become" the Self. This happened because the identity boundaries that secured the existence of an external, and constitutive, Other were now being increasingly crossed, thus losing its "frontier-effects" (Hall 1996, 3). Because it felt threatened, whiteness became more defensive and, as a consequence, more visible during the PT era. More than ever before in the history of Brazil, whiteness was interpellated, in the sense that it was increasingly "called into place" (Hall 1996). As the dominant, universal, and default identity, whiteness had more commonly been in the position of interpellating others than being, itself, interpellated. The important social changes that occurred in Brazilian society during the PT era shifted this condition as it ousted whiteness from its comfortable and powerful position of relative invisibility and neutrality.

Despite the problematic process of "inclusion via consumption" promoted by the PT administrations, the enhanced purchasing power of the poor had a crucial effect in injuring whiteness. It is widely known that consumption allows for the preservation of social distinction. Being able to consume expensive goods validates one's position in a social hierarchy, especially when that privilege is restricted to a select few. But the symbolic power of consumption is also confirmed through access to the spaces where consumption happens. In the case of Brazil, shopping malls, airports, and even airplanes were the major sites where the newfound presence of the "previously poor" created a profound unease among the traditional middle class.

As poor and Black Brazilians began to consume products and access spaces that had previously been off limits, an injured whiteness became more vocal and consequently more visible. Journalist Danuza Leão's remark that it was no longer worth visiting New York City because now even her doorman could travel there (Geledés 2012), and comments on social media such as "airports now look like bus stations,"[7] revealed not only class discomfort but also the repudiation that social sectors, historically racialized as nonwhite, could no longer be kept apart. The "social geography of race"—the racial mapping of environments in physical and social terms that enables a conceptual mapping of the Self and Other (Frankenberg 1993, 44)—was changing too dramatically for those whose identities had been firmly attached to the privilege of inhabiting exclusive spaces.

One of the most important factors in injuring whiteness among the traditional middle class was the widespread implementation of affirmative action in higher education. Although several initiatives to increase the number of Black students in public universities already existed since 2003, in 2012 President Rousseff sanctioned Law 12.711/2012, known as the Quotas Law, making mandatory that 50 percent of all the seats in federal universities be destined to poor students, and of this total, a percentage was destined to Black and Indigenous students according to the demographics of the state where each university is located. From 2003 until 2014, affirmative action increased by 178 percent the number of Black students in Brazil's federal universities, where the student body had always been almost exclusively white and from the middle and upper classes (ANDIFES 2016). Because they require racial identification on the part of potential beneficiaries, racial quotas make not only blackness more discernible and demarcated, but as a result, its historical other, whiteness, has become more visible and marked out too. As longtime Black activist and intellectual Sueli Carneiro argued, this law "forced whites to manifest as white, in defense of their interests. They promoted white activism like never before" (Carneiro 2017, 46).

Another major consequence of the upward mobility of the poor during the PT era was that many women who had previously worked as maids started to find other employment opportunities, where they were paid better, received more benefits, and were able to break away from the stigmatized and undervalued domestic work. Between 2009 and 2011, the number of domestic workers dropped from 1,652,000 to 1,554,000, while their salaries received the significant boost of 5.3 percent above inflation, compared to only 2.6 percent of all other professional categories in Brazil during the same period (Pinho 2015, 125). The traditional middle class, who had always relied on the cheap labor and high availability of maids, took that as yet another blow to their social position. A statement by a middle-class Brazilian housewife on the eve of President Dilma Rousseff's inauguration lays clear her desperation for a maid while deceitfully portraying Bolsa Família as a program that enabled poor women to quit working: "My wish for 2011 is that President Dilma discontinues Lula's Bolsa Família. I need a maid! I desperately need a maid! But with the government offering Bolsa Família poor people are not available to work as maids anymore!" (Pinho 2015, 123). The programs implemented by the PT governments were meant to enhance the income of poor families, but they did not replace the need to work for a salary. To suggest otherwise is to endorse the stereotype that poor and/or Black people are inherently lazy.

The conflation between domestic work and blackness was also made explicit when the PT government implemented the program Mais Médicos (More Doctors) with the goals of overcoming the country's deficit of medical doctors and increasing their presence in impoverished and remote areas of Brazil. Brazilian doctors, most of whom are white and from the middle and upper classes, have often refused to work in poor neighborhoods and peripheral areas of the country. The PT administration then decided to temporarily import foreign doctors, among whom Cubans were the majority. When the Cuban doctors, many of whom are Black, began arriving in 2013, they were met with hostility, if not outright bigotry, from sectors of the Brazilian elite. Journalist Micheline Borges's explicitly racist remarks epitomized these reactions: "Forgive me if it is prejudice, but these Cuban female doctors look like domestic workers. Are they really doctors? Ugh, so terrible. Doctors, generally, have the posture of doctors, and impose themselves through their appearance" (Gonçalves 2013). In an excellent analysis, aptly titled "Whiteness Is Naked," writer Ana Maria Gonçalves (2013) explained, "For Micheline Borges, the female Cuban doctors do not have 'good appearance' and, therefore, they should be domestic workers, the position in which she is used to dealing with Black people; the position from which, from the high echelon of her whiteness, she feels comfortable."

As the traditional middle class reacted stridently against the changes to the status quo, and whiteness became increasingly vocal and visible, there was a widening of what was considered acceptable political speech, normalizing statements grounded on authoritarianism and explicitly opposed to social solidarity (Miguel 2018). As Solano (2018, 13) argues, there was a "reactionary reorganization" during the PT era, which made "authoritarian and anti-democratic postures" much more explicit. The newfound ease of middle-class Brazilians to make openly reactionary remarks has been deeply critiqued by leftist scholars and activists, both online and offline.

Among the slogans to emerge in response to the boisterous injured whiteness, perhaps none is more unsettling and powerful than "A casa grande surta quando a senzala vira médica," which roughly translates as "The slave masters freak out when the slaves become doctors." The phrase gained notoriety when Suzane da Silva, a young Black woman, entered medical school in 2016 through the PROUNI, a program of the PT government that provided scholarships for impoverished students to attend private universities. Upon posting pictures of herself on Facebook, holding a poster with this slogan, she was trolled by members of Dignidade Médica, a group of doctors, who attacked her with racist comments, such as "Will she be able to enter hospitals with that hair?" Retelling the story in an event with President Dilma Rousseff in April 2016, Silva exclaimed, while holding the same poster, "Not only will I enter hospitals! I'll enter airplanes, and I'll enter the Palácio do Planalto [the official workplace of the president]!"[8]

The "Casa Grande and Senzala" binary had been made famous in the 1930s when Gilberto Freyre (1978) published his most renowned book under that title. But the dyad "master's house/slave-quarters," which had for so long been represented as an expression of the Brazilian capacity to overcome racial conflict, was now being mobilized to underscore the antagonism between Blacks and whites, and how the legacy of slavery has continuously benefited the latter, materially and symbolically. It is impossible to know who first coined the "slave masters freak out" expression, but the popularity it has gained and the intensity with which it has circulated online and offline—on banners, T-shirts, and everyday conversations—expresses a profound critique to an injured whiteness that refuses to let go of the privilege it has accrued for over more than five hundred years. The expression has thus played an important role in "outing" whiteness.

In fact, whiteness has come out of the closet in two main ways: by being outed and by outing itself as it became increasingly injured and strident. Central to both of these processes is that it was no longer possible to remain "ignorant" of the reality and effects of racism in Brazil. As Sedgwick (2008) argues, ignorance and silence are essential components of discourses. Instead of a generic lack of knowledge, ignorance is always intrinsic to a particular type of knowledge. Ignorance is thus an "epistemological privilege" as it allows the interlocutor who has or pretends to have less knowledge of a specific issue to define the terms of exchange (Sedgwick 2008, 4). The reactionary wave unleashed during the PT era rendered untenable the long-established silence around the country's long history of racism and racial discrimination. While it chose to ignore the effects of racism, whiteness had defined the parameters of the conversation around it. Now that the silence, obliviousness, denial, and evasion regarding one's own position of power are no longer tenable in Brazil, whiteness can no longer function as an "unmarked marker" (Frankenberg 1993).

FIGURE 4.1. Suzane da Silva at the event "Encontro pela Democracia" in the Palácio do Planalto, April 12, 2016
Photo by Lula Marques.

FIGURE 4.2. Suzane da Silva and President Dilma Rousseff at the event "Encontro pela Democracia" in the Palácio do Planalto, April 12, 2016
Photo by Lula Marques.

ASPIRATIONAL WHITENESS

The phenomena of the middle-class resentment and injured whiteness that were unleashed during the PT era, despite their shocking tone, are not exactly surprising in their content. Authoritarianism has long been a characteristic of Brazilian society, and it has been integral to the safeguarding of the middle and upper classes. Perhaps less predictable, however, has been the growth of the reactionary wave also among sectors of the Brazilian lower classes.

Several analyses have underscored the production of enmity as a major component of the rise of the far right in Brazil. Pinheiro-Machado and Scalco (2018), for example, argue that the election of Bolsonaro was made possible because of the fear of an "internal enemy," whom they define as an empty signifier that is "filled" according to whoever is perceived as the major threat for each constituency. Thus for religious fundamentalists, the internal enemy is the LGBTQ; for machista men (and women), it is the feminist; for the middle classes, it is the ascending poor as well as the *bandido*, the "bandit," who is implicitly or explicitly associated with blackness; and so on. In that sense, almost anyone can be classified as the enemy: Blacks, *favelados*, Bolsa Família beneficiaries, gays, feminists, and so on. What the authors do not define, though, is who is not ever classified as the enemy: middle- and upper-class, heterosexual, white men, and perhaps women, depending on whether they obediently stick to their "gender role."

Furthermore, there is one type of fear that permeates all sectors of Brazilian society: the fear of violence and the constant apprehension of being attacked and robbed, at home or in the streets. The media-induced "sense of insecurity" played an important role in fostering public support for greater police brutality against the nonwhite poor and informing the reactionary wave overall. An example of the implicit value of whiteness during this period of growing intolerance was the misrepresentation of human rights as yet another leftist pretext to defend "bandits," best exemplified in the slogan "Direitos humanos para humanos direitos" or, roughly, "Human rights for correct/appropriate/worthy humans."

For the majority of the poor, as well as for most Afro-Brazilians, besides the possibility of being themselves the victims of violence, there is also the fear of being mistaken for the "bandit," who is imagined as the quintessential perpetrator of violence. Attempting to resist this profiling, poor, and especially so, Black men have resorted to various strategies in order to prove that they are "hard workers": from always carrying picture IDs in the event that they are stopped and frisked, to managing their appearance through clothes, haircuts, and even "proper" ways of speaking Portuguese. Analyzing the effects of the worker-versus-bandit dichotomy on the lives of Black *favelados* in São Paulo, Jaime Amparo Alves (2018) argues that self-identification with the hard worker ideal is both an often failed survival strategy and an attempt to represent oneself and one's community as dignified and worthy. This happens in a country where out of the astounding rate of 180 homicides per day, Blacks make up 75.5 percent of the victims and are killed by the police at a rate of 2.5 times that of that of whites (IPEA 2019). Focusing on language and embodied knowledge, Jenifer Roth-Gordon (2016, 44) shows that impoverished youth in Rio de Janeiro attempt to avoid blackness and display "situational whiteness" through managing their speech and appearance in a context where bodies are read and heard as Black or white—not only according to skin color and phenotype but also according to linguistic practices that indicate simultaneously race and class belongings.

It is against this backdrop that fear has contributed not only to preserve class and racial boundaries but also to produce boundaries *among* the poor and nonwhites as they attempt to escape the assumption that *they* are the internal enemy. Although specific fears may have a greater impact on particular constituencies, they can also influence other groups. Discursively organized, disseminated, and mobilized, fear can be employed "as a strategy and technology of social control" with important effects over subjectivities (Teles 2018, 66). In that sense, the instrumentalization of fear was effective not only in producing an injured whiteness among the middle and upper classes but also in fostering an "aspirational whiteness" among the lower classes. Fear has thus operated across class and racial lines, functioning as a conduit for the validation and overvaluing of whiteness, even among nonwhites, and contributing to the production (or confirmation) of an even lower Other for those who are themselves already lowered and othered socially and racially.

For lower-class and nonwhite Brazilians, aspirational whiteness requires enacting an explicit disidentification from the "bandits," from the members of leftist social movements, such as the Landless Rural Workers' Movement (MST) and the Homeless Workers' Movement (MTST), who have been historically portrayed as troublemakers, as well as from the beneficiaries of income distribution programs, who are depicted as freeloaders and work averse. As Ruy Braga (2019) explains, "The popularity of certain policies, such as bolsa família or university racial quotas, strengthened a backlash from those precarious workers who, living in the informal sector or receiving low wages, did not directly benefit. In the eyes of many of these workers, the public policies of the PT era have done nothing more than stimulate laziness and political clientelism, transforming citizens into parasites and objects of electoral exploitation by corrupt politicians. The Brazilian far right managed to instrumentalize this feeling through the rhetoric of 'meritocracy,' appealing to popular resentment against the PT as the crisis deepened and decimated jobs."

The discourse of meritocracy inherently overvalues whiteness as it contributes to naturalize inequality by ignoring how individuals from different social and racial groups benefit from very distinct levels of privilege, opportunity, and various types of capital (economic, social, and cultural) that ultimately reproduce asymmetries and preserve the status quo. What is striking is how prevalent this discourse has become among the lower classes, which can perhaps be explained in light of two major factors: the dissemination of the neo-Pentecostal "prosperity theology," which influences also the worldview of non-neo-Pentecostals, and the strengthening of neoliberal subjectivities. In a reality marked by the precarity of labor and the marketization of all spheres of life, individuals are increasingly required to self-engineer and identify their successes and failures as the result of their personal merit. The production of neoliberal subjectivities was, ironically, further encouraged during the PT era through the aforementioned process of inclusion via consumption, since many viewed the ability to consume to be the result of individual effort and not a consequence of the valorization of the minimum wage and other governmental policies.

Another important factor that contributed to consolidate aspirational whiteness while simultaneously distancing the lower classes from the PT was the biased, selective, and quite hypocritical "anticorruption" discourse, which projected onto the party, and especially and revealingly so, on the figure of Lula, the stereotype of the "bandit," which represents the poor as inherently criminal and dangerous. In that sense, the dominant media's endeavor to criminalize Lula—which contributed to building public support for his imprisonment under unfounded charges—was an effortless deed because, throughout his presidencies, he was persistently portrayed as *poor*, *nordestino*, and *pau de arara*, terms that are implicitly yet deeply connected to being nonwhite. Even if these terms do not always denote blackness, they necessarily imply antiwhiteness. This is an example of how the moralist anticorruption discourse that was so selectively anti-PT, and that has contributed to the overall shift to the far right, can be better understood in light of the study of whiteness.

It is important to highlight that although aspirational whiteness has gained a new influx of energy in the context of the current reactionary wave, its premise is deeply rooted in Brazil's dominant national narrative of racial democracy and its apparently looser racial boundaries. In that sense, aspirational whiteness also builds on a more explicitly racial logic since it is made possible by Brazil's celebratory representations of *mestiçagem*, where racial blurriness historically allured nonwhite Brazilians to identify with whiteness. Although referring to the Mexican context, Monica Moreno Figueroa's (2010, 387) argument is also applicable to Brazil: "Mestizaje enables whiteness to be experienced as both normalized and ambiguous, not consistently attached to the (potentially) whiter body, but as a site of legitimacy and privilege." Even if not necessarily in a physical, phenotypical sense, anyone can aspire to become white, through desiring to enter a social stratum that is superior to one's own. In the pursuit of a higher status, many Brazilians engage in what Sean Mitchell (2017) calls practices of "everyday whitening," grounded on the fact that Brazil's ethnoracial ambiguity is skewed toward whiteness.

Paradoxically, the PT era witnessed two opposite phenomena regarding whiteness among the lower classes. On the one hand, stimulated by affirmative action and other pro-Black policies, there was a denunciation of white privilege, the overcoming of whiteness as an ideal, and the reclaiming of blackness as a dignified identity, as Suzane da Silva's speech exemplifies. On the other hand, however, and certainly more prevalent, there is a growing desire for whiteness that has been incentivized through the strategic mobilization of fear, the incentive to consume, the influence of prosperity theology, and the increasing neoliberal shaping of subjectivities. The lack of correspondence between how the subject is interpellated and what the subject desires does not prevent the aspiration of whiteness. After all, identity is more about "becoming" than "being," and it is produced within specific discursive formations and practices, where subjects make specific enunciative strategies (Hall 1996, 5).

CONCLUSION: FEAR AND DESIRE AS THE CONNECTING FACTORS

While injured whiteness results from the effort to prevent the undoing of the suture that for so long seamlessly stitched the white subject to its dominant position, aspirational whiteness is the attempt at stitching the subject that is not interpellated as white to a position of power, by summoning the discursive configuration that sustains the ideal of whiteness. In that sense, by mobilizing fear and desire, injured whiteness and aspirational whiteness mutually support one another. The strategic mobilization of the fear of the Other has a long history in Brazil (as elsewhere), having peaked in specific historical moments. The period leading into as well as the one that followed the abolition of slavery were profoundly marked by fear, especially the fear of blackness. Whether it was conceived through the concern with the alleged inability of Blacks to modernize, or as the anxiety regarding Black freedom, Black vengeance, and Black protagonism, the fear of blackness had direct implications for Brazil's conception of itself as a nation, having informed a biopolitical order that regulates policies regarding education, health, hygiene, sanitation, immigration, and a justice system that continues to justify the elimination of nonwhites, through either assimilation, incarceration, or death.

But linked to, and operating in tandem with, the fear of blackness has been the desire for whiteness. To desire can be understood as wanting or craving something, but it also refers to the attempt at attaining what is deemed lacking, and it is therefore connected to the idea of wholeness. Whether revealing of a sense of incompleteness that derives from the condition of otherness, or a longing for power from a place of powerlessness, desire is a crucial factor that propels aspirational whiteness. But desire equally informs injured whiteness; after all, the social ascension of the poor was perceived as a rupture in the boundary that kept whiteness separate and whole. Although in other contexts desire can function as a tool of collective agency in the dismantling of social hierarchies, in this case, because the object of desire is whiteness, it has served not only to preserve the status quo but, in fact, to deepen and justify an already brutally unequal system.

The narrative of racial democracy and the celebration of mestiçagem had made explicit self-identification as white in Brazil almost a taboo. Emphasizing one's racial mixture and/or cultural abilities to perform blackness (through dancing samba, for example) had conventionally been the Brazilian thing to do, at least until the social transformations brought about during the PT era. With blackness no longer remaining culturally decorative and becoming increasingly socially imperative, whiteness had no alternative but to come out of the closet. If coming out refers to something that is hidden, this expression can only be applied to an identity that is already visible and embodied when coming out is not about *revealing*, but about *affirming* and, in the case analyzed here, *confirming* one's position of power. The metaphor of the closet has a different meaning in reference to whiteness than when applied to an oppressed identity. Coming out as LGBTQ means overcoming shame and liberating from an oppressive heteronormative system, and it is therefore a step toward an inclusive society. Whiteness coming out of the closet, on the other hand, is the performative act of reclaiming privilege, for those who fear they have lost it; or the attempt to partake in it, for those who have never had it in the first place.

ACKNOWLEDGMENTS

I am grateful to the editors for organizing this important book, to my *companheiras* in the research cluster "Researching and Resisting Brazil's Reactionary Wave" for our inspiring conversations, to the UCSC Research Center for the Americas for supporting our cluster, and to photographer Lula Marques for authorizing the use of his impactful images in this chapter.

REFERENCES

Alves, Jaime Amparo. 2018. *The Anti-Black City: Police Terror and Black Urban Life in Brazil*. Minneapolis: University of Minnesota Press.

ANDIFES. 2016. *IV Pesquisa do perfil sócioeconômico e cultural dos estudantes de graduação das instituições federais de ensino superior brasileiras, 2014*. Uberlândia, Brazil: ANDIFES, 2016.

Bento, Maria Aparecida Silva. 2002. "Branqueamento e branquitude no Brasil." In *Psicologia social do racismo—Estudos sobre branquitude e branqueamento no Brasil*, edited by Iray Carone and Maria Aparecida Silva Bento, 25–58. Petrópolis, Brazil: Editora Vozes.

Braga, Ruy. 2019. "From the Union Hall to the Church." *Jacobin*, April 7, 2019. https://www.jacobinmag.com/2019/04/bolsonaro-election-unions-labor-evangelical-churches?fbclid=IwAR1wXO27S8UYAwgmlxLGjYxsVTQmpAWtB-qoDZafEMC7DszfTgN7Qo8qWkk.

Brasil, Ubiratan. 2018. "'Homofobia de Bolsonaro é da boca para fora', diz Regina Duarte." *Estadão*, October 26, 2018. https://politica.estadao.com.br/noticias/eleicoes,homofobia-de-bolsonaro-e-da-boca-para-fora-diz-regina-duarte,70002564696.

Carneiro, Sueli. 2017. Interview in *Report of the LASA Fact-Finding Delegation on the Impeachment of Brazilian President Dilma Rousseff*. Latin American Studies Association, April 25, 2017. https://lasaweb.org/en/news/report-lasa-fact-finding-delegation-impeachment-brazilian-president-dilma-rousseff/.

Flauzina, Ana Luiza Pinheiro. 2019. "Democracia genocida." In *Brasil em transe: Bolsonarismo, nova ddireita e desdemocratização*, edited by Rosana Pinheiro-Machado and Adriano de Freixo, 63–82. Rio de Janeiro: Oficina Raquel.

Folha de São Paulo. 2018a. "Pesquisa Datafolha 2018: Confira os resultados das pesquisas para presidente, governador e senador. Preta." August 30, 2018. Accessed July 1, 2019. https://arte.folha.uol.com.br/poder/eleicoes-2018/pesquisa-datafolha/#/presidente/segundo/brasil/intencao-de-voto-estimulada-votos-validos/total/cor/preta.

———. 2018b. "Pesquisa Datafolha 2018: Confira os resultados das pesquisas para presidente, governador e senador. Mais de 2 a 5 S.M." August 30, 2018. Accessed July 1, 2019. https://arte.folha.uol.com.br/poder/eleicoes-2018/pesquisa-datafolha/#/presidente/segundo/brasil/intencao-de-voto-estimulada-votos-validos/total/renda-familiar-mensal/mais-de-2-a-5-s-m.

Frankenberg, Ruth. 1993. *White Women, Race Matters: The Social Construction of Whiteness*. Minneapolis: University of Minnesota Press.
Freyre, Gilberto. 1978. *Casa grande & senzala: Formação da família brasileira sob o regime da economia patriarcal*. 19th Brazilian ed. Rio de Janeiro: José Olympio, 1978.
Geledés. 2012. "O perigo de dar de cara com o porteiro do próprio prédio. Danuza Leão pede desculpas a porteiros e leitores." *Portal Geledés*, December 2, 2012. https://www.geledes.org.br/o-perigo-de-dar-de-cara-com-o-porteiro-do-proprio-predio-danuza-leao-pede-desculpas-a-porteiros-e-leitores/.
Gonçalves, Ana Maria. 2013. "A branquitude está nua." *Portal Geledés*, September 11, 2013. https://www.geledes.org.br/branquitude-esta-nua/.
Hall, Stuart. 1996. "Who Needs 'Identity'?" In *Questions of Cultural Identity*, edited by Stuart Hall and Paul du Gay, 1–17. London: SAGE.
IPEA. 2019. *Atlas da violência 2019*. Brasília: Instituto de Pesquisa Econômica Aplicada. http://www.forumseguranca.org.br/wp-content/uploads/2019/06/Atlas_2019_infografico_FINAL.pdf.
Klein, Charles, Sean T. Mitchell, and Benjamin Junge. 2018. "Naming Brazil's Previously Poor: 'New Middle Class' as an Economic, Political, and Experiential Category." *Economic Anthropology* 5 (1): 83–95.
Maia, Suzana. 2017. "A branquitude das classes médias: Discurso moral e segregação social." In *Branquitude: Estudos sobre a identidade branca no Brasil*, edited by Tânia M. P. Müller and Lourenço Cardoso, 107–123. Curitiba, Brazil: Appris.
Miguel, Luis Felipe. 2018. "A reemergência da direita Brasileira." In *O ódio como política: A reinvenção das direitas no Brasil*, edited by Esther Solano, 17–26. São Paulo: Boitempo Editorial.
Miskolci, Richard. 2012. *O desejo da nação: Masculinidade e branquitude no Brasil de fins do XIX*. São Paulo: Editora Annablume.
Mitchell, Sean T. 2017. "Whitening and Racial Ambiguity: Racialization and Ethnoracial Citizenship in Contemporary Brazil." *African and Black Diaspora: An International Journal* 10 (2): 114–130.
Moreno Figueroa, Monica. 2010. "Distributed Intensities: Whiteness, Mestizaje and the Logics of Mexican Racism." *Ethnicities* 10 (3): 387–401.
Müller, Tânia M. P., and Lourenço Cardoso, eds. 2017. *Branquitude: Estudos sobre a identidade branca no Brasil*. Curitiba, Brazil: Appris.
Pinheiro-Machado, Rosana, and Lucia Mury Scalco. 2018. "Da esperança ao ódio: A juventude periférica Bolsonarista." In *O ódio como política: A reinvenção das direitas no Brasil*, edited by Esther Solano, 53–69. São Paulo: Boitempo Editorial.
Pinho, Patricia de Santana. 2009. "White but Not Quite: Tones and Overtones of Whiteness in Brazil." *Small Axe: A Caribbean Journal of Criticism* 29 (13/2): 39–56.
———. 2015. "The Dirty Body That Cleans: Representations of Domestic Workers in Brazilian Common Sense." *Meridians* 13 (1): 103–128.
Piza, Edith. 2000. "Branco no Brasil? Ninguém sabe ninguém viu." In *Tirando a máscara: Ensaios sobre o racismo no Brasil*, edited by Antonio Sérgio Alfredo Guimarães and Lynn Huntley, 97–125. São Paulo: Paz e Terra.
Pragmatismo Político. 2014. "Professora da PUC debocha de 'passageiros pobres' em aeroporto." February 7, 2014. https://www.pragmatismopolitico.com.br/2014/02/professora-da-puc-debocha-de-passageiros-pobres-em-aeroporto.html.
Ribeiro Corossacz, Valeria. 2018. *White Middle-Class Men in Rio de Janeiro: The Making of a Dominant Subject*. Lanham, Md.: Lexington.
Roth-Gordon, Jennifer. 2016. *Race and the Brazilian Body: Blackness, Whiteness, and Everyday Language in Rio de Janeiro*. Berkeley: University of California Press.
Santos, Hélio. 2018. "Não votar em Bolsonaro: para os negros uma questão de amor próprio." *Portal Geledés*, October 15, 2018. https://www.geledes.org.br/nao-votar-em-bolsonaro-para-os-negros-uma-questao-de-amor-proprio/.
Santos, Sales Augusto dos, Eliane Cavalleiro, Maria Inês da Silva Barbosa, and Matilde Ribeiro. 2008. "Ações afirmativas: Polêmicas e possibilidades sobre igualdade racial e o papel do estado." *Estudos feministas* 16 (3): 913–929.
Sedgwick, Eve. 2008. *Epistemology of the Closet*. Berkeley: University of California Press.
Solano Gallego, Esther. 2018. "Apresentação." In *O ódio como política: A reinvenção das direitas no Brasil*, edited by Esther Solano, 13–16. São Paulo: Boitempo Editorial.
Souza, Jessé. 2016. *A radiografia do golpe: Entenda como e por que você foi enganado*. São Paulo: Editora LeYa.
Sovik, Liv. 2009. *Aqui ninguém é branco*. Rio de Janeiro: Aeroplano.

Teles, Edson. 2018. "A produção do inimigo e a insistência do Brasil violento e de exceção." In *O ódio como política: A reinvenção das direitas no Brasil*, edited by Esther Solano, 65–72. São Paulo: Boitempo Editorial.

Yahoo! Notícias. 2019. "Jean Wyllys atribui vitória de Bolsonaro à homofobia." February 28, 2019. https://br.noticias.yahoo.com/jean-wyllys-atribui-vitoria-de-bolsonaro-homofobia-194929765.html.

NOTES

1. Social classes in Brazil are classified according to a descending A-B-C-D-E system, where A = richest and E = poorest.
2. Implemented in 2003 by President Lula, Bolsa Família was a program of cash transfer for impoverished families in return for keeping their children in school and making preventive health care consults.
3. The traditional middle class encompasses the already established professional class and inherited-money elite, characterized by home ownership, college education, and elevated social and cultural capital (Klein et al. 2018), in addition to an identification with the upper class and sharp distinction from the lower classes.
4. Sullivan (this volume) makes a similar point, that Bolsonarismo represents the continuity and acceleration of racial hatred.
5. See Muller and Cardoso's (2017) important collection of recent studies of *branquitude* in Brazil.
6. Technically, most of the poor who ascended socially entered class C. For a thorough analysis of this phenomenon, see Klein et al. (2018).
7. The comment that airports began to look like bus stations became common in everyday conversations and social media, but some cases became particularly famous, such as when a college professor posted a similar remark on her Facebook page (Pragmatismo Político 2014).
8. Silva's powerful and moving speech is available at https://www.youtube.com/watch?v=uNrfjgrooec, April 15, 2016, accessed June 26, 2019.

PART II CORRUPTION AND CRIME

5 · CRUEL PESSIMISM

The Affect of Anticorruption and the End of the New Brazilian Middle Class

SEAN T. MITCHELL

Between 2015 and 2018, I attempted to conduct ethnographic research on a disappearing—or, perhaps, never existing—object: Brazil's so-called new middle class.[1] These were years of economic decline for the tens of millions of people who had risen out of poverty and into this alleged (e.g., by Neri 2014) new class.[2] That socioeconomic mobility had principally occurred during the 2003–2016 administrations of Workers' Party (Partido dos Trabalhadores; PT) presidents. Those administrations, under Luiz Inácio Lula da Silva (hereafter, Lula) and Dilma Rousseff (hereafter, Dilma), had taken advantage of a global boom in the price of Brazilian exports in order to adopt many successful social democratic redistributive measures. The years 2015–2018 also marked the period that Lava Jato (Car Wash), a massive ostensible anticorruption investigation, would transform Brazil's politics and economics. The investigation was led by a once-heralded judge, Sérgio Moro, and linked to the impeachment of PT president Dilma, and to the imprisonment of 2018 presidential frontrunner, former PT president Lula. Politically, these years culminated in the election of a far-right figure, Jair Bolsonaro, who, in campaign discourses, promised a historic "cleansing" of his political enemies (*Carta Capital* 2018). Those years were also characterized by ever-clearer revelations that the "anticorruption" investigation was itself politicized and corrupt.[3]

I argue in this chapter that (1) the dashing of economic hopes and mobility among the previously socioeconomically ascendant, coupled with (2) the ever-clearer corruption and venality of the "anticorruption" campaign that reshaped Brazilian politics, have (3) fostered widespread sentiment of what I call cruel pessimism, which (4) was one important condition of possibility for the election of Bolsonaro and the turn in Brazilian politics toward the far right.

Lauren Berlant (2011, 1) has influentially described a form of affect prevalent under neoliberalism in the United States, cruel optimism: the affect of a failed American Dream. Berlant (2011) describes cruel optimism as the imperative to strive for goals that are unreachable, which leads people to accept hopes, plans, and behaviors that are harmful to their well-being. "A relation of cruel optimism," Berlant writes, "exists when something you desire is actually an obstacle to your flourishing." Drawing on Berlant, Dia Da Costa (2016, 1) turns away from the affluent United States to examine the "historical present of those born into a pervasive and intractable sense of marginality and insecurity," coining the helpful term *cruel pessimism*, which I borrow for this chapter.

As I use it in this chapter, cruel pessimism is not the imperative to strive for the impossible and self-defeating that Berlant describes but, rather, the sense that all forms of collective striving for the public good are doomed to failure, because of the deficiencies and corruption of the would-be strivers themselves. I argue here that three interlocking factors have cultivated cruel pessimism among Brazil's previously ascendant. Those factors are (1) dashed hopes of social mobility; (2) an awareness of the hypocrisy of anticorruption, compounding long-standing awareness of the venality of corruption itself; and (3) pervasive and hypervisible injustice and structural inequality.[4] This process is self-reinforcing because cruel pessimism is the consequence of these three factors, but once cruel pessimism takes hold, the very explanations that people give to understand these factors rely on cruel pessimism, reinforcing the affective dynamic.

Before I present the ethnography that informs this argument, I want to make it as clear as possible, abstracting the argument and some of that ethnography in ideal-typical form. In recent years, my interlocutors in urban working-class Brazil would frequently lament the end of social mobility, the poverty of public services, and the untrustworthiness of political leaders. The most common explanation that my interlocutors gave for these things was some version of "we have these problems because we Brazilians are corrupt and thus collective projects are doomed to fail." This is cruel pessimism, a consequence of the three factors I describe above and one condition of possibility for Brazil's swing to the far right at the end of the twenty-first century's second decade. In this chapter, I map out the characteristics of cruel pessimism using ethnographic examples, and I reflect on the profound implications of this affective formation for Brazilian politics.

CRUEL PESSIMISM IN A NORTH RIO DE JANEIRO CONDOMINIUM

In 2016, I rented a room for a few months in the small—but tidy and comfortable—condominium of a family in Rio de Janeiro's North Zone.[5] I was beginning a long-term collaborative research project, for which my colleagues and I had recently received funding. Collaborating with a local team of researchers, I was carrying out an extensive survey in a series of working-class neighborhoods in Rio.[6] While working on that survey, I chose to stay in the Rio Comprido neighborhood, located between the city's center and its North Zone. I chose the area primarily for its easy access to the different subway, commuter train, and bus lines leading to the different neighborhoods in the city's North and West Zones in which we were conducting the survey, and in which I was carrying out interviews and ethnographic research on class mobility and politics.

In that Rio Comprido condominium of three small bedrooms, just beginning to show scuffs on a crisp renovation carried out in 2011, I became a frequent conversation partner of the matriarch of the family, Marilda.[7] Her trajectory of rapid class ascent and decline mirrored—in perhaps exaggerated fashion—that of millions of other Brazilians during a period of widespread, and tragically short-lived, poverty reduction in the country. Marilda had been born poor in São João de Meriti, one of the industrial suburbs of the Baixada Fluminense, north of the city proper. When asked how she understood her class position, she would refer to herself as a member of the "improved poor" (*pobre melhorada*).[8] Between 2004 and 2014, Marilda had run a successful business. Trained as a radiology technician during a period of expanding educational opportunities in the country and able to secure credit during a period of expanding access, the ambitious Marilda founded a school offering preparatory courses for aspiring radiology technicians. The school had, for a time, placed her family very comfortably in the middle class.

However, in 2014, as Brazil was showing the early signs of an economic downturn from which the national economy had scarcely recovered even before the COVID-19 pandemic, Marilda lost her business. When I lived in her apartment in 2016, she was contributing to her husband, Raul's, modest retirement income by renting and tending to the room I stayed in. I found out only later that they displaced their only grown son to the tiniest room in the apartment in order to accommodate me and the other renters who came through from time to time when I was not there. The son was a university student, and that income helped the family support him. Marilda also managed and rented another condominium that the family owned in a beach town a few hours up the coast. They had purchased both properties at the end of the previous decade—during times that were economically flush for the family and for much of Brazil. But by mid-2016 when I stayed with them, Brazil was well into a prolonged period of economic decline and political upheaval. The assets the family had purchased during the boom times of 2004–2014 allowed them to hold on to a bare semblance of a middle-class lifestyle, although they then strenuously avoided luxuries. And like many of those who had been economically ascendant at the start of Brazil's twenty-first century, they struggled to pay off the debt they had accumulated during those easier times.

Just as the family's economic rise and fall had an arc parallel to that of the national economy during the first decade-and-a-half of the twenty-first century, so too did Marilda's experience and perceptions of Brazilian politics. They also shed light on some affective aspects of the precipitous political shifts of the period between the impeachment of PT president Dilma Rousseff in 2016 and the election of the far-right Jair Bolsonaro in October 2018, especially among the tens of millions who exited poverty during the PT administrations of 2003–2016.

Marilda frequently told me that she hated politics and politicians, a common enough sentiment among my many interlocutors in Brazil—especially during those years of economic decline and political disillusion. Like most people in the neighborhood, she frequently lamented the poor quality of public transportation, sewage, education, and especially, the always-present fear of crime. And she spoke frequently of the problem of corruption whenever the topic of politics and politicians came up. In an August 2018 interview, when former president Lula was imprisoned on (highly politicized and thin) corruption charges, Marilda told me, laughing nervously when I asked about him, that she hoped Lula would "die behind bars."

This was not a surprising sentiment. One would be hard-pressed to find defenders of Lula in 2018 among the Rio de Janeiro petite bourgeoisie—whether present, former, or merely aspirational holders of that class position. By 2018, Lula's base of support was solidly among the urban and rural poor and in the country's poorest region, the northeast. But Marilda was ever conscious of her roots among the urban poor, and she paused, considered, and continued, partially reversing her sentiment: "But the truth is [Lula's presidency] was the period when we had the most opportunities . . . he may have robbed, but the population wasn't suffering nearly as much as we started to when he left. . . . I don't even know whether I think he should return. You see? Because things are so bad that, if he came back, maybe things would get better."

She laughed nervously again and went on,[9] "But I'll never vote again for him. I'll never vote for anyone. I'll annul my vote."[10]

She had enthusiastically supported Dilma's impeachment when I lived with the family in 2016, but when I asked about it again in 2018, she told me that "it was a failure. They [the agents of the impeachment] just wanted to rob too."

Her statement was typical among people who might be categorized as the "previously poor" (Klein, Mitchell, and Junge 2018) of the Rio neighborhoods of the North and West Zones where I have carried out research. The PT dominated presidential elections for much of the century in those neighborhoods.[11] That changed in 2018, when Jair Bolsonaro won in all neighborhoods but one in, not only the city of Rio, but all of Rio de Janeiro State in the decisive second round that pitted the far-right wing congressman and former army captain against former São Paulo mayor and PT education minister Fernando Haddad.[12]

When I asked Marilda what might be done to improve Brazil, she made her bleak sentiment even clearer: "I think it could even stay the same or get worse but get better? Doubtful. Here in Brazil nothing can get better. If a meteor shower comes raining down on us, maybe. In Brazil, everything must end and start again."

It was August of 2018, just two months until the first round of the 2018 presidential elections. Few respectable commentators inside or outside of Brazil thought that Bolsonaro could win. However, with the imprisonment of frontrunner Lula, a virally spreading social media campaign aimed against the PT's then likely candidate Haddad,[13] and the surprise far-right electoral successes of Brexit in the United Kingdom and Donald Trump in the United States, it was beginning to appear that Bolsonaro's campaign might genuinely have a path to victory. So I asked Marilda about Bolsonaro and whether she would vote for him. Her reply expressed a ubiquitous sentiment in my conversations about politics in Brazil of 2018, even among those who had been enthusiastic about the PT years earlier, or among those who had been enthusiastic about the impeachment of Dilma, as had Marilda. Marilda told me, as she had before, that she would annul her vote. She continued, "I now think that everyone is a crook [*ladrão*]. I now believe that there's so much thievery [*roubalheira*] that I no longer believe in politicians. To me, politician is the profession for a crook."

In my reading, Brazil's corrupt and politicized anticorruption politics—something very distinct from a genuine attempt to create a less corrupt political economy—had dashed all the forms of enthusiasm for collective politics at the national level that Marilda had felt in recent years. The anticorruption politics of Lava Jato—and its many proximate political and mass-media projects, such as the imprisonment of Lula and impeachment of Dilma—had dampened her prior enthusiasm for the antipoverty politics of the PT, which she acknowledged she had benefited from. The hypocrisy and venality of those who professed anticorruption, moreover, soured her on institutional anticorruption politics itself. All this left her profoundly cynical[14] about the possibility of political improvement in Brazil, which could only be carried out by something as violent and destructive as her "meteor shower."[15]

That meteor shower arrived. In another reversal, Marilda's sentiments toward Bolsonaro shifted in September 2018. Although she had disavowed the incendiary figure a month earlier, by September, Marilda was enthusiastically backing Bolsonaro, frequently posting pro-Bolsonaro memes to Facebook and WhatsApp. A typical meme that she shared combined anticommunism with the aestheticization of violence and the nation, all crucial elements in Bolsonaro's campaign: "Brazil will never again be red. It will only be red if it needs our blood to keep it green and yellow" (the colors of the Brazilian flag). She shared many other memes along those lines.

I focus this chapter on Marilda's narrative, because like her socioeconomic arc, it traces, in exaggerated form—almost as an ideal type made flesh—a trajectory I saw repeated again and again during those years of tumult: from poor to middle class, and then precipitously down again (although Marilda rose higher and did not fall nearly as far as many).

As an explicit trajectory of political sentiment, Marilda's journey also marked out a perfectly clear instance of a pattern I witnessed frequently. She went from (1) qualified support for the state-based social mobility facilitated by the PT during the years that it was effective; to (2) support for the impeachment of PT president Dilma when that mobility faltered and amid a constant drumbeat of corruption accusations in Brazilian mass media; to (3) an antipolitical rejection of all politics as the hypocrisy of the impeachment was made clear; to (4) the sense that, in Brazil, collective forms of social progress for some sort of public good were simply impossible; and to (5) eventual support for the candidacy of a politician who promised to wipe the slate through violence.

THE END OF THE NEW MIDDLE CLASS

This chapter (and this book) chronicles Brazil's tumultuous passage from a widely hailed, apparent social-democratic success story under the PT, through seemingly unending economic and political crisis, and to the assumption of the presidency by Jair Bolsonaro, a figure who can be called, with some justification, neofascist.[16] I do not attempt to provide all the *reasons* for those broad changes—although that is a goal of my current book project.[17] Such an endeavor is a much broader task than that which I undertake here.

Any thorough explanation of why Brazil changed as it did would have to consider factors outside the purview of the ethnographic methods on which this chapter is based: factors such as changes in the global political economy; a transition from Brazil's 1964–1985 military dictatorship that left many structures and personnel from that era intact and empowered; and the covert and overt influence of conspiratorial actors, Brazilian and foreign (Mier and Hunt 2019). It is important here to note that those actors include agents and agencies of the U.S. federal government. Leaked documents have made it clear that, in violation of Brazilian law, the U.S. Department of Justice and FBI were closely involved in Lava Jato (Fishman, Viana, and Saleh 2020; Viana and Neves 2020). These crucial matters are beyond the scope of this chapter. Here I am focused simply on unpacking some of the affective and experiential consequences and conditions of possibility for Brazil's political transformation.

Moreover, even in the realm of affect, cruel pessimism isn't the only cause of Brazil's swing to the right. For example, many Evangelical Christians, and many political conservatives, see a national moralization in the rise of the right and cast their votes for Bolsonaro with a kind of optimism (see chapters by Biondi; Kalil, Pinheiro-Machado, and Scalco; Jarrín; and Junge in this volume). And the forms of affect that Rojas, Olival, and Spexoto Olival, and Kopper describe in this volume ("despairing hope" and "negative hope," respectively) are testaments to the complexity of affective shifts in recent Brazilian politics. I think that "cruel pessimism" identifies an aspect of these shifts that helps us understand the dizzying political transformations of the period this book chronicles.

The research that this chapter is based on was conceived at the start of the twenty-first century's second decade. Brazil under the PT was lauded internationally for its success at reducing poverty and inequality and for making itself an important world power. In the pages of the *New York Times*, for example (Cohen 2011), Brazil was taken as demonstrating the possibility of a "giddy convergence"—of a reduction of economic inequalities on a global scale. As I sought out a new research project during that "giddy" period, and while working on completing my analysis of earlier long-term research based in Alcântara, Maranhão, Brazil—research that eventually became *Constellations of Inequality: Space, Race, and Utopia in Brazil* (Mitchell 2017)—poor and working-class friends and interlocutors from the states of Maranhão and Rio de Janeiro (where my closest ties in Brazil are) told me frequently how much their lives had improved over the last decade. Afro-Brazilian young people from the *quilombos* of Maranhão[18] and the favelas and suburbs of Rio de Janeiro whom I spoke to were attending prestigious universities—which would have been unthinkable for their parents—with wages on a steady upward trajectory. Despite the emergence of protest movements in 2013, and widely reported unrest during the 2014 Brazilian World Cup, when I spent some time just in Alcântara, just after that World Cup, people's euphoria about their improving life conditions remained palpable. And people in Alcântara were also very clear about whom they would vote for in what would be a highly contested presidential election of 2014: the PT candidate, incumbent president Dilma Rousseff.

Given the anecdotal observations of my interlocutors and the scholarly corroboration of massive poverty reduction and the rise of the so-called, albeit disputed, "new middle class" (Klein, Mitchell, and Junge 2018; M. Neri 2012; Pochmann 2014; J. de Souza 2010; A. de Souza and Lamounier 2010), it seemed obvious to me at the time that this was a key example of what Piketty (2014) had recently shown to be extremely rare in world history: largescale inequality reduction in a capitalist economy, and in one of the most brutally and violently unequal countries on earth. Here was an opportunity to study something of undoubted importance, and fundamentally hopeful.

However, what my colleagues and I chronicled over years of research on this project, from 2016 through the present, was a story of decline: of democratic institutions, economic fortunes, national sovereignty, and public well-being. But most crucial for this chapter was the loss I have perceived when talking to those poor and once-poor people who had expressed such optimism in 2011, when I had not yet conceived of this research project—the loss of that optimism and the rise of cruel pessimism.

THE CRUEL PESSIMISM OF CORRUPTION AND ANTICORRUPTION

The dashing of people's aspirations amid this widespread economic decline is one crucial factor that fostered this affect of cruel pessimism—this sense of the impossibility of collective and public striving, because of the insufficiencies of the strivers themselves. The use and abuse of corruption and anticorruption is another. Many different political concerns run through the interviews and conversations I collected over these years of research in which I, contrary to my original plans, ended up studying the tragic decline of the so-called new middle class. People in the North and West Zone neighborhoods of Rio de Janeiro whom my research collaborators and I spoke to were alternately worried about education, infrastructure, public sanitation, violence, employment, poverty, sexual morality, sexual liberty, racial disorder, racism, inequality, communism, and much more. But corruption was, by far, the most common lament when people talked politics. And "corruption," along with its dialectically inevitable partner, "anticorruption," formed the most common idiom—or metadiscourse—for discussing politics.

A kind of floating signifier, "corruption" can be made to refer to any of the worries listed above and more. It is polysemic and can be stretched widely—both deliberately and unconsciously—and understood very differently by different publics. When Marilda spoke of corruption, for example, she sometimes seemed to be referencing some inherent moral deficiency, some quality of abjection that "inheres in what people are, rather than what they do," as Ansell has written of one mode of corruption discourse in Brazilian politics (Ansell 2018, 312). This is what Marilda seemed to mean when, for example, I heard her derisively use corruption language when talking about organizers of a union-led general strike in 2017, on one occasion, and of *travesti* sex workers and their clients, on another.

But more often for Marilda and her husband, Raul, and many of my other interlocutors during this period, corruption was used as a catchall explanation and language for why things did not work as they thought they should. Why were schools poor, roads mottled by potholes, the bay filled with sewage, and the nation wracked by economic and political crises that just seemed to worsen each year? Because, the answer went, people in public office had stolen money, and because such thievery was ubiquitous in Brazil. This was a mode of political explanation in wide use in Brazil at the time. And when deployed by politicians and pundits of the right or center right or by the major organs of Brazil's mass media, this anticorruption discourse most frequently, and opportunistically, identified politicians of the PT as the chief culprits (see, Feres and Sassara 2018).

The very flexibility of anticorruption discourse is likely one reason it is so compelling for political figures, especially those of the right: It can simultaneously mean many different things to different constituencies, and it favors moral reforms and punishment, more than it does any structural transformations. But the metadiscursive use of "corruption" as an explanation for other problems in Brazil—and in people's neighborhoods, families, and lives—was its most common use in interviews, among people with widely varied ideological commitments.

Consider this August 2018 interview with Zé Luís, a retired mechanic from the Rio de Janeiro West Zone neighborhood of Padre Miguel with generally left-leaning political sentiments and commitments. When asked about PT-era federal programs to provide student loans for private higher education,[19] Zé Luís responded emphatically, "[Higher education] should be free! The country has the money. You understand? It should all be free; and you shouldn't have to pay anything after graduating because the government has the money. If they would just stop stealing! Just stop stealing in a country that is rich like this! A rich country! You plant something here on top of a rock and a plant grows! But everyone takes something for themselves!"

While less severe than Marilda's call for a meteor shower as the only cure for endemic corruption, Zé Luís's and Marilda's analyses share a commonality that is an important feature of the "cruel pessimism" this chapter describes. Both analyses identify pathological corruption as an omnipresent quality of Brazil and Brazilians, preventing the nation from achieving its potential. For Zé Luís and Marilda, it is not some mutable condition that blocks collective progress. Such a conditional barrier to progress might give rise to a more productive, less cruel, kind of pessimism. Instead, for Zé Luís, Marilda, and many others, a collective improvement that only recently seemed in reach has come to seem impossible because of the nature and/or culture of the people involved. This pessimistic mode of thinking about corruption in Brazil was common among my interlocutors, and it is a very common idea in scholarship and punditry as well.

To take one example among many from the border between scholarship and punditry, consider the work of Alex Cuadros, a U.S. journalist who wrote a widely read, well-researched, and highly informative book about Brazil's wealthiest during the Lula years. Drawing on Raymundo Faoro (1958), Cuadros (2016, 50) precisely distills the culturalist ethos I am identifying as important to cruel pessimism: "Brazilians never drew a clear line between public and private. This is one reason corruption in Brazil is so entrenched. Corruption is part of the culture, even the language."

As different as they all are, for both Marilda and Zé Luís, and also for Cuadros (as for his source, Faoro), corruption is a profound Brazilian characteristic. And such corruption makes collective forms of social progress difficult or impossible.

Let me state clearly three points that I have partially developed and that I will further develop below:

First, while these culturalist conceptions of corruption have a long history in Brazil, the hypocrisy of anticorruption politics during the years that they were weaponized against the PT acted as a kind of intensifier, transforming such conceptions into the deep despair of cruel pessimism. It is one thing to think that there is a lot of corruption. And indeed, there is plenty of bribery and graft in Brazil. However, it is another to see the supposed enemies of corruption revealed to be corrupt themselves. And amid economic decline, it is still worse to see the supposed enemies of corruption actively undermining the social progress that had recently seemed to make your life better. All this produces ideal conditions for the spread of cruel pessimism. Second, the cruel pessimism thus generated helps produce support for economic policies that give the reins to foreign capital, rather than to Brazilians—all to the benefit of foreign actors who are hardly free from corruption. If Brazilians are convinced that collective progress, or even efficient management, is simply impossible in Brazil, then why not hand over control to those foreigners who might administer things efficiently?

And third, as I have already described in the case of Marilda, cruel pessimism was one of the affective conditions that made it possible for Bolsonaro to win the presidency by promising a violent cleansing (*Carta Capital* 2018). For example, one young man, Edvaldo, a migrant from

Maranhão, lives in the Bonsucesso neighborhood of Rio's North Zone. In 2018, without formal employment, he supported his young family through odd jobs as a handyman. When I spoke to him in 2014, when he was in his early twenties, he was much better off than he was by 2018, and he was very excited about the reelection of PT president Dilma Rousseff, emphasizing how much the lives of his family members in the rural northeast had improved under PT governments. He had also won a house through the federally funded housing subsidy, Minha Casa Minha Vida (see Kopper, this volume). But when I spoke to him in 2017, he had been laid off by the national oil company, Petrobras, during a wave of layoffs precipitated by both declining oil prices and the effects of the Lava Jato operation. He told me in July 2018, when I was questioning him about October's presidential election: "It's better that we let them privatize Petrobras and everything else. Brazilians are so corrupt that they'll rob everything."

And he expressed pessimism not only about Brazilian industry but also about the housing program that had gotten him a condominium: "It's all corruption and thievery [*roubalheira*] around there and the people living here have already ruined this place. I was lucky to get this apartment, but Minha Casa Minha Vida lets in too many criminals."

And when I asked Edvaldo in August 2018 whom he would vote for in October's presidential elections, he replied without hesitation, "Bolsonaro. He'll get rid of criminals and the corrupt." Here Edvaldo's loss of faith in collective Brazilian projects—whether development projects, such as Petrobras, or social projects, such as Minha Casa Minha Vida—joins with an affect of pessimism about Brazil and about the inevitability of corruption.

The sociologist Jessé Souza, in one of the much-read critiques of the direction of Brazilian culture, politics, and scholarship he has published in recent years, provides a different frame for thinking about corruption politics in Brazil than the culturalist one I described discussing Cuadros, Faoro, and many of my interlocutors. I translate a short passage from J. Souza (2017) here: "Conflict between classes is distorted and becomes unrecognizable, as it is substituted by a false conflict between the patrimonial and corrupt state and the virtuous market."

In contrast to Cuadros and Faoro, who see corruption as a deeply rooted feature of Brazilian culture, in Souza's analysis, corruption and anticorruption are terms by which the powerful legitimate their domination and expropriation of the weak. For Souza, talk of corruption in Brazilian society provides an obfuscation of class domination and a legitimation of the appropriation of public goods by a privatized market bearing only the facade of incorruptibility.

Souza's critique might also be applied with some validity to the ideologues of libertarianism in the United States. But the pessimism of culturalist corruption discourse is especially cruel in the Global South. One of the imperatives of the sort of corruption discourse mobilized by Edvaldo is to remove from Brazilians any responsibility for managing elements of the economy—this is most clearly carried out through the privatization of public goods. It is now a cliché in international political accounts to say that Jair Bolsonaro is a "nationalist" (e.g., Faiola and Lopes 2018), but this is a misreading of his repositioning of Brazil as subordinate within international hierarchies. In previous decades, Bolsonaro did take economically nationalist positions, but his administration has been eager to privatize many industries and resources that Brazilian nationalists once fiercely guarded.[20] The aesthetic nationalism of Bolsonaro's sloganeering is oddly matched with a willingness to relinquish Brazilian industries and resources to the management and benefit of companies from wealthier nations.

Exemplary of this is the airplane manufacturer Embraer, the world's third largest. The creation of Embraer was a great success of developmentalist policy under the 1964–1985 military dictatorship that Bolsonaro frequently lauds for violence and repression. And Embraer was once a great source of pride (not to mention revenue) for successive Brazilian governments. Yet under the

Bolsonaro administration, an 80 percent stake in Embraer's commercial aircraft division was sold to the U.S. corporation Boeing—a company that is itself buried in corruption that has had deadly consequences (Stoller 2019).[21] During 2019, I asked some people who support Bolsonaro what they think about the plan to sell Embraer, trying to understand the changing fate of Brazilian economic nationalism. Raul's answer was exemplary: "It's good," he told me. "Brazilians will just steal from it. Politicians will just steal from it."

Unlike Berlant's "cruel optimism," the "cruel pessimism" I describe in this chapter is a sentiment of the structurally subordinate, reaching for an explanation for that subordination in the insufficiency—in the corruption—of the subordinate actors, or the subordinate nation, themselves.

CONCLUSION

I have argued in this chapter that (1) the unscrupulous deployment of anticorruption politics by political figures of the center and the right, (2) during a time of economic decline and the reversal of substantial social-democratic gains, have fostered, especially for the previously socially ascendant, (3) a hopelessness about the possibility of collective social projects, and (4) a sense of the inevitable ruinousness of corruption in Brazil—a cruel pessimism.

Of course, such phenomena and sentiments have long been present in Brazil. They are not themselves new—as the culturalist historical analyses of Cuadros and Faoro make clear. But the political and economic circumstances of recent Brazilian history have been such that this cruelly pessimistic affect has been kindled among members of the once-ascendant so-called new middle class, as they saw a precipitous decline in their fortunes since 2015.

Forms of affect, like other social forms, are shared, structural, and as unpredictable in their transformations as is history itself. Having sketched here the sad historical transformations that have led cruel pessimism to be such a pervasive form of affect in contemporary Brazil, I can only hope that historical circumstances shift again to render cruel pessimism obsolete and forgotten.

REFERENCES

Anderson, Perry. 2019. *Brazil Apart: 1964–2019*. New York: Verso.
Ansell, Aaron. 2018. "Impeaching Dilma Rousseff: The Double Life of Corruption Allegations on Brazil's Political Right." *Culture, Theory and Critique* 59 (4): 312–331.
Berlant, Lauren. 2011. *Cruel Optimism*. Durham, N.C.: Duke University Press.
Brasil Wire. 2019. "New Revelations Show Sérgio Moro and Lava Jato Were Central to Brazil's Coup." September 8, 2019. https://www.brasilwire.com/moro-lava-jato-lula-dilma-coup/.
Carta Capital. 2018. "Bolsonaro ameaça: 'Vamos varrer do mapa esses bandidos vermelhos.'" October 21, 2018. https://www.cartacapital.com.br/sociedade/marcha-das-mulheres-negras-a-marcha-que-faz-sentido-7941/.
Cohen, Roger. 2011. "Brazil's Giddy Convergence." *New York Times*, July 4, 2011, Opinion. http://www.nytimes.com/2011/07/05/opinion/05iht-edcohen05.html.
Costa, Dia Da. 2016. "Cruel Pessimism and Waiting for Belonging: Towards a Global Political Economy of Affect." *Cultural Studies* 30 (1): 1–23.
Cuadros, Alex. 2016. *Brazillionaires: The Godfathers of Modern Brazil*. New York: Profile.
Faiola, Anthony, and Marina Lopes. 2018. "Bolsonaro Wins Brazilian Presidency." *Washington Post*, October 28, 2018. https://www.washingtonpost.com/world/the_americas/brazilians-go-the-polls-with-far-right-jair-bolsonaro-as-front-runner/2018/10/28/880dd53c-d6dd-11e8-8384-bcc5492fef49_story.html.
Faoro, Raymundo. 1958. *Os donos do poder: Formação do patronato político brasileiro*. Rio de Janeiro: Editora Globo.
Feres, João, Jr., and Luna de Oliveira Sassara. 2018. "Failed Honeymoon: Dilma Rousseff's Third Election Round." Translated by Frutuoso Santana. *Latin American Perspectives* 45 (220): 224–235.
Fishman, Andrew, Rafael Moro Martins, Leandro Demori, Glenn Greenwald, and Amanda Audi. 2019. "'Their Little Show': Exclusive: Brazilian Judge in Car Wash Corruption Case Mocked Lula's Defense and Secretly Directed

Prosecutors' Media Strategy during Trial." *Intercept* (blog), June 17, 2019. https://theintercept.com/2019/06/17/brazil-sergio-moro-lula-operation-car-wash/.

Fishman, Andrew, Natalia Viana, and Maryam Saleh. 2020. "'Keep It Confidential': The Secret History of U.S. Involvement in Brazil's Scandal-Wracked Operation Car Wash." *Intercept* (blog), March 12, 2020. https://theintercept.com/2020/03/12/united-states-justice-department-brazil-car-wash-lava-jato-international-treaty/.

Goel, Vindu. 2020. "Boeing Terminates $4.2 Billion Deal to Buy Stake in Embraer Unit." *New York Times*, April 25, 2020, Business. https://www.nytimes.com/2020/04/25/business/boeing-embraer-acquisition-coronavirus.html.

Boito, Armando, Jr. 2020. "Avanços do conservadorismo e do neofascismo no brasil recente: entrevista com Armando Boito Jr." Inteview by Bruna Andrade Irineu and Leonardo Nogueira. *Revista direitos, trabalho e política social* 6 (10): 352–362.

Junge, Benjamin. 2018. *Cynical Citizenship: Gender, Regionalism, and Political Subjectivity in Porto Alegre, Brazil.* Albuquerque: University of New Mexico Press.

Klein, Charles H., Sean T. Mitchell, and Benjamin Junge. 2018. "Naming Brazil's Previously Poor: 'New Middle Class' as an Economic, Political, and Experiential Category." *Economic Anthropology* 5 (1): 83–95.

Mello, Patrícia Campos. 2018. "Empresários bancam campanha contra o PT pelo WhatsApp." *Folha de São Paulo*, October 18, 2018. https://www1.folha.uol.com.br/poder/2018/10/empresarios-bancam-campanha-contra-o-pt-pelo-whatsapp.shtml.

Mier, Brian, and Daniel Hunt, eds. 2019. *Year of Lead: Washington, Wall Street and the New Imperialism in Brazil.* San Francisco: Blurb.

Mitchell, Sean T. 2017. *Constellations of Inequality: Space, Race, and Utopia in Brazil.* Chicago: University of Chicago Press.

———. 2018. "Empire as Accusation, Denial, and Structure: The Social Life of US Power at Brazil's Spaceport." In *Ethnographies of US Empire*, edited by John F. Collins and Carole McGranahan, 369–390. Durham, N.C.: Duke University Press.

———. 2019. "O Acordo de Alcântara sacrificaria a soberania, o desenvolvimento, e os direitos dos quilombolas brasileiros, por Sean T. Mitchell." *GGN* (blog), September 6, 2019. https://jornalggn.com.br/artigos/o-acordo-de-alcantara-sacrificaria-a-soberania-o-desenvolvimento-e-os-direitos-dos-quilombolas-brasileiros-por-sean-t-mitchell/.

Neri, Marcelo. 2012. *A nova classe média: O lado brilhante da base da pirâmide.* São Paulo: Saraiva.

Neri, Marcelo Côrtes. 2014. "Poverty Reduction and Well-Being: Lula's Real." In *Brazil under the Workers' Party*, edited by Fábio de Castro, Kees Koonings, and Marianne Wiesebron, 102–125. London: Palgrave Macmillan.

Piketty, Thomas. 2014. *Capital in the Twenty-First Century.* Translated by Arthur Goldhammer. Cambridge, Mass.: Belknap.

Pinheiro-Machado, Rosana. 2019. *Amanhã vai ser maior: O que aconteceu com o Brasil e possíveis rotas de fuga para a crise atual.* São Paulo: Planeta.

Pochmann, Marcio. 2014. *O mito da grande classe média: Capitalismo e estrutura social.* São Paulo: Boitempo Editorial.

Saad-Filho, Alfredo, and Lecio Morais. 2018. *Brazil: Neoliberalism versus Democracy.* London: Pluto Press.

Schwarcz, Lilia Moritz. 2019. *Sobre o autoritarismo Brasileiro.* São Paulo: Companhia das Letras.

Silva, Ana Paula da. 2014. *Pelé e o complexo de vira-latas: Discursos sobre raça e modernidade no Brasil.* Niterói: EDUFF.

Singer, André. 2015. "Quatro notas sobre as classes sociais nos dez anos do Lulismo." *Psicologia USP* 26 (1): 7–14.

Souza, Amaury de, and Bolivar Lamounier. 2010. *A classe média brasileira: Ambições, valores e projetos de sociedade.* Rio de Janeiro: Elsevier.

Souza, Jessé. 2017. *A elite do atraso: Da escravidão a Bolsonaro.* Rio de Janeiro: Estação Brasil.

———. 2010. *Os batalhadores brasileiros: Nova classe média ou nova classe trabalhadora?* Belo Horizonte: Editora UFMG.

Stoller, Matt. 2019. "Boeing's Travails Show What's Wrong with Modern Capitalism." *Guardian*, September 11, 2019, Opinion. https://www.theguardian.com/commentisfree/2019/sep/11/boeing-capitalism-deregulation.

Viana, Natalia, and Rafael Neves. 2020. "Como o FBI influenciou procuradores da Lava Jato." *Agência pública* (blog), July 1, 2020. https://apublica.org/2020/07/0-fbi-e-a-lava-jato/.

NOTES

1. The help of many people and institutions made this research possible. Bruno Coutinho, Janine Targino, and Pamella Liz Pereira, and Thayane Brêtas are important research collaborators. The research, which I carried out

collaboratively with Benjamin Junge and Charles Klein, was funded by a three-year collaborative grant from the National Science Foundation's Division of Behavioral and Cognitive Sciences, Cultural Anthropology Program. The project is titled "Collaborative Research: Social Mobility, Poverty Reduction, and Democracy in an Emerging Middle Class" (grants 1534606, 1534621, and 1534655).

2. Many scholars disputed whether this "class" should indeed be considered a "new middle class" or a class at all (see, for example, Pochmann 2014; Singer 2015; J. de Souza 2010; and, for an overview of these debates, see Klein, Mitchell, and Junge 2018).

3. The corruption of "anticorruption" politics was long clear to many in Brazil. However, it became clearer still in June 2018, when the *Intercept Brasil* was given a vast trove of leaked conversations among the key protagonists of the Lava Jato investigations, including judge Sérgio Moro—who was appointed Bolsonaro's justice minister after assuring Bolsonaro's election through the imprisonment of frontrunner Lula, and who left the Bolsonaro government in April 2020. In my evaluation, the leaks have left no reasonable doubt that Dilma's impeachment (Brasilwire 2019) and Lula's imprisonment (Fishman et al. 2019) were politically, not legally, motivated.

4. I should be clear that awareness of ubiquitous political corruption, and even awareness of the manipulation of anticorruption, are not new in Brazil. But the toxic stew of factors I describe in this chapter were specific to this historical period and did generate novel forms of political despondency.

5. The vast municipality of Rio de Janeiro is divided among North, South, and West Zones. Each of these zones is marked by significant internal economic stratification, but the poorer North Zone has long been a supplier of labor to the wealthier South Zone, as has, increasingly, the city's West Zone, which has surged in population in recent decades. Beyond the tripartite city proper extends a vast metropolitan area to the north and across the bay to the south and east.

6. My collaborators, Benjamin Junge and Charles Klein, were carrying out parallel surveys in Recife and São Paulo. The first publication that utilizes data from this survey is Klein, Mitchell, and Junge (2018).

7. As with all other ethnographic interlocutors in this chapter, "Marilda" is a pseudonym.

8. All translations from the Portuguese are mine.

9. There were other details that she gave when discussing Lula, which I omit for clarity, that underscore her ambivalence toward the ex-president. Notably, Marilda said that she never liked Lula because "he reached the presidency without even attending middle school," expressing common grounds of class-based disdain for the ex-president, who had been born poor and made his name as a labor leader.

10. Voting in Brazil is obligatory, and one is issued a (small) fine if one does not show up to vote. However, one can annul or leave blank their ballot without penalty.

11. The PT dominated presidential elections in those neighborhoods, although rarely elections for local offices, which tend to be shaped by local patronage networks.

12. The only Rio neighborhood that Bolsonaro did not carry in the 2018 second round was Laranjeiras, a comfortable and leafy middle-class neighborhood that is famously the home to many intellectuals, professors, and artists.

13. Haddad's candidacy was not announced until it was clear Lula would not be able to run. The highly effective viral social media campaign was conducted in violation of Brazilian electoral laws (Mello 2018, see also Medeiros et al., this volume).

14. On cynicism in Brazilian politics, see Junge (2018).

15. It would take me beyond the scope of this account, but such pessimism about Brazil has frequently had racial (and racist) overtones in Brazilian history and is sometimes referred to as the *complexo da vira lata*, or the mutt complex—the idea that it is Brazil's racially mixed character that leads the country to fail (see Silva 2014).

16. In a published interview, Boito characterizes Bolsonaro's neofascism as a kind of politics that combines traditional political elements of fascism ("authoritarianism, anticommunism, the cult of violence, negativism, irrationalism, sexism, etc.") with "ultra-neoliberal economics" (Boito 2020).

17. Many are now attempting the task of explaining this shocking transformation. For some notable recent works, see Anderson (2019); Mier and Hunt (2019); Pinheiro-Machado (2019); Saad-Filho and Morais (2018); Schwarcz (2019).

18. A quilombo is a designation for Afro-Brazilian communities in Brazil, principally rural communities and frequently populated by descendants of people who escaped slavery. Quilombo land is protected by Brazil's postdictatorship 1988 constitution. Alcântara, Maranhão, is a peninsula with large-scale quilombo settlements on the border between Brazil's northeast and Amazon regions. It is also the site of the launching hub of Brazil's space program and extensive conflict over land, race, inequality, national sovereignty, and technological development, all of which I have written about extensively (Mitchell 2017).

19. These initiatives were accompanied by a large-scale expansion of the free public university system under PT governments.

20. See, for example, Bolsonaro's switch on the accord to cede Brazil's northeastern Satellite Launch Center to the United States, which I have written about here (Mitchell 2019). He was fiercely opposed to such a deal on nationalist grounds in 2001, when he was a congressman, and when the accord was promoted under the neoliberal presidency of Fernando Henrique Cardoso (see Mitchell 2018). However, Bolsonaro has aggressively pursued such a deal in his own presidency.

21. In April 2020, Boeing terminated this deal, alleging that Embraer did not meet unspecified conditions. More likely Boeing is trying to conserve cash in the wake of the grounding of its 737 jets and a pandemic-era drastic reduction of demand (Goel 2020).

6 · THE EFFECTS OF SOME RELIGIOUS AFFECTS

Revolutions in Crime

KARINA BIONDI

In 2015, seven years after carrying out fieldwork in Brazilian prisons while visiting my husband (who was in prison for more than five years awaiting trial), I started a new research project in similar prison facilities. This time, I entered prison as an official researcher instead of a visitor. This meant I didn't have to wait for hours in the visitors' line or undress in front of female guards. Although the research project was new, I brought with me, in addition to a notebook and a pen, more than ten years of research experience with prisoners, former prisoners, and people linked to criminal activities, especially those affiliated with the First Command of the Capital (Primeiro Comando da Capital; PCC), said to be South America's largest criminal cartel.[1] If in the academic world my research produced books and papers, in the *malandragem* (criminal) world, the result of my interaction with criminals was what they call *visão* (view), a kind of wisdom about modes of functioning and conduct that supports our ability to perceive what's happening, to evaluate possibilities, to predict what could happen and, consequently, to formulate strategies in order to be successful in actions (Biondi 2018).

This acquired skill led me to conclude that private dialogues with prisoners in private settings could generate suspicions that, in turn, could lead prisoners to refuse to speak to me. Or worse, it could harm one of them, such as when my husband's cell mate became the prime suspect for having reported an escape plan because he had had an appointment with his lawyer the day prior to the plan's discovery. In cases such as these, what is at play is the adherence of prisoners to one side of the criminal/police divide, which then helps sustain the existence of the PCC. I describe this adherence as a double-sided policy: "peace between criminals and war against the police" (or against the "system"). This means in practice that the permanence of a suspected traitor among prisoners is put in question, which can be solved by his murder or, if he is lucky, by his transfer to another prison ruled by enemies of the PCC (rare in São Paulo, where more than 90 percent of correctional facilities are "command prisons").

My weekly meetings with the prisoners took place then at the institution's library, with the presence of at least three of them and permission for others to circulate there. Eventually, those others who had not volunteered to talk to me also ended up participating in our conversations. On the first day, I told them about my past as a visitor, to which they replied, "So your husband has already been through the pain. And you too, right? Because the family suffers together." My past "suffering" opened up a certain flow of affection that resulted then and there in a feeling of sharing and trust that allowed for more open conversations, with less distrust and estrangement.

FIGURE 6.1. Prison yard at the Santo André prison, showing Evangelical worshippers on visiting day
Photo by author.

In this atmosphere, we talked about all kinds of subjects. One day when we were talking about literary preferences, a prisoner who was a member of the PCC and still supported their ideas told me that all he read in prison were Pastor Silas Malafaia's books. I was surprised, because Pastor Malafaia, besides being one of the leaders of the Assemblies of God in Brazil, is well known for his ultraconservative stance and his political influence. In his speeches, he takes a strong position against abortion and the legalization of drugs, he criticizes feminism and homosexuality, he calls for the participation of churches and Christian ideology in the direction of the country's affairs, and he presents biblical arguments for harder criminal punishments, including the death penalty.

Along with other representatives with equally conservative ideas, Malafaia formed a multiparty alliance known as "BBB" (Bibles, Bulls, Bullets), which fully supported Dilma Rousseff's impeachment in 2016. On the day the impeachment was decided, Bolsonaro, then one of Malafaia's allied representatives, formalized his religious conversion with a baptism in the Jordan River in Israel and became part of the same Evangelical denomination to which Malafaia belongs. In 2018, Bolsonaro was elected president of Brazil, benefitting from the massive backing of Evangelical churches and the support of their adherents. Seventy percent of the Evangelical vote (which represents almost a third of the Brazilian population) went to Bolsonaro, which was decisive for his election (Almeida 2019). Two days after the election, Malafaia and Bolsonaro celebrated their victory together in a service at the Assembly of God.

In his campaign, Bolsonaro professed the same conservative values defended by Malafaia for years. Some of those values, following the BBB line, mixed religious and moral issues with public security. Adopting the notion that *bandido bom é bandido morto* (the only good criminal is a dead criminal), supported by Malafaia and other religious people, Bolsonaro defended projects that introduced the death penalty in Brazil. Although this discourse dates back to the military dictatorship and has never completely ceased to exist, it became stronger with the growth of the conservative wing in the National Congress, already quite visible in the 2014 elections. Thus in 2015, when that prisoner stated that he liked reading Malafaia's books, the pastor was already known for speaking out against criminals and, consequently, against prisoners.

This contradiction between Malafaia's discourse and the prisoners' very existence caught my attention and I asked myself how a prisoner could possibly appreciate Malafaia's writings. Furthermore, while the PCC claims to have worked a revolution in prisons and poorer neighborhoods in the state of São Paulo, how could people who view themselves as revolutionaries against what they call "state oppression" agree with the discourse of such a conservative politician?

This apparent contradiction is not very different from the one that motivated Cesarino's research (2020), addressing the question of how Bolsonaro secured the vote of people whose moral inclinations and behavioral profiles are so different from his. I include some examples in order to make the contradiction clearer: Why did gays vote for a homophobe? How did women decide to vote for a sexist? What made people who defend democracy declare their vote for someone who glorifies dictatorship? Why did people who thrived economically under the PT's social programs choose neoliberal alternatives? (See Mitchell, this volume.) In short, how was it possible that more than half of Brazilian voters chose a candidate with authoritarian inclinations? This question deeply permeates this book and requires some analytical creativity to escape from old explanatory categories that, as Collins (in this volume) points out, are inadequate to understand this particular moment in Brazilian history.

In the 2018 presidential campaign, there was no official support from the PCC for the candidacy of Bolsonaro and his backers. On the contrary, although the majority of prisoners are not even allowed to vote, there was a mobilization for their relatives to miss visits and go to the polls. I followed a campaign on social media with the slogan "Um dia por uma vida" (One day for a life), in which prisoners' relatives mobilized people to vote against Bolsonaro. This position, however, was not unanimous: There were relatives of prisoners—all Evangelical—who declared and defended the Bolsonaro vote, with the argument that the PT is to blame for the conditions—economic, spiritual, and moral—that resulted in the arrest of their relatives. Collins's approach (in this volume) can be fruitful to analyze how new consumption patterns driven by PT's economic and social policies were rationalized. There was also a cosmological rationality, however, in the arguments of Evangelical relatives of prisoners, linked to the struggle between good and evil, in which people's moral degradation is seen as stemming from political choices that made the world a place prone to the action of the forces of evil.

The same Evangelical orientations that supported the argument for Bolsonaro as president have also been circulating for many years in the poor neighborhoods where I conducted my research and, specifically, in the PCC itself. A viewpoint at one end of the political spectrum gives rise to the discourse that "the only good criminal is a dead criminal." A viewpoint on the other end promotes a "revolution" against the oppression of the police state. Several rationalities also emerge between one extreme and the other. But it is those two extremes that were put side by side on that day in 2015 when the prisoner stated that he liked Malafaia's books.

In this chapter, I will keep these two extremes in mind in order to highlight, through ethnographic examples, the circulation of religious statements with an Evangelical slant in the practices surrounding the PCC. I argue that, in different formations, mixed with different elements, these statements are capable of producing different affects that, in the end, can result in opposing attitudes, orientations, thoughts, and votes. I agree with the editors of this book who, in the introduction, claim that we are facing a "complex panorama of sentiments" and that "affect is a useful analytic to consider the momentous political shift in Brazil." Inspired by the definition put forward by Gregg and Seigworth (2010), the authors state that affect "is not merely individual emotion but, rather, a description of collective capacities to feel and generate feelings in others, as affect is being constantly transmitted between bodies" (see Introduction, this volume). Following that definition, I will identify some traces of Evangelical Christianity that can be found within the PCC in order to show how religious ideas mix with the daily practices of criminals, producing affects that support what they call a "revolution" against the oppression of the police state—different, therefore, from the affects that guided Bolsonaro's votes. First, however, I will expound on some general features of the PCC.

A REVOLUTION IN CRIME

The PCC was founded in 1993 by a group of prisoners who deemed it necessary to unite in order to address what they saw as "state abuses." Events such as the Carandiru Massacre, in 1992, when police forces invaded prison premises to suppress an inmate uprising and killed 111 inmates, are seen by prisoners as the pinnacle of such "abuses." At the time, the PCC was one of many gangs that fought for space inside São Paulo's prisons. Their distinctive feature was not the use of force—all gangs were violent. The proposal consisted of prisoners uniting to face a common enemy—that is, the state. According to prisoners, the group's proposal was alluring, which explains the speed with which it obtained a high number of adherents. Two general guidelines were born together with the PCC: peace between criminals and war against the oppressive (prison, police, judiciary) system (Marques 2014). According to prisoners who experienced those times, it was this way of thinking (guided by the PCC motto "Peace, Justice, Freedom and Equality") that made the PCC's expansion possible in the state of São Paulo.

By the first decade of the twenty-first century, the group had already become a hegemonic criminal force in São Paulo, both inside and outside the prison system, and had been classified by the authorities as a large and well-structured criminal organization. Not many prisons in São Paulo have inmates opposed to the PCC; likewise, *quebradas* (poor neighborhoods) led by other criminal gangs are now virtually unheard of. The PCC's supremacy in São Paulo is so great that its members often use the word *crime* itself as a synonym for PCC. The disappearance of sexual violence among prisoners, of trivial deaths, of inmates being robbed by other inmates leads many prisoners to conclude that São Paulo's *quebradas* and prisons are now at peace. Most disputes that previously led to deaths have vanished. In São Paulo, in 1999, 117 deaths were recorded among a population of a little more than fifty thousand prison inmates, while in 2016, there were only fourteen killings among more than 230,000 inmates. After that, with the PCC's growth outside the prison system, there was also a sharp decline in the rate of intentional homicides in the state of São Paulo (from 123 intentional homicides per 100,000 inhabitants in 2001 to sixteen per 100,000 inhabitants in 2014).

The government of the state of São Paulo celebrated the decline in the rate of intentional homicides, linking it to an improvement in its public safety policies and prison system: more police, better training for public security agents, investments in police intelligence, enhanced crime-fighting and prisoner-control technology, purchase of crime-fighting equipment (weapons, vehicles, etc.), and above all the building of new prisons and the consequent growth in the number of imprisonments. Some researchers, like Carneiro (2010), endorse the discourse of the authorities. Some studies, however, point to other reasons. For Manso (2012), the PCC is the result and not the cause of the falling homicide rate in São Paulo, and for Darke (2018), this is an effect of what he calls cogovernance. Nonetheless, for studies that base themselves mostly on ethnographic research, the main reason for the decrease in the number of homicides is the PCC. The decrease in violence was already indicated in Dias (2008) and Biondi (2006) for the prison context, as well as Feltran (2020a) and Hirata (2018) for urban environments. It did not take long for the association between the reduction in the number of homicides with the actions of the PCC to explicitly appear in research results (Biondi 2016; Marques 2014; Feltran 2020a; Telles and Hirata 2010; Dias 2011; Willis 2015). However, according to ethnographers who work or have worked in prisons and poor neighborhoods, including me, prisoners and residents were unanimous in saying that killings had gone down "because of the PCC" (Biondi 2016; Feltran 2020a).

For people from favelas and prisons with whom I talked during my research, lower homicide rates are a direct result of a change in the way of life inside prisons and in the "world of crime," where slogans such as "Ninguém é melhor que ninguém" (No one is better than anybody else), "Ninguém é obrigado a nada" (No one is bound to do anything), and "É de igual" (It's all about equals) are constantly repeated.[2] And precisely because all were equal—criminals or not—their lives had the same value and, therefore, nobody could be killed in the absence of a complex process of deliberation in which all sides were necessarily heard. This system—called *debates*—found support among the residents of the *quebradas* (favelas or poor neighborhoods) who, instead of calling the police, resort to the *irmãos* (brothers, the term by which PCC members are called) to solve their problems without the need for the use of brute force or even state forces, keeping the "*quebradas* in peace." These are the reasons why people connected to crime say the PCC has worked a "revolution" in the prisons and poor neighborhoods of the state of São Paulo.

CRIME AND RELIGION

The presence of Evangelical religions in the world of crime, or the presence of the world of crime in Brazilian religion, are phenomena that are being studied by several researchers (Birman 2012; Dias 2008; Lins and Silva 1990; Machado 2014; Medrado 2016; Vital 2015). The most noteworthy instance was presented by Marques (2015): a PCC brother who is also a "church brother" and reconciles both affiliations.

In fact, from the very beginning, the religious formulas that I came across during my research on crime caught my attention. Inside prisons, Evangelical churches are the main Christian denominations. According to prisoners I talked to, the Catholic Church, especially through its prison pastoral care, is one of the main institutions vouching for the defense of prisoners' rights. An inmate said, "But they are so distant, a little arrogant, you know? They don't touch us, they don't ask how we feel, they are so formal. Instead, the brothers of the Evangelical churches give us more attention, they bring spiritual comfort to us. Furthermore, every week the Evangelicals are here with us and the Catholics only appear once in a while." In short, despite maintaining relations with both religions, prisoners state that while the Catholic Church is seen as an institution that defends their rights, Evangelical religions are seen as sources of spiritual support. They are able to provide an affective engagement that the Catholics cannot.

I want to stress another reason, however, why Evangelical religions have a larger presence. This is not only because Evangelicals are the ones who do most of the pastoral work in the prison environment but also because their discourses and guidelines are those that manifest the most in inmates' behavior. The expansion of the PCC, the enhancement of its activities, and the decrease in violence (inside and outside the prison system) as measured by official statistics coincide with the incorporation of religious formulas in the discourse of those who participate in the existence of the PCC.[3] Biblical quotations, Christian references, and moral reasoning based on religious teachings can be found in a diffuse form in the discourses of the inmates in "PCC prisons." In an Evangelical radio station, hours of programming are dedicated to prison inmates. Religious services are held every week by Evangelical preachers inside prison units, while all expressions of religions of African origin are forbidden among inmates.

This rapprochement between the PCC and Evangelical churches is not a matter of complicity or a relation between two different institutions. For years, I have argued that the PCC is constituted by heterogeneous dynamics without defined contours, this being the reason why it is not appropriate to approach it as a coherent and cohesive unit (Biondi 2016). In the same way, some authors criticize the attempt to fit the complex dynamics of Evangelical religions and each one of their denominations inside fixed, unidirectional, and predetermined frameworks (Almeida 2019; Teixeira 2016). So instead of thinking about involvement between churches and criminal organizations as if they were defined and coherent units, or as if religion and crime were two separate domains similar to a Durkheimian sacred/profane categorization, I prefer to look at the acts, beliefs, and sentiments that cross ethnographic realities. Contrary to the theoretical approach that presumes the pureness of things (and in which blurry boundaries become empirical and analytical problems), my ethnographic research reveals that the Evangelical discourse pervades—not without distortions—the whole existence of the PCC.

According to criminals I talked to, for someone to be seen as a reputable man in crime, it is not enough to abide by the rules of the PCC. It is also necessary to follow a host of guidelines that determine even the most subtle words, gestures, and actions that constitute an inmate's life in prison. While talking to me about some of those guidelines, an inmate drew my attention to the substance of those laws: "When you come to think of it, it all boils down to the Ten Commandments."

If at first sight that seems to indicate a confrontation between two opposite ethics, what ethnography reveals is how both those ethics share the same religious discourse, and the consequent coexistence of this discourse with different ethics, producing different sentiments and outputs in each one. This becomes obvious when we take as an example the end of the "mourning period." Some years ago, the mourning period for the death of a "brother" ideally lasted a week—"ideally" because in actual practice, it could be cut short by other events, such as visit days. But while it lasted, games and sports activities were suspended and the volume of radio or television sets was turned down. More recently, mourning has been replaced by a kind of homage to the deceased. Every day, the inmate responsible for a particular prison makes contact with "brothers" from other prisons to get information on mourning or some other announcement (known as a salve). He then passes on the information to the prisoners responsible for each prison wing. Each of them relays it to the brother who will tell the "population"[4] whether the day is a normal day or if a prayer service will be held in a few minutes. In the latter case, the "population" then gathers—usually in the prison courtyard—to listen to the brother's account of what happened. A prisoner has given me some examples of the opening sentences of such speeches: "Unfortunately, brother X has passed away." Or "Unfortunately, X has passed away in a confrontation with the police, in which he was brutally and cowardly murdered."

After the announcement, inmates start what Father Valdir João Silveira, coordinator for prison pastoral care in São Paulo, calls a "strange liturgy." This begins with the Our Father and Hail Mary prayers and proceeds to a kind of war cry:

BROTHER: One for all!
POPULATION: All for one!
BROTHER: United...
POPULATION: ...we shall conquer!
BROTHER: 15–3—3!

POPULATION: PCC!
BROTHER: Victory is . . .
POPULATION: . . . ours!

Except for the last sentence, each part of the dialogue is repeated three times by both the brother and the population. The brother then calls the meeting to a close: "That is it, family. A good day to all of us."

This is a situation in which reverence for the Christian God and reverence for the Command are joined together. For the inmates, this is not seen as a problem or a contradiction. The only exception is that Evangelicals do not take part in either the (Roman Catholic) Hail Mary or the war cry, for conversion implies giving up both "the life of crime" and "the things of this world." Therefore, there is an attempt to maintain a distinction between their religious choices and all criminal activity. To make this distinction explicit is important because of the treatment they receive. If a person becomes an Evangelical, the commitment to crime is no longer required and some previous moral debts are no longer demanded and collected; but they must at all times prove the sincerity of their conversion, giving up all worldly things.

On the other hand, this does not prevent religious elements from being used by those who strike a "commitment with crime." It is common for an inmate to ask the church brother (note that both the member of the PCC and the Evangelical convert are called "brothers") to pray for someone, usually a member of his family, whom he deems to be in need. Also, it is common for Evangelical denominations to use the language of the prisoners. The instance that appealed to me the most was a flyer in which inmates' family members were called to a church service: "Come and pray for Justice, Peace, and Freedom." Although the words were not used in the same order, they were the same as those that made up, at the time, the PCC's motto, "Peace, Justice, and Freedom." Finally, biblical texts mentioning the prison experiences of Jesus and some of his apostles are constantly read by Evangelicals' preachers. Jail is presented as a test that the prisoner is subjected to, which should be endured with courage. Inmates often make statements such as "Whoever doesn't come to God through love, comes to Him through pain"; however, this is typically qualified with statements like "God does not like weaklings and cowards, He likes fighters. . . . Even when he was imprisoned and tortured to recognize Caesar's reign, Jesus went on saying that His king was the king of kings." These statements, among others, serve as an encouragement for the prisoner to see his prison sentence as a stage he must go through without bowing before the oppressor. It produces a sentiment of determination to fight and resist. Inmates appreciate this kind of resistance against the established order, which helps dissolve the contradiction implied in the use of violence as a means to achieve peace.

In other words, biblical statements are used as cries of resistance, especially when God is envisaged as the one and only judge, the one being who is truly just, fair, and capable of meting out "true justice." Psalm 23 becomes a symbol of such resistance and is frequently recited by inmates, especially this verse: "Though I walk through the valley of the shadow of death, I will fear no evil: for God is with me." Among the most common statements uttered as means of comfort and motivation, we find the following: "When man closes a door, God opens two doors," "Remember that God never gives us a cross to carry that is heavier than we can bear, and that suffering nourishes our courage even more," and "Even though I am a sinner, God loves me just as I am."

This perspective allows crime to be seen as a sin like any other; all sins are put on an equal footing and all comparative judgments of severity are annulled. Thus homicide, adultery, and blasphemy are seen as equally severe, for all of them trespass against Christian principles—that is, all can be pardoned by God, who is understanding and merciful. This mercy and understanding enable Him to mete out "the one and only true justice," which is divine justice. Thus armed robbery—seen as the prime example of crime in São Paulo—is no more serious than the greed of a businessperson. This idea enables the criminal to perceive himself as a sinner like any other, capable of being pardoned by God in spite of the verdict imposed by the "justice of men."

According to the religious discourse of Evangelical preachers who visit prisons (many of whom are former convicts who give testimony about how they got out of the *vida do crime*—life of crime), inmates who are capable of handing their lives over to Christ acquire a kind of freedom that has nothing to do with the freedom of movement ruled upon by the judiciary. This new freedom can be conquered even behind bars, in a spiritual dimension, as prisoners drive off the forces of evil and recover from the desire for the things of the world, which imprisons people inside a consumerist system. Along with freedom as understood according to the "justice of men" (the one that is regained when prisoners are released) and the freedom given by the "justice of God," inmates talk about freedom as a way of resisting against and not submitting to the (prison, judicial, political) "oppressive System"; even in the latter context, though, religious formulas are maintained, so that the distinction between "divine justice" and "the justice of men" becomes a discourse of opposition against the System. In the same way in which the quest for peace among prisoners is promoted by religious formulas, these formulas also play a role in reinforcing confrontation against those who mete out the "justice of men" (policemen, prison agents, judges, prosecutors, police deputies), characterized as imperfect and inaccurate when compared with "divine justice."

More than that, this triggers a sentiment of willingness among the prisoners to face the oppressor, motivating them to do the "revolution," in this case through the PCC. After all, this formation is a way of gathering prisoners together and offering them the shelter and the backing they need to confront the state.

SPREADING THE WORD OF GOD AND THE REVOLUTION

One day, while I was carrying out fieldwork in *favelas* to study how the PCC acted outside prison facilities, a PCC brother gave me a ride in his car. His radio was on loudly as he listened to gospel music and sang together with the artist while driving well above the speed limit. At a certain point, he stopped the music and said, "Pay attention to what he will say now!" and then he sang excitedly along with the singer. He stopped the music once again, repeated the same words, recalled the time he spent in prison, and said, beating his hand hard on the steering wheel, "Amen! Isn't it so? Isn't it exactly like that?" The close contact with Evangelical Christianity they had in prison is often maintained by the brothers when released from prison. Another brother told me he goes to church service every week. When I expressed surprise ("You go to services?"), he answered, "Of course! You cannot remember God only when you're in prison, can you?"

And indeed, it is impossible not to remember God when one is with the brothers. For example, the brothers of a favela where I did research used to stay at a place adjoining a small Evangelical church whose services incorporate loud, live music. When the service is over, brothers from the church mingle with those from the PCC. They greet each other with respect, many of them know each other, and some are relatives. But this intercrossing and intermingling is not limited to church brothers and PCC brothers. The mixture of biblical formulas and prison slang found inside jails has spread throughout the poor neighborhoods. It is on the lips of old people, children, workers, and other people who often have nothing to do with crime or with the church.

It is interesting to notice that the growth of the PCC—now regarded as the largest criminal group in Latin America, being represented in almost all Brazilian states—has happened alongside a great growth of Evangelical churches in the country. Evangelicals were 9 percent of the Brazilian population in the 1991 census, reached 16 percent in 2000, 22 percent in 2010, and are over 30 percent of Brazilians in 2020. The PCC was founded in 1993, showed its hegemonic criminal force in São Paulo in 2006, and in 2020 its presence is noticed in all Brazilian states and even in some countries abroad.

The revolution made by the PCC in São Paulo has not been replicated in other states. The feeling of encouragement produced by the religious discourse that led the prisoners of São Paulo to unite in order to face the oppression of the state, a movement that also spread out through all *quebradas*, resulting in what they call a revolution, made possible the expansion of the PCC throughout Brazil, but it has not been able to produce the same effect elsewhere. In some places, the arrival of the PCC was met with resistance from other groups, which has been causing conflicts inside and outside prisons. Thus instead of diminishing the number of homicides, as occurred in São Paulo, the arrival of the PCC in other states has increased their number. The revolution, measured by the peace that it achieved in São Paulo's *quebradas*, has nothing to do, therefore, with the expansion and dominance of the PCC, but rather with the effects of peace that it produced. In that sense, its revolution did not reach the other states.

On the other hand, biblical formulas with an Evangelical slant are even more present in everyday talk, and not only in *quebradas* or prisons (although they are still strong in these spaces). Upon hearing the Word of God, people say they feel comfort, peace, self-esteem, and freedom. Some women feel empowered (Teixeira 2016). Furthermore, it is not just the prisoners who, when they hear religious speeches, feel courage and determination to face their enemies. Although the feelings are the same for a fair share of the Brazilian population, the affective engagement, the enemies, and the revolution in play are different.

And here we come to the point highlighted by Feltran (2020b): What prevails in Brazil is not an authoritarian state but a mass movement that, motivated by religious discourses, fights for moral and cultural hegemony within the framework of the Old Testament. Homosexuals, perverts, Satanists, pedophiles, criminals, rapists, murderers, leftists: These were some of the descriptors (often bundled together) that qualified the enemies of Bolsonaro during the 2018 electoral campaign. For those who participate in this movement, fighting against them is the only way to save the world from the forces of evil, their greatest fear. A few years ago, these were scattered ideas found at the level of local speeches. Nonetheless, other processes also underway joined to give them a direction. This is what Leirner (2020), who has studied the military world for twenty years, presents in his new book as a "hybrid war," in which the Brazilian military aim at a profound transformation of reality through the conquest of hearts and minds around a cultural project for Brazil. The other process that was underway is more comprehensive: a process of confiscation of the ability to distinguish between the real and the unreal, of total detachment from the truth by means of technological tools (Villela 2020) or, as per Meg Stalcup's definition, a new regime of veridiction (Graan et al. 2020). Thus the feelings incited by the religious discourse were intertwined with the idea of a cultural—and moral—project for Brazil and gained a vehicle for dissemination in which links with the truth take place under another regime, that of "my opinion" (Villela 2020).

The Word of God, in this scheme, gains more speed and greater reach, intertwining with a greater number of subjects, issues, and discursive repertoires. Questions about religion, sexuality, politics, economics, education, cosmology, and security are all blended in the same formulations, in a mass movement that, according to Feltran (2020b), is supported by three discursive matrixes: police militarism, Evangelical anti-intellectualism, and entrepreneurial monetarism. Their aim is a social transformation that Bolsonaro and his supporters call a "revolution":

My campaign was based on a Biblical verse "You shall know the truth, and the truth shall set you free." I always dreamed about freeing Brazil from the harmful ideology of the Left. One of my greatest inspirations is standing right beside me, to my right: Professor Olavo de Carvalho. He is admired by the youth of Brazil and we owe the revolutions we are living today to him. Despite Olavo de Carvalho, Brazil is not an open terrain where we can plan to build things for our people. (Jair Bolsonaro's speech at the Brazilian Embassy in the United States, March 17, 2019; quoted by Feltran 2020b)

In fact, Olavo de Carvalho (a popular pseudointellectual and friend of U.S. president Donald Trump ally Steve Bannon) was very skilled at handling the available feelings, projects, discursive elements, and technological tools and bringing them together for a single purpose: the revolution. According to Meg Stalcup (Graan et al. 2020), there is not only an affective engagement in William Mazzarella's sense but also a "mode of truth, a popular epistemology." On the other hand—to return to my own argument—this popular epistemology that is the basis of the "revolution we are living" not only has as its main ingredient the Evangelical discourse but also exists because of the feelings this discourse triggers.

CONCLUDING REMARKS

In this chapter, I have explored a research question: How could a prisoner related with the PCC—that claims to have worked a revolution against the oppressive state—appreciate the books written by a pastor and deputy known for his ultraconservative stance, including his proposal for introducing the death penalty in Brazil and his endorsement of the idea that "the only good criminal is a dead criminal"? This question is significant not only due to the strong support given by Evangelicals to Bolsonaro's election but also in view of the intensive use of biblical formulas in the formal and informal electoral campaign. That is why I think it is not possible to understand this moment in Brazilian history without considering the fastest growing religion in the country.

Based on ethnographic material accumulated over fifteen years, I have tried to show that the same religious orientation that supported the argument for Bolsonaro as president has also been circulating for many years in the poor neighborhoods where I conducted my research, and specifically inside the PCC itself. Nonetheless, the effects of the Evangelical discourse vary a lot. I have argued that religious discourse is able to trigger different feelings, including encouragement and the determination to fight. This affective engagement, mixed with different social arrangements, can result in movements for revolutions based on opposing orientations and aims.

The authors whose works are compiled in this book agree that traditional and predetermined conceptual templates, as well as the broad conceptual categories used for political analysis, are not enough to explain what is happening in Brazilian democracy. Our contribution as ethnographers does not consist of proposing other categories or concepts in order to provide definitive explanations. On the contrary, we strive to show the complexity of the phenomena. I hope I have contributed to this task.

REFERENCES

Almeida, Ronaldo. 2019. "Bolsonaro presidente: Conservadorismo, evangelismo e a crise brasileira." *Novos estudos CEBRAP* 38 (1): 185–213.

Biondi, Karina. 2006. "Tecendo as tramas do significado: As facções prisionais enquanto organizações fundantes de padrões sociais." In *Antropologia e direitos humanos 4*, edited by Miriam Pillar Grossi, Maria Luzia Heilborn, and Lia Zanotta Machado, 303–350. Florianópolis, Brazil: Nova Letra.

———. 2016. *Sharing This Walk: An Ethnography of Prison Life and the PCC in Brazil*. Translated by John Collins. Chapel Hill: University of North Carolina Press.

———. 2017. "'It Was Already in the Ghetto': Rap, Religion and Crime in the Prison: Interview with Djalma Oliveira Rios, aka Cascão." *Prison Service Journal*, no. 229, 45–47.

———. 2018. *Proibido roubar na quebrada: Território, hierarquia e lei no PCC*. São Paulo: Terceiro Nome.

Birman, Patricia. 2012. "O poder da fé, o milagre do poder: Mediadores evangélicos e deslocamento de fronteiras sociais." *Horizontes antropológicos* 18 (37): 133–153.

Carneiro, Leandro Piquet. 2010. "A sedução do PCC." *Jornal estado de São Paulo*, May 2, 2010.

Cesarino, Letícia. 2020. "Como vencer uma eleição sem sair de casa: A ascensão do populismo digital no Brasil." *Internet e sociedade* 1 (1): 91–120.

Darke, Sacha. 2018. *Conviviality and Survival: Co-producing Brazilian Prison Order*. London: Palgrave Macmillan.

Dias, Camila Caldeira Nunes. 2008. *A igreja como refúgio e a Bíblia como esconderijo: Religião e violência na prisão*. São Paulo: Humanitas.

———. 2011. "Da pulverização ao monopólio da violência: Expansão e consolidação do Primeiro Comando da Capital (PCC) no sistema carcerário paulista." PhD diss., Universidade de São Paulo.

Feltran, Gabriel de Santis. 2020a. *The Entangled City: Crime as Urban Fabric*. Manchester: Manchester University Press.

———. 2020b. "The Revolution We Are Living." *HAU: Journal of Ethnographic Theory* 10 (1): 12–20.

Graan, Andrew, Adam Hodges, and Meg Stalcup. 2020. "Fake News and Anthropology: A Conversation on Technology, Trust, and Publics in an Age of Mass Disinformation." *PoLAR: Political and Legal Anthropology Review*, February 16, 2020. https://polarjournal.org/2020/02/16/anthropology-and-fake-news-a-conversation-on-technology-trust-and-publics-in-an-age-of-mass-disinformation/.

Gregg, Melissa, and Gregory J. Seigworth, eds. 2010. *The Affect Theory Reader*. Durham, N.C.: Duke University Press.

Hirata, Daniel Veloso. 2018. *Sobreviver na adversidade: Mercados e formas de vida*. São Paulo: Edufscar.

Leirner, Piero. 2020. *O Brasil no espectro de uma guerra híbrida: Militares, operações psicológicas e política em uma perspectiva etnográfica*. São Paulo: Alameda.

Lins, Paulo, and Maria de Lourdes da Silva. 1990. "Bandidos e evangélicos: Extremos que se tocam." *Religião e sociedade* 15 (1): 166–173.

Machado, Carly Barboza. 2014. "Pentecostalismo e o sofrimento do (ex-)bandido: Testemunhos, mediações, modos de subjetivação e projetos de cidadania nas periferias." *Horizontes antropológicos* 20: 153–18.

Manso, Bruno Paes. 2012. "Crescimento e queda dos homicídios em SP entre 1996 e 2010: Uma análise dos mecanismos de escolha homicida e das carreiras no crime." PhD diss., Universidade de São Paulo.

Marques, Adalton. 2014. *Crime e proceder: Um experimento antropológico*. São Paulo: Alameda.

Marques, Vagner Aparecido. 2015. *Fé e crime: Evangélicos e PCC nas periferias de São Paulo*. São Paulo: Fonte Editorial.

Medrado, Lucas. 2016. *Cristianismo e criminalidade: A adesão de bandidos ao Universo Cristão Pentecostal*. São Paulo: Fonte Editorial.

Teixeira, Jacqueline Moraes. 2016. *A mulher universal: Corpo, gênero e pedagogia da prosperidade*. Rio de Janeiro: Mar de Ideias.

Telles, Vera da Silva, and Daniel Hirata. 2010. "Ilegalismos e jogos de poder em São Paulo." *Tempo social* 22 (2): 39–59.

Villela, Jorge Mattar. 2018. "Prison and Coup d'État." In *Authoritarianism and Confinement in the Americas*, edited by Karina Biondi, Jennifer Curtis, and Randi Irwin, 54–59. São Luís: Editora UEMA.

———. 2020. "Confiscações, lutas anti-confiscatórias e antropologia modal." In *Insurgências, ecologias dissidentes e antropologia modal*, edited by Jorge Mattar Villela and Suzane Alencar Vieira, 277–307. Goiânia, Brazil: Editora da Imprensa Universitária.

Vital, Christina. 2015. *Oração de traficante*. Rio de Janeiro: Garamond.

Willis, Graham Denyer. 2015. *The Killing Consensus: Police, Organized Crime, and the Regulation of Life and Death in Urban Brazil*. Oakland: University of California Press.

NOTES

1. The years that intervened between my two periods of research inside prisons were dedicated to other research about the PCC's performance outside prisons, especially in *favelas* and poor neighborhoods.

2. This argument is very well synthetized in an interview I did with the rapper Cascão (Biondi 2017).
3. It is important to point out that participating in the existence of the PCC is not confined to its actual members, the "brothers." The inmates who inhabit prisons influenced by the PCC are not mere spectators of its existence or victims of its oppression. They actively collaborate with the PCC's existence, or, as inmates say, they "share this walk" with the Command (Biondi 2016). The same can be said of people who live in areas influenced by the PCC.
4. The name given to those inmates who do not have a position of responsibility in prison.

7 · "LOOK AT THAT"

Cures, Poisons, and Shifting Rationalities in the Backlands That Have Become a Sea (of Money)

JOHN F. COLLINS

"Ô pa isso" (look at that), Agnaldo commented to no one in particular as a pair of four-wheel-drive vehicles belonging to the Bahian Military Police (PMBA) bounced along the dirt road that separates Agnaldo's Bar from a cattle field ringed by cacti and barbed wire. Inside the thirty-three-year-old man's establishment, an assortment of cowboys, family members living nearby, small-scale agriculturalists, relatives visiting from the state capital of Salvador, and a lone anthropologist celebrated the beginning of the *festas juninhas*, or the June 2019 cycle of Catholic saint festivals central to social life in Brazil's Northeast. Women shouted and men pounded the bar, sharing hand-rolled cigarettes or wiping, with the backs of their hands, spatters of sugar cane alcohol from their mouths. Some roasted corn at the bonfire outside, and salty food circulated as country music played loudly. People pressed their mouths to others' ears in order to be understood and to make material their familiarity. Those assembled in this isolated corner of the Bahian *sertão* (backlands) knew one another well. Most were relatives, by blood or marriage, and all who did not share kin ties had lived alongside one another for decades. Perhaps for this reason—or perhaps because of its still-novel aspects—the revelers seemed to bend in unison as, less than half an hour after the police convoy passed for the first time, we noticed a dust plume as the police passed again, automatic rifles bristling. "Lá vem eles, de novo" (Here they come, again), commented Agnaldo's father, Antonio, as a thick-necked officer peered out, sweeping an automatic rifle across the group.

The patrol lurching through the crossroads that I will call "Riacho Seco" was returning from a nearby hamlet, which I will call "Pedro Malasartes." There, police sought to eliminate a cocaine-dealing network that locals described as a branch of the Primeiro Comando da Capital (PCC), said to be South America's largest and most powerful criminal cartel. The presence of this organization founded in prisons in São Paulo, nearly two thousand kilometers away, was both shocking and not unexpected given the salience of migration to that city from this corner of Bahia. It thus seemed both apt and provocative when Agnaldo's mother, a dour woman, who over the last four years had beaten breast cancer into remission, remarked, "Yup, Lula got me my [cancer] medicine. But those guys in Pedro Malasartes sell a very different type of medicine." I laughed, slightly painfully. Recalling how difficult access to local health posts and doctors in the state capital had been just a decade earlier, I inquired further, "Dona Josefina, has it really gotten better? Do you get your medicines without problems these days? Is it really better?"

"Sure," she responded,

Look at Nivaldo and his shiny motorcycle! That damned thing. He's gonna fall off, drunk. Look at me! Not only am I getting fat like everyone else, but, heck, two days a week there's a doctor at the health post in Cassutinga. And if not, or if there's something wrong, the ambulance takes me to Salvador and I'm back by night. I sleep in my own bed. The problem is those boys over the hill in Pedro Malasartes. They're a problem. Now that there's money here, there's junk here. I want nothing to do with those guys. *But I know how to take my medicine alongside the poison, and pretend it doesn't exist. It does exist. Not everyone knows how to do that.* (italics by the author)

What does it mean to take medicine alongside poison, as Dona Josefina puts it, and how does such a negotiation impact political processes? How might citizens and academics make clearer sense out of a situation in a stigmatized and still impoverished region where new sources of aid, and increasing flows of cash that lead to a real sense of well-being, have improved life in certain ways while also generating—or at least correlating with—poisons like cocaine dealers, drug addiction, and the police who seek to repress them? How has a contradictory historical moment in which residents benefitted from an expanding national economy and received increasing attention and aid from their state come to be translated into views of that state, and of democratic participation and the polity? These questions are useful for understanding more clearly how in 2018 voters selected dire opponents of the left-leaning presidential regimes that had over the last decade implemented what residents themselves describe as improvements in their lives. They also provide ethnographic attention to how previously cash-poor, working-class populations experience a ragged insertion into the consumption-based economies typical of global capitalism today. This chapter is thus both a detailed look at a changing sertão and an examination of rationality, a much-discussed and much-criticized term within ethnographic explorations of subaltern communities, politics, and worldviews.

Rationality—especially "economic" rationality—has been central to debates about peasants, modernity, capitalism, and the ostensible "naturalness" of economic thought. But here I approach rationality a bit differently. Rather than imagining that I know what rationality is, and thus attaching it to a particular form of logic or claims of decision-making in the world that accords to my models of empiricism, permitting me to evaluate who is or is not "rational," I hew to the most absolutely basic insights of those arch social constructivists, Max Weber and Michel Foucault. This means that I do little more than associate rationality with institutions and, above all, with mediating idioms. Hence I treat rationality semiotically, approaching rationalities as habits or patterned means of engaging social challenges that come to make sense to the people embedded in these social actions. Such an attempt to pick up the most basic chords of modernist social constructivism positions what I am calling "rationalities" as but ragged means of getting by and performing political subjectivities (Mitchell 2013).

This recalls and builds on ethnographic explorations of contradictory and yet effective forms of working-class politicization in Porto Alegre as detailed by Benjamin Junge (2018), as well as ethnographic approaches to patron-client structures in the state of Piauí (Ansell 2014) and in the city of Salvador (Collins 2015). It also recalls Lucia Cantero's careful ethnographic treatment in this volume of the ways that citizens' narrative and affective engagements with state-based resources shape political subjectivities. From such perspectives, as crystallized by Ansell in relation to his *piauense* interlocutors, patronage is not just an antithesis or precursor to democracy but also a fundamental aspect of democratic politics in northeastern Brazil, where "the permanent reduction of persons to numerically instrumentalized selves ... manifests a version of Kant's categorical imperative, that people not treat one another as means to ends" (Ansell 2018, S130). Or, put another way, patron-client relations offer a remainder, or a space of difference, in which the ostensibly powerful and the supposedly disempowered may at times rework the terms of politics, personhood, and community. What is key then is not patronage as an ideal or generalized form but rather the nature of the interactions that peasants engage in so as to produce what social scientists call "patronage" (Collins 2008).

A more subtle, and disambiguated, approach to patronage encourages analysis of fine-grained negotiations of social worlds in ways that destabilize broad conceptual categories in favor of the realization that those categories are contradictory and somewhat different from what political science alleges. In the present chapter, I take similarly small steps—which are, as ethnographers recognize, in fact rather foundational—to draw on nearly thirty years of experiences in a particular corner of the sertão in order to examine those social idioms I dub "rationalities." These idioms are undergoing change at a moment when the wealth, food, and access to consumer goods that supposedly improves lives threatens also to bring down new forms of violence and to energize and unleash new state institutions upon a *sertanejo* populace that typically seeks autonomy from that state. As a result, I do little more in this chapter than look at how political economic shifts may be altering pragmatic, everyday formations in which people make do and make themselves. I do not yet feel competent to propose new political categories that emerge from these interactions or explain voting patterns in their light. Nonetheless, an archaeology of these shifts in form—or what Michael Herzfeld has called "localized social dramas that allude to great historical events now reproduced in quotidian performance" (2015, 18)—promises to make clearer the microinteractions, perceptual cues, and genres of evidence that undergird and construct public and private social forms and political institutions.

To document and understand more clearly quotidian interactions and interpretive footings in Bahia, a region where in 2018–2019 the electorate overwhelmingly supported the Workers' Party (PT) candidate for presidency *against* the conservative Jair Bolsonaro, is especially important. It is important because rural, working-class, Afro-Bahians who supposedly piggyback upon an "assistentialist" state are precisely the demographic group against which substantial portions of the generally whiter and wealthier Bolsonaro electors aimed their ire. They are also important because, as Agnaldo and his mother, Josefina, recognize, the political economic shifts and moral environment catalyzed by successive PT governments at the national, state, and local levels are filled with contradictions. How people—even those people who continue to support the PT—navigate these contradictions at a local, everyday level is significant in explaining political support, moral outrage, feelings of disempowerment, and thus political opinions and voter choice. So while this chapter does not scale up into electoral issues, it is directed at both the conditions and perceptions commonly understood to condition political behavior. In short, it is aimed at understanding the everyday microinteractions taking place in a sertão in which people gain new forms of access to cash economies in ways that both disempower and empower, almost like a medicine or cancer treatment that threatens to overcome the subject it is supposed to cure.

A PUMP AND A CROSSROADS IN BRAZILIAN DEVELOPMENT AND THE BAHIAN SERTÃO

Cacti, *umbu* trees, and dry fields—now in large part planted in imported grasses that nourish cattle for beef exports—mark the inland, northern part of the state of Bahia, a region covered mostly in thorny scrub forest (*caatinga*) until the 1990s when deforestation and technological advances made cattle raising more common. Like the sertão more generally, this corner of Bahia bordered

FIGURE 7.1. Sunset across the Sertão
Photo by author.

by Pernambuco and Sergipe has been marked for centuries as an exceptional, originary, and yet denigrated national space associated with banditry, factional violence, glaring inequalities and its inhabitants' independent spirit and strange "nature" (da Cunha 1964). In part as a result, across the late twentieth century, and until the election of Luis Inácio Lula da Silva, local people maintained a vexed and contradictory relationship to their state. For the most part, they forewent engagements with bureaucratic apparatuses in favor of personalized appeals to officials like mayors and aldermen who might mediate, or even step in themselves, to provide the services solicited.

Often configured as favors, rather than obligations to a citizenry, government responsiveness to residents of Riacho Seco during previous decades was largely limited to the presence of a mechanic who maintained the artesian well that provided water to people and livestock in a wide radius; attempts to gain retirement pensions in offices in the county seat; scattered and largely unsatisfying visits to government medical clinics; the provision of musical entertainment for June and carnival festivals in the plaza of the county seat; and moments of attention by political candidates during elections. Nonetheless, since 2004, when the reforms following the 2002 election of Lula began to be put in place, residents have gained running water. This resulted in the deactivation of the artesian well in 2017. Electrical power has reached Riacho Seco and most surrounding communities. A school bus takes children to the county seat, some eighteen kilometers down the road. Local people also benefit from visits from health workers and even pedagogical visits from government functionaries who, during the years that the PT was in power nationally, encouraged residents to recognize themselves as Black.

Residents with children in school participate overwhelmingly in Bolsa Família, a conditional cash transfer program whereby those who send their children to school receive a small, bimonthly payment.[1] These supplement incomes from small-scale farming in this region that has not seen rains adequate for agriculture since 2004. They also provide some autonomy to women with children who seek to separate from abusive partners. And payments to mothers have broken the rural tradition of sending pubescent girls to cities to work as domestic servants, where they may be subject to abuse and interruption of education. The payments also maintain a space at home—and provide food—for boys who might otherwise migrate to Salvador, where some join the ranks of what outsiders often generalize as "street children." Clearly then, and in spite of the presence of a new breed of what residents refer to as "Rio de Janeiro–style" drug dealers in their midst, much has improved in Riacho Seco.

Emblematic of the changes is the trajectory of Agnaldo's bar and the family that runs it. The bar, standing at a dusty crossroads, abuts a shuttered engine repair shop owned by his father, Antonio; an empty elementary school building, where Dona Josefina, his mother, once taught; a home whose occupants have moved to São Paulo; and seven occupied single-story family dwellings built of brick and concrete. Riacho Seco gained form in the early 1960s as a cluster of wattle and daub homes. At that time, as part of the development initiatives grouped under the Superintendency for the Development of the Northeast (SUDENE) established during the government of President Juscelino Kubischek, technicians perforated the hard clay. Cowboys employed by large landowners soon flocked to the crossroads to water herds of goats, sheep, and cattle, as well as the horses and donkeys used for transportation at the time. Riacho Seco became a meeting point that supported the livestock sold in the nearby county seat or transported to the commercial hub of Feira de Santana.

In the late 1970s, the state government established a schoolhouse at Riacho Seco. There, Dona Josefina, the daughter of a cowboy who oversaw a nearby farm belonging to a politically important landowner (*coronel*), began to teach. The majority of her students dropped out before the third grade, due primarily to the long distances, lack of transportation, and a need to help out with household economies. Most children, and nearly all girls, would leave the region by the time they were teenagers in order to try their luck in cities like Salvador, the state capital of Bahia, and especially São Paulo.

In 1980, Josefina married Antonio, who would come to be the mechanic in charge of the government artesian well maintained previously by his father. Across the 1980s and the 1990s, the two raised a family of eight children, six of whom survive today. But the government salaries paid to the teacher and the mechanic were often delayed by up to six months. This eroded their buying power during periods of high inflation prior to the 1994 Plano Real. Antonio hunted songbirds and small game with a flintlock rifle, supplementing the beans, milled manioc (*farinha*), coffee, and sugar cane derivatives (*rapa dura*) that formed the core of most diets in the region. Josefina gathered licorí, a small coconut; umbú (*spondius tubarosa*)—a sour, citrus-tasting fruit from a tree able to survive by storing water in its roots—and barrel cactus (*cabeça de frade*). Eventually, Antonio purchased a third-hand automobile from his brother, who lived in São Paulo. Antonio became a driver in the informal transport networks based on pickup trucks with a long pole gripped by those who pack these vehicles, or "parrots perches" (*pau de arara*). At one point Antonio opened a small bar. But due to the expense of bringing in supplies and the small number of impoverished people living nearby, it soon closed.

Antonio and Josefina struggled. Their daughter, Nenca, moved to town to work as a domestic servant. She became pregnant, had twins, and then separated from their father. Josefina found herself raising the twins after her daughter returned to domestic service and then married her second cousin, a cowboy. Nenca and her husband now live on a thirty-hectare ranch down the road from Riacho Seco. Given the increasing aridness, the ranch no longer produces vegetables. Instead, it supplies beef to a local packing plant and the family enjoys watching YouTube and Brazilian movie streaming services by piggybacking on a neighbor's wireless internet connection. One of Nenca's brothers now works in São Paulo, where he maintains go-carts at an amusement park. Another brother works in a jewelry store in Salvador, owned by immigrants from China. Nenca's

FIGURE 7.2. Red Label and Campari, June Festivals, Bahian Sertão 2019
Photo by author

remaining siblings remain in Riacho Seco, where Agnaldo reopened Antonio's bar after he returned from an unsatisfying time in São Paulo. All those still in Bahia help out at the bar, whose profits accrue to the family as a whole, albeit mostly to Agnaldo. His other two siblings survive through small-scale farming on plots the family owns in the region (*roças*).

The family's economics revolve most basically around their occupation of space—they own all but one of Riacho Seco's buildings—and cash transfers from the federal government in the form of Bolsa Família and their parents' pensions. The guaranteed, minimum cash income provided by Bolsa Família has allowed family members to acquire cell phones and eat regularly, and well. In the evenings, all gather around a fire at the crossroads, pulling out chairs from their homes, to swap stories while watching YouTube, updating Instagram, or chatting with age-mates in China, India, and across Brazil.

The "da Silva" family has followed a trajectory repeated across the sertão, and rural Brazil during the PT years: People who just barely scratched by and often suffered hunger up through the presidential administration of Fernando Henrique Cardoso (1995–2002) now consume striking quantities of animal protein, imported electronics that link them to the world in new ways, and manage steady supplies of cash that support small business projects. Many take advantage of credit that ranges from small loans to credit cards offered by a government bank. Rather than drinking cachaça and visiting friends by donkey, they use WhatsApp and ride motorcycles to visit friends who offer them Johnny Walker Red whiskey in homes that now boast electricity but still often lack basic sanitary infrastructure and potable water.

WHEN THE SERTÃO BECOMES A SEA: COPING WITH CASH AND CHANGE IN AND AFTER THE LULA YEARS

In 2006, Agnaldo took the nearly thirty-hour bus ride to Brazil's most populous city to try his luck. But he detested São Paulo. The cold, the work, the city folk, and the noise and pollution "nearly drove [him] crazy." After two years, he returned home and began a project behind his father's bar. He diverted some of the water from the government artesian well maintained by Antonio into a new concrete-and-tile swimming pool. Approximately seven meters long, three meters wide, and one and a half meters deep, the swimming pool was an immediate success.

Men from across the region stop by after work for drinks, changing into shorts and going for a dip, or even sipping a cold beer poolside. Entrance costs R$5 (US$1.25). On weekends, children and younger people enter, although adult women rarely do. The resultant cash flow has allowed Agnaldo to expand, becoming, as his siblings put it, "a nightlife entrepreneur." In 2017, he put together Riacho Seco's first-ever *lavagem*, or street party with electrified sound trucks atop which performers play live music. Such a party, repeated in 2018 and 2019, would have been—and indeed was—unthinkable just fifteen years earlier, when Riacho Seco offered water only to livestock and housed impoverished families, most of whom scratched out a living raising beans, manioc, and sisal. People got their water from the well or from systems of gutters and concrete reservoirs that channeled runoff across V-shaped roofs.

The principal reason that a lavagem would have been unthinkable a decade earlier involves cash. During the 1980s and 1990s, cash was practically worthless to residents since, due to inflation, it lost significant value for people who lacked the hedging mechanisms available to middle-class and wealthy Brazilians. Thus most "economic" exchanges in the Riacho Seco region were balanced or generalized forms of reciprocity, whereby people often offered up to age-mates, kin, and neighbors surpluses of whatever they had. Walking home from the fields, one might drop off beans to a family noted for its cashew trees, thus returning with a bit of tasty cashew fruit or some nuts stored by the family after having been collected and dehusked by burning in the fires that mark the June saints' holidays. Happening upon an open door in an informal bar further along one's journey, one might enter and place some of the nuts upon the counter, as a barfly or the owner offered sugarcane alcohol in turn. A neighbor might then appear with a guinea pig–like rodent he had just shot (*preá*), or a bit of intestine received in exchange for slaughtering a sheep. After the proprietor roasted it or the hunter built a small fire on the side of the road, all assembled would eat a bit while passing meat around, proclaiming out of politeness that they were sated, but would nonetheless do their best to eat the meat because it looked so tasty. Such exchanges of goods and labor, unmediated by cash but strictly governed by quotidian convention, were not simply common but, in fact, how people survived.

Today, as cash circulates throughout the sertão, residents engage in hybrid forms of consumption and exchange. Old rules about receiving visitors, milking cows and sending milk to neighbors, and sharing fruits or what one brings back from the caatinga, still apply. And yet residents of Riacho Seco routinely buy airplane tickets to São Paulo, rent vehicles, and purchase widescreen televisions. In this context, it bears noting that the only enjoyable aspect of his time in São Paulo remembered today by Agnaldo involved bumping into people he knew from Riacho Seco and surrounding villages. One young man whom Agnaldo socialized with in São Paulo, although they had never been close in Bahia, was Dilmario. An age-mate born and raised in Pedro Malasartes, Dilmario worked for a time as a mason's assistant in São Paulo and then dropped out of view. After Agnaldo returned to Bahia, the two lost contact. However, around 2012, Dilmario reappeared in Pedro Malasartes:

FIGURE 7.3. Pedro Malasartes, June 2019
Photo by author.

I wasn't really paying attention. A few guys smoked marijuana. That we knew. Always in secret, however. But then one day they killed Quisinho. That Quisinho was the biggest thief I knew. He needed to die. I mean, he took a cell phone off the lady right down the road here, in broad daylight. That never, ever, used to happen in Barreiro Preto! That's stuff for Rio. The guy was robbing all over. The guys (*os cara*) came looking for him. Two guys on a motorcycle, with helmets. Then we found him bound and shot through the head. Good riddance . . . Dilmario's boys who did it. They don't want any thieves around here. They might draw the police. They have their own business and don't want any small-time thieves messing it up!

Dilmario had returned and set himself up in business in Pedro Malasartes. But instead of running a bar and organizing parties, he led a group of men who hung out in front of a tire shop. Located atop a hill, it is a perfect point from which to make out any automobiles that approach the village. Drawing on contacts that Dilmario had gained when incarcerated for an armed robbery in São Paulo, the group sold small, usually R$5 and R$10, portions of cocaine shipments carried to northern Bahia by people said to be affiliated with the PCC. Dilmario soon gained fame. He and his compatriots walked around in brand-name clothing bought in Salvador, often brandishing weapons and using new slang. For example, in spite of the high altitude of his drug-selling point, Dilmario used the term *quebrada*—valley, or low-lying neighborhood—that is used also in São Paulo to describe a region of a favela dominated by a particular group. Residents of Pedro Malasartes and surrounding communities flocked to this high region, where they exchanged their cash for cocaine as part of an economy that, again, would have been unthinkable just a decade earlier.

In June of 2019, I traveled nearly daily to conduct business at legitimate establishments, visit friends, and gossip in bars in Dilmario and his gang's section of Pedro Malasartes. Upon arrival, Agnaldo and his relatives would greet the assembled young men formally, with the slightly stiff and yet soft handshakes employed by men not bound by kin ties. Dilmario's men would respond in kind, welcoming formally their neighbors. They would reciprocate once again when they came through Riacho Seco, buying a drink at Agnaldo's bar and behaving respectfully.

Antonio once recounted an example of such "respect":

> I was sitting out front and two guys I've seen before, two kids I know... came up on a motorcycle talking real fast and sweating. They said "*Tio* [uncle], can we drink a beer?" So I got the key, and opened the establishment for them [pantomiming a quick, but stiffly-formal-in-a-connotation-of-respect series of movements]. They stood at the bar. "What can I serve you?"
>
> "Voop," then they drank their beer. Then they asked for another. "Tio, can we go into your bathroom?" I knew just what was up.
>
> "Of course, make yourselves comfortable."
>
> "When they came out, they were shaking and wiping their noses, crazy-eyed. Like this [makes a snorting noise]."
>
> They drank their beer and paid. "Thanks Tio, you're good people," and they got on their motorcycle and left. They haven't been back since, thanks be to God!

Such interactions are normal in the sertão, where isolated groups maintain lasting, and intimate, ties that may devolve quickly into violence if participants fail to adhere to social norms. For example, the verbal insults common across the Bahian capital of Salvador or in its surrounding rural plantation belt known as the Recôncavo are not usually tolerated in the region around Riacho Seco. One example involves the day that Agnaldo's uncle was drinking in a different local bar and a man jokingly called him a *filha da puta* (son of a bitch, feminized) as part of a longer, jocular conversation of a sort rather normal in Salvador. Since the uncle had stepped into the bar after work and carried his spurs in his hand, he immediately raked his tools across the offensive bar patron's chest, opening up a series of gashes, saying softly but firmly, "Don't ever insult my mother!"

Such actions introduce something important to the present analysis—given a history of worker exploitation by a powerful elite and the relative absence of the state in terms of the provision of security, people living in small groups like the agglomeration of houses in Riacho Seco typically band together in a manner that makes the violation of local norms rather dangerous (Villela 2004). They do so for safety, and for issues of honor and reputation that are tied to safety as well as to scapegoating mechanisms. People often repeat, "You can know a man, but you never know what he is capable of." Certain families are recognized as especially fierce, not to be trifled with (*retados*). Often this designation arises simply from the fact that a family has many sons, who mobilize to meet threats. At other moments it may be related to the power of influential women or the fact that one family member is a hit man (*pistoleiro*) or an enforcer for a nearby rancher (*jagunço*). Yet such violent possibilities are typically avoided, or assuaged and veiled, by social conventions that lend a highly formal, stereotyped quality to gendered interactions like greeting a neighbor, "respecting" women, or walking into a bar. This mix of intimate violence, threat, and convention is a basic facet of everyday interactions and broader political structures in the sertão, or what are typically called "patron-client" relations or even *coronelismo* in scholarly analyses (Leal 2012). What most interests me are not the patron-client structures themselves but the vocabularies, intonations, embodied affectations, and thus everyday grammars and rituals so often identified as basic to them, as well as the more horizontal relations between people who are more socially equal.

SHIFTING RATIONALITIES

This chapter is not about the transformation of some precapitalist order into a neoliberal regime. The Bahian sertão and its agriculture have long been tightly integrated into global circuits. Nor was the region around Riacho Seco once pacific, with people living in a harmony indexed by exchange rather than cash-based relations. On the contrary, the sertão has historically been a region of conflict and banditry. Agnaldo's grandfather, today a 105-year-old retired cowboy, recounts fleeing into the caatinga with his mother and siblings for safety when the infamous bandits Lampião and Maria Bonita would pass through the region in the late 1920s.[2] But what does seem to be different are the mediating forms to which people look in inflecting, avoiding, or exacerbating violence. Such forms are what I take to be "rationalities," or shared public conventions, that people employ to explain, or make comprehensible, the world.

While we were hunting in the caatinga, Antonio once pointed to a house:

> That belonged to the family of my buddy, Marquinhos. We shot our slingshots, set our traps, and dived into cattle troughs as kids. We stayed close. But we never talked about certain things—he was a pistoleiro. Then one day, Laercio down the road started talking about another pistoleiro, Manuel da Ford. Manuel didn't like that. He shot Laercio and buried him in the caatinga. No one could prove anything, and no one really talked about it. But Marquinhos thought that was wrong. Why kill a neighbor because he talked a little too much? Talk to him, show him what's right. So Marquinhos took out Manuel, in turn. Manuel's family didn't like that either. So they paid a pistoleiro from Pernambuco to get rid of Marquinhos . . . shot him in the head right here at the crossroads. The body lay for two days, gathering flies.

Revenge killings, domestic violence, and pistoleiros were staple subjects of gossip networks. Such gossip was in previous decades limited by sanctions of the sort that got "Laercio down the road" killed by Manuel, thus setting off revenge killings that took Antonio's childhood friend. These roiling waves of violence are key topics in social scientific, popular, and literary analyses of the sertão. Yet today gossip networks as shared, mediating forms for explaining the unexplainable, the secret, or the confusing aspects of life seem to be more increasingly directed at and by stories of police movements and police killings than they are aimed at murky actors among one's neighbors. In a region in which homicide used to be limited for the most part to revenge killings, domestic violence, and the actions of individual, hard-to-pin-down pistoleiros, drug dealing now generates the majority of murderous violence. This is a public violence, generated by young men who dominate a section of their city, frighten neighbors, and consume ostentatiously.

A perusal of the online networks that link people in the Pedro Malasartes region reveals constant stories, reminiscent of those about the peripheries of Rio de Janeiro or São Paulo, of young men killed in the drug trade. Rival gangs (*facções*) have invaded Pedro Malasartes in order to "take" Dilmario's drug-dealing spot. Principal among these is Katiara, a grouped tied to Rio de Janeiro's Comando Vermelho. Katiara is active in the Bahian Recôncavo and is a rival to Bonde dos Malucos (BDM), the largest of the Bahian gangs and one linked to São Paulo's PCC. In most areas of Bahia, PCC and BDM are synonymous, but in Pedro Malasartes, residents speak only of the PCC. This reflects the Pedro Malasartes region's tighter ties to distant São Paulo than to the Bahian capital of Salvador, only some three hundred kilometers away. Such criminal groups tied to national-level gangs have brought a novel police presence to the backlands. In fact, up until the last decade, it was nearly impossible to come across a military police patrol in the region. Disputes were typically dealt with by families, even as people recognized the power and the corrupting influences of local civil police officers (*delegados*).

Agnaldo, his brothers, his cousins, and his brothers-in-law maintain a cordial if distant relationship to Dilmario's gang. They behave correctly when visiting Pedro Malasartes. They are careful to be good hosts and to demonstrate masculine daring, a willingness to commit to violence, and possession of firearms as part of a corporate group whenever anyone from Pedro Malasartes arrives in Riacho Seco. Dilmario and his group seem wary of Agnaldo's family, due in part to their control of a definite piece of territory, their fame as a united group with "disposition" (*disposição*), and decades of engagement between people who have known one another since childhood. In this respect, relations between Dilmario's group and residents of Riacho Seco correspond in important ways to the subrelations between groups of peasants allied with distinct patrons, or landlords, so much a part of the literature on the sertão. However, today there is a major difference in this relationship. This has little to do with formalized interactions, which still seem to accord tightly with what I have observed in the region since the beginning of the 1990s.

Across their lives, Antonio and Agnaldo have maintained rather distinct types of ties to lawbreakers. I understand this difference as generational, and indicative of the changes that accompany the flow of cash into the sertão. Antonio's relationship to a pistoleiro was intimate and characterized by "real" friendship. But in spite of this real friendship, the two would never talk about being guns for hire or any illicit activities at all. Meanwhile, even as Dilmario and his gang shield their activities from Antonio, moving to the bathroom to snort cocaine as part of an unspoken agreement, when they engage with Antonio's son Agnaldo they do little to shield their activities. "Vou dar um teco" (I'm gonna do a line), they announce. Agnaldo, who consumes alcohol but no drugs, once commented, "They know I don't approve. But they don't need to respect me as they do the elderly. They respect me as a man. Sometimes I think they're afraid we'll go to the police, which we'd never do. When the cops kill one of them I'm like, 'good riddance,' but I'd never squeal." While denials of drug use and serving as a police informant are notoriously unreliable, years of interactions have taught me to take Agnaldo at his word. And yet I have often watched as rumors of the exploits of the Pedro Malasartes drug traffickers are repeated, and Agnaldo and his age-mates take great joy in traffickers' confounding of the police. In fact, it is these police that I link here to shifts in social life in the sertão, to what may be looming on the horizon, and to the words by Agnaldo's mother, Dona Josefina, that I reported in opening this chapter.

CONCLUSION: MEDIATIONS

I have spent hundreds of hours discussing with Dona Josefina the extent to which she has spent a life negotiating between her family and neighbors, men and women, landowners and those, like most of her family, who work for them or are subservient to their enormous power in rural Bahia. Today, however, those landowners appear increasingly distant. They no longer maintain everyday relations with her family. For example, the farm owner from Feira de Santana, some two hours away by car, now visits his ranch that Josefina's brother manages by helicopter. The property includes a Lear jet runway and a helicopter pad next to the farmhouse. The farmer's daughters live in Miami, and while people in Riacho Seco still consider him "good people," he no longer maintains the tight relations that have long characterized his exploitation of the ranch, his control over large groups of men who might impose his will on the countryside, and his relationship to the mayors of nearby towns.

At the same time, Agnaldo, whose own relatives have long made up that group of men subservient to the landowner, tells me that he has begun to hire his own security forces for the parties he throws annually at Riacho Seco. These guards are the same military police who glanced at us menacingly after returning empty-handed from Pedro Malasartes. "Yeah, you just gotta get the sergeant alone, because he doesn't want to share the loot with the lieutenant," Agnaldo told me. "And the lieutenant charges too much. I slip them a couple hundred, and they crack some heads for me during the lavagem. NO ONE acts up!"

Here as part of a growing cash economy, nonelite actors employ security practices typically confined historically to the bourgeoisie and elites in manners akin to what João Costa Vargas (2006) documents for a peripheral community in Rio. It seems that the very bases of sociability, of understandings of public and private, inside and outside, right and wrong, and belonging and exclusion are currently in play. This is not some simple accounting of who is on top, or who has money, and thus who replaces whom on an airport line or in a congressman's office. At least in places like Riacho Seco, it is a relational performance in which social idioms like secrecy, double entendre, patron-clientship, silence, and metacommentary and rumor seem to be undergoing changes, even as they carry with them practices from earlier moments (Collins 2015). And these performances, or idioms I refer to above as "rationalities," are what make the world intelligible, and real.

To point out that poor people put together a gated condominium in Rio (Costa Vargas 2006) or that a *sertanejo* barkeep hires the police is not to argue simply that these "new" consumers are usurping an established place in Brazil. It is to suggest, instead, as Sean Mitchell also points out in his contribution to this volume, the emergence of new rationalities. So rather than alleging that invasions of middle-class space generate middle class, reactionary rancor that explains much about the country's recent rightward shift, I wish to suggest that more than middle-class rancor is at stake, and in play.

Dona Josefina's words at the beginning of this chapter gesture at something of what is at play. To repeat, when speaking of her relative enrichment and access to cancer treatments, alongside the sale of illegal drugs in Pedro Malasartes, Josefina exclaimed, "But I know how to take my medicine alongside the poison, and pretend it doesn't exist. It does exist. Not everyone knows how to do that." This statement recalls the Greek concept of the *pharmakon* as both a remedy and a poison, as expanded upon by Jacques Derrida (1981). For Derrida and the Greeks, the poison always carries with it something of the medicine, and vice versa. I understand Josefina to be telling me that her curative cancer medicine is made possible by the sorts of economic leaps that permit young men to market drugs in a town in which residents could barely afford bread a generation ago. Josefina is clear that she knows how to take medicine alongside poison. Here, it would seem, she sums up what I have been trying to put together across these pages—with the ambiguous but very real gains of the Lula and Dilma years, there have arisen also a series of poisons. The question of politics, and ethics and survival, thus becomes that of learning how to take one's medicine—understood as the positive aspects of increased cash flow in a market economy—alongside the poison.

Josefina's outlook suggests the value of ethnographic considerations of ambiguity and everyday life, rather than facile pronouncements about shifts in the categories considered by earlier analysis. Thus it seems that looking at how people consume and, for example, dubbing them a "new middle class" is much less analytically useful than seeking to understand how people survive, and enter into new forms of power and new market relationships, on the basis of new institutions. A fine example in Riacho Seco is the police, who now take on a role that is more akin to their roles in favelas in Rio de Janeiro than their traditional absence in the face of private armies in the sertão. These police, who do not yet enter Riacho Seco in search of miscreants, nonetheless eye its inhabitants. And Josefina senses that trouble is on the horizon—that along with the good will come a series of changes to Riacho Seco that may threaten her children and grandchildren.

In pointing out Josefina's prescience, and positioning her as engaging in a hermeneutics of ambiguity, I am not celebrating tricksters. I am emphasizing that the enormous political change confronting Brazil today involves questions of minor idioms and muffled, ambiguous statements. These are roads into the rationalities through which people make do and survive. Riacho Seco and its new cash flows face a collision of values associated with earlier patron-client relations, with prohibitions on verbalizing dissent, and with injunctions against individualism or "selfishness" (Kottak 2017). Such conventions have functioned, for some time, even as they never remained static. But in their alteration today, we might recall what happens when people pick at a roasted bit of rodent put atop a bar. The small animal will never fill the bellies of all assembled. In such situations, I often long for my own *preá*, to spirit away and eat alone to satisfy my hunger. But when everyone pecks at, and consumes a bit of, the meat, everyone survives. It is *how* we peck, and how we deal with medicine alongside poison, that I suggest is in play in Brazil today and that we must make visible in order to survive.

REFERENCES

Ansell, Aaron. 2014. *Zero Hunger*. Chapel Hill: University of North Carolina Press.

———. 2018. "Clientelism, Elections, and the Dialectic of Numerical People in Northeast Brazil." *Current Anthropology* 59 (18): S128–S137.

Collins, John. 2008. "Patrimony, Public Health, and National Culture: The Commodification and Redemption of Origins in Neoliberal Brazil." *Critique of Anthropology* 28 (2): 237–255.

———. 2015. *Revolt of the Saints: Memory and Redemption in the Twilight of Brazilian Racial Democracy*. Durham, N.C.: Duke University Press.

Costa Vargas, João. 2006. "When a Favela Dared to Become a Gated Condominium: The Politics of Race and Urban Space in Rio de Janeiro." *Latin American Perspectives* 33 (4): 49–81.

Cunha, Euclides da. 1964. *Rebellion in the Backlands*. Translated by Samuel Putnam. Chicago: University of Chicago Press.

Derrida, Jacques. 1981. "Plato's Pharmacy." In *Dissemination*, edited and translated by Barbara Johnson, 63–171. Chicago: University of Chicago Press.

Herzfeld, Michael. 2015. "Anthropology and the Inchoate Intimacies of Power." *American Ethnologist* 42 (1): 18–32.

Junge, Benjamin. 2018. *Cynical Citizenship: Gender, Regionalism, and Political Subjectivity in Porto Alegre, Brazil*. Albuquerque: University of New Mexico Press.

Kottak, Conrad. 2017. *Assault on Paradise: The Globalization of a Little Community*. New York: Waveland.

Leal, Vitor Nunes. 2012. *Coronelismo, enxada e voto: O município e o regime representativo no Brasil*. São Paulo: Companhia das Letras.

Mitchell, Timothy. 2013. *Carbon Democracy: Political Power in the Age of Oil*. New York: Verso.

Villela, Jorge Mattar. 2004. *O povo em armas*. Rio de Janeiro: Ediouro.

NOTES

1. See, for example, Ansell 2014 and the chapter on Bolsa Família by Jessica Jerome in the present volume.

2. His story is supported by the historical record, which indicates that Lampião crossed the San Francisco River in northern Bahia in 1928 and spent the end of 1929 conducting various operations in the cities surrounding Riacho Seco.

8 · "THE OIL IS OURS"
Petro-Affect and the Scandalization of Politics

LUCIA CANTERO

> Capital bequeathed to mankind from other living beings.
> —Jean Paul Sartre, on oil ([1977] 2004)

Petrobras was once the apogee of Brazilian pride. At the height of Workers' Party (Partido dos Trabalhadores; PT) leadership and commodity boom, Petrobras went public on September 24, 2010, with a valuation that then-president Luis Inácio Lula da Silva (hereafter Lula) exalted as the "highest in the history of capitalism." It was an undeniably euphoric moment. Petrobras had become the largest company in Latin America, with market capitalization and revenues outshining all others. Only days before Dilma Rousseff (hereafter Dilma) was to be elected in 2010, Lula graced the BOVESPA Stock Exchange in São Paulo, along with his team, to address the heads of Brazilian banks, politicians, citizens of the nation, and beyond. Wearing a white hardhat and neon orange jacket, he reminded the public of a sovereignty that Petrobras had recently made possible with the discovery of presalt.[1] This, in the backdrop of the 2008 global economic crisis, which spared Brazil, seemed to make Lula even more ecstatic. He asserted that, unlike in the past, Petrobras achieved what it could never do before: capitalize on the future modes of productivity over time and reconcile all worries that it would "debilitate the state or alienate the public patrimony." He declared, "Brazil is very proud of Brazil. What is materializing here [today] is the decision of a *sovereign society* to capitalize their future, to capitalize the future of their modes of productivity for the present and for generations to come. Petrobras is an extraordinary triumph for Brazil's development."[2] The national ceremony adjourned in characteristically festive form, and like a sports team, the president and his council huddled together, pressing a button that released metallic confetti and sounded the very same sonic BRASIL heard when a goal is scored. This moment marked an exemplary time in 2010[3], when Petrobras rocked the financial records as the most profitable valuation project ever, successfully capitalizing the highest profit going public to foreign shareholders in economic history at that time (Gall 2011).

Today Petroleo Brasileiro S.A. (Petrobras) is a semipublic, majority state-owned company occupied mostly with oil and gas exploration, refining, and transport. It is, nominally, Brazil's largest company. Headquartered in downtown Rio de Janeiro, Petrobras's history is charged; stories of blood absorbed in a national struggle to defend "the riches of the land," and "sovereignty," as some of my interlocutors called it. An affective connection to this company, first enunciated in the 1949 slogan "O Petróleo é Nosso" (hereafter "The Oil Is Ours"), ebbs and flows with changing moments that reflect deep structures of feeling (Williams 1977) and consciousness: from the euphoria of the presalt discovery and its valuation at BOVESPA and more recently, the public outcry, shame, and vitriol—which ultimately targeted the Workers' Party and the very political foundation on which it stood. The oil or "crude sovereignty" that Lula invoked turned rather quickly from euphoria to dystopia, or as this edited volume conveys, from hope to despair in governance as the associated *petróleo* corruption scandals emerged and shook Brazilians and the very meaning of democracy.

The "Operation Car Wash" (hereafter Lava Jato) task force was deployed to investigate the details of the graft, revealing a mammoth bribery scheme that exposed countless connections to Petrobras and huge swaths of Brazilian politicians. The scandal dominated mainstream media, and the juridical politics around these conditions led to the impeachment—also understood by many as a soft coup—of Dilma and landed ex-president Lula in prison. Vice President Michel Temer stepped in as acting president on May 12, 2016, after Dilma was impeached and then became full-time president on August 31 after Dilma was convicted and removed from office; it was against this backdrop that extreme-right candidate Jair Bolsonaro was elected to the presidency in 2018.

The chapter begins with a euphoric valuation to convey the ways that Petrobras reflects, not only how Brazilians forge nationalism and notions of sovereignty, but also how this imbrication hinges on affective attachments that coproduce political subjectivity. In other words, I demonstrate how Petrobras serves as a charged symbol of the nation, its cultural politics, and Brazil's relationship to globalization. I explore the affective attachments and contestations that emerge around three distinct moments in Petrobras's history and enduring social life: (1) inaugural and foundational push under then-president Getúlio Vargas to stay public or state-owned; (2) the aforementioned moment of capitalization under Lula in 2010, or going public; and (3) the 2014 *Petrolão* corruption scandal exposed by Lava Jato. The first section of this chapter explores the history of Petrobras and considers discourse that emerged in 2011 from interlocutors in Rio de Janeiro about the historical 1943 "The Oil Is Ours" campaign to examine affective attachments to Petrobras and the effervescent disenchantment around corruption and increasingly privatizing state resources. This ethnographic data was culled from interlocutors who responded to queries and surveys around Petrobras propaganda and memory pooled in 2011. The section that follows explores the dynamics of the *petróleo* corruption scandal and the juridico-politics of anticorruption measures, including the ways in which sovereignty shifted. By exploring these moments, I argue, moreover, that affective linkages and accompanying media spectacles obscured the extractive and imperial nature of the graft, making both the state and Petrobras vulnerable to lawfare ushered in from anticorruption measures that increasingly internationalized the Brazilian Public Prosecutor's Office (Ministerio Público Federal; MPF).

THE OIL SLICKS OF DEVELOPMENTAL NATIONALISM

Here I draw from conversations and interviews with Cariocas (Rio residents) in 2011 (well before the scandal) that recalled the landmark "The Oil Is Ours" campaign to recount Petrobras's creation story. Soliciting the contents of collective historical memory allows contemporary ethnographers to assess the enduring quality of affect, as memory is a metric that imprints onto the body in compelling soma-ethical ways (Hirschkind 2006). As Lula's 2010 speech recounted, Petrobras in Brazil has historically been a cipher for expressing political alliances, patriotism, and nationalism. In the commemorative speech, he harkened back to a time under Vargas when many citizens feared the debilitation of the state through privatization, or "selling out" (known as *entreguismo*) in favor of protecting it as national patrimony, governed by the state for public coffers. The sellouts defended foreign investment in the name of development and modernization. Since 1939, when oil was discovered in Lobato, Bahia, this resource has carried the symbolic weight of the nation and, under dictatorship, citizens staged grassroots campaigns to defend their land's "richness," thereby protecting the state's territorial resources through advocacy.

The fear of losing access to one's patrimony motivated many citizens to voice their concerns over national commodities under a Brazilian developmental nationalism. During the Vargas regime and under U.S. imperialism, many incited resistance to foreign investors in the fight over the discovery of petroleum. A seventy-year old Botafogo resident named Daniel recalls the historical conflict over the creation of Petrobras: "I remember the fight, when I was a student, to create a Petrobras so that we could say the oil was ours." This was part of Vargas's agenda of that time and, as early as 1939, he established the National Council on Petroleum (CNP) with a law that sanctioned it as patrimony of the Union.

When pressed to think about this historical campaign, another interlocutor immediately remembered the staunch nationalist writer Monteiro Lobato. His famed *Letter to Getúlio* outlined his ideas as for neither international big oil nor state monopolies but rather local small-scale and regional Brazilian companies. In *Viscount's Oil*, published in 1937, he warned of the U.S. exploitation of Brazil's raw material solely for consumer markets—that is, without development or accompanying infrastructures.[4] This landed Lobato, with his then-radical views and witty pen, in prison under the Vargas regime. Fifty-two-year-old Copacabana resident Marcos said the slogan made him "think of the injustices under Getúlio Vargas and Dutra against Monteiro Lobato; they wanted to turn over [*entregar*] the oil, and Monteiro Lobato wrote a book that made the slogan ['The Oil Is Ours'] famous."

After World War II in 1945, when Brazil had been an ally to the United States, Brazilian nationalists launched a fierce anti-imperialist campaign, with constituencies ranging from the Communist Party to ex-military officers led—ironically—by former president Fernando Henrique Cardoso's father, General Leônidas Cardoso. Luz Contreiras, who was arrested during the height of this activism, noted somberly that "folks still had to carry cans of gas marked Standard Oil" (Carrion 2003). This campaign fomented, moreover, a sense of citizenship and democratic participation, and with Getúlio Vargas finally elected by popular vote in 1951, helped to sustain a sense of nationalism around these resources. The efficacy of public opinion and propaganda to represent the interests of the nationalists instilled a pride around a patrimony. "The Oil Campaign was effectively the biggest and most original contribution to the creation of a 'nationalist Brazilian democratic' attitude," confirmed activist Maria Miranda in her 1983 text *The Oil Is Ours*.

On October 3, 1953, Getúlio Vargas finally approved Law 2004 (*lei 2004*), which created Petrobras as the arbiter of the patrimony of oil and its derivatives, management, and exploration, and the following year inaugurated refineries in Cubatão, São Paulo, and Mataripe, Bahia. Vargas's words betrayed the bloodied struggle to defend the monopoly, rhetorically solidifying the victory of developmental nationalism and the push toward industrialization under the following declaration, which came only a year before his suicide: "The Congress has just substantiated the law and governmental plan for the exploration of our oil. Petrobras will secure not just the development of the national petroleum industry, but also decisively limit our invasions and supplies. Consisting of capital, technology, and labor exclusively Brazilian, Petrobras results from a firm national economic policy. It is with satisfaction and patriotic pride that today I sanction the Law approved by the legislature that constitutes a new mark in our economic independence" (Carrion 2003). Vargas's words conveyed a deep concern around turning over Brazilian resources to foreign investment and control. The launch of 1943's "The Oil Is Ours" was a campaign, moreover, that signaled citizen pride over public goods, and as my ethnographic research conveyed, is continually remembered today in popular public opinion as citizens lamented the loss of national commodities to foreign investors, as in the case of Vale (Brazil's largest mining company, which was sold under Fernando

Henrique Cardoso to a Spanish corporation for "the price of bananas" in the 1990s under initial privatizations, under earlier neoliberal policies). Evelyn, a young lawyer from Catete was also an intern at the Oil Industry Workers Union (SindPetro) and recounted the salience of the slogan. She recalled, "I remember the culture of not letting our rich national resources and the technology that we patent get 'sold.'" Indeed, this opinion represented over a quarter of my respondents, who recalled that the campaign urged in them a nationalist nostalgia and fervor to protect, even today, the riches of Brazil's national territory. This natural inclination to keep Petrobras public and—for Brazilians—found resonance in many recent social movements, as represented by the forum "O Pré-sal é Nosso," (the pre-salt is ours) which advocated for the protection of presalt for public coffers so that taxpayers can defend their voice in the parceling of the patrimony.

Some of the more ubiquitous responses conveyed a concern over "selling out," much in the way it had played out in the past. As one middle-class, middle-aged Centro resident named Heitor put it plainly, "The oil should really be ours, but with globalization, lots of companies started to exploit the riches, and the people don't reap the advantages of that. Look at the price of gasoline." He felt that as a citizen of a country that is purportedly "rising," he should reap some benefits of this process too. That the company stays "national," however, carries with it expectations that all citizens have a voice in how these resources are parceled. "What comes to mind," said a woman from Vila Isabel named Clarice, "is Petrobras's monopoly and the debate over whether to 'liberate' oil to foreign exploration. It ends up not being ours." For many, "The Oil Is Ours" meant just that. They were more interested in making sure the resource would stay precisely that to the citizens of the nation: a public good. And it wasn't exactly all about a nationalist sensibility to them either. Rather, nationalist would be too broad an analytical category for the ways in which these subjects were circumscribing their relationship to this good. Indeed, it was more about a sense of "rights to patrimony," Rafael from Rio Comprido described oil as "the riches of the national territory" and as such, "a public good" that should benefit all citizens in the kind of progressive nationalism Dilma had promised.

This pronounced sense of entitlement over Petrobras was not only "distributive" as research on state projects has revealed (Mitchell 2017) but also resoundingly protectionist: "I don't agree with the privatization of ANY natural resource whatsoever," declared another interlocutor. For others, it recalled not just protecting oil for public coffers but also elevating the commodity in a "tournament of value" (Appadurai 1986). "I think it is Brazil's gold," exalted one younger interlocutor named Paolo from Barra de Tijuca. "Where you drill, you find oil in Brazil," exclaimed Carmen from Leblon. And despite this lack of scarcity, others cautioned, "I think we should give more value to the riches of the country." Still, others took direct entitlement over the resource; "The Oil *Is* Ours" was a common response. "I think we 'the people' are the owners, as it grants us autonomy," said Mariana from Flamengo. The questions posed to interlocutors adhered to the "methodological fetishism" that Appadurai (1986, 5) urges: "We have to follow the things themselves, for their meanings are inscribed in their forms, their uses, their trajectories." In this way, to follow the social life of oil on the ground is to also understand the ways in which these kinds of goods enunciate affective attachments. Following the narratives over Petrobras on the ground revealed, indeed, the ways in which subjects embodied an affective connection to patrimony that indexed sovereignty, in particular. "It's ours, it's our sovereignty" said a young man named Thiago from Méier. If, for some, oil signaled sovereignty, then protecting the resource meant voicing this concern over selling out.

The kinds of reactions culled from interlocutors about this hallmark Petrobras campaign were various, but what became certain was that subjects felt they had a relationship to the resource as both consumers and citizens. Not all sentiments "protected the patrimony" through exaltations of the riches of "their" nation, for there were considerable voices of dissent from my respondents about the "real" fruits of the land. The subjects asserted their consumer rights to public revenue from these resources. Common responses complained about the prices of gas, asking "if the so-called oil is mine" or "where's my piece?" or stating the familiar "the oil is theirs, the corrupt." Whether tongue-in-cheek or truly disgruntled, these responses indicate a hungry public awaiting the "trickling-down" of this latest privatizing victory. What these responses also revealed was that notions of corruption, too, were hard to locate. In the years that followed, this reigning and amorphous category of corruption later gets shaped, polished, and weaponized against the PT.

The history of Petrobras was already a charged one when I first posed these questions in 2011, long before the slogan "The Petroleum Is Ours" reemerged and became popularized again in the public sphere through labor protests. Shortly after the epic June 2013 protests, on October 21, 2013, union strikers organized protests outside Barra de Tijuca's Windsor Hotel, where "Libra," the offshore oil field, faced a multibillion-dollar bid over production rights. As Lília from Santa Teresa noted, "The slogan signals a kind of nationalism, a collective sentiment of sharing and taking advantage of a high valued good and of the purported valorization of said product." This kind of nationalism also recapitulated the promises of populism conferred by governments in the past and, purportedly, rearticulated under Lula and Dilma's terms. As Marcelo from Jacarepaguá reminded me, "The government will give back to society all the benefits obtained with that prime material. In various forms: improvement in education, health care, infrastructure, transportation, et cetera." It was, indeed, the growing recession, and failure to see better access to the above forms, that drove many citizens to publicly demand these rights in the massive June 2013 protests. This progress, as it were, faced a halt when protesters gathered to "protest democracy" (Dent and Pinheiro-Machado 2013) and Dilma was forced to respond to the very concerns voiced by citizens in my fieldwork interviews years before. In her response to these protests, she assured the populace that their voices as citizens were being heard, and she promised a platform of actions that earmarked Petrobras profits for health care, education, and other social programs. It was in this context, and at that moment, that the maelstrom of megaevents ushered in a volatile political climate. The inaugural protests in 2013 hailing from the "free pass movement," which centered on access to basic infrastructures like public transportation, incited a multitude of other voices in dissent. These slogans, as affective attachments, get exploited by many parties of competing interests and, of late, even reinvigorated by right-wing discourse and Bolsonaro fans for their purposes.

CORRUPTING THE LAW AND THE SCANDALIZATION OF POLITICS

The *petróleo* corruption scandals exposed by Lava Jato beginning in 2014, the details of which I will soon explore, undoubtedly changed the nature of Brazilian pride around Petrobras, pronouncing an affective shift—quite literally—from hope to despair. Not only did these scandals rupture the existing social and political order, but they also conflated various forms of dissent, as witnessed with Dilma's impeachment in 2016 (Ansell 2018). Corruption has a long and contested history both in practice and in anthropological literature, and in Brazil it permeates as an enduring cultural trope. As I demonstrated in the previous section, the conversations about Petrobras with interlocutors at the time it was potentially most warm and fuzzy revealed corruption as a long durée descriptor of governance and public resources. Anthropologists are "justifiably wary of reproducing clichéd images of political dysfunction, especially in postcolonial and other contexts that routinely bear the brunt of transnational governance" (Gupta and Muir 2018, 1). Following reinvigorated anthropological interest in "corruption anti-corruption complexes" as it reveals tensions between public and private (Nugent 2018), this section interrogates the mechanics of these forms of politics and the ways they shape governance both at the level of the nation-state and internationally.

The tethering of massive corruption charges and impeachment in Brazil are not at all new, yet the specificities of this particular moment, as this volume explores, require further analysis. In 1990, Fernando Collor de Mello, who had just been elected president, remarked, rather ironically, "It is one thing to talk about austerity. It is another thing to practice it" (Brook 1992). With these words, and a *cara de pau* (a lot of nerve), he announced he would live in a modest ranch house in Brasilia in early 1990. Instead, Brazilians later learned that he was finalizing the "construction of a three-acre garden oasis that would ultimately include eight artificial waterfalls, a 1,000 square foot swimming pool and a triple level lagoon stocked with Japanese carp" (Brook 1992). If not new, what is novel about the *petrólão* scandal was the way in which forms of corruption allowed for systematic jockeying and even what can be understood as juridico-extraction through lawfare, as I will explore shortly. (Two years later, Mello resigned amid an impeachment trial; after he left office, the Senate convicted him, barring him from future office.)

In 2016, Brazil's most influential newspaper, *Folha de São Paulo*, reported that ex-president Lula's defense team hired an expert in "lawfare" to help in the defense of the money laundering and corruption charges upward of ten billion *reais* purportedly involving him and many Workers' Party leaders via the state-based oil giant Petrobras (Bilenky 2016). In the landscape of this "lawfare," John Comaroff (whose face graced the cover of that very newspaper) defined broadly the political instrumentalization of law in postcolonial societies (Comaroff and Comaroff 2006). Comaroff argued that the allegations violated the law by litigating under "a presumption of guilt" by Judge Sergio Moro, charged to lead the case administered by the MPF. Comaroff, moreover, suggested substituting federal judges to avoid further conflict (sanguine advice that, of course, was not heeded). This lawfare, he insisted, placed Lula and the Workers' Party as the media centerpiece of the corruption. Indeed, lawfare often operationalizes media in ways that shape an affect, which also has the potential to spill onto adjudication and other legal procedures (Clarke 2019). In this way, scandals are weaponized politically as spectacle, allowing for the kind of judicialization that shook the structure of sovereignty in Brazil.

The *petrólão* corruption scandal was deemed the largest bribery scandal in history and stretched well beyond Petrobras. Marcelo Odebrecht was sentenced to sixteen years in prison for thirty million in bribes to Petrobras executives. According to the Transparency International website, a key player in this anticorruption lawfare, there were "more than 240 criminal charges, 118 convictions totaling 1,256 years of sentence time, record breaking asset recovery (US$200 million returned to Petrobras, US$735 million in frozen assets) and fines of US 11.3 billion . . . easily the largest corruption investigation ever conducted in Brazil which counted on the collaboration of 30 countries authorities."[5] Roberto Leonel de Oliveira Lima, the tax authority auditor for the task force, confirmed the big construction companies received the highest penalties, upward of six hundred million dollars in taxes, fines, and interest.

It was in this context, a scandalization of politics, from which federal judge Sergio Moro emerged as a superhero who would purportedly install justice and order. Indeed, Moro was called Batman by many and even quoted Batman and Spider-Man's notions of justice in his court cases. His sidekicks, as intimated above, were global anticorruption agencies like Transparency International, called in to rescue the citizens of Brazil from these high-end corruptors. Massumi suggests that in these times of crisis, the first impulse is to "restore trust in the system" (2015, 6). "We need order in Brazil," said Edilson from Irajá in 2016. "I don't trust the leadership on the left or right—they are all corrupt. Let's just put them all in prison; this is what happens with too much *jeitinho*." As he noted, "the Brazilian *jeitinho*—or 'favor'—makes small-scale corruption a norm but are common and notable practices of giving favors" (Barbosa 1992; Jarrín 2017). An enduring culture in Brazil of accepted corruption through clientelist loyalty witnessed in the famous *rouba mas faz* (steal yet do) idiom in Brazil reflects this paradox (Pereira and Melo 2015). This creates social norms whereby politicians are seen as corrupt by nature and officials are elected as such so long as they serve their constituency through other measures.

As corruption discourse proliferated well beyond the usual talk of *jeitinho*, mainstream media like Globo TV circulated narratives that increasingly targeted the PT. It was not until journalist Glenn Greenwald published an analysis of several leaked conversations in the *Intercept Brasil* that the public was made aware this superhero could be more akin to villain, and what was seen as Sergio Moro's staunch defense of rule of law ultimately delegitimized when he accepted Bolsonaro's offer to join him as the minister of justice (Londoño and Casado 2020). Indeed, Greenwald's investigation confirmed what many believed had been collusion and Moro's influence on the prosecutors of Lava Jato. Deltan Dallagnol, one of the lead prosecutors who had dramatically portrayed "corruption [as] a serial-killer disguised as potholes, lack of medicine and street crime,"[6] soon became the face of another form of legal manipulation or legal corruption himself. Lava Jato, ultimately, revealed not only the depths of corruption but also the various ways in which politically motivated litigation could shake a precarious democracy. Indeed, Bolsonaro's leadership continues to use law in pernicious ways, charging Glenn Greenwald with criminal activity for what he defends is merely good journalism and free speech—hallmarks of a healthy democracy. But the question remains, how did one federal judge come to have such power? What was at stake? In what ways did this global lawfare operate?

GASLIGHTING AND OTHER IMPERIAL EXTRACTIONS

In conventional development literature, corruption is often framed as a symptom of poor governance. Global watchdog organizations like Transparency International envision their roles, by ranking and filing metrics of democracy, as monitoring states to help usher along order and rule of law. The conditions that allowed for these agencies to collaborate with federal jurisprudence in Brazil did not happen overnight. Since the early 2000s, international development agencies sought to export democracy and governance through collaborative efforts in Latin America (Dezalay and Garth 2002), effectively forging independent power structures based in courts and public ministries (Engelmann and Menuzzi 2020). This autonomous judiciary, structurally separate from the political sphere in Brazil, saw full force in Lava Jato. However, it was the slow and gradual internationalization of the MPF, and accompanying technocratic production, that created the conditions for corruption and anticorruption measures to work in such political ways.

In 2010, the CleanGovBiz was launched in several countries by the Organisation for Economic Co-operation and Development (OECD), which deployed anticorruption toolkits and trained public servants. The National Program for the Dissemination of International Legal Cooperation (Grotius Brazil), for example, had trained 364 agents by 2012 (Engelmann and Menuzzi 2020). Between 2000 and 2019, thirteen anticorruption laws were introduced to Brazilian jurisprudence. The 2000 Law of Fiscal Responsibility, 2009 Transparency Law, the 2013 Plea Bargaining Law, the 2016 Anti-Terrorism Law, and the 2019 Anti-Crime Packages are a few notable laws that became especially important for this judicialization. In that same time, eleven international agreements were conferred, including the Inter-American Convention against Corruption, the UN Convention against Corruption in International Commercial Transaction, and others that gradually encroached more and more directly in cooperation with the MPF—like the 2015 MPF and World Bank Memorandum. As Engelmann and Menuzzi argue, the internationalization of the MPF "forges a corporate path that goes beyond the original prerogatives set forth in the laws of the 1988 Constitution" (2020). Of these juridical innovations, the coupling of the anticorruption laws *with* the introduction of plea bargains created the conditions and mechanics for the "scandalization" of politics.

Within this context of global lawfare, the casualties of these new forms of power are clear. As Lava Jato took down corruption, it also stripped Petrobras of the crude sovereignty it once declared. After years of being the very bedrock of developmental nationalism—a solid symbol and reflection of the Brazilian state, that very inaugural moment in this chapter (and history of capitalism) when Petrobras launched its IPO leaves the residues of perhaps the quietest of corruption consequences—and yet easily the most excessive. Indeed, the transnational layer made possible by the reconfiguration of the international political economy and the ways that Petrobras's promiscuous connection to these big companies, of which Odebrecht dominated, are endemic to a neoliberal globalization that marks a particular habitus in the history and social life of Petrobras. Indeed, Petrobras has, in these years since the soft coup, gone from 40 percent para-petrol that were national to over 72 percent owned by Halliburton (Colombini 2020). Taken together, my interlocutors in 2011 were prophetic themselves when they suggested the "oil was sold long ago."

As I have conveyed throughout this chapter, the affective attachments and symbolics around Petrobras have shifted tremendously since Lula's terms. Within this backdrop, this chapter exposes how Brazilian anticorruption laws, officialized during PT leadership, were instrumentalized to target Petrobras and PT. Ultimately, global civil society and governance, NGOs like Transparency International enacted a "vertical topography of power" (Ferguson 2006) that operationalized innovations in jurisprudence that supported federal judge turned minister Sergio Moro, as a form of global justice hero against endemic corruption in Brazil. This obscured, rather perniciously, the extractive nature of the Petrobras corruption, which ultimately paid out 2.95 billion dollars in fines to the U.S. Department of Justice under the Foreign Corrupt Practices Act of 1977 (CNBC 2020). Indeed, this is one of the largest securities fraud settlements after Enron. To this day, Petrobras denies the accuracy of the wrongdoings but still had to pay out—revealing a deeper layer in this example of anticorruption politics that not only reifies the U.S. fiscal and hegemonic dominance but also begs the question of whom these corruption scandals ultimately benefited. Indeed, it reveals that lawfare and legal extraction via fines can accompany the shaming of the Global South using corruption as imperial practices of capital accumulation.

CONCLUSION

I began this chapter by recalling the feelings of euphoria when Petrobras's—and national—pride was at an all-time high in Brazil. I demonstrated the various ways in which political subjectivity is shaped by a subject's attachment to the resources of their national land, as patrimony, to interrogate the ways that subjects built a sense of national pride around these public goods in the face of neoliberal shifts in political economy. I then considered the "scandalization of politics" using the Petrobras corruption case to evaluate the ways in which the Brazilian judiciary increasingly gained autonomy since the 2000s. I argue that corruption and lawfare—especially the mechanics of anticorruption politics—operationalized during the Lava Jato also exploited the intimacies created during developmental nationalism and obscured the U.S. imperial and extractive nature of the graft, as Petrobras did not just "sell out" but rather was sold through the excesses of this exchange and complex legal warfare.

REFERENCES

Ansell, Aaron. 2018. "Impeaching Dilma Rousseff: The Double Life of Corruption Allegations on Brazil's Political Right." *Culture, Theory and Critique* 3 (1): 312–331.

Appadurai, Arjun. 1986. *The Social Life of Things: Commodities in Cultural Perspective*. New York: Cambridge University Press.

Barbosa, Lívia. 1992. *O jeitinho brasileiro: A arte de ser mais igual que os outros*. Rio de Janeiro: Editora Campus.

Bilenky, Thais. 2016. "Professor de Harvard ve 'presunção de culpa' contra Lula na Lava Jato." *Folha de São Paulo*, April 11, 2016. https://www1.folha.uol.com.br/poder/2016/11/1829175-professor-de-harvard-ve-presuncao-de-culpa-contra-lula-na-lava-jato.shtml.

Brooke, James. 1992. "Looting Brazil." *New York Times*, November 8, 1992, sec. 6. https://www.nytimes.com/1992/11/08/magazine/looting-brazil.html.

Carrion, Raul. 2003. "O Petróleo é Nosso: Mobilizaçao nacional grantiu monopólio estatal do ouro negro no Brasil." Jornal Eletrônico Novo Milênio, June 5, 2003. http://www.novomilenio.inf.br/cubatao/cfoto012.htm#Autor.

Clarke, Kamari. 2019. *Affective Justice: The International Criminal Court and the Pan-Africanist Pushback*. Durham, N.C.: Duke University Press.

Colombini, Iderley. 2020. "Golpe quebrou 40% das para-petroleiras nacionais e aumentou em 72% contratos da Halliburton com a Petrobras." *Revista Forum*, January 23, 2020. https://revistaforum.com.br/politica/golpe-quebrou-40-das-para-petroleiras-nacionais-e-aumentou-em-72-contratos-da-halliburton-com-a-petrobras/.

Comaroff, Jean, and John L. Comaroff. 2006. *Law and Disorder in the Postcolony*. Chicago: University of Chicago Press.

Dent, Alexander S., and Rosana Pinheiro-Machado. 2013. "Protesting Democracy in Brazil." Society for Cultural Anthropology, December 20, 2013. https://culanth.org/fieldsights/series/protesting-democracy-in-brazil.

Dezalay, Yves, and Bryant G. Garth. 2002. *The Internationalization of Palace Wars: Lawyers, Economists, and the Contest to Transform Latin American States*. Chicago: University of Chicago Press.

Engelmann, Fabiano, and Eduardo de Moura Menuzzi. 2020. "The Internationalization of the Brazilian Prosecutor's Office: Anti-corruption and Corporate Investments in the 2000's." *Brazilian Political Science Review* 14 (1): 1–35.

Ferguson, James. 2006. *Global Shadows: Africa in the Neoliberal World Order*. Durham, N.C.: Duke University Press.

Gall, Norman. 2011. "Oil in Deep Waters: Will Offshore Discoveries Change the Course of Brazil's Development?" *Braudel Papers*, no. 45.

Gupta, Akhil, and Sarah Muir. 2018. "Rethinking the Anthropology of Corruption." *Current Anthropology* 59 (S): S4–S15.

Hirschkind, Charles. 2006. *Ethical Soundscape: Cassette Sermons and Islamic Counterpublics*. New York: Columbia University Press.

Jarrín, Alvaro. 2017. *The Biopolitics of Beauty: Cosmetic Citizenship and Affective Capital in Brazil*. Berkeley: University of California Press.

Londoño, Ernesto, and Leticia Casado. 2020. "Glenn Greenwald in Bolsonaro's Brazil: 'I Trigger a Lot of Their Primal Rage.'" *New York Times*, January 25, 2020. https://www.nytimes.com/2020/01/25/world/americas/glenn-greenwald-brazil-blsonaro-cybercrimes.html.

Massumi, Brian. 1995. "The Autonomy of Affect." In "The Politics of Systems and Environments, Part II," special issue. *Cultural Critique*, no. 31 (Autumn): 83–109.

———. 2015. *The Power at the End of the Economy*. Durham, N.C.: Duke University Press.

Miranda, Maria Augusta Tibiriçá. 1983. *O petróleo é nosso*. Petrópolis: Editora Vozes.

Mitchell, Sean T. 2017. *Constellations of Inequality: Space, Race, and Utopia in Brazil*. Chicago: University of Chicago Press.

Nugent, David. 2018. "Corruption Now and Then: Managing Threats to the Nation in Twentieth Century Peru." *Current Anthropology* 59 (S18): S28–S36.

Pereira, Carlos, and Marcus André Melo. 2015. "Reelecting Corrupt Incumbents in Exchange for Public Goods: Rouba Mas Faz in Brazil." *Latin American Research Review* 50 (4): 88–115.

Pierson, Brendan. 2018. "Brazil's Petrobras to Pay $2.95 Billion to Settle US Class Action Lawsuit over Corruption." CNBC, January 3, 2018. https://www.cnbc.com/amp/2018/01/03/brazils-petrobras-to-settle-us-class-action-lawsuit-over-corruption.html.

Sartre, Jean Paul. (1977) 2004. *Critique of Dialectical Reason.* Vol. 1, *Theory of Practical Ensembles.* Translated by Alan Sheridan-Smith. London: Verso.

Williams, Raymond. 1977. *Marxism and Literature.* Oxford: Oxford University Press.

NOTES

1. Presalt is offshore natural gas and oil rich preserves, of which rich sources were discovered in 2007 off the Brazilian coast.
2. Planalto, "Presidente Lula Discurso na Bovespa" clip available at https://www.youtube.com/watch?v=NltjeqlqxkU&feature=relmfu (accessed September 11, 2020).
3. In 2013, Pré-Sal Petróleo S.A. was also established to manage related projects and funds, many of which were earmarked for antipoverty and education.
4. He also wrote a manuscript *The Size Switch* (*A Chave do Tamanho*), published in 1942, of which the central themes were the role of science and technology in generating a pace so fast humans would be "eaten" (anthropophagy is a recurring theme here). Other themes included the beliefs that war only resulted from political alienation of the masses, racial prejudice, and corporate greed.
5. Transparency International, "Operation Car Wash Task Force: Anti-corruption Award Winners 2016," clip available at https://www.youtube.com/watch?v=gHK9HhzaPog (accessed June 8, 2018).
6. Transparency International.

PART III INFRASTRUCTURES OF HOPE

9 · DESPAIRING HOPES (AND HOPEFUL DESPAIR) IN AMAZONIA

DAVID ROJAS, ALEXANDRE DE AZEVEDO OLIVAL,
AND ANDREZZA ALVES SPEXOTO OLIVAL

One afternoon in late November 2010, in a rural area some sixty miles from the village of Jaíli in the state of Mato Grosso in southern Amazonia, one of us (David) sat with Helena, a non-Indigenous peasant, watching images of Brazilian military police using helicopters and armored troop carriers to occupy several *favelas* in Rio de Janeiro.[1] A decade before, Helena and hundreds of other landless peasants, most of them of African and Indigenous heritage, occupied a dense forest on public lands, divided the area into hundreds of plots, and then pressured state officials to recognize the place as the official *assentamento* (rural settlement) of Novo Horizonte. Official recognition gave the *assentados* (people living in the *assentamento*) access to rural development programs that the center-left PT (Workers' Party) implemented during its tenure (2003–2016) with the stated intention of benefiting poor rural families. Immediately after meeting David, Helena invited him to spend an afternoon talking about all that she had endured (and achieved) in Novo Horizonte. But when the anthropologist arrived, they both remained staring at the television in silence, their attention captured by images of state violence originating thousands of miles away.

When Helena finally spoke, she connected, in a way that was surprising to David, the military-style invasion of Rio's *favelas* with her own experiences in the *assentamento*. She expressed contempt for *all* politicians (PT members included) who, she argued, claimed to work for the poor in places like Rio and the state of Mato Grosso but did nothing but advance the cause of the powerful. The PT rural development programs she had benefited from for more than a decade had not made Helena into one of the party's supporters but rather left her feeling profound contempt for the political establishment at large. Her stance in this regard was like that of a majority of people in rural Mato Grosso who, when the PT was ousted from power by an administrative coup d'état in 2016, did not display much support for the center-left party. The mass demonstrations in defense of the PT that took place in Rio, São Paulo, and other urban areas were absent from small cities in Mato Grosso such as Jaíli, the town in which Novo Horizonte was placed (Ríos Vera 2018). Such lack of support from the poor was also manifest in the electoral results of the 2018 presidential elections in which more than 60 percent of Mato Grosso's electorate voted for Jair Bolsonaro's extreme-right authoritarian project (Makino 2020; Rojas de Carvalho and Santos 2019).

Helena's comments on the military-style invasion of Rio's *favelas* open a window into some of the most significant affects that shaped non-Indigenous peasants' political life in the run-up to the 2018 presidential elections. Following Brazilian philosopher Vladimir Safatle's (2015) invitation to consider the political significance of affects such as abandonment, hope, and despair, we consider how political behaviors of *assentados* such as Helena were shaped by their sense that the PT, its social program notwithstanding, had abandoned them to grapple with destitution—and the powerful economic forces at its roots—on their own. When Helena shared with David the story of her life, she alluded to something akin to what Elizabeth Povinelli (2011) calls an "economy of abandonment" insofar as she had been treated as cheap, disposable labor even when the PT was in power. The open wounds left by such experiences made Helena doubt that the PT's center-left political agenda could help her keep her smallholding afloat. Instead of committing herself to party platforms of ideals, she attached her hopes to patronage interactions with local elites who gave her access to government programs and rural commodity markets in exchange for her vote and labor (on the situated transactions out of which patronage relations emerge, see Collins, this volume).

But such hopes were, crucially, infused with profound despair insofar as she knew that working with landed elites meant contributing to economic dynamics that undermined the economic viability of the settlement of Novo Horizonte that she had worked so hard to establish. We allude to the affective ambivalence expressed by people such as Helena using the term *despairing hopes*. By that we mean an affective condition under which persons and groups come to sense that the best path forward is one that requires attaching themselves to relationships that they know are harmful to their dreams (see Bangstad, Bertelsen, and Henkel 2019; Berlant 2011). Such despairing hopes, we argue, drive the attachments to authoritarian efforts, which, in contemporary Brazil and elsewhere, are grounded on the nihilistic sense that, as Sean T. Mitchell (this volume) puts it, "all forms of collective striving for the public good are doomed to failure." From this perspective, all that remains possible is pursuing aggressively individualistic goals while mounting nihilistic attacks on established political ideals, institutions, and agendas (see Brown 2019, 177–179).

If, however, despairing hopes feed into authoritarian dynamics, in this chapter we also show that grassroots political efforts can generate affective conditions that carry the promise of nonauthoritarian politics. This part of our argument focuses on the peasant-led grassroots organization, Instituto Ouro Verde (IOV), which works in southern Amazonia with some twelve hundred non-Indigenous peasant families who live in twenty-five *assentamentos* and thirty rural communities across eight municipalities. IOV members are for the most part nonwhite community leaders who came to southern Amazonia as landless peasants and became involved in rural development projects being implemented by the military government (1964–1985). Having lived in Amazonia for decades, they acutely sense that those with no cash will see no relief from their plight anytime soon and that political institutions will offer very little help as they struggle to preserve their lands and livelihoods. Such a sense of abandonment does not, however, lead IOV members to seek favors from landed elites; instead, they join networks of mutual support through which peasants provide one another with resources that help them endure profoundly adverse socioeconomic conditions. Such efforts are grounded in an affective condition we call "hopeful despair," in which, as Robyn Marasco (2015) suggests, disheartenment is not debilitating but instead fuels "a restless passion that keeps things moving as earthly projects and purposes fall into disrepair" (13–14). To understand how this may be the case, we shall first return to Helena's 2010 comments on the authoritarian actions of the Brazilian state in Rio's *favelas*.

AN AMAZONIAN VIEW ON THE LIMITS OF THE PT'S DEVELOPMENT APPROACH

Sitting beside a silent Helena, David assumed, wrongly, that she was appalled by a military-style invasion that, by targeting a *favela*, undermined self-construction efforts analogous to those she had advanced in Novo Horizonte. To be sure, there are fundamental differences between urban *favelas* and rural *assentamentos*. The former are built in densely populated areas by vibrant communities that have to endure violence at the hands of the police, paramilitary forces, and gangs (Willis 2015; Larkins 2015). *Assentamentos*, on the other hand, are built in rural areas by cash-poor non-Indigenous peoples who cut trees to make space for settlements while resisting efforts from agribusiness and other extractive operations to appropriate their hard-won lands (Ioris 2017; Rojas 2016; Rojas, Azevedo Olival, and Alves Spexoto Olival 2020). These crucial differences notwithstanding, both *favelas* and *assentamentos* are self-built spaces constructed by peoples who struggle against socioeconomic exclusion and political disenfranchisement (Holston 1991; Otsuki 2013). Both spaces, moreover, were included in the PT's development policies as areas in which state institutions should support cash-poor communities and carve neighborhoods out of hills and settlements out of forests (Holston 2008; Lara 2013).

Given the role played by such spaces in the PT's development agenda, the military-style invasion in Rio laid bare the contradictions of the party's approach. To be sure, the PT did not plan or implement these operations itself. The city and state governments in Rio de Janeiro were controlled by the Democrats party (DEM) and the Brazilian Democratic Movement party (MDB), respectively. The invasion, however, was advanced in preparation for the 2014 World Cup and 2016 Summer Olympics, which took place in Rio, thanks in large part to the PT's aggressive lobbying of international sporting bodies. The federal government saw these global events as opportunities to invest billions of dollars in projects that would benefit a "new middle class" (Mitchell, this volume) while generating tax revenues that could be used in pro-poor national programs. These federal projects were used in places like Rio by parties such as the DEM and the MDB to fund projects designed to attract a global elite that, they assumed, had to be reassured that it was safe to invest in Rio. It was in this way that the PT's pro-poor agenda became complicit with the so-called pacification of the *favelas* in a performance of state violence, whereby more than two thousand special forces members using armored troop carriers and military helicopters invaded Rio's *favelas* and criminalized its inhabitants so that national and global elites would invest in the city (Larkins 2018).

With these thoughts in mind, David sat waiting for the moment that Helena would comment on the contradictions of a pro-poor federal development agenda that paradoxically led to militarized police forces targeting people like her. And yet when Helena spoke about the images on the screen, she did so in admiration for "the military," which, she claimed, "steals but gets things done." In places like Rio and Mato Grosso, she argued, all political parties catered to the rich while pretending to advance projects for the poor. From her perspective, the military-style invasion did not betray a political agenda in which she could place any hopes but rather showed her that the military police, compared to political parties, acted in ways that were refreshingly unambiguous in their violence.

SOUTHERN AMAZONIA'S ECONOMIES OF ABANDONMENT

Helena's interest in the TV images disappeared when David, skeptical about her comments regarding the military, said "but things improved after the end of the military government, right?" She responded with a story she recounted with the tense patience of someone struggling to be polite while correcting someone clueless.

Some of the worst things she had lived through, Helena said, did not occur during the military regime but rather in Jaíli's rainy season of 2003–2004. Having just started to open her smallholding in Novo Horizonte, she had only cleared enough forest to make space for a makeshift tent and a small garden. There was no road between Novo Horizonte and Jaíli at the time, and the *assentamento* remained mostly uninhabited as many *assentados*, Helena's husband included, were forced to spend months in faraway locations working to gain the cash they needed to open their smallholdings. Living alone and isolated in her makeshift tent, she struggled with critters that came out of the surrounding forest to raid the garden in which she grew the food crops on which she relied. Her situation deteriorated further as the rainy season brought floods that blocked the trail to Jaíli and undermined her food crops. Even forest animals, it seemed, were having a hard time as they began attacking Helena's garden with increased frequency. Lacking food, Helena grew increasingly weak, eventually falling ill and having to spend days in a bed under which her injured dogs cowered as the rain poured in through her tent's plastic roof.

The worst was yet to come, though, delivered not by rains or the forest but by state officials whom Helena met when she finally dragged herself to Jaíli's clinic, sick and emaciated. Her requests for food assistance and health care were met with dismissive questions about her provenance, the reasons she was establishing a smallholding in public forests, and evasive answers regarding what state officials could do to help someone like her who lacked proof of residence in Jaíli. She was treated, Helena said, not as a person whose life was at stake but as an "animal" that should be abandoned to its fate. "They treated me like a dog," she told me, "and I could not stay [in Jaíli] begging them [state officials] for food, so I came back here [to Novo Horizonte] to suffer with my dogs, surviving any way I could, until [my husband] came back."

David's assumption that Helena's living conditions had improved during democratic times was focused on the violence promoted by the military government when it allowed white entrepreneurs to move into Amazonia from southern Brazil claiming the land of forest peoples as their own (Schmink and Woods 1992). Helena reminded the anthropologist of another continuing "slow violence" (Nixon 2011) that kept burning long after the military regime ended. What Helena described was the harm of economies of abandonment in which persons are reduced to cheap, disposable laborers who are expected to toil in dangerous conditions enduring exploitation in silence and out of sight. And this violence, as Povinelli (2011) claims and Helena's story confirms, was perfectly compatible with liberal, center-left democratic agendas like those advanced by the PT.

By 2010 Helena's makeshift tent and half of the trees on her property were gone and in their place stood two modest brick houses surrounded by pastures. The *assentamento* as a whole had also undergone major changes. Thousands of acres of forests had been transformed into pastures, a dirt road now made it possible to reach Jaíli by a four-hour bus ride (organized by a local supermarket twice a week to attract customers), and in 2009 it had been connected to the federal electricity grid. All these improvements were related to large-scale rural development programs pursued at the federal level by the PT, such as Luz para Todos (Light for Everyone; LpT) and the Programa Nacional de Fortalecimento da Agricultura Familiar (National Program for Strengthening Family Agriculture; PRONAF).

Despite their impact in places like Jaíli, for Helena these programs had done nothing to counter the forces that pushed her nearly to starvation seven years earlier. From her perspective, one could see how these programs and the lofty ideals on which they were based did little to undermine the grip that local elites had on people like Helena. LpT, for instance, was advanced by PT officials who rejected the long-standing argument that it was impossible to connect cash-poor rural communities to the electricity grid as this would not generate the monetary returns needed to cover the initial investment (Freitas and Silveira 2015). Making equity rather than efficiency their principle, LpT officials connected more than fifteen million of Brazil's poorest people to the grid by 2016 (Freitas and Oliveira 2017). However, besides leaving behind some possible beneficiaries and suffering cutbacks in the last days of PT rule (see Camargo and Ribeiro 2015) in places like Jaíli, LpT was rolled out in such a way that it was co-opted by local elites.

Powerful families in Jaíli, for instance, seemed capable of determining the order in which LpT reached particular *assentamentos* and families. Novo Horizonte, a settlement established with the acquiescence of local elites who encouraged marginalized people to move in so that they could hire them at low wages and capture their votes in local elections, was electrified in 2009. In contrast, by 2012 other settlements in the municipality in which landless peasants were engaged in land struggles against landholders were still waiting for electrification crews. Similar dynamics were apparent at the level of individual properties. When Helena wanted to establish two connections on her smallholding—one for each of the two houses that she and her husband built—she petitioned a powerful rancher to whom she was renting her pastures. Although they were a couple, she argued, one house was hers and the other was her husband's, so they needed two separate connections. Although the petition ran against LpT's regulations mandating one connection per family, the electrification crew—which working far from managers and overseers had significant discretionary powers—linked both buildings to the grid in a way that Helena and her neighbors thought showed the clout of local elites over the federal program.

The sense that abstract ideals such as equity were less important than the influence of local elites in the rollout of federal programs had a profound impact on the electoral behavior of *assentados*. In 2012, six months before that year's municipal elections, David participated in animated discussions with Novo Horizonte's smallholders, who talked about how much money they would make by selling their votes and whether it would be more profitable to sell them one by one or as a set that would comprise the votes of all family members. Besides making cash, *assentados* discussed how by selling their votes they could establish close relationships with local elites and thus have privileged access to government programs.

These conversations had no room for abstract generalities such as political ideals or party platforms. In fact, not even one of the political parties to which various local elites belonged were mentioned with any regularity. Instead of ideological commitments or partisan affiliations, *assentados* focused their attention on how situated interactions with particular persons and families could result in relationships that they hoped would provide them with some stability in deeply precarious conditions (see Collins, this volume). These hopes, however, were enveloped by a sense of despair. They came with the understanding that the life trajectories of people like them were at the mercy of unaccountable elites who, the favors they offered them notwithstanding, trapped smallholders in subordinate political and economic relationships.

Despairing hopes in Novo Horizonte were also associated with other federal efforts such as PRONAF, a program designed to support family agriculture. Once the electrical grid reached the *assentamento*, a dairy company began installing cooling units in which people like Helena stored the milk they produced until a refrigerated cistern truck picked it up for transport to the village, where it was pasteurized and commercialized. Most of the pastures on which these milk cows grazed were established with PRONAF loans, which *assentados* did *not* receive in cash but as packages of inputs and tools crafted by technicians working for the municipality. Although federal instances often stressed that the program's funds could be used to support agro-ecology initiatives and women-led undertakings (Sabourin 2007), in Jaíli PRONAF technicians systematically encouraged settlers to establish pastures that they could rent to powerful ranchers or use themselves to graze milk cows whose produce they would sell to the one dairy company in town.

As a result, PRONAF did not challenge established economic relations but rather transformed *assentados* into buffers that landholders used to manage their exposure to market risks. Once PRONAF was in place, landed elites could capitalize on favorable economic conditions without engaging in the costly and lengthy process of cutting trees and seeding grasses to produce milk or beef. Rather, they could simply rent pastures that *assentados* had already established with PRONAF funds or buy more milk in the *assentamento*. And if market conditions turned sour, elites could limit their losses by quickly withdrawing from *assentamentos*, leaving settlers starved of cash. In such conditions, while PRONAF awarded landholders significant freedom of choice regarding the allocation of their investments, it trapped peasants in the risky business of maintaining healthy pastures that could sustain milk production or attract renters.

Even those *assentados* who managed to establish profitable pastures faced precarious long-term prospects. Both milk-production and pasture-renting agreements involved slim margins that left smallholders with just enough money to cover living expenses. As Helena told David that November afternoon in 2010, her pastures were sustaining cows just fine, and she was making enough to get by renting to a rancher whose cattle we could see through the living room window. Yet she knew that parts of her smallholding had already been covered by grass for more than five years and that grazing would soon deplete the soil. Although it was theoretically possible to till and fertilize her land, she had been unable to save the money this would have required, and she faced the possibility she would soon be able to graze fewer and fewer cows in her land. This, in turn, would mean living with less and less money year after year until eventually she would be forced to sell her land, falling back into the landless condition in which she had endured much harm.

When David last visited Jaíli in 2015, it was obvious that, as Helena had anticipated, PRONAF had done little to help smallholders keep their land in Novo Horizonte. From friends in the settlement, he learned that about 30 percent of the smallholdings had been sold by their proprietors. Lack of customers meant the supermarket in Jaíli cut the frequency of its bus route to the settlement in half to only once per week. Still, Helena and others had managed to use their relations with landed elites to keep their pastures healthy. But even those who managed to retain their land had no future as *assentados*. The future seemed to hold only two alternatives: most of them would fall back to the condition of landless living, while a lucky few would consolidate relatively large properties and transition to the status of landholders.

Despite injecting large sums of money into Novo Horizonte, by 2015 LpT and PRONAF had failed to prevent smallholders such as Helena from feeling as abandoned as they had felt in 2003 at the start of the PT's thirteen-year rule. In their everyday lives, they witnessed how the PT's propoor rural development plans did little to avoid exposing *assentados* to systematic dispossession. In Helena's experience, political parties of all stripes—the PT included—touted grand platforms and ideals but operated in a profoundly pragmatic way (Mendes Loureiro and Saad-Filho 2019), which ultimately benefited the rich and powerful. Little wonder then that *assentados* could not see the PT as an institution deserving of their support were it to be attacked (as was the case since 2016) by authoritarian forces in Brazilian politics. While placing their hopes in patronage relationships, they despaired about the sheer impossibility of collective politics (Collins, this volume) and invested in authoritarian political relationships that undermined their own flourishing (Berlant 2011; Marasco 2015). It was in this context that in the 2018 presidential elections more than 60 percent of people in Jaíli voted for Jair Bolsonaro.

HOPES OUT OF DESPAIR

Helena's story teaches us how, while succeeding in the technocratic task of investing billions in pro-poor programs, the PT failed in the essential affective task of eliciting hopes in collective politics among the rural poor in Mato Grosso. This story of despairing hopes, however, is only one of many one can find in Amazonia. When two of us, Alexandre and Andrezza, first arrived in Mato Grosso as veterinary doctors interested in programs that supported family agriculture, they learned from smallholders about socioeconomic systems that, having exploited and dispossessed them for generations, were unlikely to disappear anytime soon. However, from the same smallholders, Alexandre and Andrezza also learned that hope can flourish even amid pervasive despair.

Both insights informed Alexandre's and Andrezza's taking part in the creation of the IOV, a grassroots organization led by peasants who in 2003 began operating in the city of Alta Floresta in the state of Mato Grosso. While other environmental organizations ground their work on the understanding that socioecological catastrophe in Amazonia is now "unavoidable" and all there is to do is lessen profound devastation (Rojas 2020), the work carried out at the IOV is more hopeful. This is clear in the organization's flagship project Seeds of the Portal, which was designed to assist peasants in helping each other remain on their smallholdings and grow back some of the forest that had been cleared. The objective, however, is not to bring back native vegetation to meet conservation objectives but rather to establish agroforestry systems in which native trees grow side-by-side with crops that peasants use for their own consumption or commerce. These unnatural but livable ecological configurations are established using seeds that project members themselves gather in remaining forests, store in community seed banks (which are managed by peasants themselves), and give to project participants for free.

The role of Alexandre and Andrezza in this project is unlike that of PRONAF technicians, who see themselves as knowing best what smallholders should do. In contrast, Seeds of the Portal was born out of smallholders' demands for mechanisms that could allow peasants to share with each other their own knowledge and labor. In meetings regularly held by IOV participants, *assentados* share with one another seed gathering techniques and planting strategies that are useful when planting native and nonnative seeds together. Among the things they collectively learn is how by mixing species it is possible to enrich soils and protect waterways. This means that for their smallholdings to flourish, they may not rely on pasture monocultures or landed elites. In this sense, what results from IOV projects are "material hopes" (Kopper, this volume) or spaces in which smallholders, despite their sense of abandonment and despair, can imagine a future in which marginalized peoples and nonhuman species work together to create a rural world that has a place for people like them (see Rojas, Azevedo Olival, and Alves Spexoto Olival, 2020).

What we call hopeful despair can be seen embodied in the house of Nathalia (see figure 9.1), a woman in her sixties who Alexandre and Andrezza met in 2007 when they began working with the IOV in the municipality in which she lived. Whenever she talked to us about what she had accomplished by taking part in IOV programs, she did not stress soil fertility, crop yields, or waterway protection as much as taking part in a grassroots movement that enabled her to inch closer to a place she saw in a recurrent dream she had since her teenage years. In the dream, she was standing at the end of a trail in Amazonia, and from there she could see a piece of land she knew was hers—a land in which she would be able to live a life worth living. When she woke, she took note of the trail's distinctive traits in the hope that, if she came across it one day, she would be able to recognize it. It was because of this that she memorized the image of two large rocks, one rounded and one sliced, that stood at the beginning of a trail that then went around a small lake that led to a sixty-foot tree by a ditch. The dream-space at the end of this path generated a bundle of affects in the subjective space of Nathalia's sleeping mind. And yet the dream and the hopes it nourished were not a purely subjective affair insofar as it had emerged against landscape defined by economic exploitation and social discrimination that shaped Nathalia's affective attachments (see Navaro-Yashin 2009).

Although Nathalia was very introverted as a result of people in her town questioning her morality as a survivor of sexual abuse and as a worker in a *buteco* (small bar), she opened up to Alexandre and Andrezza, thanks to their common involvement in IOV's grassroots movement. They not only had time to know one another during workshops and meetings but sometimes spent the

FIGURE 9.1. The house that Nathalia built in the late 1980s, abandoned in the late 1990s, and returned to in 2018
Photo by David Rojas, 2018.

night together with other IOV participants as storms or other unexpected events prevented meeting attendees from traveling back to their places of origin. It was thus that Alexandre and Andrezza came to know that Nathalia's family had always had profoundly precarious attachments to the land. She was a toddler when her family fled their native state of Paraná in southern Brazil, escaping violent land struggles. During the following years, they moved around southern Brazil, unable to settle down permanently in part due to Nathalia being denied entry to public schools because she was Black. Only at age eleven did her family settle in a place that was safe and in which she had access to education—but only three years later, she left school and began working at her family's smallholding. Then at age nineteen, only four days after giving birth to her first daughter, she hopped on a truck with her husband and embarked on a sixteen-day trip to Mato Grosso, where life proved to be just as hard as it had been in Paraná.

After bearing her second daughter and determined to control some of the factors that were defining the course of her life, Nathalia began saving as much money as she could from low-paying jobs to undergo a sterilization procedure. But before she saved enough, her father presented her with an opportunity that, for her, was as definitive as choosing how many children she would have: land speculators were selling a smallholding for a price that she could afford with her current savings. She decided to make the purchase when her father told her that he had seen the place, a beautiful land that could be reached by walking down a trail that featured two large rocks, one rounded and one split, then went around a small lake, and finally reaching a large tree that stood by a ditch. So it was that, in the late 1980s, having abandoned her plans for the surgery, she felt close to making reality a dream she had since she was a teenager.

As it was for most settlers with whom Alexandre and Andrezza work in southern Amazonia, Nathalia's purchasing of the land did *not* mean she now had a hold on it. The smallholding was completely covered with dense forest, the nearest village could only be reached by a long walk, and after moving there, she and her husband were not able to generate the income needed to sustain their two infant daughters, the youngest of whom was only six months old. Unable to breastfeed because she herself lacked proper nourishment, Nathalia resorted to feeding her baby watered-down powdered milk while working as hard as she could clearing as much forest as they could and establishing pastures that they could rent to local ranchers. As the years went by and the trees fell, Nathalia's family kept growing. She gave birth to three more daughters at this smallholding, which, despite all their efforts, a full decade after she first set foot on it, still did not generate a livable income. Living in destitution in a place with no school that her daughters could attend, the family's situation deteriorated, and Nathalia's husband became increasingly violent toward her and his daughters.

By the late 1990s, as her land slipped through her fingers, Nathalia divorced her abusive husband and moved to the city where she endured harm similar to that experienced by Helena in Jaíli where, as in other Brazilian settings, systemic violence against Afro-Brazilian women is not rare. Without a job, Nathalia was unable to afford the mandatory uniforms needed to send her five daughters to public school. As their economic situation deteriorated, she was forced to feed her family discarded produce she found in the trash. "I was all alone," she said, recalling that time. "I had nothing, and do you know what nothing was?" In her story, nothing was seeing her daughters starve, losing all her teeth due to malnourishment, experiencing her own mental and physical health deteriorate to the point of suffering a near-complete breakdown, and feeling so awkward in her frail body that when Alexandre and Andrezza first met her, she barely talked in public, and when she did, she dared not look her interlocutors in the eye.

And yet at the very limits of what her mind and body could endure, she refused to sell the land of her dreams. People who knew her at the time told her, she recounted, "You are crazy, you starve because you want to, you have a smallholding you can sell." To this she replied, "And once I have spent the money [provided by the selling] of the smallholding, then what will I eat?" Such a profound despair contains the seeds of a particular kind of hope: because all was in a sense lost, there was not much to gain from giving up on her dream.

With the help of a woman Nathalia knew in town, in the early 2000s she was able to open a *buteco* (small bar) that allowed her to feed her children and send them to school. Still, this job provided her no pathway back to her smallholding and left her stuck in a job that exposed her to sexual violence. Still searching for a way back to her smallholding, Nathalia joined, in 2007, an IOV women-led program that taught artisanal skills; later, the program became involved in the Seeds of the Portal project. "These people are crazy," Nathalia first thought about those who were working hard to grow trees in places in which the forest had been cleared at immense personal and economic cost. Her doubts notwithstanding, she wanted to remain part of the IOV's community of peers, many of them women who had lived through life experiences similar to hers. Seeds of the Portal, moreover, gave her a reason to go back to her smallholding, not to live in it initially, but to work long hours in a small reforestation plot she established using only native tree species.

She changed her mind about agroforestry when she traveled with other IOV members to reforestation smallholdings in which other Seeds of the Portal members grew a wide range of native plants together with species that yielded fruit and raw materials. Drawing inspiration from her peer's experiments, she designed agroforestry projects that could produce fibers for making crafts and, eventually, she then helped organize a group of women who used these materials to make baskets, decorative weavings, and placemats (see figure 9.2). After Mato Grosso's ranching economy had left Nathalia with "nothing," other smallholders gave her seeds and knowledge that, together with the other women in the group, made it possible to gain her land back. Over the next decade,

FIGURE 9.2. Stalks grown by Nathalia as part of the work she carries out with a group of women
Photo by David Rojas, 2018.

Nathalia's health recovered; she was able to pay for dental work, which bolstered her confidence; and in 2019 she represented the IOV at a national agro-forestry conference.

Her dream had been rekindled and transformed in fundamental ways. To hold on to her land no longer meant establishing grass monocultures to rent to local elites; instead, she worked alongside marginalized people who affirmed abandonment as a condition of contingency that opened possibilities for working alongside others seeking alternative modes of living (Safatle 2016, 21).

CONCLUSION

Since 2013, a dramatic affective swing has defined Brazilian political life. Within the span of a few years, a country that gave people around the world hopes in new progressivist approaches became one of the hubs of an international wave of extreme-right government. After the uncommonly high popularity rates of PT officials collapsed in 2013 and an administrative *coup d'état* derailed the PT's center-left agenda in 2016, an extremist known for his authoritarian, racist, classist, and homophobic sentiments was elected president (see Holston 2014; Anderson 2019).

In rural *assentamentos* in Amazonia, the shift unfolded in less dramatic ways than in urban settings. Whereas major Brazilian cities were shaken by popular protests during the final years of the PT regime, *assentamentos* and small cities in southern Amazonia remained relatively calm (the celebration of Jair Bolsonaro's victory in late 2018 with fireworks and shots fired in the air being among the loudest expressions of political opinion that we the authors of this chapter have experienced during this time). Part of the reason is that in places like Jaíli, there was no affective swing from pink hopes to authoritarian despair, as *assentados* never developed strong affective attachments to the PT's institutional agenda or the ideas on which said agenda was based. This was clear in the story recounted by Helena as the televised invasion of Rio's *favelas* played in the background, and her hopes were reduced to the despairing sense that the best she could do was to attach herself and her smallholding to elites whose actions were harmful to her (on such behaviors, see Bangstad, Bertelsen, and Henkel 2019; Berlant 2011; Mitchell, this volume; Stewart 2017).

Acknowledging despairing hopes among *assentados* makes it easier to understand how, despite substantial investment by the PT in poor rural communities in southern Amazonia, people like Helena turned their backs on the party and instead supported Jair Bolsonaro's elitist, racist, protofascist project. The PT's center-left strategies not only failed to grow a durable political base but created a situation in which a nihilistic idea blossomed: that nothing could be expected from ambitious social undertakings and there was nothing to do but to ingratiate oneself with unaccountable elites who promise nothing beyond a fragile sort of protection (see Safatle 2016; Mitchell, this volume).

And as we consider despairing hopes, we can also understand that, as scholars working on the politics of affect have shown, affective attachments to authoritarian relationships are neither a subjective issue nor the expression that something is "wrong" with disaffected publics (Stewart 2017). Rather, this affective condition is a result of relationships that persons and groups have established with material landscapes and other people over the course of their lives (Massumi 2015; Kopper, this volume). In this sense, Helena's and Nathalia's sense of abandonment did not express the inner worlds of two Afro-Brazilian women so much as it demonstrated how they were systematically marginalized and exploited. And because they were both manifesting "affects generated by space and the non-human environment" (Navaro-Yashin 2009, 4), their affects were not theirs alone but generated by sprawling monocultures, isolated *assentamentos*, and increasingly depopulated rural areas that exuded hope enveloped by despair (Navaro-Yashin 2009).

From this perspective, we argue that the affective work involved in breaking out of authoritarian, protofascist attachments cannot be carried out individually but requires horizontal networks of support that are capable of carrying out material interventions of the kind that alter relations between subjects and landscapes (Navaro-Yashin 2009). Such is the work that, we argue (and we hope), IOV participants perform as they engage in reforestation efforts that not only yield economic outcomes but establish complex multispecies formations that reshape dreams and hopes. As Nathalia told us, as she worked with other smallholders and visited agro-forestry smallholdings, the land of her dreams ceased to be one covered by pastures rented out to local elites, becoming instead an agro-forestry smallholding established by sharing seeds, knowledge, and experiences with other *assentados* like her.

At a time when the rise of authoritarian projects across the globe is the cause of much despair, Nathalia reminds us that the wounds opened by extreme loss do not necessarily need to result in inaction or authoritarian behaviors but can result in hopeful despair. Here abandonment is asserted as a condition that opens possibilities for people seeking alliances with peers with whom they may try to correct what ails them (Povinelli 2011, 103, Safatle 2016). To say that *assentados* like Nathalia have found ways to keep their struggles alive against all odds does not however mean that we should see them as having found the secret for defeating authoritarian dynamics. Such an argument would do nothing less than place on the shoulders of dispossessed populations the responsibility for finding a way out of a global political predicament driven by exceedingly wealthy and powerful groups.

While thus far IOV participants have been able to build networks of mutual support while enduring extreme harm, under the Bolsonaro administration, the funding on which the grassroots organization relied has all but disappeared. Meanwhile, environmental crimes spike, deforestation rates explode, massive forest fires rage every dry season, and monoculture plantations rapidly expand. And in 2020, Brazil became one of the global epicenters of the COVID-19 pandemic, and Bolsonaro and his administration not only rejected scientific advice on the disease and how to contain it but actively undermined any collective measure that could provide relief to the pandemic. Due to COVID-19, Alexandre and Andrezza have been forced to suspend meetings and gatherings that were already scaled back due to funding issues, thus limiting exchanges through which smallholders help one another. These compounding dynamics undermine not only agroforestry smallholdings but also, more importantly, the material conditions that have enabled people like Nathalia to keep alive a restless passion even when it is clear that dire times await her. Hopeful despair then is not in itself an antidote against protofascistic authoritarianism but rather a reminder that establishing solidarity networks and novel relations with nonhumans is required if generous modes of living are to flourish out of the ruins of yesteryear's hopes.

REFERENCES

Anderson, Perry. 2019. "Bolsonaro's Brazil." *London Review of Books* 41 (3): 11–22.
Bangstad, Sindre, Bjørn Enge Bertelsen, and Heiko Henkel. 2019. "The Politics of Affect." *Focaal*, no. 83, 98–113. https://www.berghahnjournals.com/view/journals/focaal/2019/83/fcl830110.xml.
Berlant, Lauren Gail. 2011. *Cruel Optimism*. Durham, N.C.: Duke University Press.
Brown, Wendy. 2019. *In the Ruins of Neoliberalism: The Rise of Antidemocratic Politics in the West*. New York: Columbia University Press.
Camargo, Ednaldo José Silva de, and Fernando Selles Ribeiro. 2015. "Programa luz para todos: Avanços e retrocessos–um novo estoque de excluídos." Paper presented at the 10th Congresso sobre Geração Distribuída e Energia no Meio Rural, São Paulo University, São Paulo, November 11–13, 2015.
de Carvalho, N. R., and Orlando dos Santos Jr. 2019. "Bolsonaro and the Inequalities of Geographical Development in Brazil." *Journal of Latin American Geography* 18 (1): 198–202.
Freitas, Gilmar Fialho de, and Marcelo Leles Romarco de Oliveira. 2017. "Uma análise do programa luz para todos do governo federal." *Revista de extensão e estudos rurais* 6 (2): 143–155.
Freitas, Gisele de, and Suely de Fátima Ramos Silveira. 2015. "Programa luz para todos: Uma representação da teoria do programa por meio do modelo lógico." *Planejamento e políticas públicas*, no. 45, 1–22.
Holston, James. 1991. "Autoconstruction in Working-Class Brazil." *Current Anthropology* 6:447–465.
———. 2008. *Insurgent Citizenship: Disjunctions of Democracy and Modernity in Brazil*. Princeton, N.J.: Princeton University Press.
Ioris, Antonio A. R. 2017. "Encroachment and Entrenchment of Agro-Neoliberalism in the Centre-West of Brazil." *Journal of Rural Studies* 51:15–27.
Lara, Fernando Luiz. 2013. "Favela Upgrade in Brazil: A Reverse of Participatory Processes." *Journal of Urban Design* 18 (4): 553–564.
Larkins, Erika Robb. 2015. *The Spectacular Favela: Violence in Modern Brazil*. Berkeley: University of California Press.
———. 2018. "Police, Hospitality, and Mega-Event Security in Rio de Janeiro." In *The Anthropology of Police*, edited by Kevin G. Karpiak and William Garriott, 139–152. New York: Routledge.
Makino, Rogério. 2020. "Bolsonarismo e branquitude: Notas sobre as eleições presidenciais de 2018 em mato grosso." *Geografia: Ambiente, educação e sociedades* 3 (1): 125–136.
Marasco, Robyn. 2015. *The Highway of Despair: Critical Theory after Hegel*. New York: Columbia University Press.
Massumi, Brian. 2015. *Politics of Affect*. Cambridge, UK: Polity.
Mendes Loureiro, Pedro, and Alfredo Saad-Filho. 2019. "The Limits of Pragmatism: The Rise and Fall of the Brazilian Workers' Party (2002–2016)." *Latin American Perspectives* 46 (1): 66–84.
Navaro-Yashin, Yael. 2009. "Affective Spaces, Melancholic Objects: Ruination and the Production of Anthropological Knowledge." *Journal of the Royal Anthropological Institute* 15 (1): 1–18.
Nixon, Rob. 2011. *Slow Violence and the Environmentalism of the Poor*. Cambridge, Mass.: Harvard University Press.
Otsuki, Kei. 2013. *Sustainable Development in Amazonia: Paradise in the Making*. New York: Routledge.
Povinelli, Elizabeth A. 2011. *Economies of Abandonment: Social Belonging and Endurance in Late Liberalism*. Durham, N.C.: Duke University Press.
Ríos Vera, Luis José. 2018. "Tres etapas del golpe 'blando' en Brasil: Hacia una rearticulación social del capital." *Revista de ciencias sociales* 31 (43): 183–204.

Rojas, David. 2016. "'This Is Not Science Fiction': Amazonian Narratives of Climate Change." In *Anthropology and Climate Change: From Actions to Transformations,* edited by Susan A. Crate and Mark Nutall, 271–279. New York: Routledge.

———. 2020. "Crisis Progressive: Environmental Ethics in a Time of 'Unavoidable' Ecological Destruction in Amazonia." *Ethnos,* 1–23. https://doi.org/10.1080/00141844.2020.1736596.

Rojas, David, Alexandre de Azevedo Olival, and Andrezza Alves Spexoto Olival. 2020. "Cultivating Alternatives to Authoritarian Populism in Amazonia." *Journal of Latin American and Caribbean Anthropology* 24 (4): 958–981.

Sabourin, Eric. 2007. "Que política pública para a agricultura familiar no segundo governo Lula?" *Sociedade e estado* 22 (3): 715–751.

Safatle, Vladimir. 2016. *O circuito dos afetos: Corpos políticos, desamparo e o fim do indivíduo.* São Paulo: Cosac Naify.

Schmink, Marianne, and Charles H. Wood. 1992. *Contested Frontiers in Amazonia.* New York: Columbia University Press.

Stewart, Kathleen. 2017. "In the World That Affect Proposed." *Cultural Anthropology* 32 (2): 192–198.

Willis, Graham Denyer. 2015. *The Killing Consensus: Police, Organized Crime, and the Regulation of Life and Death in Urban Brazil.* Oakland: University of California Press.

NOTE

1. We use pseudonyms when referring to all places and persons (other than the authors) mentioned in this chapter.

10 · TEMPERED HOPES

(Re)producing the Middle Class in Recife's Alternative Music Scene

FALINA ENRIQUEZ

In 2011, in the capital city of Recife, Pernambuco, the mostly middle-class musicians who were part of the metropolitan area's alternative scene (*cena alternativa*) were struggling to make ends meet as they sought to maintain music as their sole profession.[1] Independently produced bands, like A Roda, blended genres like rock, soul, and Afro-Beat with elements of traditional folk. Although A Roda had recently released a new album, it was not audible on mainstream, national media, and it mostly performed to local audiences. Nonetheless, at the time, state sponsorship—in the form of publicly funded music festivals and grants—provided a platform for the band to think big. When I asked the nine band members about the near future, they envisioned performing on bigger stages with more professional accoutrements, such as sophisticated lighting designs. André "Mucuim," the bassist, described the band's intentions to "pave the path for a tour" around the country, while Andret, the keyboardist, specified that A Roda aimed to tour in Argentina and the United States the following year. Their expectations coincided with those of their peers in the scene and dovetailed with a general sense that Brazil was in a moment of ascendancy.

However, more recently, alternative musicians in Recife have been contending with dramatic economic and political shifts that have pushed them to recalibrate their aspirations and hopes. Rather than striving to play larger and more sophisticated shows around the world, most of these musicians have been devising smaller-scale approaches since 2014, such as performing in intimate bars and private homes, and trying new strategies—like using crowdfunding campaigns—to make ends meet. As they alter and pare down their professional activities, musicians are also tempering their hopes for the future. In early 2018, when I asked Túlio, a member of a postrock band called Kalouv, about the band's plans, he did not express the optimism that A Roda's members had described seven years earlier.[2] Instead, he described Kalouv as being at a crossroads; its members were unsure if they would be able to continue as a band due to the financial and emotional stresses they were facing. Meanwhile, when I asked another musician on the scene about his hopes for the future, he focused more on politics than music, stating, "My hope is that Bolsonaro isn't elected." He, along with other alternative scene music professionals, was against Jair Bolsonaro's racist, homophobic, and misogynist presidential campaign as well as the rising tide of nostalgia for the dictatorship that undermines the legitimacy of democratic governance (Silva and Larkins 2019).[3] Musicians in Recife's alternative scene are aware that the rising precariousness of Brazilian democracy threatens their livelihoods and lives. As a man I call Heitor told me in 2011, during the dictatorship in Recife, being a musician meant being "a *marginal* [outcast], even if you studied classical music." He had begun his musical career in the 1970s, so he remembered well that "it was dangerous to be a rebel [*ser rebelde*]; the military dictatorship would apprehend young people. Many of our friends disappeared."[4]

This chapter examines shifting outlooks, professional strategies, and subjectivities among musicians and promoters in Recife's alternative scene to better understand how members of the traditional Brazilian middle class, particularly those involved in cultural work, are negotiating mounting precarity.[5] In a similar manner to members of the working class and the tenuous new middle class, these traditionally middle-class Brazilians have had to cope not only with an ongoing economic crisis but also with a loss of government support (see Mitchell, this volume). While social assistance programs were key to the social mobility that working-class Brazilians experienced during the country's economic boom during the 2000s and early 2010s (Barrientos 2013), cultural and creative workers, including from the traditional middle class, benefited from an expansion of cultural sponsorship at federal and local levels that focused on expanding cultural rights and promoting multiculturalism (Moehn 2007). In Recife, municipal and state support helped the city's mostly middle-class alternative scene musicians to record and publicize albums as well as to go on tour, while also encouraging them to formalize and professionalize their work. Sponsorship, and emerging bureaucratic mechanisms, including the federal tax status known as MEI (Microempreendedor Individual; Individual Microentrepreneur), not only gave musicians a modicum of economic security, but in formalizing their labor, these processes also enabled middle-class musicians to attain the patina of professionalism normally reserved for more white-collar professions and historically unavailable to musicians.[6]

In employing entrepreneurial strategies, alternative scene music professionals are not seeking to emulate traditional middle-class white-collar workers. Rather, their priorities lie in fulfilling their artistic passions and meeting their basic needs. Moreover, while middle-class Brazilians have generally experienced the crisis as a loss of income and a decline in life chances (Fonseca 2019; Pinheiro-Machado and Scalco 2020), Recife's alternative-scene professionals do not necessarily understand their circumstances in terms of loss, but as a continuation of what they have always had to negotiate: scarcity and precariousness. In 2018, Eduardo, a former member of A Roda approaching his forties, was not anxious about the economic downturn; as a musician, he has always had to endure periods of feast and famine. Given these experiences, he differentiates himself from white-collar professionals who are "impatient with the crisis" because they expect regular employment and benefits. However, while Eduardo and his peers are used to facing financial insecurity, the combination of lost sponsorships, political instability, and changes in cultural work has made their lives more precarious.

In discussing the professional trajectories and perspectives of people like Eduardo, I argue they are shifting their ambitions in ways that change what it means to be middle class in Brazil. I situate my analysis of Recife's alternative musicians in dialogue with scholars who reveal that precarity is no longer exclusive to working-class and poor populations but is also becoming central to middle-class life around the world (Han 2018; Jefferson 2013; 2015). Scholars define precarity in various ways, but I follow anthropologist Clara Han (2018, 331) in defining it as the conjuncture between "unstable contract labor and a loss of state provisioning," because it concisely describes what Recife's alternative music professionals have recently faced. The rising formalization and growing acceptance of entrepreneurialism are key to musicians' shifting ambitions. As anthropologist Maureen O'Dougherty (2002) revealed, during the Brazilian economic crises of the 1990s, members of the traditional middle class approached project-based, entrepreneurial work as a temporary, and for some, embarrassing, substitute for more formal employment. However, for middle-class music professionals, entrepreneurialism has become not only normative but also appealing. In 2011, Eduardo wanted to register as an MEI to achieve "the mark of a business" and shed his identity as a freelancer. By 2018, he was a partner in a small-scale audio production company and had resolved his traditional middle-class parents' skepticism about his desire to pursue music. The increased normativity and respectability surrounding musical entrepreneurship in Recife are intertwined with the domestic and global rise of the "new economy," a labor regime characterized by a transnational flow of capital and project-based, temporary work that pushes laborers to be autonomous, flexible, and able to capitalize on their skills, assets, and relationships (Dávila 2012; Gershon 2017; Scharff 2018; Urciuoli 2008). In trying to keep up with the material and symbolic demands of the new economy, Eduardo and his peers are part of a global set of cultural workers who are managing contractions in government support and pressures to become autonomous entrepreneurs who do not burden the state (Bishop 2012; McRobbie 2015).

The intensification of precarity among Recife's middle-class music professionals includes not only budget cuts and a lack of stable employment but also a sense of social fracture and a lack of safety. While many of the people I discuss in this chapter are motivated by their passion for music—and adjust their labor practices to maximize it—some of their recent lifestyle choices are also shaped by the affective impacts of precarity, which, as Anne Allison (2013) argues, includes hopelessness and a sense of estrangement. In 2018, musicians and other members of Recife's traditional middle class reported a sense of hopelessness related to a rising tide of violence, including muggings and robberies in neighborhoods once thought to be relatively immune from such problems. One musician I have known for years was no longer living in his detached home because it was robbed. He reported the crime, but the police apparently did nothing other than warn him the robbers would probably return. Fearing for their safety, he and his family moved to a modest apartment a few miles away. Zé, a close friend of mine and a retiree, lamented that rising violence is driving residents of Recife (*Recifenses*) and Brazilians, more generally, to leave the country, despite having long been accustomed to economic oscillations. Moreover, with the 2018 presidential election about six months away, Zé reported feeling that Brazil had become "a polarized country." Similarly, a friend of mine and adjunct university professor lamented that he could no longer speak openly about politics with his girlfriend's family because of how "polarized" the political landscape had become (see also Junge, this volume).

Despite being dismayed by rising violence and political tensions, in early 2018, alternative musicians from Recife had not fully embraced hopelessness, cynicism, or the kinds of cruel pessimism that posit the country's ruin as an inevitable condition (see Mitchell, this volume). In part, their relative lack of despair is structural: as unracialized members of the middle class, they can adjust their lives by, for example, moving to a new neighborhood. However, their musical practices are also crucial to cultivating a sense of tempered hope amid precarity. Alternative musicians are not aiming for fame, fortune, or even the stability and amenities of traditional middle-class life that their parents might have experienced. Rather, music motivates them to weather the storm of instability. In the process, they are forging more intimate and collaborative relationships with each other and their audiences. Recent forms of precarity are informing music professionals' tempered hopes, but their circumstances and affective dispositions have also precipitated from cultural policies that have reshaped musical entrepreneurialism in Recife's alternative scene.

NEW POLICIES AND ENTREPRENEURS IN RECIFE'S ALTERNATIVE SCENE

Recife's current alternative scene mostly took shape during the early 1990s, when another economic recession hampered efforts to redemocratize the country, including enforcing Brazilians' newly instituted constitutional cultural rights. Federal cultural policies of the time sought to offset the cost of publicly funding culture to the private sector. In 1991, the Federal Cultural Incentive Law provided the structure for corporate and individual tax deductions to fund cultural projects (Olivieri 2004); it entailed an application system that required cultural workers, including musicians, to fend for themselves and take on the role of self-promoting entrepreneur (Dent 2009; Moehn 2012).[7] Under President Luiz Inácio Lula da Silva (2003–2011), the federal government augmented these policies through multicultural programs that posited cultural production as a conduit of democratic participation and economic development (see, for example, Moehn 2007). These efforts echoed contemporaneous transnational neoliberal policies and discourses that transformed culture and cultural workers into multifunctional resources whose value is subordinated to market principles (Chaui 2014; Collins 2015; Comaroff and Comaroff 2009; Dávila 2012; Yúdice 2004).

Despite these federal initiatives, the Recife area's alternative scene and the rise of neoliberal entrepreneurialism within it were arguably most affected by local interventions.[8] The early 1990s were especially dire in Recife. High rates of poverty, unemployment, pollution, and violence put it among the worst cities in the world in which to live, according to the U.S.-based Population Crisis Committee (Teles 2012, 15). In response, a set of middle and working-class young people across the metropolitan area sought to revitalize the city through an aesthetic movement known as mangue beat. Bands like Chico Science and Nação Zumbi, who blended (trans)national styles—including rock, samba, and hip hop, as well as traditional local genres, like *frevo*—sparked their peers' interest in traditional music.[9] Their success in the world music market showed that Recife was relevant beyond its regional confines and despite its negative reputation. Although mangue beat strengthened the alternative scene, it would not have survived without sponsorship since, as Carlota, an artist and promoter in his forties described, the scene was "precarious, like the situation of the country itself."

Mangue beat informed how a succession of Workers' Party (PT) mayors adapted multiculturalism to address Recife's needs. In 2001, the municipal government anticipated federal multicultural programs by rebranding the city's Carnival celebration as "the Multicultural Carnival," which, in addition to featuring traditional genres and middle-class pop, now included alternative music (Lyra 2016). In step with local and federal programs, from 2007 to 2014, Governor Eduardo Campos made multiculturalism a central part of expanding the state's cultural industry in order to enhance Pernambuco's appeal among "First World" tourists and investors. While Brazilian multicultural policies and social assistance programs from the 2000s and early 2010s were ostensibly focused on democratization, cultural sponsorship in Recife echoes scholarly insights that these were nonetheless premised on transforming citizens into entrepreneurial subjects (Ansell 2014; L'Estoile 2014; Larkins 2015).

Multiculturalism and the cultural sponsorship programs associated with it lost momentum due to Brazil's economic crisis and associated political shifts. In 2015, Recifenses faced the biggest economic decline in Pernambuco in two decades and the sharpest decrease in quality of life in the country (*Globo Pernambuco* 2016; Diário de Pernambuco 2017). These economic factors promoted significant cuts to the state's budget and seemingly accelerated the state government's shift away from multiculturalism and toward promoting entrepreneurialism more overtly (Santos

2015).[10] In 2017, Pernambuco established a new sponsorship policy, the System of Cultural Incentives (SIC), which aims to "incentivize groups' and cultural agents' autonomy and economic sustainability" (translation mine).[11] It fosters entrepreneurialism among cultural workers by offering grants, including some specifically for MEIs, and loans to finance cultural projects. The SIC coincides with policies in other countries where governments manage high rates of unemployment by incentivizing cultural work, while diverting most of the risk and responsibility—financial and otherwise—onto individuals (Bishop 2012; Dávila 2012; McRobbie 2015).

While cultural sponsorship within the state of Pernambuco has changed direction, on a national level, it has largely been deprioritized. Already in 2014, the federal government cut the Ministry of Culture's budget by 21 percent (Miranda 2015). These and other austerity measures contributed to the fire that nearly destroyed Rio de Janeiro's National Museum (*Museu Nacional*) in 2018 (Watts et al. 2018). During Jair Bolsonaro's administration, the federal government has, in effect, dismantled the Ministry of Culture, which had been a cornerstone of federal efforts to enhance cultural rights since 1985, and subsumed it under the Ministry of Citizenship, which also manages sports and communications (Simões 2019). Brazilian musicians, artists, and politicians, including former president Lula da Silva, have publicly decried Bolsonaro's policies as efforts to limit freedom of expression and undermine human rights (Buarque et al. 2020; Matos 2019).

Budget cuts and political realignments have weakened cultural policies and in turn, exacerbated the effects of the recession on musicians. As sponsorship has receded, middle-class alternative musicians in Recife have become increasingly entrepreneurial to survive in the city's competitive and limited music industry. Although it is home to approximately four million residents, the metropolitan area lacks enough affordable, appropriately sized venues. Consequently, music professionals are forming collectives where they host performances and pool resources. Given these limitations, musicians and promoters have continued enrolling as MEIs because it streamlines their financial interactions and provides a thin, yet otherwise inaccessible lifeline to resources like unemployment insurance.[12] Recife's contemporary alternative scene is a product of intersecting socioeconomic trends and institutional policies that have increasingly interpellated cultural workers as formalized entrepreneurs who ostensibly develop private markets without overburdening the state.

LIFESTYLES OF THE NOT SO RICH AND FAMOUS

Most of the alternative music professionals I know grew up in households with parents who were civil servants (*concursados*), lawyers, business owners, psychologists, and teachers. Although most do not share their parents' financial stability, they are nonetheless embedded in powerful social/professional networks. They began establishing these networks during the 1980s and 1990s, while attending private primary and secondary schools and later, prestigious federal universities, where elites and traditional middle-class people have long consolidated power (Levine 1978). Until recently, these institutions did not teach the pop and folk music that members of the alternative scene enjoy; however, they were nonetheless important places for aspiring alternative scene music professionals. As Hugo, an audiovisual artist and musician in his thirties explained, his journalism degree did not directly help his career, but it "afforded me the chance to meet people and likewise, to put me in contact with that universe of [audiovisual production]." Thus in keeping with Pernambuco's film industry, in the absence of formal training, generationally based social networks established in universities serve as social infrastructure (Nogueira 2014). This suggests that amicable interpersonal relationships are crucial resources not only for Pernambuco's poor but also for middle-class people who, albeit to a lesser degree, are now experiencing economic crisis as an ongoing process (L'Estoile 2014).

Knowing the right people is especially useful for cultural promoters because they have historically learned their trade via informal apprenticeships they arrange through friends and acquaintances. Rute is now an experienced promoter in the Recife area who bridges alternative and traditional music. However, in the mid-2000s, she was a journalism student who spent her leisure time volunteering in small theatrical and film productions. Eventually, she took on more responsibilities and gained the skills and confidence to form a production company, registered as a microbusiness, with her business and life partner, Maciel Salú, a prominent traditional and alternative musician in Recife. Yet her career path troubled her father, a lawyer who grew up poor. He wanted her to follow in his footsteps to have economic security. As she recounted, "In the beginning he was very unsure [about it], [but] now he's my biggest supporter." However, whereas Rute was able to transform her passion into a career, others in her position pursue their interests more informally. Guilherme, also known as "Bota," worked at a publicity firm, but he had grown up wanting to play percussion. However, his conservative father was "highly repressive" (*altamente repressor*) and forbade him from doing so because he thought it would derail Bota's studies. Yet Bota kept music in his life by organizing parties at friends' houses and when I met him in 2010, he worked as A Roda's manager. However, given the demands of his day job, at times, he was unable to prioritize the band as much as a full-time manager would have. While Rute and Guilherme pursued their interests in different ways, both had ambitions that clashed with their fathers' focus on financial stability. Relative to their parents and traditional middle-class peers, creatively inclined professionals therefore have different standards about what constitutes a good life.

While cultural promoters encounter tensions in pursuing their ambitions, musicians also face pressure from friends and family to pursue more conventional and prestigious careers. Marquinhos, a conservatory-trained saxophonist, said his father wanted him to either help with his tractor repair business or join the military police even though he was making "good money" from gigging and teaching music. Similarly, Andret, A Roda's keyboardist, felt like his nonmusician peers looked down on him because they did not consider music to be a viable career. He said, "In my generation there's a bit of that prejudice. [They ask], 'What else do you do besides music?' as if it were a hobby.... They treat you as if you were inferior."

Becoming a music professional in the alternative scene thus means eschewing some of the norms that encompass traditional middle-class life. It is also a counterculture that many see as a haven for young/middle-aged people who might smoke marijuana, wear tattoos, and embrace LGBTQI+ identities and people, practices that are not uniformly accepted among members of the traditional middle class and are increasingly part of the culture wars that have consumed public debates in Brazil (see also Jarrín and Junge, this volume). These values are reflected in and constructed through musical approaches that blend high/low and local/(trans)national genres in ways that do not necessarily overlap with commercial trends. Consequently, insiders on the scene claim alternative music is something "that the market doesn't see," as a cultural promoter stated, and therefore attracts audiences that insiders describe as "brainy" (*cabeça*), relative to their mainstream counterparts who ostensibly prioritize entertainment over art.

In rejecting traditional middle-class expectations, alternative scene professionals tend to live modest lifestyles. Hugo splits an apartment with a roommate in the lower-middle-class neighborhood of Casa Amarela. When I asked if he makes enough to pay the bills, he commented, "It's enough to survive, but for now, it's not enough cash to travel and have a really cushy life." Hugo and his peers invest their income on equipment related to their profession, like computers, instruments, and cameras, rather than on travel and luxurious consumer goods. Consequently, they do not tend to have elegant furniture or decorations in their homes, a characteristic that contrasts with more typical homes occupied by members of Brazil's traditional middle class (Maciel 2018;

O'Dougherty 2002). His comment that it is enough to survive "for now" also points to how alternative scene professionals are operating on a long timeline, one that, as Eduardo commented, requires more "patience" than those imagined by their white-collar counterparts.

From the perspective of older generations, the lifestyles these creative professionals lead seems to constitute an extended adolescence. While some of the artists I know are married—or divorced—with children, many others live in rented apartments either alone or with roommates. The few who own their homes tend to have inherited them from their families. In some cases, some of them live with their parents to save money. Members of the instrumental postrock band Kalouv were able to dedicate themselves to executing a crowdfunding project because they were living with their parents and did not have to worry about paying bills. This parallels the experience of creative workers across Latin America who are living with their parents due to economic insecurity (Dávila 2012). To some extent then, choosing to work as a creative professional within the alternative scene trades the stability and relative luxury of a traditional middle-class lifestyle for a more modest one focused on the pleasure attained from pursuing one's passion.

While the creative professionals I know often worry about their finances, the joy they get from their work keeps them motivated. Mery, a cultural promoter, explained, "I really like what I do." Her romantic and professional partner, Juliano Holanda, a performer, composer, and producer, sees this enjoyment as a metric of success: "Success is enjoyment" (*sucesso é curtir*). Similarly, I asked Guga, A Roda's former percussionist, why he chose to pursue music professionally. He said, "Passion . . . [music] took over my life." This passion also fuels Carlota, who has worked as a stage manager and roadie for over twenty years. For him, seeing a performance come together is the most satisfactory and "cool" (*bacana*) part of his job: "You put everything together and see everything working, the whole machinery working, the lights working, the guy singing, everything rolling, and you know that you . . . helped all that happen."

Even when the pay is insufficient, he explained, "personal satisfaction has no price. I feel really happy to know that I can manage to live from art here in Recife." The passion people like Carlota experience is palpable: their eyes light up when they describe their latest ventures despite the stress they face. However, such passion is also a normative expectation within the knowledge-based economy that drives workers to sacrifice their physical and emotional health and prioritize work over other obligations; in other words, ideologies about passion fuel (self)-exploitation (Gershon 2017; Scharff 2018). Yet Christina Scharff (2018) shows how classical musicians' pleasure in performing helps them forge connections to their audiences. Similarly, as recifense music professionals cultivate tempered hopes, their artistic passion helps them create solidarity among themselves and with their audiences.

DOING BUSINESS

As alternative scene music professionals formalize their entrepreneurial efforts amid austerity and economic stagnation, they are also trying to depend less on state sponsorship. Yet relying on the private sector is not much better given Recife's limited venues for alternative shows. Although new small bars and cafés have emerged, most are unequipped to host bands with more than a few members and moderate followings. Moreover, they tend to be ephemeral due to economic instability and bureaucratic/legal conditions that affect owners' abilities to maintain them (Nova 2018). In response, people have been improvising performance spaces, including performing in private homes. Others pursue more formal approaches like joining the Sixth-Floor Collective. In 2015, when I visited the Collective's office in Recife's busy yet dilapidated downtown, I thought it was a co-working space. However, Hugo specified that the self-employed musicians, promoters, and audiovisual artists who constitute it do not rent out space to work; rather, they pool their resources, collaborate on artistic projects, and cohost multimedia events. The Collective is not just about compensating for reduced state funding and a deficient private sector but also about creating community. This suggests that economic instability along with the kinds of entrepreneurialism generated through the neoliberal new economy can foment solidarity. Mery, a core member of the Collective, emphasized how their events focus on creating more interactions between artists and audiences; they enable people to "not just to watch a show, but to also enjoy the space, the people, to interact. I think that this somewhat influenced the city ... and is making it possible for other people to do this [too]."

However, these activities are not necessarily translating into overt forms of political mobilization. In fact, alternative scene professionals remain relatively fragmented as an interest group even though many participate in protests and other activities to advocate for more equitable cultural policies.[13] An alternative scene musician approaching his fifties I call Ricardo, explained musicians' financial instability and the fact that they do project-based work "makes it difficult to mobilize." Factory workers can strike to demand better wages even if the higher wage they gain might still be unjust. However, for musicians it is "more complicated" because they must always "chase" (*correr atrás*) opportunities without guarantees or financial safety nets. Some musicians go months without performing or earning any money, leaving them open to any opportunity, regardless of whether it is exploitative. This fragility, as he put it, "disarticulates everything" (*desarticula todo*). Similarly, Carlota talked about how roadies are paid poorly, which he thinks is "kind of unjust because they don't have a union." In contrast, "in France, artists go on strike. If we went on strike here, we would starve." For Carlota, the lack of unions and the absence of a "principle of collectivity" among music professionals is a major obstacle in the ability of alternative scene professionals to attain more equitable wages and receive more infrastructural support—in the form of more professional training and financial backing for more venues—from the government. This suggests that as individuals become enterprises within the new economy, they do not necessarily mobilize around common professional interests.

Relatedly, these processes are changing how Recife's music professionals imagine their relationships to the state, which they see as a potential business partner more than a patron or enforcer of rights. Malícia Champion is an alternative band that includes former members of A Roda. They cover 1970s and 1980s romantic dance music (*brega*) and Caribbean dance genres, like bachata and cumbia, with an insouciant, rock sensibility. During the past five years, the band has gained significant success performing exclusively at private venues, rather than at state-sponsored events. In 2018, Charles, the band's drummer and de facto manager, lamented that the economic crisis and the deprioritization of cultural democratization among local government agencies was amplifying clientelism and cronyism. Although potential performers must submit formal applications to perform in sponsored events, Charles reportedly knows musicians and band managers who subvert this process by appealing to bureaucrats in person. However, he specified that he and his band oppose this practice: "I'm not going to say, 'Put my show [in Carnival], please' [because] it's not a favor, it's a business." Charles's narration suggests that professionalized forms of entrepreneurialism are reshaping how creative professionals envision their relationships to the state; rather than seeing the government as an entity that upholds his constitutional rights to produce and access culture, he approaches it as a potential client (see also, Enriquez 2018). Thus the "business-to-business" relationships Gershon (2017) observes between U.S. white-collar employers and employees are also operational between entrepreneurial citizens and the state in Recife. While Malícia Champion relies on a well-formed fan base to pursue privately funded opportunities, younger bands use social media and crowdfunding to finance their projects and cultivate their audience. Although these resources entail their own challenges, the instrumental postrock band Kalouv has found these digital tools useful in forging more intimate connections with their collaborators and fans.

THE HIGHS AND LOWS OF NEW MEDIA

Kalouv's members are approximately ten to fifteen years younger than most of the aforementioned alternative scene professionals. They formed the band as undergraduates at Pernambuco's Federal University (UFPE) in 2010, but once they graduated and could invest more in the band, the recession took hold. In 2017, the band followed the example of other alternative bands in the area by using Catarse, one of Brazil's most popular crowdfunding sites, to finance its third album, *Elã* (Elan). Crowdfunding appealed to them because it seemed like a more feasible route than applying for sponsorship, which would not only require them to write an application, but Túlio, the band's lead guitarist, believed state institutions were now less receptive to nontraditional music, especially from a relatively unknown band. More importantly, unlike state funding, crowdfunding provided a way to make the audience part of the "journey" of bringing the album to fruition. As Túlio explained, the band wanted to try crowdfunding in order to generate gains that "were not just financial" by "involv[ing] people in our project."

The collaboration Kalouv envisioned was successful since it reached—and slightly exceeded—its funding goal of $6,222 (R$19,683). It also became acquainted with its audience in a more intimate way. Inspired by the crowdfunding campaign, fans used social media to reach out to the band. A young man posted an Instagram video of himself dancing with a Hula-Hoop to Kalouv's album, which prompted Túlio to correspond with the dancer about potentially collaborating with him in a music video. People also took pride in having funded the project. They posted pictures of themselves across social media platforms with the new album and the merchandise they had received from contributing. One fan even sent Kalouv a photo showing their tattoo of the new album's cover art on their arm. For Túlio, these interactions revealed that "everyone felt like they were part of [the album's] construction," because in participating in the crowdfunding campaign, they "suffered and won with us." The social and emotional connection crowdfunding and social media helped them establish with their audience was, as Túlio described, "the most beautiful thing" because "we really felt the[ir] embrace."

Nevertheless, this embrace did not translate into personal income for band members since their earnings from crowdfunding went toward paying their collaborators, including the artist who designed the album art, and the costs of manufacturing and mailing CDs and merchandise. Overall, the process was more challenging than they anticipated. As Basílio, the band's bassist, described it, "Everything we went through was really stressful," because it required systematically reaching out to potential funders both in person and across social media platforms; collaborating with artists to design merchandise; and anxiously waiting to see if their "all or nothing" funding approach would succeed. Moreover, due to manufacturing delays, months after the crowdfunding project had ended, Basílio was still driving around town delivering rewards to local funders. Given his persistent lack of income, Basílio began leaning on his psychology degree. Yet following his mother's example by working as a psychologist was not providing a steady flow of income either. He wanted to expand his private practice—which is more lucrative than working through the public health system—but after eight months, he was having trouble recruiting patients since many people cannot afford private therapy sessions. However, Basílio's heart is in music, not psychology; ultimately, he said, "I don't want to leave music." Accordingly, in early 2018, he started playing in a cover band that plays Anglophone and Brazilian pop/rock. Such bands are in high demand at nightclubs, parties, and weddings. Even though this is not his preferred aesthetic, he hoped playing in the band would enable him to remain a musician and "at least have something stable each month." Basílio was not alone in expanding his musical opportunities. Túlio planned to take a class in audio production in São Paulo, and another band member was working as a roadie for wedding bands. Other musicians I know have been supplementing their incomes by driving traditional taxis or working for Uber, which started in the city in 2016.[14] Both gigs enable them to earn money while accommodating their inconsistent schedules and frequent late nights. As the economy becomes more precarious for everyone, musicians are building on the flexibility that has long been a necessary part of their professional lives and tempering their hopes.

NEW HORIZONS

The collected experiences of Recife's alternative music professionals reveal that within the last twenty years, and more importantly, between 2011 and 2018, they have experienced significant changes. These Recifenses went from benefiting from a level of state support and broad economic growth that they—and arguably most Brazilians—had never experienced, to having the proverbial rug pulled out from underneath them. This constitutes a shift from a general sense of precariousness—a lack of stable employment and a remote relationship to the state—to one of *precarity*—a lack of stable employment *and* a loss of state support. Nonetheless, rather than abandoning their ambitions, these professionals are taking on new skills, collaborating more, and making use of new technologies and policies to preserve music's central role in their lives. Fueled by passion and bolstered by their structural advantages as members of the middle class, these music professionals imagine lifestyles and career paths that diverge from those their parents imagined for them. Although they still struggle to earn the respect of their white-collar parents and peers, they reveal that relative to the 1990s, entrepreneurialism is not only more respectable, and desirable, but it has enabled people like Eduardo, Rute, and Mery to imagine new professional and aesthetic horizons. However, the lack of concentrated political mobilization among them suggests precarity is disabling forms of political action that could promote more equity among workers in the new economy. These issues are symptomatic of Brazil's current circumstances and emblematic of global economic and ideological shifts that are intensifying precarity among the previously insulated middle classes. In tempering their hopes and ambitions, middle-class people are redefining what being middle class entails. Moreover, rather than giving in to hopelessness, my interlocutors are anchoring themselves around music in ways that foster new communities and sensibilities through which they can collectively imagine better futures.

REFERENCES

Agência Brasil. 2013. "Brasil terá 3 milhões de empreendedores individuais segundo Dilma." May 6, 2013. http://memoria.ebc.com.br/agenciabrasil/noticia/2013-05-06/dilma-brasil-tera-3-milhoes-de-empreendedores-individuais.
Allison, Anne. 2013. *Precarious Japan*. Durham, N.C.: Duke University Press.
Ansell, Aaron. 2014. *Zero Hunger: Political Culture and Antipoverty Policy in Northeast Brazil*. Chapel Hill: University of North Carolina Press.
Barrientos, Armando. 2013. "The Rise of Social Assistance in Brazil." *Development and Change* 44 (4): 887–910.
Bishop, Claire. 2012. *Artificial Hells: Participatory Art and the Politics of Spectatorship*. London: Verso.
Buarque, Chico, Caetano Veloso, Sebastião Salgado, Arnaldo Antunes, Djamila Ribeiro, Milton Hatoum, Petra Costa, and others. 2020. "Democracy and Freedom of Expression Are under Threat in Brazil." *Guardian*,

February 7, 2020, Opinion. https://www.theguardian.com/commentisfree/2020/feb/07/democracy-and-freedom-of-expression-are-under-threat-in-brazil.

Chaui, Marilena. 2014. *Cultura e democracia, o discurso competente e outras falas*. São Paulo: Cortez Editora.

Collins, John F. 2015. *Revolt of the Saints: Memory and Redemption in the Twilight of Brazilian Racial Democracy*. Durham, N.C.: Duke University Press.

Comaroff, John L., and Jean Comaroff. 2009. *Ethnicity, Inc.* Chicago: University of Chicago Press.

Dávila, Arlene M. 2012. *Culture Works: Space, Value, and Mobility across the Neoliberal Americas*. New York: New York University Press.

Dent, Alexander S. 2009. *River of Tears: Country Music, Memory, and Modernity in Brazil*. Durham, N.C.: Duke University Press.

Diário de Pernambuco. 2017. "Pesquisa aponta o Recife como a capital com a maior queda de qualidade de vida." August 28, 2017. https://www.diariodepernambuco.com.br/noticia/vidaurbana/2017/08/pesquisa-aponta-o-recife-como-a-capital-com-a-maior-queda-de-qualidade.html.

Dunn, Christopher. 2016. *Contracultura: Alternative Arts and Social Transformation in Authoritarian Brazil*. Chapel Hill: University of North Carolina Press.

Enriquez, Falina. 2018. "Business, Transnationalism, and Patrimony: Comparing Entrepreneurial Musicians in Recife, Pernambuco." *Suomen antropologi* 43 (1): 6–27.

Fonseca, Iolanda. 2019. "Brazil's Recession Has Decreased Workers' Real Income by 16 Percent in Five Years." *Rio Times*, June 24, 2019. https://riotimesonline.com/brazil-news/politics-and-societysocietybrazillife/the-recession-in-brazil-has-decreased-workers-income-by-16-percent-in-five-years/.

Globo Pernambuco. 2016. "Em 2015, PIB de Pernambuco teve a maior queda dos últimos 28 anos." March 23, 2016. http://g1.globo.com/pernambuco/noticia/2016/03/em-2015-pib-de-pernambuco-teve-maior-queda-dos-ultimos-28-anos.html.

Gershon, Ilana. 2017. *Down and Out in the New Economy: How People Find (or Don't Find) Work Today*. Chicago: University of Chicago Press.

Goldstein, Donna M. 2003. *Laughter Out of Place: Race, Class, Violence, and Sexuality in a Rio Shantytown*. 1st ed. Berkeley: University of California Press.

Han, Clara. 2018. "Precarity, Precariousness, and Vulnerability." *Annual Review of Anthropology* 47 (1): 331–343.

Hertzman, Marc A. 2013. *Making Samba: A New History of Race and Music in Brazil*. Durham, N.C.: Duke University Press.

Jefferson, Anna. 2013. "Narratives of Moral Order in Michigan's Foreclosure Crisis." *City and Society* 25 (1): 92–112.

———. 2015. "'Not What It Used to Be': Schemas of Class and Contradiction in the Great Recession." *Economic Anthropology* 2 (2): 310–325.

Kallen, Stuart A. 2012. *The History of Alternative Rock*. Farmington Hills, Mich.: Lucent.

Klein, Charles H., Sean T. Mitchell, and Benjamin Junge. 2018. "Naming Brazil's Previously Poor: 'New Middle Class' as an Economic, Political, and Experiential Category." *Economic Anthropology* 5 (1): 83–95.

Larkins, Erika Robb. 2015. *The Spectacular Favela: Violence in Modern Brazil*. Oakland: University of California Press.

L'Estoile, Benoît de. 2014. "'Money Is Good, but a Friend Is Better': Uncertainty, Orientation to the Future, and 'the Economy.'" *Current Anthropology* 55 (S9): S62–S73.

Levine, Robert M. 1978. *Pernambuco in the Brazilian Federation, 1889–1937*. Stanford: Stanford University Press.

Lima, Maria. 2013. "Rompimento do PSB com o governo irá além da entrega de cargos, diz Campos." *O Globo*, September 19, 2013. https://oglobo.globo.com/brasil/rompimento-do-psb-com-governo-ira-alem-da-entrega-de-cargos-diz-campos-10013661.

Lyra, Carla. 2016. "O bairro do Recife e a economia criativa: do carnaval multicultural ao paço do frevo." *Pragmatizes: Revista latino americana de estudos em cultura* 6 (11): 109–121.

Maciel, Louise Claudino. 2018. "Pode entrar: Manifestações de gosto no âmbito da moradia e da decoração das elites culturais na região metropolitana de Recife." PhD diss., Universidade Federal de Pernambuco, Recife.

Matos, Willian. 2019. "'Querem destruir o Brasil começando pela cultura', afirma Lula, sobre governo Bolsonaro." *Journal de Brasília* (blog), December 19, 2019. https://jornaldebrasilia.com.br/politica-e-poder/querem-destruir-o-brasil-comecando-pela-cultura-afirma-lula-sobre-governo-bolsonaro/.

McRobbie, Angela. 2015. *Be Creative: Making a Living in the New Culture Industries*. Cambridge, UK: Polity.

Miranda, André. 2015. "Ministério da Cultura terá orçamento menor em relação a 2014." *O Globo*, May 28, 2015. https://oglobo.globo.com/cultura/ministerio-da-cultura-tera-orcamento-menor-em-relacao-2014-16280312.

Moehn, Frederick. 2007. "Music, Citizenship, and Violence in Postdictatorship Brazil." *Latin American Music Review* 28 (2): 181–219.

———. 2012. *Contemporary Carioca: Technologies of Mixing in a Brazilian Music Scene*. Durham, N.C.: Duke University Press.

Moura, Mariama da Mata Leite. 2017. "A influência do movimento manguebeat na cena Cultural do Recife: Um estudo a partir da identidade e do consumo." Master's thesis, Universidade Federal Rural de Pernambuco, Recife.

Nogueira, Amanda Mansur C. 2014. "A brodagem no cinema em Pernambuco." PhD diss., Universidade Federal de Pernambuco, Recife.

Nova, Leonardo Vila. 2018. "Porto Musical debate o 'gigante mundo das pequenas casas.'" *PorAqui*, February 2, 2018. https://poraqui.com/recife-antigo-centro/porto-musical-debate-o-gigante-mundo-das-pequenas-casas/.

Oakes, Kaya. 2009. *Slanted and Enchanted: The Evolution of Indie Culture*. New York: Henry Holt.

O'Dougherty, Maureen. 2002. *Consumption Intensified: The Politics of Middle-Class Daily Life in Brazil*. Durham, N.C.: Duke University Press.

Olivieri, Cristiane Garcia. 2004. *Cultura neoliberal: Leis de incentivo como política pública de cultura*. São Paulo: Escrituras.

Pinheiro-Machado, Rosana, and Lucia Mury Scalco. 2020. "From Hope to Hate: The Rise of Conservative Subjectivity in Brazil." *HAU: Journal of Ethnographic Theory* 10 (1): 21–31.

Salazar, Leonardo. 2011. "Governo anuncia ampliação do simples nacional e do microempreendedor individual." *Música Ltda. O Negócio da Música para Empreendedores* (blog), August 10, 2011. http://www.musicaltda.com.br/2011/08/governo-anunciaampliacao-do-simples-nacionale-do-microempreendedor-individual/.

Santos, Giselly. 2015. "Governo de Pernambuco anuncia corte de mais R$ 600 milhões." *LeiaJá*, August 24, 2015. https://www.leiaja.com/politica/2015/08/24/governo-de-pernambuco-anuncia-corte-de-mais-r-600-milhoes/.

Scharff, Christina. 2018. *Gender, Subjectivity, and Cultural Work: The Classical Music Profession*. Abingdon, UK: Routledge.

Silva, Antonio José Bacelar da, and Erika Robb Larkins. 2019. "The Bolsonaro Election, Antiblackness, and Changing Race Relations in Brazil." *Journal of Latin American and Caribbean Anthropology* 24 (4): 893–913.

Simões, Mariana. 2019. "Brazil Dissolves Its Ministry of Culture." *Hyperallergic*, January 23, 2019. https://hyperallergic.com/481163/brazil-dissolves-its-ministry-of-culture/.

Teles, José. 2012. *Do frevo ao manguebeat*. 2nd ed. São Paulo: Editora 34.

Urciuoli, Bonnie. 2008. "Skills and Selves in the New Workplace." *American Ethnologist* 35 (2): 211–228.

Watts, Jonathan, Dom Phillips, and Sam Jones. 2018. "Brazil National Museum Blaze in Rio Blamed on Austerity." *Guardian*, September 3, 2018, World News. https://www.theguardian.com/world/2018/sep/03/brazils-national-museum-blaze-blamed-on-austerity-cuts-amid-olympics-spending.

Yúdice, George. 2004. *The Expediency of Culture: Uses of Culture in the Global Era*. Durham, N.C.: Duke University Press.

NOTES

1. Insiders also call this the "independent scene" (*cena independente*); however, I heard "alternative" more often. The scene is historically connected to Brazilian countercultural movements that began during the 1960s among members of the middle class who cultivated cosmopolitan tastes informed by leftist politics (Dunn 2016). It is also informed by U.S. alternative/indie music markets and scenes; in both Brazil and the United States, alternative/indie scenes are informed by a punk-inspired "do-it-yourself" attitude to musical production and circulation that involve independent record labels and distribution networks (Kallen 2012; Moura 2017; Oakes 2009).

2. Postrock music diverges from rock's conventional verse-chorus-verse song structure, while incorporating a greater variety of time signatures as well as synthesized sonic effects and textures.

3. On this nostalgia and critiques of it, see this volume's introduction and the chapter by Jarrín.

4. *Marginal* is a racializing, criminalizing term that pejoratively describes people who occupy society's social and geographic peripheries (Dunn 2016; Goldstein 2003).

5. In keeping with Klein, Mitchell, and Junge (2018), "traditional middle class" contrasts with the "new middle class"—that is, the formerly working-class populations that recently ascended into the middle class.

6. Brazilian musicians have long earned money from performing and composing; however, they have historically operated within the informal economy and lacked social recognition as professionals (see, for example, Hertzman

2013). MEI (Microempreendedor Individual) tax status was established in 2006 through the Lei Complementar 123; it gives self-employed people a chance to formalize their businesses while contributing to and benefiting from Social Security as well as health and workers' compensation insurance (Salazar 2011; *Agência Brasil* 2013).

7. Lei Federal de Incentivo à Cultura, law no. 8.313, December 23, 1991.

8. Olivieri (2004) argues that the Cultural Incentive Law benefited industrialized, high-income states like São Paulo, more than rural, less-populated states like Pernambuco.

9. On *frevo*, a Carnival genre from the late nineteenth century mostly played by brass ensembles, and other Carnival music from Recife, see Teles (2012).

10. Governor Eduardo Campos (1965–2014) was a key proponent of Pernambucan multiculturalism. However, even before he resigned in 2014 to run for president, Campos was dismantling multicultural programs. In 2013, he severed the alliance between his party, the center-left Brazilian Socialist Party (PSB), and the PT, which had championed multicultural policies on the federal level. On this shift, see Lima.

11. Law 16.113, Chapter I, Article 2, section XII. https://www.sefaz.pe.gov.br/Legislacao/Tributaria/Documents/legislacao/Leis_Tributarias/2017/Lei16113_2017.htm.

12. MEI tax status allows one to submit a bill of sale (*nota fiscal*) to clients without having to pay a third party. By 2015, most of the alternative scene music professionals I knew had enrolled as MEIs or registered as other kinds of businesses, like *microempresas* (microbusinesses).

13. For example, in 2016, after decades of protesting and organizing, a coalition of music professionals and other citizens succeeded in establishing the public radio station Rádio Frei Caneca.

14. On subjectivities among Uber drivers in Recife amid rising precarity, see Junge and Álvaro (2020).

11 · WITHERING DREAMS

Material Hope and Apathy among Brazil's Once-Rising Poor

MOISÉS KOPPER

Things proved complicated when I set out to implement the second round of questionnaires among first-time homeowners of a social housing complex in the city of Porto Alegre, Southern Brazil. It was early 2017, and two years had passed since 160 families moved to Residencial Bento Gonçalves—a model project of Brazil's Minha Casa Minha Vida (MCMV) public housing program. The Workers' Party (Partido dos Trabalhadores; PT) introduced the initiative in 2009, toward the end of Luiz Inácio Lula da Silva's second term as president, as part of the government's Growth Acceleration Program (PAC), which promised to infrastructurally upgrade Brazil's big ailing cities through decentralized public-private investments. Ten years later, Brazil's first-ever large-scale social housing program had delivered over four million two-bedroom apartments[1]—one-third of which was reserved for families earning up to three monthly minimum wages (some US$650).[2]

Injecting fifty-five billion dollars in subsidies and outright investments, MCMV helped reduce the housing deficit from 10.4 percent in 2009 to 7.3 percent in 2013. The program was widely hailed as a timely antidote against the growing effects of the 2008 international crisis, revamping the civil construction industry and creating 3.5 million job posts. By asking questions about socioeconomic status and political and cultural dispositions, I wanted to understand how PT's postneoliberal paradigm of poverty governance—blending governments, markets, and activist citizens—was changing the everyday lives and political subjectivities of the beneficiaries residing in these projects.

Assisted by two research assistants, I had already visited my interlocutors' new homes shortly after they moved in September 2014. We mostly found happy and welcoming families, eager to comment on their new sociomaterial status. Now after weeks of delicate mediation with leaders of the housing association and the building manager, I had finally been allowed into a condominium meeting to pitch residents on why they should participate in my survey. Before I could finalize talking about the advantages of data collection for better community politics, I was interrupted by a disgruntled resident squealing from the audience: "I don't feel like responding to any questionnaire. And nobody can force me to change my mind."

The head of household of an apartment constructed under the PT's poster policy, and the beneficiary of a range of other social programs, the fifty-five-year-old complainant is representative of a splintering divide in Brazilian national politics. Urban peripheries were prominent recipients of the

FIGURE 11.1. Residencial Bento Gonçalves, January 2017
Photo by the author.

redistributive effects generated during the PT era (2003–2016), which brought access to consumer markets and services for over forty million low-income citizens (Arretche 2015; Andrade 2008). Yet peripheries have also stood at the center of two competing electoral patterns long in the making. Whereas voters of these areas massively supported the PT during the presidential elections of 2002 and 2006, a shift toward the center-right PSDB occurred in 2010 and 2014 and then more dramatically to the far-right PSL in 2018 (Richmond et al. 2020). While such numbers seem to indicate a move toward political conservatism, a second—mostly overlooked—pattern has been the mounting number of abstentions among low-income voters between 2010 and 2018 (Junge 2019).

Here I wish to move beyond prevailing explanations of the 2018 presidential elections that recast the poor either as a mass of clientelist voters waiting to be manipulated by their wealthier counterparts[3] or as conservative political subjects ready to engage in "social wars" beyond their everyday well-being.[4] More sophisticated and nuanced theories about the poor, their livelihoods, and political consciousness are long overdue. Only analyses that take into consideration the roles of ambivalence, cynicism, and apathy, and the multiscalar realities in which they gain traction, can help explain how the individual hopes produced and engaged by the PT policies coexist with electoral ambiguity and collective apathy in Brazil's urban peripheries today.

Ambivalence and apathy remain understudied topics in the development literature on political participation and subjectivity, which overemphasizes best practices for achieving good outcomes (Ellison 2018). Even on-the-ground accounts are frequently overclouded by normative assumptions about the political behavior of the poor and the militant proclivities of researchers themselves (Junge 2018). Taking stock of the "orientations" whereby the future is made actionable in the present (Bryant and Knight 2019), I explore the alternative hypothesis that apathy as a response to collective engagement perceived as fruitless is indeed a desperate attempt at holding on to the promises of "material hope."

Simply defined, material hope refers to the sociotechnical infrastructures that enabled people to aspire to and realize their dream of homeownership during the years of economic prosperity that led to the construction of Residencial Bento Gonçalves. It includes the yearning for a better life as envisioned in relation to the material and sensorial aspects of housing. By retreating to private spheres of comfort and middle-class respectability, individuals and families strive to avoid falling into a condition I label "negative hope," in which the sociomaterial footing that once upheld hope is preempted, and all that is left are the dreams of bygone upward mobility.

Between 2003 and 2014, Brazil figured among the fastest growing economies in the developing world. A range of successfully implemented social and economic policies reduced inequality to levels only seen before the "Economic Miracle" of the 1970s, when Brazil also grew significantly, albeit without income redistribution. Starting in 2014, however, a series of self-enforcing political and economic events led the country into a deep-seated period of political instability and financial unpredictability.

Much like the notions of "cruel pessimism" (see Mitchell, this volume) and "despairing hope" (see Rojas, Olival, and Spexoto Olival, this volume), negative hope is the affect of a withering dream that creeps in amid faltering economic and political structures. Trailing the aftermath of boom-and-boost cycles, negative hope exemplifies a condition of "frustrated freedom," when "agency can exceed [collapsing] opportunity structures, thwarting aspirations" (Fischer 2014, 144).

Yet the specter of negative hope also evinces how a jittery national politics can intersect with the micropolitics of everyday life, creating situations in which the locality both mimics and repurposes the moral repertoires of apathy deployed elsewhere. As this chapter shows, people become skeptical of collective mobilization not *only* because of the signs of a national economy on edge, like indebtedness and unemployment. Apathy also reveals itself across spatial-temporal scales—as political events and disruptions unfolding at the national level travel, refashioning the locality and, in this case, informing political strategies and emotional frictions between housing residents and their leaders. When the promises of developmental inclusion fail and governments and markets are called out on the limits of their projects, community politics relying on participation protocols that mimic those of democratic institutions replicate some of the same apathy and ambivalence that have characterized the citizenry's relationship to politics at large.

The material I draw from is part of a postdoctoral research project in which I examined the long-term effects of policy implementation and the emergence and effacement of individual and collective forms of hope. Ethnographic research for this project was carried out between 2012 and 2015 among collectively organized first-time homeowners in Porto Alegre's Partenon neighborhood. It was complemented by two sociodemographic surveys in 2015 and 2017 and follow-up visits and interviews in 2016 and 2017.

In what follows, I reflect on how the methodological challenges posited by survey implementation expose the making of ambiguous political subjectivities, as these intersect with a disintegrating political economy and the recasting of individual hopes in the wake of the housing program. I then identify instances where national political dynamics and events overlap, in complex and unforeseen ways, with everyday communitarian governance in the projects. This gives insight into the sociocultural and voting patterns of low-income groups building to the rightward turn in the 2018 presidential elections.

NEGATIVE HOPE

After four years of diligent ethnographic fieldwork, following meetings of the housing association, and visiting joyful families in their homes—old and new—people seemed to have suddenly grown uninterested and apathetic. "It's too much research that ends in no real change. People are fed up with giving interviews and being met with empty promises," I heard here and there, as I dug deeper to understand why people chose to refrain from participating. During two months in early 2017, my assistants and I attempted to reach all 160 heads of households in their apartments, working around the clock to schedule individual appointments; circulating in between building corridors early in the mornings to catch stay-at-home moms (*donas-de-casa*), late in the afternoons to meet individuals at the end of their workday, and full days during weekends; advertising financial contributions to those willing to take twenty minutes of their time to respond; negotiating with the building manager to use the party saloon as headquarters to conduct interviews; and even distributing pamphlets containing my picture and information about the research goals, with details on when and where to find the researchers.

The story behind the harsh response to my survey pitch begins six months earlier, in September 2016. I had just defended my dissertation and was now setting the ground for a postdoctorate fieldwork project. I stand on the second floor of the former home of the president of the housing association, now remade into the headquarters of an ambitious electoral campaign. Benedita[5] storms through the door carrying piles of papers that displayed her name, picture, and ballot number. It was her second attempt running for city counselor. Four years earlier, she received some twenty-five hundred votes, placing her favorably on the waiting list. This time, she switched political parties and gathered an even larger entourage of community leaders to mobilize an aggressive campaigning plan. This included working face-to-face with community residents who had not been selected as housing beneficiaries and first-time homeowners who needed to be "reminded" of the collective efforts that brought them to the projects.

Many leaders present in the room, and snacking on finger food, had been at odds with Benedita for years, some since the last election. Benedita rose to prominence after building a communitarian coalition to assemble the housing association in 2009—shortly after MCMV's announcement by then chief of staff Dilma Rousseff. Benedita soon gathered hundreds of families from among informal settlements in the Partenon neighborhood to mobilize for housing. Cleverly, she conditioned the allocation of units to families registering with the association's bureaucracy and participating in their biweekly meetings, festivities, and other political events, including those of the Participatory Budgeting (OP) scheme. As Benedita worked her way up within OP's forums, earning the trust of governmental authorities and the autonomy to indicate 150 families to move to the project, other leaders felt they were bypassed in the decision-making process. To appease them, Benedita promised housing quotas in exchange for political support. All went well until after the 2012 elections, when the Municipal Housing Department suddenly changed its housing policy, forcing Benedita to cut back on the commitments made.

Benedita was indeed a controversial figure amid community circles. Seu Juliano—a longstanding activist, and the leader's brother—had a jarring relationship with Benedita. Over the years, I documented his grievances about housing allotments through cycles of approximation and disconnection from the leader. On that afternoon of September 2016, I spotted Seu Juliano among other guests. He greeted me without the same enthusiasm of past times. After sharing a beer, we sat on plastic chairs in the backyard of Benedita's house. "I'm supporting my sister for all she has achieved in the projects, different from other political candidates who only make promises," he said.

Then Seu Juliano went back to telling the default story of painstaking collective struggles, past communitarian achievements, and the leadership his sister had displayed—a narrative I had heard him question many times before: "We need this effort documented because people tend to forget, they are not grateful." He was referring, at once, to the photographic archive I had accrued over years of fieldwork, and to those beneficiaries who begrudged voting for Benedita. The connection here was that a well-articulated narrative could persuade swing voters. "We see so many untrue stories on TV, in the newspapers. . . . Why not tell this story that indeed happened, which people won't believe, because it's so hard to imagine if you haven't lived it?"

There was apprehension in Seu Juliano's words. The rapid expansion of Evangelicals in the projects and their problematic overlapping of religion and politics could thwart his sister's candidacy: "The church forces them to vote for their candidates. Talking to people, I sense a commitment to our project, but they can't voice it because of their religious bonds. We know that they are on our side." He suggested that even though not publicly supportive, Evangelicals were still loyal voters to Benedita.

"These are memories worth evoking," said Seu Juliano as he stared at me once again. "Maybe you and Ricardo could figure something out to support Benedita's campaign." Without expecting an answer, he kept voicing concerns. Because TV advertisements were too expensive, community leaders had to rely on online social networks, such as WhatsApp and Facebook, for internal communication, and the broadcasting of fliers and paid ads. Ricardo, the other interlocutor mentioned by Seu Juliano, nodded agreeably to the suggestion of using his computational skills to thrust Benedita's online campaign. He worked as an IT expert for technology companies in the wealthier parts of the city and had been nominated building manager by Benedita as soon as Residencial Bento Gonçalves opened in September 2014.

Not far away, on the building's second story, I ran into Matias, one of Benedita's sons. Inside, his wife and an eight-month-old baby shared the space with tables full of campaign materials. "Preparations are going great," he reported. "We managed to put supporters in many neighborhoods of Porto Alegre, and each one is doing her part." This was a great political moment to elect somebody like Benedita, I was told. Prominent political figures had been worn off during the latest corruption investigations, and new, more strict electoral legislation set an expenditure ceiling, which made it more straightforward for community candidates to compete for the poor's votes.

A third person joined the conversation. The man, apparently in his fifties, had just arrived on his motorcycle and came to collect campaigning materials to distribute among local supporters. Matias introduced me somewhat passionately, praising my dissertation as a truthful account of the housing association and its accomplishments. Before we realized it, what had been an exchange of pleasantries ran into heavy topics, such as the consequences of the country's elastic immigration policies and the proliferation of racial quota systems in Brazil's public universities during the Lula years. The man argued that a medical professor with whom he had recently conversed complained that, within a few years, the quality of public higher education would deteriorate significantly due to the increased presence of people of color in universities. He also did not understand why Brazil had become so receptive of Haitian and African immigrants. His opinion was that "wherever four people lunch well, five can't be adequately served."

Clearly disturbed, Matias said he was fed up with exclusionary comments that dropped all the burden on the most vulnerable. In his reasoning, there was always room for "one more person," much like Benedita opened the association's doors for those in need. "In their countries, immigrants don't have the option to say 'no' to drug trafficking before getting shot." He alluded to his own fight to remain on the "right path," a story I had heard Benedita tell on the microphone many times to corroborate her mothering and leading qualities.

"What we really need is better basic schools and more attention to functional family environments that enable access to knowledge from an early age," the man concluded. "There was a time when public schools were a reference for quality, but now . . . I believe the middle class needs to create a fund to help the poor pay for their access to education." Matias could not bear another word. He said he would not accept charity or crumbs from the "white middle class" only "to give them the satisfaction" of morally indebting the poor. "I want to build my own path, no matter what. People need good examples and self-esteem to improve their lives"—again, words I had heard many times from a range of leaders like Benedita and Ricardo to justify the allocation of housing and instill the will to mobilize in their members.

In the wake of the move to Residencial Bento Gonçalves, these encounters are glimpses into what I gloss as "material hope": orientations of future well-being that emerge out of the texture of everyday mobilization for housing and that are rooted in a quest for material improvement. Material hope refers to both the infrastructures upon which these expectations are ascribed—consumer goods, college degrees, the fruits of social programs—and the physical vessels perceived as legitimate to achieve such well-being—hard work, self-esteem, individual effort, and communal mobilization. Material hope is as much about the "textility" of objects (Ingold 2011, 12) as it is about the political act of staking citizenship claims on future expectations of material improvement (Kopper 2019a).

To both Seu Juliano and Matias, transforming infrastructure (decorating the house, obtaining a degree, telling digital stories with objects) was a way of improving the material livelihood of their family, but it was also about buttressing social distinction *through* access to the fruits of public policies. Crucially, materialities were associated with new forms of narrating individual and collective merit that blend policy outcomes, personal effort, and communal meritocracy.

In this sense, material hope illuminates both the poetic and political dimensions of infrastructure, its temporal aspiration, and spatial interconnection (Larkin 2013; Anand, Gupta, and Appel 2018). Material hope is more than "the wish for something to come true" (Swedberg 2017, 43). It is also about resisting *negative hope*: the specter of losing control over the opportunity structures that led one to hope for and attain better futures. Material hope then is *the wish for something to remain true*.

APATHY

In my earlier ethnographic forays, I documented a growing dissatisfaction with the PT national politics and their policy designs. In an interview conducted in January 2015, an Afro-Brazilian woman in her thirties reported that, after becoming the recipient of Bolsa Família and accessing higher education through the racial quota system, she "now sees politics differently." Attending college at a prestigious public university while receiving financial support from the government, Jussara was able to keep her domestic environment "functional." Bolsa Família "was the cash for kitchen gas, groceries, clothes for our daughter to go to school, sneakers for me to go look for a job." Cash transfers allowed the family to set aside *time* to think about long-term projects while adjourning difficult decisions.

Yet, in our conversations, Jussara also voiced a piercing critique of the social programs she was a part of. Like Matias and many younger-generation heads of households in the condominium, Jussara believed social housing programs should not cater to all, at least not to the poorest among the poor. Instead, state-distributed benefits should operate as springboards whereby inner aspirations meet (otherwise improbable) chances for a better life. As I show elsewhere (Kopper 2019b), notions of personal development and success were firmly anchored on ideals of the nuclear family, to the extent that a "structured" and "normalized" familial arrangement was seen as both a precondition to and the consequence of well-implemented policy designs.

For Jussara, people were not equally prepared to take advantage of opportunities made available via governmental intervention. Some people would need support before committing to a house mortgage, while others would first need to see value in paying for a home, a persuasion process at which community leaders excelled. Indeed, Benedita was known for drawing extensively on the parable of the "carroceiro" with sixteen kids—an irresponsible wandering man who lives under the bridge, whose occupation is to recycle trash to survive. "How can the government just dump such person into the projects, without giving him any kind of long-term guidance or assistance?" Benedita would marvel during meetings, only to convey that "here we ought to do differently. We ought to build a model community." Potential beneficiaries like Jussara were thus encouraged to believe that their "deservedness" to earn a house hinged solely on their participatory deeds and consistent effort to conform to a version of the activist citizen.

However, the results of the 2016 municipal elections were disconcerting for Benedita. She received seven hundred fewer votes than in 2012 for a seat on the city council. By November 2016, she was nowhere to be found in the condominium. In talking to neighbors, family, and friends, I learned she had retreated to a beach house for some personal time. Meanwhile, essential condominium decisions, including the charging of fees for the installation of surveillance technologies, had been made—unilaterally, some claimed—by Ricardo, often regarded by many as Benedita's right arm.

After unsuccessfully trying to reach Benedita, I strived to schedule conversations with Ricardo, who responded evasively and sometimes dismissed my queries. One day, walking out of one of the towers, I spotted Ricardo and his family arriving by car. After exchanging pleasantries, he invited me to join him at the party saloon. During our exchange, he went into details about the gradual and painful process of trying to separate his image from Benedita's; how he was forced to make difficult decisions following her absence; and his aversion for what he called ungrateful, unreasonable, and complaining neighbors. Ricardo wanted to drop the leading role and resume thinking about his professional and aspirational future, perhaps even consider applying for college at the public university. He described how his accumulating responsibilities as building manager were causing fissures in his family and the ways his unpopular measures of bringing improvements to the condominium's common areas and infrastructures were tainting his reputation.

Overall, I sensed an increasing lack of command over what the future might hold for Ricardo. Younger heads of household like him and Jussara, who conceptualized success at the juncture of personal effort and opportunity, had become disgruntled with the increasing gap between the allures and projects that living in Residencial Bento Gonçalves initially meant for them, and the means to realize such ideals of well-being. Retreating to their new domestic environments to pursue individual and familial projects was a desperate attempt at trying to secure and hold on to futures—of material comfort, familial privacy, and personal development—ever siphoning through their hands.

"People are tired of being researched," Ricardo went on to say. "They want to see real impact." As we discussed the difficulties of meeting residents at home, Ricardo voiced criticism of all parties who sought to "interpellate" people's hopes and future expectations—whether those parties were researchers, community leaders, journalists, or politicians—in times when such hopes were fulfilled or threatened to collapse.

In our efforts at taking stock of "the poor"—Ricardo's thought prompted me to think—could it be that we all might have muddled our grasp of the *actual* circumstances, expectations, and subjective realities of the people we work with?

Community leaders, policymakers, and scholars usually converge in that they expect the poor to provide an endless reservoir of answers and testimonies of their vulnerability and will to thrive. Meanwhile, the poor themselves come to hope and behave as though they need to "subjectivize" their poverty condition to have their demands heard (Fassin 2011; Auyero 2001). Refusal, apathy, and concerns about privacy then reveal the idealized dimensions of upward social mobility among the once-rising poor: a path envisioned as the arrival of new horizons of possibility in which one leaves behind the "supplicating subject of need" and seeks control over the future. As we shall see later (in the section "Private Democracies"), such control is also exerted as the struggle to enact a narrative of self-worth, hard work, and meritocratic effort—often against the backdrop of decaying present-day social and economic realities.

FABRICATING A COUP

Eventually, I got to meet with Benedita again in January 2017. Realizing that the environment had changed, and respecting people's decision to forgo answering questionnaires, my research assistants and I installed ourselves in the condominium's party saloon for a few days per week. There, we would attend to those interested in coming to us and participate in the survey. One of these days, I noticed Benedita watching us from her apartment window. Ultimately, after countless unanswered calls and WhatsApp messages, she decided to give us an "exclusive interview."

"Ask me anything," she giggled to my research assistants, who were meeting her for the first time. Benedita was eager to entertain their questions and construe her agency as an exemplary figure that gets things done amid economic precarity. Yet much like other residents, who feared that exposing their vulnerabilities and broken expectations would upend dreams of homeownership, Benedita was battling her own insecurities in the wake of the election results. Her reputation had been rapidly depreciating as families retreated to their homes and coped privately with economic recession.

"People are so ungrateful," she lamented, "they forget too easily the harsh times of suffering and all we did to help." As I would later discover, her reputation was also affected by what residents increasingly perceived as a "controlling and egoistical personality." Benedita's predicaments were gradually likened to those of a politician: someone who would show up strategically, take credit for collective achievements, and conveniently disappear right after. While many were not appeased by Ricardo's decisions, residents still appreciated his effort to face difficult choices following Benedita's withdrawal.

"I will tell you openly," she continued, "my relationship with Ricardo has become strained. People associate the unpopular and unilateral decisions he is making with me, as if I directed him to do so. They can't distinguish the housing association from the condominium administration. Consequently, my name suffers," she rued. "He leaves me with no other option but to stage a coup!"

Benedita was unabashedly using the language that had become so current in Brazil's mainstream media, following the trial and ouster from office of former president Dilma Rousseff in August 2016. For months, Rousseff and her supporters argued that efforts to impeach her were politically motivated, to the point that *coup* became shorthand for accusing political opponents of exploiting the law and subverting democracy. Now Benedita was mocking the PT's political language, repurposing the term to signify her own attempt to stop unpopular measures and reinstate herself into power.

"I can take over the administration for an indefinite term until things calm down, and then summon elections for a new manager," she said. Similar to Rousseff's objection, which rested on justifying a minor charge by defending a greater public good,[6] Benedita also advocated curtailing the condominium bylaws to cater to an elusive greater good. Here the survey became an inconvenient instrument of truth, revealing the *actual* preferences and anxieties of residents and their disconnect from the expectations of community leaders.

Soon enough, in talking to other residents and leaders like Seu Juliano, I learned that people's apathy toward community participation stemmed, to a significant degree, from the backlash of enduring friction between Benedita and Ricardo. The survey implementation had been caught between their dispute for power over the new body politic that was crystallizing as people struggled to make their new living ecosystem viable.[7]

While such dispute had little to do with people's *real* concerns and everyday battles, it nonetheless sheds light on how research instruments can become unintended political actors in their own right. As such, they can be the targets of apathy and ambivalence, even when they are born out of a desire to uncover power asymmetries that hijack people's hope in the first place.

PRIVATE DEMOCRACIES

Given this delicate reality, only ninety-nine heads of household—of a total of 160 apartments—responded to the questionnaire in 2017. Still, survey data shows that 70 percent were dissatisfied with the performance of their leaders, and 44 percent said that the housing association was doing a poorer job compared to 2014. While Benedita distanced herself from the concerns and anxieties of her constituency, residents coped with new senses of domesticity and comfort that contracted the space and scope for political action. Meanwhile, Ricardo pushed for collective investments and efforts to refurbish common areas, engaging residents by relying on their voluntary work and remaking the condominium as a platform for private participation against the deficient agencies of the state, the market, and the housing association.

Survey data illuminates how such a turn toward domesticity and privacy interacts with people's perception of safety. From democratic institutions to one's intimate life, numbers reveal a decreasing spiral of confidence: 18.1 percent of respondents feel unsafe inside their apartments; 35.5 percent in the condominium's common areas; 61.3 percent in the condominium's surroundings; 60.2 percent in the neighborhood; 82.8 percent in the city center; 82.6 percent in public transportation; and 89.2 percent in the city in general. Distrust in political figures and institutions is equally widespread: 86 percent of respondents distrust the president (at that time, Michel Temer, PMDB); 84.9 percent, congresspeople and senators; 86 percent, the governor; 76.3 percent, the mayor; 74.2 percent, municipal authorities; and 48.4 percent, the judiciary.

Sweeping skepticism and ambivalence toward social institutions and media exist as well: for instance, distrust in churches (35.9 percent); social media (52.7 percent); the internet (45.1 percent); newspapers (23.7 percent); TV channels (41.3 percent); and the police (38.7 percent). Distrust in market services exists as well, including bank managers (40.9 percent); call centers (82.4 percent); online commerce (60.4 percent); and salespeople (51.1 percent). There is also distrust in the following: building managers (38.7 percent); community leaders (40.9 percent); condominium neighbors (48.4 percent); next-door neighbors (37.6 percent); and friends (30.1 percent). Kin, however, remains a stark source of confidence, with only 12.9 percent of distrust. Overall, these responses draw a robust map of people's spaces of circulation, as 71 percent are not interested in party politics and 88 percent have the TV as their main information provider.

Whereas democracy is conventionally defined as the predominance of the common good over private interests (Marres 2012), I use the term *private democracies* to signal the shifting scales of political interest whereby translocal power dynamics come into contact with private senses of well-being. Rather than concerning themselves with the fate of national electoral politics, or the ideological proclivities of municipal authorities, housing residents are absorbed by everyday political disputes directly associated with the future state of their projects and material well-being. Yet far from being detached from national or municipal politics, such forms of experiencing and locating the political overlap with the languages and dynamics of politics elsewhere.

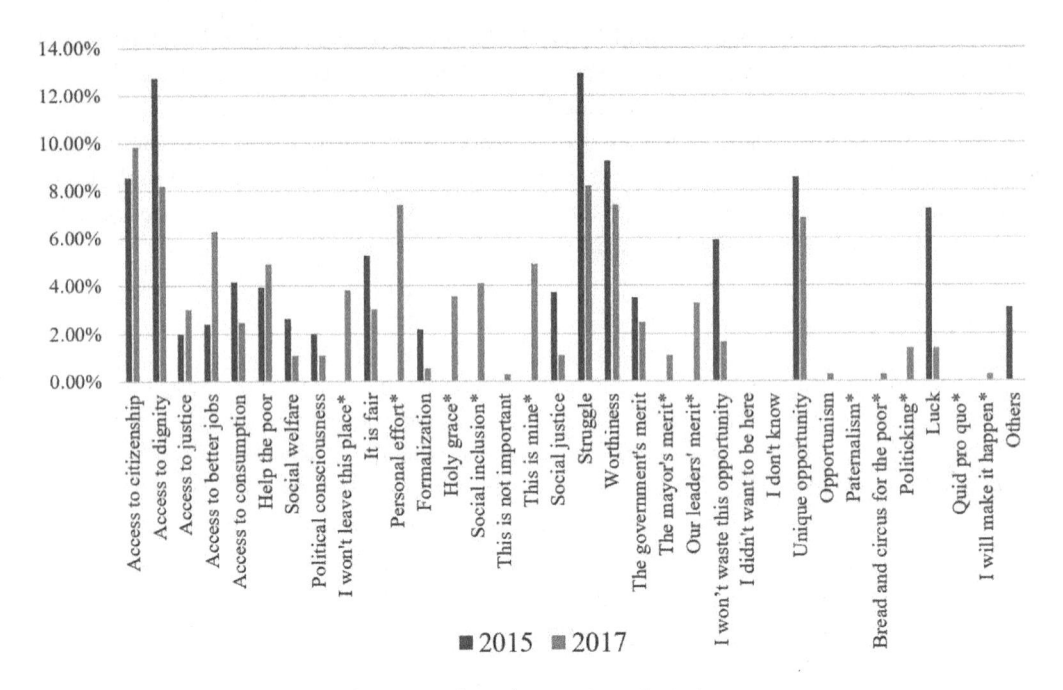

FIGURE 11.2. What does it mean to live in Residencial Bento Gonçalves? Created by the author.

The notion of private democracies describes the spatial-affective milieus that emerge as housing beneficiaries remake political interests and allegiances; withdraw to their homes; and embrace consumption practices and concepts of the nuclear family. It helps specify what political scientists generally gloss as "disinterest in politics" by locating ambivalence and apathy within different zones of interest. While broader political dynamics taking place at the national level have a reduced impact on the life of individuals, and people often feel disconnected from and distrustful of the political system, these dynamics find less conspicuous ways to creep into the common areas and social architectures of the condominium. Whereas residents often disregard the political ramifications of Rousseff's impeachment, they do grasp and care about the future of social programs or the pervasive impacts behind Benedita's threat to dethrone Ricardo from his position as the building manager. And while these scales of political life are not directly associated, they nevertheless carry affective isomorphisms that shape the political consciousness of beneficiaries in Brazil's current climate.

People like Jussara saw the transformation of their political subjectivity as a critical by-product of the inclusion through consumer markets of the PT years. The accrued knowledge and independence bolstered by her participation in economic and social programs led Jussara to hone expectations for her own political career: "I want to do something meaningful, applied to our reality. I want to have the power to change [*poder da caneta*]." Jussara had clear and incisive suggestions on how to perfect the implementation of such programs; on how to "help" the poor through comprehensive follow-ups and case-by-case assessments, without undermining their freedom to choose or infringe on their human dignity.

In these people's view, pro-poor policies did not have to mean pro-poor politics: poor people should not be automatically preconditioned to vote for parties who claim to defend their interests or even carry out projects from which they ended up profiting electorally. Instead, they saw themselves as responsible for putting up the hard work of engaging with these programs, the painstaking everyday work of meeting the eligibility criteria of these programs, and the moral rules superimposed by leaders who claimed to steer them onto the way of state benefits.

This is reflected in the lexicon of expressions residents used to define what it means to live in Residencial Bento Gonçalves. Respondents were asked to pick up to five words in a pool of dozens of expressions inductively compiled from five years of ethnographic fieldwork.

In 2017, interviewees associated their apartments with expressions such as access to citizenship, access to dignity, personal effort, struggle (*luta*), worthiness (*merecimento*), and unique opportunity. Compared to 2015, the 2017 survey also reveals a sharp decline in terms commonly associated with the experience of being part of collective mobilization, including access to dignity, luck, "I won't waste this opportunity," social welfare (*assistencialismo*), and struggle (*luta*). Interestingly, values like personal effort, "this is mine," "I won't leave this," holy grace (*graça divina*), and social inclusion were on the rise, pointing to new spheres of belonging and social action that foreground personal development and privacy. Moreover, apartments were associated with access to justice and better jobs, confirming data on employment that suggests a gradual formalization of job posts among working-age residents.

Still, most respondents in 2017—78 percent—had voted for the reelection of Dilma Rousseff in 2014. Though I do not have firsthand data on electoral preferences and voting patterns for 2018, I suspect that many apathetic electors who in 2014 voted for Dilma Rousseff claiming a logic of "the lesser of two evils" swung to Jair Bolsonaro in 2018. Such results would be consistent with the electoral dynamics encountered in other Brazilian peripheries (Richmond, 2020).

Table 11.1 illustrates the voting results per census tracts for the Partenon neighborhood and adjacencies—the electoral colleges of my interlocutors. While they still paint a small advantage of the PT candidate Fernando Haddad, they also reveal that 47.42 percent of the voters in these low-income areas opted for the PSL candidate, Jair Bolsonaro.

In the aftermath of policy implementation, broader political dynamics continuously and productively pervade people's experience of the house, becoming figures of thought-shaping political exchange, leadership expectations, and power imbalances among residents of MCMV projects. Political technologies—including the construction of walls (Kopper 2019c) and the architecture

TABLE 11.1. Vote distribution per census tracts in Partenon, 2018 presidential elections

Census tract (Partenon)	% Fernando Haddad (PT)	% Jair Bolsonaro (PSL)
Morro da Cruz	59.1	40.9
Rua Nove de Junho	54.2	45.8
Rua Vidal de Negreiros 1	53	47
Rua Vidal de Negreiros 2	51.6	48.4
Rua Dona Firmina	54	46
Rua Saibreira	58.2	41.8
Rua Tenente Ary Tarragô	54	46
Rua D Quadra	45.7	54.3
Santa Luzia Obra Social	50.7	49.3
Rua Juarez Tavora	50.3	49.7
Cel. Aparício Borges	47.1	52.9
Paulo da Gama	49	51
Otávio Rocha	54.8	45.2
Rua Mario de Artagão	54.4	45.6
Average for the above tracts	**52.57**	**47.42**
State of Rio Grande do Sul	36.8	63.2
National result	44.9	55.1

of "coups"—coexist with participatory designs seeking to expunge nepotism and corruption and to promote transparency and accountability. These materialities inform everyday sociality and place-making amid private democracies of consumer-citizens.

CONCLUSION

Hailed as an inconvenient truth in a political dispute involving community leaders of a social housing project and facing enduring criticism about the applicability of science in people's everyday lives, the socioeconomic survey carried out in 2017 was an improbable achievement. The study—and the erratic conditions of its implementation—echoed broader transformations in the course of Brazil's political economy: the decoupling of communitarian politics and the interests and anxieties of residents, apparent in Benedita's frustrated political endeavors; the spreading concerns about falsehood and lies, noticeable in Seu Juliano's storytelling; the making of reactionary opinions regarding beneficiaries of economic and social programs such as the racial quotas system; the broader disconnect between once progressive political parties like the PT and their envisioned constituencies, evident in Jussara's criticism; and the desperate act of retaining control over one's crumbling future amid economic stagnation and political instability, manifest in people's hesitation in participating in communitarian activities. These factors, together, harbored distinct forms of hope and apathy that paved the way for the election of Jair Bolsonaro in 2018. Yet they were hardly analyzed together or acknowledged as elements shaping the everyday lives of the poor in the years preceding Brazil's rightward turn.

By examining how these mechanisms coalesced around the implementation of a socioeconomic survey in an MCMV project in Porto Alegre, I sought to interrogate the spatial-affective interface that opened up between national politics and local power dynamics. Concerns about the role of science, fake news, walling practices, and political coups are vessels whereby ideas about democratic rule and governing instruments travel and repurpose, landing in localities that mimic, mock, suspend, or sequester the state and its material and isomorphic qualities.

"Government, as it disperses itself," write the Comaroffs (2006, 139), "becomes less an ensemble of bureaucratic institutions, more a licensing-and-franchising authority"—a thick interstitial space amenable to political disorders and market liberalizations. Since Brazil's redemocratization, organized social movements have sustained relationships with the state that at once fetishize, recreate, and contest the law, its ways, and means (Szwako and Gurza Lavalle 2019). The concept of private democracies illuminates the antithetical logics by which beneficiaries disavow institutional politics and remake political action within the privatized spaces of housing projects. More than merely mocking the state, consumer-citizens organizing in private democracies actively repurpose national politics to invest local disputes with meaning and authority.

This analytical leap moves beyond apathy as only "disinterest in politics" to consider the granular textility of the materials and hopes that undergird the experience of ambivalence. Apathy is not merely a global variable in quantitative instruments; neither does it relate exclusively to the dynamics of national politics. Apathy beseeches ethnographic inquiry into the everyday struggles, micropolitical disputes, and subjective ambiguities whereby scales of concern weave together.

Understanding the roles of ambivalence and apathy in today's political and economic climate is critical for the future of Brazil's democracy. Surveys tell us about the corroding impacts of large-scale corruption investigations, economic recessions, and political disruptions. But people on the ground are also deploying apathy as a way to hold on to ideals of upward mobility they were promised by community leaders and politicians involved with the implementation of social and economic programs. Much like *favela* residents in Rio de Janeiro are cynical about local leaders and civic groups to protect a vision of good citizenship (Savell 2015), so too are housing residents in Porto Alegre crafting new ways of being politically engaged that protect them from falling into negative hope. Similar to Mitchell's (this volume) use of the term *cruel pessimism* to describe the deadening affect of anticorruption, negative hope depicts a condition in which the opportunity structures that caused individuals to invest their hopes into collective structures of aspiration sharply disintegrate—an affective state that is steadfastly becoming the norm as the Bolsonaro administration defunds MCMV.

Resisting negative hope is as much about preserving the economic sustainability of the good life as it is about cultivating self-worth, or the possibility of retaining control over telling a story of pride and hard work as one deems fit. Thus remaining critical about the government's policies, the intents of local leaders, and the usefulness of scientific research are also ways of experiencing the politically enfranchising project of becoming upwardly mobile. By acting as critical consumer-citizens, residents construct discursive spaces in which they can give fruition to projects and exercise control over the institutions and agents to which they attribute their social and economic achievements. Thus to move beyond the "suffering subject of aid" projected by leaders, politicians, and intellectuals means to regain control over deciding who is entitled to administer one's private hopes, who is allowed to claim the deeds over accomplished fates, and who should be held responsible when things go downhill.

By retreating to private spheres of well-being in the process of regaining such control, the once-rising poor mimic elements of privacy and seclusion of Brazil's traditional middle classes (Caldeira 2000), while also giving way to a political subjectivity that is disconnected from partisan politics, conventional social movements, and conservative representations about poverty. Attention to the interactions between material hope, micropolitical dynamics, and critical future orientations is vital to envision new pathways for Brazil's democracy in the years to come.

ACKNOWLEDGMENTS

This chapter was prepared during my stay as a Visiting Postdoctoral Researcher at the Max Planck Institute for the Study of Societies (MPIfG), Cologne. I thank the Alexander von Humboldt Foundation and the Coordination for the Improvement of Higher Education Personnel (CAPES) for their financial support.

REFERENCES

Anand, Nikhil, Akhil Gupta, and Hannah Appel, eds. 2018. *The Promise of Infrastructure*. Durham, N.C.: Duke University Press.
Andrade, Luiz Antônio Evangelista de. 2008. "Espaço, política e periferia: As políticas sociais na reprodução ade relações sociais de produção." *Terra Livre* 24 (2): 33–48.
Arretche, Marta, ed. 2015. *Trajetórias das desigualdades: Como o Brasil mudou nos últimos cinquenta anos*. 1st ed. São Paulo: Editora UNESP; CEM.
Auyero, Javier. 2001. *Poor People's Politics*. Durham, N.C.: Duke University Press.
Bryant, Rebecca, and Daniel M. Knight. 2019. *The Anthropology of the Future*. Cambridge: Cambridge University Press.
Caldeira, Teresa. 2000. *City of Walls: Crime, Segregation, and Citizenship in São Paulo*. Berkeley: University of California Press.
Comaroff, Jean, and John Comaroff. 2006. "Law and Disorder in the Postcolony." *Social Anthropology* 15 (2): 133–152.
Ellison, Susan Helen. 2018. *Domesticating Democracy: The Politics of Conflict Resolution in Bolivia*. Durham, N.C.: Duke University Press.

Fassin, Didier. 2011. *Humanitarian Reason: A Moral History of the Present.* Berkeley: University of California Press.
Fischer, Edward. 2014. *The Good Life: Aspiration, Dignity, and the Anthropology of Wellbeing.* Stanford: Stanford University Press.
Ingold, Tim. 2011. *Being Alive: Essays on Movement, Knowledge, and Description.* New York: Routledge.
Junge, Benjamin. 2018. *Cynical Citizenship: Gender, Regionalism, and Political Subjectivity in Porto Alegre, Brazil.* Albuquerque: University of New Mexico Press.
———. 2019. "Our Brazil Has Become a Mess: Nostalgic Narratives of Disorder and Disinterest as a 'Once-Rising Poor' Family from Recife, Brazil, Anticipates the 2018 Elections." *Journal of Latin American and Caribbean Anthropology* 24 (4): 914–931.
Kopper, Moisés. 2019a. "A Politics of Hope: The Making of Brazil's Post-neoliberal New Middle Class." MPIfG Discussion Paper 19/7. Cologne: Max Planck Institute for the Study of Societies.
———. 2019b. "House-ing Urban Kin: Family Configurations, Household Economies and Inequality in Brazil's Public Housing." Special issue, *Articulo*, 20. https://journals.openedition.org/articulo/4400.
———. 2019c. "Porous Infrastructures and the Politics of Upward Mobility in Brazil's Public Housing." *Economic Anthropology* 6 (1): 1–13.
Larkin, Brian. 2013. "The Politics and Poetics of Infrastructure." *Annual Review of Anthropology* 42 (September): 327–343.
Marres, Noortje. 2012. "Introduction to the Paperback Edition." In *Material Participation: Technology, the Environment and Everyday Publics*, ix–xvi. London: Palgrave Macmillan.
Pinheiro-Machado, Rosana, and Lucia Scalco. 2018. "The Bolsonaro Effect." *Jacobin*, October 4, 2018. https://jacobinmag.com/2018/10/brazil-election-bolsonaro-corruption-security-pt.
Richmond, Matthew. 2020. "Narratives of Crisis in the Periphery of São Paulo: Place and Political Articulation during the Rightward Turn." *Journal of Latin American Studies* 52 (2): 241–267.
Richmond, Matthew, Moisés Kopper, Valéria Oliveira, and Jacqueline Garza. 2020. "Introdução: Espaços periféricos, ontem e hoje." In *Espaços periféricos: Política, violência e território aas bordas da cidade*, edited by Matthew Richmond, Moisés Kopper, Valéria Oliveira, and Jacqueline Garza, 13–40. São Paulo: UFSCAR/CEM.
Savell, Stephanie. 2015. "'I'm Not a Leader': Cynicism and Good Citizenship in a Brazilian Favela." *Political and Legal Anthropology Review* 38 (2): 300–317.
Souza, Jessé. 2019. "100 Days of an Idiot in Power." *Brasil 247* (blog), April 8, 2019. https://www.brasil247.com/blog/os-100-dias-de-um-idiota-no-poder.
Swedberg, Richard. 2017. "A Sociological Approach to Hope in the Economy." In *The Economy of Hope*, edited by Hirokazu Miyazaki and Richard Swedberg, 37–50. Philadelphia: University of Pennsylvania Press.
Szwako, José, and Adrian Gurza Lavalle. 2019. "'Seeing like a Social Movement': Symbolic Institutionalization and Cognitive State Capacities." *Novos estudos CEBRAP* 38 (2): 411–434.

NOTES

1. MCMV condominiums usually comprise several five-story towers placed next to each other and organized in a way to maximize inward sociability. Units follow a strict thirty-nine-square-meter floor plan established by Caixa Econômica Federal—the public bank upholding endorsements, financing constructors, and issuing mortgages. Units are made of two bedrooms, a living room, a dining room, one bathroom, a kitchen, and a laundry area.
2. In MCMV's entry-level bracket, the government subsidizes up to 81 percent of the property cost, which Caixa Econômica Federal estimated to be US$20,000 for 2009.
3. See Souza (2019).
4. See Pinheiro-Machado and Scalco (2018).
5. All names have been anonymized to preserve identity.
6. Dilma Rousseff was tried on charges of concealing a budgetary deficit by borrowing from state-owned banks to finance public expenditures, including the maintenance of social assistance programs.
7. Supporters of Benedita feared that questionnaires had been ordered by Ricardo to speculate on Benedita's allegiances and vice versa.

12 · BOLSONARO WINS JAPAN
Support for the Far Right among Japanese Brazilian Overseas Labor Migrants

SARAH LEBARON VON BAEYER

On May 15, 2019, within his first six months in office as president of Brazil, Jair Bolsonaro was approached by an Asian tourist who wished to take a photo with him at the airport in Manaus, the capital of Amazonas. The president obliged, but not without slipping in a potentially offensive joke while he was at it: "Tudo pequenininho aí?" he asked the tourist in Portuguese, holding his thumb and index fingers close together in a diminutive gesture. "Everything tiny there?"[1] Reactions to the event among Japanese Brazilians were mixed. Raul Takaki, president of the *Nikkey Shimbun* newspaper in São Paulo, was quoted in *Gazeta Online* (2019) as saying, "I don't know if he meant that to refer to height or what. If he meant it in terms of genitalia, that's really unfortunate." Indeed, it is impossible to know what the president's actual intentions were in that moment. More likely than not, though, Bolsonaro was playing into pervasive and pernicious stereotypes that routinely emasculate men of East Asian descent. In Brazil, people of Japanese descent in particular have long been associated with studiousness and discipline; on the other hand, they have also been stereotyped as short, lacking sensuality, submissive, and, in the case of men especially, poorly endowed sexually (Lesser 2013; Ribeira 2011). Given this context, it is very probable indeed that Bolsonaro intended the sexual innuendo of his comment, and that the comment itself was degrading—even though the tourist he said it to most likely did not understand enough Portuguese to be offended.[2]

Since Bolsonaro was elected as president, it has become commonplace for international media to report on his offensive remarks, most of which tend to be aimed at people of African descent, Indigenous groups, women, and LGBTQ communities (see, for example, Faiola and Lopes 2018; Londoño and Darlington 2018; Schipani and Leahy 2018; Spektor 2018). Although this anecdote from Manaus was not picked up by major media outlets outside of Brazil, I raise it here as an example of his pejorative behavior being directed specifically at someone of East Asian descent.[3] As I explore in this chapter, despite his vocally racist and antiminority position, Bolsonaro enjoys tremendous popularity among Japanese Brazilians living and working overseas. In fact, of the Brazilian nationals in Japan—most of whom are of Japanese descent—who voted for president in 2018, an overwhelming 90 percent or more elected Bolsonaro in the second term.[4] While Brazilians in Japan have a history of voting against Workers' Party (PT) candidates such as Dilma Rousseff and Luiz Inácio Lula da Silva—a majority voted for Aécio Neves in the 2014 elections and for José Serra in the 2010 elections,[5] both of whom represented the centrist Brazilian Social

Democracy Party (PSDB)—support for Bolsonaro and his Social Liberal Party (PSL) was especially strong. How is it that Bolsonaro—the type of politician who publicly mocks Asian men for their supposed lack of sexual prowess—won over so many ethnically Japanese voters living overseas? In other words, how did Bolsonaro win Japan?

In order to understand support for the far right among Brazilians in Japan, I suggest that one must first examine the ongoing double precarity that transnational labor migrants moving between Japan and Brazil have faced over the last several decades. In doing so, it is easier to grasp how, to these voters, the figure of Bolsonaro has come to represent ideals of safety, order, and transparency—ideals that are equated with life in Japan or the Global North, but not Brazil under PT leadership. To many Brazilian labor migrants in Japan, then, an eventual return to Brazil is only imaginable should the country "clean itself up," return to the "good, old values of the past," and join the same "civilized," First World ranks as Japan—something Bolsonaro and his party were deemed capable of achieving.

Brazilians in Japan constitute one of the largest groups of overseas Brazilians eligible to vote in presidential elections, second only to Brazilians residing in the United States (see Caesar 2018). Most Brazilians in Japan are of Japanese descent due to a special ethnicity-based visa loophole that, in an effort to curtail severe labor shortages across many sectors, has been a part of Japan's immigration policy from the early 1990s to the present day. Specifically, this visa allowance renders people of Japanese descent and their spouses eligible for long-term residence and employment for what is deemed unskilled labor in Japan (Kondo 2015). The result has been a marked increase in the number of Latin Americans, particularly Brazilians, of Japanese descent registered as residents in Japan. From the outset, the population of Brazilians in Japan has included relatively balanced numbers of women and men, many of them accompanied by their young children (Toma 2000; Yamanaka 2003). In 1985, there were only 1,955 Brazilian residents in Japan, but by 2007, at their peak, there were 316,967, representing a significant majority of Japan's nearly 400,000 Latin American residents registered that year (Chiavacci 2016; Ministry of Justice, Japan 2019). This number started to decline in 2008–2009, following the global financial crisis, and continued to do so in the years immediately following the Fukushima triple disaster of 2011 when, concomitantly, Brazil's economy and overall political situation looked increasingly bright. As of 2015, however, the Brazilian population in Japan began to gradually increase again, so that by mid-2018, the total population had reached 196,781 (see figure 12.1).[6]

Since this migratory movement began some thirty years ago, Brazilian workers have been largely marginalized within Japan's segmented labor market primarily as a result of the system of *haken gaisha*, or employment brokerage firms, whereby third-party companies act as a go-between linking Japanese factories and most foreign, unskilled workers (see, for example, Tanno 1999). As a number of scholars found (e.g., Roth 2002; Tsuda 2003), these employment brokerage firms often allow for significant discrimination and exploitation, and they determine the limited nature of interactions encouraged between Japanese and Brazilian workers. Thus fragile working conditions, as well as gaps in the housing, education, and social spheres resulting from the segmented labor market and *haken gaisha* system, rendered early Brazilian migrants to Japan relatively isolated from broader Japanese society.

Between 2009 and 2019, I worked with Japanese Brazilian transnational labor migrants, conducting ethnographic fieldwork in both Japan and Brazil on issues such as education, labor, religion, and class mobility and aspirations across generations. Based on this research, I found that over the past several decades, Brazilians in Japan have by and large continued to work on temporary contracts in brokered, unskilled labor, whether they arrived as adults or grew up there as the children of labor migrants. Through the process of transnational migration, Brazilian laborers in

Population of Brazilians in Japan (1985-2018)

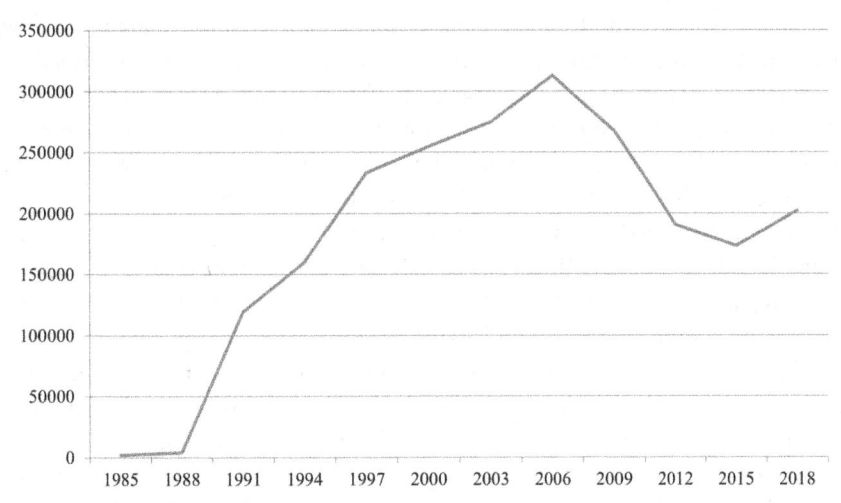

FIGURE 12.1. Number of Brazilian residents in Japan, 1985–2018
Sources: Foreign Resident Statistics [*Zairyū Gaikokujin Tōkei*], compiled by the author. Yearly statistics for the 2000s accessible online at Japan's Ministry of Justice's website: http://www.moj.go.jp/housei/toukei/toukei_ichiran_touroku.html (accessed August 1, 2020) as well as Statistics of Japan website: http://www.e-stat.go.jp/SG1/estat/List.do?lid=000001111183 (accessed February 1, 2015); numbers for the 1980s and 1990s adapted from Sasaki, Elisa. 2009. *Ser ou Não Ser Japonês? A Construção da Identidade dos Brasileiros Descendentes de Japoneses no Contexto das Migrações Internacionais do Japão Contemporâneo* (To Be or Not to Be Japanese? Identity Construction of Nikkei-Brazilians in the Context of Contemporary Japan's International Migration). Campinas: University of Campinas. Dissertation thesis, University of Campinas, 667 pages.

Japan have also experienced a kind of double precarity since a return to Brazil is made tenuous by their lack of professionalization and/or education acquired while in Japan. Although they may make significantly higher wages in Japan than they would in comparable or even higher status jobs in Brazil, labor migrants rarely acquire the kinds of skills that are transferable to white-collar workplaces in Brazil. Furthermore, for those who did have higher education prior to moving to Japan, years outside the job market in Brazil make it difficult to return. These challenges have, in turn, only increased in recent years as a result of Brazil's prolonged economic crisis that began in 2014.

Furthermore, as I explore in my book *Living Transnationally between Japan and Brazil: Routes beyond Roots* (2020), in focusing on the downward social and cultural mobility of Brazilian labor migrants in Japan, scholars may have overemphasized Japanese Brazilians' white-collar or middle-class status to begin with. There is a general notion—among both lay audiences and academics familiar with Brazil—that Brazilians of Japanese descent are largely middle class and well educated compared to the broader Brazilian population. Certainly, since urbanizing in the 1950s and 1960s, Japanese Brazilians have experienced considerable social mobility *as a whole* in the context of Brazil, contributing to a widespread model minority stereotype attached to the term *japonês* (see Adachi 2004). This does not mean, however, that the Japanese Brazilians who have migrated to Japan are necessarily middle class, nor that they achieved high educational and occupational status before leaving Brazil. In fact, many of the people I interviewed considered themselves to be from *humilde* (humble) origins and felt looked down upon by more "elite" members of Japanese Brazilian communities, who tended to distinguish between those who "made it" in Brazil and those who did not and had little choice but to go to Japan for work. In this sense, a significant number of Brazilians in Japan consider themselves just as much "economic refugees" or "economic prospectors" as do many Brazilian immigrants in the United States (Margolis 2008). Of course, like their counterparts in the United States, as well as international migrants everywhere, they exhibit considerably more privilege of mobility than the poorest classes of Brazilians (see Castles et al. 2014). Still, many of the Japanese Brazilians who move to Japan to work do not feel they can claim the same model minority / middle-class status as their counterparts who never migrated; it is partly the lack or loss of such a status, in fact, that leads them to yearn nostalgically for a Brazil of yore. As Suma Ikeuchi (2019) convincingly demonstrates, the ethnic prestige they once embodied in Brazil disappears in the Japanese context, and they become stereotyped as a backward, even delinquent, Brazilian minority. Thus their nostalgia for a past they perceive as secure and orderly has at least in part to do with the desire to reclaim their previous model minority status, one that marked them as solidly middle class, and as honest, correct, and disciplined.

While the bulk of my fieldwork on issues of mobility and precarity among Japanese Brazilian migrants took place in the years 2011–2012, in later visits to Japan and Brazil, I noticed conversations taking a decidedly more political turn than before, especially in the lead-up to Brazil's 2018 presidential elections. As a result, I increasingly focused my research on voting behavior among transnational Brazilian labor migrants and their families. Between July 2018 and August 2019, in addition to visits to both Japan and Brazil to follow up with people I had worked with since 2009, I also followed their social media posts from afar and set up structured phone interviews with key interlocutors on the subject of Brazilian politics in general and Bolsonaro in particular.

As it turned out, many of my interlocutors in Japan voted for Bolsonaro in the 2018 Brazilian presidential election. Brazilians in Japan were far from the only overseas supporters of Bolsonaro, however (Moreira 2018). In the United States, for example, nearly forty-three thousand Brazilians, or close to 82 percent of the eligible votes, went for Bolsonaro. More than 60 percent of eligible votes in Portugal, the UK, and Italy, all of which have sizeable Brazilian populations, also went for Bolsonaro (Germano 2018). In fact, overseas voters exhibited a much higher percentage of votes for Bolsonaro, at more than 70 percent, as opposed to 55 percent of domestic votes.[7] Nowhere in the world, though, was home to as large a majority of votes for Bolsonaro as Japan. There, a total of 27,078 votes—more than 90 percent of all votes counted as valid in Japan—went to Bolsonaro in the second term (see table 12.1).

Roughly a quarter of the Brazilian labor migrants I worked with in Japan identified as practicing Evangelical Christians, though I did not find a significant correlation between their religious

TABLE 12.1. Percentage and number of valid votes for Bolsonaro in the first and second terms in Japan by municipality, 2018[1]

Municipality	Hamamatsu (%)	Nagoya (%)	Tokyo (%)	Total # of valid votes
First term	78.47	76.61	70.70	22,186
	(3,915 votes)	(8,815 votes)	(9,456 votes)	
Second term	92.14	92.03	89.33	27,078
	(4,677 votes)	(10,538 votes)	(11,863 votes)	

1 Numbers here are drawn from the *Gazeta do Povo*'s special edition on 2018 election results, which provides a breakdown of the overseas votes that Bolsonaro received in the first and second terms per municipality. In Japan, there were three municipalities, each of which corresponded to the jurisdiction of one of three Brazilian consulates: those of Nagoya, Hamamatsu, and Tokyo. Available online at https://especiais.gazetadopovo.com.br/eleicoes/2018/resultados/municipios-exterior/presidente-candidato-jair-bolsonaro/ (accessed June 10, 2019).

identity and political positioning. Nor did their views on Brazilian politics seem in any way connected to Japanese politics; in fact, few of my interlocutors followed Japanese politics or concerned themselves with the conservative, right-leaning activities of Japanese prime minister Shinzō Abe. As I demonstrate below, key reasons for supporting Bolsonaro had to do with the desire to put an end to corruption in Brazil, protect Brazil from the left/communism, and return to "good, old" values of the past. Further reasons included general disillusionment with the political status quo and a deep distrust of mainstream media. Similar attitudes have been observed in nationalist populist movements around the world (see, for example, Evans 2017; Gusterson 2017; Mikus 2016; Shoshan 2016), and while they are likely familiar to Bolsonaro supporters besides those voting from Japan, in this case they are also couched within the specific context and precarity of transnational labor migration between Japan and Brazil.

To begin with, to many Brazilian labor migrants in Japan who voted for Bolsonaro, the Workers' Party (PT), represented corruption and a lack of transparency, especially following Dilma Rousseff's impeachment in 2016 and Lula's imprisonment in 2018. In fact, corruption was the topic that came up the most across all my conversations and interviews with interlocutors concerning the 2018 Brazilian presidential election.[8] Ricardo (age forty-one, who first went to work in a factory in Japan at the age of fifteen and had been moving back and forth between Japan and Brazil for work ever since) spoke of corruption in the following terms: "Look, I live along the border of Brazil and Paraguay. There on the border things changed a lot because there was a lot of drug trafficking, weapons trafficking. The military stopped it all, is stopping it all. Lots of smuggling of gold, dollars, illegal money, drugs, heavy weapons, all of it going to Rio, São Paulo. So the border closed. Brazil is a very violent country, there were a lot of drugs, a lot of corruption. And he [Bolsonaro] put an end to that. Brazil was practically out of control." Thus Ricardo saw corruption first and foremost as a local-level challenge, something that affected the specific region of Brazil he was from in ways that needed to be addressed. He felt that, since being elected as president, Bolsonaro had successfully cracked down on the chaos of this border region in a way that the PT never would have.

Other interlocutors spoke of corruption at the national level, either in general terms (e.g., "there has been so much robbery and corruption [under the PT]") or more specifically, citing Petrobras and the Brazilian Development Bank (BNDES) in particular as examples.[9] In general, they saw Bolsonaro as the answer to ridding Brazil of "corrupt thieves." From their perspective, this thievery and corruption percolated from the government—led specifically by the PT—all the way down to individual Brazilian citizens, particularly those of lower socioeconomic standing. As Samuel (age forty-four, who, like Ricardo above, had moved back and forth between Brazil and Japan since he was a teenager) put it:

> The PT is all about you going after land for free, getting a house for free. These people from the left, without land, without homes, they're the people who get *Bolsa Família, Bolsa Gás, Bolsa Escola*,[10] they suck at the teat of the government. People from the *favelas* [slums] are all PT. Because Lula and Dilma made it easy for them to borrow money. Today they're all in debt, but in their heads, Lula gave them opportunities. To them, Lula is amazing because he gave them the chance to feel what it's like to have a car, an iPhone, a good TV, a computer, etc. They couldn't pay for them, their names are tainted now, but it doesn't matter, the government gave it to them.[11] And Bolsonaro, he's not giving that to people.

Similarly, another interlocutor in her fifties, Meire, lamented how "now poor people don't admit that they're poor. That's what happened under the PT. Back in my day, poor people worked hard to save up for things." In other words, from the point of view of Samuel or Meire, the PT had instilled a kind of dishonest, freeloading mentality on the part of poorer Brazilians who, instead of working hard for things themselves, simply took things for free from the government or else engaged in a system of easy credit. For many Brazilians who had spent years, if not decades, working as manual laborers in Japan in order to save up for the trappings of a middle-class lifestyle—for example, a home, a car, a university education, name-brand goods, and the like—they saw the rise of poor Brazilians through PT's initiatives such as *Bolsa Família* to be unfair, even akin to corruption.[12] Why, they wondered, should they toil for years in factories in Japan, facing discrimination and displacement there, while other Brazilians stayed in the comfort of home benefiting from the PT administration's handouts? In many ways, this attitude echoes what Arlie Hochschild found in her 2016 work among Obama-era Tea Party activists, who felt that the U.S. government had become an instrument of redistribution to the undeserving. More broadly, Julián Castro Rea (2018) defines the contemporary right across different contexts as an ideology based on the notion of merit or deservedness; rights belong not to all people equally but to those who "prove" their value. For Japanese Brazilians, this was further exacerbated by the model minority stereotype that suggests that they have always worked hard for and therefore deserved their position ahead of other groups.

When I asked interlocutors about accusations of corruption against Bolsonaro himself, they usually deflected, saying that the evidence was either unproven or unjustified, or else that the media was simply out to slander Bolsonaro. They also defended Bolsonaro for not being able to combat all of Brazil's corruption at once or on his own; as they saw it, it would take many years to undo the damage wreaked by the PT, and Bolsonaro should not be expected to clean up the country in one fell swoop. Several interlocutors referred in particular to Sérgio Fernando Moro, a former federal judge heavily involved in criminal investigations of the high-profile corruption scandal known as Operação Lava Jato (Operation Car Wash) and appointed by Bolsonaro as minister of justice and public security, as a hero who would help the PSL administration battle through the front lines of corruption in Brazil.

Connected to the belief that Bolsonaro and his government would lessen, if not end, corruption was a firm conviction that the PT represented not only the left but communism in particular. Interlocutors who supported Bolsonaro would regularly refer to the PT presidential candidate Fernando Haddad not by his actual name but by the nickname *o comunista* (the communist), as opposed to Bolsonaro, whom they dubbed *o militar* (the military officer) or even *o radical* (the radical). To them, an alternative to the PT was necessary in order to protect Brazil from descending into communism. Many people compared the fate of Brazil under PT leadership to that of Venezuela under Nicolás Maduro. As Samuel (quoted above) put it, "Brazil [under the PT] was no longer a democracy. It was a kind of socialist-communist state, like Venezuela, Russia, or China—only one party ever won." In a similar vein, Ricardo (also quoted above) said,

> Since we've spent many years here in Japan, working, saving our money, a safety net for when we get older, we were afraid [that Brazil] would become a kind of Venezuela, a communist country. Because Venezuela, Argentina, Cuba, they were all on the side of communism, and we were afraid that the other side would win—the Workers' Party, the opposite of Bolsonaro—and that the country would undergo an internal revolution, with invasions of land, assets, homes. That was our biggest worry. Not that Bolsonaro is 100 percent. He's kind of radical. But between the radical and the communist, we preferred the radical.

Even interlocutors who had themselves grown up during Brazil's military dictatorship spoke of a return to military rule as a necessary antidote to the PT in order to protect the country from communism. For example, Vera (age sixty-six, who was raised by her Japanese immigrant parents in the interior of São Paulo State in the 1950s and 1960s and had worked in factories in Japan since 1991), spoke of the PT administration as "a communist dictatorship." Regarding Brazil's military rule that lasted from 1964 to 1985, she said, "I was raised during the military era, and everything the military did is still functioning today. Manners were totally different, during military times people had more respect. More discipline. Today Brazil is lost. Those people who were tortured wanted to establish communism in Brazil. People talk about a dictatorship, but it wasn't a dictatorship, it's that the people were communist, they were trying to bring about a revolution. So they were exiled and badly treated, but it wasn't for nothing. No one was tortured for no reason." In short, communism was a major concern because interlocutors were afraid that, should the left continue to lead Brazil, they would lose everything they had worked so hard to accumulate as labor migrants in Japan. Though they admired the organization, safety, and convenience of life in Japan, many of them still hoped to return to Brazil one day and feared that continued PT leadership would jeopardize their chances of doing so, or of having a good life once there.[13] "We're living in a developed country, everything's so orderly here, while over there it's all a mess [*bagunçado*]," one interlocutor (female, age forty-eight) lamented. In order for Brazil to eventually join the same, "developed world" ranks as Japan, many of my interlocutors felt the country needed to take a different, less precarious path from what they had seen unfold from afar under PT leadership—even if that meant a return to military rule.

In fact, to many of the people I spoke with, life before the PT came to power was often idealized as a time of discipline and order, as well as "good family values." Bolsonaro was regularly praised by my interlocutors for "believing in family"—specifically, the heteronormative, nuclear unit of man, woman, and children. Under Lula, life had become too permissive, they felt, allowing for an unraveling of the social order and modesty that had existed in previous times. As Samuel put it, "I already think it's bad enough seeing straight people kissing each other at the mall. I think there are certain things you should do at home, in a more private place. And that's what Bolsonaro wants to do, he wants to bring order, lay down the law—put anyone who's whoring around on the streets in jail. The PT gave a lot of freedom, and that's why Brazil is what it is now." To people like Samuel, the "excessive freedom" that the PT had instilled in Brazil meant that the country now suffered from a general lack of respect for authority. Many of my interlocutors lamented not only the sexual immodesty and liberal attitudes of contemporary times but also the problems associated with current education in Brazil. "Today, people go to school to fight and kill, to dance to funk music," one interlocutor in his midforties complained. Another interlocutor in her late thirties spoke of how today "students beat up teachers, not like the days when I was in school, when there was discipline, and you had to sing the [Brazilian] national anthem every Friday. Those were the values I was raised with." In many ways, these sentiments were not any different from those of Bolsonaro supporters found throughout Brazil. As Matias Spektor (2018) notes in *Foreign Policy*, Bolsonaro is popular in part because of his defense of "family values" and his opposition to abortion, drugs, and "homosexual propaganda"; in short, he is admired for his attempts to regulate morality. For many transnational Japanese Brazilian labor migrants, who have often spent more years living in Japan than in Brazil over the last three decades, they are perhaps even more likely to associate the "good, old" values of the past with the years preceding the PT's rise to power. Thus they hope that Bolsonaro will in effect turn back the clock to the days before they ever left for Japan, when life in Brazil was familiar and, in many ways, more understandable to them. This diasporic, premigration nostalgia represents an added layer to what the authors of the introduction to this volume describe as an increasing desire for law, order, and traditional hierarchies found throughout Brazil in the pivotal period of diminishing hopes between 2013 and 2019.

In my conversations and observations among transnational Japanese Brazilian labor migrants, all these factors, from the desire to curb corruption and protect Brazil from the left/communism to the hope of safeguarding heteronormative family values and the morality associated with discipline and order, trumped other issues, including environment, health, or foreign policy. Most people admitted that they did not fully endorse all of Bolsonaro's statements or positions, and some would have instead voted for another candidate such as João Amoêdo from the libertarian Partido Novo (New Party) had he stood a better chance of winning. Still, even for people who viewed Haddad as a better-equipped candidate for president than Bolsonaro, the point was not the individual; it was the political party and the need to change the status quo from PT to something—perhaps anything—else. Thus Vera (quoted above) rationalized her choice for Bolsonaro over Haddad in the following way: "He [Haddad] was educated, but he's from the left, and it's the left that would have ruled. Nothing would have changed. I voted for Bolsonaro to try to change things. You can see that things are changing, corruption, everything. It was too much. Haddad might have been educated, he might even have been better trained than Bolsonaro to be president. Because Bolsonaro was a military officer who wasn't prepared to be president. Sometimes he says things he shouldn't. But there was no option. Things had to change." This disillusionment with the political status quo was widespread among my interlocutors, and it is an important part of the puzzle as to why a vocally antiminority candidate could prove so popular among an ethnic minority such as Japanese Brazilians living overseas. As noted in the introduction to this volume, many who voted for Bolsonaro did so out of disenchantment and disillusionment rather than a deep-seated right-wing ideology. As long as he did not represent the PT, Bolsonaro could do or say just about anything and still garner voters' support. Similarly, in the United States, Smith and Hanley (2018) found that pro-Trump voters primarily wanted a president who would "shake things up," and that they valued a candidate's ability to "bring change" far above experience. Bolsonaro, for all his shortcomings, certainly represented change.

Finally, it is important to note the role of media in shaping the attitudes of overseas voters. Most of my interlocutors regularly followed Brazilian mainstream media in Japan, primarily via cable/satellite TV or the internet. They also frequently shared or followed news stories in Portuguese via Facebook and WhatsApp. The TV channels they watched most were Globo, SBT, Rede TV, and Bandeirantes. However, in many cases, I noticed that in the months preceding the 2018 presidential election, people who had previously watched Globo news on a regular basis were growing steadily more frustrated with it. They started to perceive Globo in particular, the free-to-air TV network with by far the most viewers in Brazil, as itself an instrument of corruption, dishonesty, and even "fake news." For example, one woman in her thirties commented, "I don't even watch Globo now. I prefer Bandeirantes or Record because Globo only knows how to criticize [*meter o pau no*] Bolsonaro. I used to watch it but once the campaign [for president] started, I got too mad at Globo." Another man in his midforties said, "Ever since he [Bolsonaro] started running for president, there was that false media saying he wouldn't win, and so I stopped following it [*desisti da mídia*] a little bit. There's a lot of fake news out there, they're saying things that aren't true." And finally, a man in his fifties said, "Media only says one thing. It says what is convenient. And Globo is on the side of the PT." Clearly, there are parallels here with the decline of trust and confidence in mainstream media that the United States experienced, particularly among Republicans in the lead-up to the 2016 presidential election of Donald Trump (see Allcott and Gentzkow 2017). Distrust in mainstream media also affected the position of Brazilian voters in Japan, who increasingly associated outlets such as Globo with bias and corruption.

To conclude, in reflecting on fieldwork among far-right activists, Agnieska Pasieka (2019) warns of the dangers of othering or exoticizing interlocutors with very different political views from her own. My goal in offering an analysis of the reasons Bolsonaro enjoyed so much support among Japanese Brazilian labor migrants has not been to explain away their "unlikeable beliefs" (Pasieka 2019). Rather, I have tried to put forward a perspective that is rarely accounted for in depictions of the far right in Brazil—that is, the views of people who are at once an ethnic minority in Brazil and who live far away from what they tend to consider their home. For many Brazilians in Japan, especially those who grew up partly or fully in Brazil, they wished they had never been compelled to leave Brazil in the first place. "My grandfather is Japanese, you know, I'm proud to be in Japan," Ricardo explained. "But I wish I had been more successful in Brazil, so that I didn't need to come here to work." Further, they often dreamed of returning to Brazil one day, but ideally to a Brazil that offered them the same material opportunities that life as a manual laborer in Japan did. As Samuel put it, "We who work hard here in Japan, we wish we were in Brazil, doing what we do here while still enjoying the same perks [*regalia*] that we do here. That's what we want, a Brazil that's fairer [*mais justo*], for everyone to be able to live well there and have things like we do here." Thus their support of Bolsonaro and his administration was guided first and foremost by a desire to enjoy the stability and comforts of Japan—a country where they continued to face both immobility and marginalization—in a place they could actually call home.

REFERENCES

Adachi, Nobuko. 2004. "*Japonês*: A Marker of Social Class or a Key Term in the Discourse of Race?" *Latin American Perspectives* 31 (3): 48–76.

Allcott, Hunt, and Matthew Gentzkow. 2017. "Social Media and Fake News in the 2016 Election." *Journal of Economic Perspectives* 31 (2): 211–236.

Alternativa. 2017. "Relembre: Aécio foi o candidato mais votado por eleitores no Japão em 2014" [Remember: Aécio was the candidate most voted for by voters in Japan in 2014]. *Alternativa*, May 19, 2017. https://www.alternativa.co.jp/Noticia/View/68747/Relembre-Aecio-foi-o-candidato-mais-votado-por-eleitores-no-Japao-em-2014.

———. 2018. "Bolsonaro vence em Nagoia e Oizumi com mais de 90% dos votos válidos" [Bolsonaro wins in Nagoya and Oizumi with more than 90% of valid votes]. October 28, 2018. https://www.alternativa.co.jp/Noticia/View/78333/Bolsonaro-vence-em-Nagoia-e-Oizumi-com-mais-de-90-dos-votos-validos.

Arcanjo, Daniela, and Joelmir Tavares. 2020. "Ofensa a Japoneses amplia rol de declarações preconceituosas de Bolsonaro" [Offense to Japanese expands list of Bolsonaro's prejudiced statements]. *Folha de São Paulo*, January 26, 2020. https://www1.folha.uol.com.br/poder/2020/01/ofensa-a-japoneses-amplia-rol-de-declaracoes-preconceituosas-de-bolsonaro.shtml.

Bevins, Vincent. 2013. "Credit-Card Binge Leaves Many Brazilians Deep in Debt." *Los Angeles Times*, November 26, 2013. https://www.latimes.com/business/la-fi-brazil-credit-squeeze-20131126-story.html.

Caesar, Gabriela. 2018. "EUA, Japão e Portugal têm maior eleitorado inscrito para votar no exterior nestas eleições" [The US, Japan, and Portugal have the largest registered electorates to vote overseas in these elections]. *Globo*, September 12, 2018. https://g1.globo.com/politica/eleicoes/2018/eleicao-em-numeros/noticia/2018/09/12/eua-japao-e-portugal-tem-maior-eleitorado-inscrito-para-votar-no-exterior-nestas-eleicoes.ghtml.

Castles, Stephen, Hein de Haas, and Mark J. Miller. 2014. *The Age of Migration: International Population Movements in the Modern World*. 5th ed. New York: Guilford.

Chiavacci, David. 2016. "Migration and Integration Patterns of New Immigrants in Japan: Diverse Structures of Inequality." In *Social Inequality in Post-growth Japan: Transformation during Economic and Demographic Stagnation*, edited by David Chiavacci and Carola Hommerich, 233–249. New York: Routledge.

Evans, Gillian. 2017. "Brexit Britain: Why We Are All Postindustrial Now." *American Ethnologist* 44 (2): 215–219.

Faiola, Anthony, and Marina Lopes. 2018. "How Jair Bolsonaro Entranced Brazil's Minorities—while Also Insulting Them: Opponents Call the Presidential Candidate a Racist. So Why Are Brazilians of Color Backing Him?" *Washington Post*, October 23, 2018. https://www.washingtonpost.com/world/the_americas/how-jair-bolsonaro-entranced-brazils-minorities--while-also-insulting-them/2018/10/23/a44485a4-d3b6-11e8-a4db-184311d27129_story.html?noredirect=on.

Gazeta Online. 2019. "Japoneses que vivem no Brasil temem piadas de Bolsonaro" [Japanese living in Brazil fear Bolsonaro's jokes]. May 28, 2019. https://www.gazetaonline.com.br/noticias/politica/2019/05/japoneses-que-vivem-no-brasil-temem-piadas-de-bolsonaro-1014182876.html.

Germano, Felipe. 2018. "Em quem votaram os Brasileiros que vivem no exterior?" [Who did Brazilians living overseas vote for?]. *Superinteressante*, October 29, 2018. https://super.abril.com.br/sociedade/em-quem-votaram-os-brasileiros-que-vivem-no-exterior/.

Gusterson, Hugh. 2017. "From Brexit to Trump: Anthropology and the Rise of Nationalist Populism." *American Ethnologist* 44 (2): 209–214.

Hochschild, Arlie. 2016. *Strangers in Their Own Land*. New York: New Press.

Ikeuchi, Suma. 2019. *Jesus Loves Japan: Return Migration and Global Pentecostalism in a Brazilian Diaspora*. Stanford: Stanford University Press.

IPC Digital. 2014. "Eleições 2014: Resultado oficial da apuração das urnas do Japão" [2014 Elections: Official Results of Ballots Counted in Japan]. October 6, 2014. http://www.ipcdigital.com/comunidade/eleicoes-2014-resultado-oficial-da-apuracao-das-urnas-do-japao/.

Istoé. 2019. "Bolsonaro compara Hélio Negão a 'maracujá pretinho' e faz piada com chineses" [Bolsonaro compares Hélio Negão to a "little black passionfruit" and jokes about Chinese]. October 11, 2019. https://istoe.com.br/bolsonaro-compara-helio-negao-a-maracuja-pretinho-e-faz-piada-com-chineses/.

Kondo, Atsushi. 2015. "Migration and Law in Japan." *Asia and the Pacific Policy Studies* 2(1): 155–168.

LeBaron von Baeyer, Sarah. 2020. *Living Transnationally between Japan and Brazil: Routes beyond Roots*. Lanham, Md.: Rowman and Littlefield.

Lesser, Jeffrey. 2013. *Immigration, Ethnicity, and National Identity in Brazil: 1808 to the Present*. New York: Cambridge University Press.

Londoño, Ernesto, and Shasta Darlington. 2018. "Jair Bolsonaro Wins Brazil's Presidency, in a Shift to the Far Right." *New York Times*, October 29, 2018. https://www.nytimes.com/2018/10/28/world/americas/jair-bolsonaro-brazil-election.html.

Margolis, Maxine. 2008. "September 11th and Transnationalism: The Case of Brazilian Immigrants in the United States." *Human Organization* 67 (1): 1–11.

Mikus, Marek. 2016. "The Justice of Neoliberalism: Moral Ideology and Redistributive Politics of Public-Sector Retrenchment in Serbia." *Social Anthropology* 24 (2): 211–227.

Ministry of Justice, Japan. 2019.「在留外国人統計」[Foreign resident statistics]. Accessed June 10, 2019. http://www.moj.go.jp/housei/toukei/toukei_ichiran_touroku.html.

Moreira, Assis. 2018. "Bolsonaro é o mais votado pelos brasileiros que vivem fora do país" [Bolsonaro is most voted for by Brazilians living overseas]. *Valor Econômico*, October 7, 2018. https://www.valor.com.br/politica/5909485/bolsonaro-e-o-mais-votado-pelos-brasileiros-que-vivem-fora-do-pais.

Pasieka, Agnieska. 2019. "Anthropology of the Far Right: What If We Like the 'Unlikeable' Others?" *Anthropology Today* 35 (1): 3–6.

Payne, Leigh, and Andreza Aruska de Souza Santos. 2020. "The Right-Wing Backlash in Brazil and Beyond." *Politics and Gender* 16 (1): 32–38.

Rea, Julián Castro. 2018. "Right-Wing Think Tank Networks in Latin America: The Mexican Connection." *Perspectives on Global Development and Technology* 17 (1–2): 89–102.

Ribeira, Fábio Ricardo. 2011. "O estranho enjaulado e o exótico domesticado: Reflexões sobre exotismo e abjeção entre nipodescendentes" [The strange caged and the exotic domesticated: Reflections on exoticism and abjection among Japanese descendants]. In *Japonesidades multiplicadas: Novos estudos sobre a presença japonesa no Brasil* [Multiplied Japaneseness: New Studies on the Japanese Presence in Brazil], edited by Igor José de Renó Machado, 87–114. São Carlos: EdUFSCar.

Roth, Joshua. 2002. *Brokered Homeland: Japanese Brazilian Migrants in Japan*. Ithaca, N.Y.: Cornell University Press.

Sarmento, Claudia. 2010. "Milhares de brasileiros votam no Japão onde pesquisas apontam vitória de serra" [Thousands of Brazilians Vote in Japan Where Studies Point to Victory for Serra]. *O Globo*, October 31, 2010. https://oglobo.globo.com/brasil/eleicoes-2010/milhares-de-brasileiros-votam-no-japao-onde-pesquisas-apontam-vitoria-de-serra-4983084.

Schipani, Andres, and Joe Leahy. 2018. "Brazilian Discontent Trumps Distaste for Bolsonaro." *Financial Times*, October 26, 2018. https://www.ft.com/content/9d3e4668-d47a-11e8-a854-33d6f82e62f8.

Shoshan, Nitzan. 2016. *The Management of Hate: Nation, Affect, and the Governance of Right-Wing Extremism in Germany*. Princeton, N.J.: Princeton University Press.

Smith, David Norman, and Eric Hanley. 2018. "The Anger Games: Who Voted for Donald Trump in the 2016 Election, and Why?" *Critical Sociology* 44 (2): 195–212.

Spektor, Matias. 2018. "It's Not Just the Right That's Voting for Bolsonaro. It's Everyone." *Foreign Policy*, October 26, 2018. https://foreignpolicy.com/2018/10/26/its-not-just-the-right-thats-voting-for-bolsonaro-its-everyone-far-right-brazil-corruption-center-left-anger-pt-black-gay-racism-homophobia/.

Tanno, Kiyoto (丹野清人). 1999.「在日ブラジル人の労働市場―業務請負業と日系ブラジル人労働者」 [Zainichi Brazilians' labor and lives]. *Ohara Shakai Mondai Kenkyūjo Zasshi* 487:21–40.

Toma, Christiane Yuri. 2000. *A experiência feminina dekassegui* [The experience of women Dekasegi]. Londrina: Editora UEL.

Tsuda, Takeyuki. 2003. *Strangers in the Ethnic Homeland: Japanese Brazilian Return Migration in Transnational Perspective*. New York: Columbia University Press.

Veja. 2018. "Japão: Em seção de Nagoia, Bolsonaro vence com 93% dos votos" [Japan: In Nagoya polling station, Bolsonaro wins with 93% of votes]. October 28, 2018. https://veja.abril.com.br/politica/em-secao-de-nagoia-bolsonaro-vence-com-93-dos-votos/.

Yamanaka, Keiko. 2003. "Feminization of Japanese Brazilian Labor Migration to Japan." In *Searching for Home Abroad: Japanese Brazilians and Transnationalism*, edited by Jeffrey Lesser, 163–200. Durham, N.C.: Duke University Press.

Zarur, Camila, Hellen Guimarães, and Rafael Nascimento. 2019. "Bolsonaro faz piada com oriental: 'Tudo pequenininho aí?'" [Bolsonaro jokes with Asian: "Everything tiny there?"]. *Globo Extra*, May 15, 2019. https://extra.globo.com/noticias/brasil/bolsonaro-faz-piada-com-oriental-tudo-pequenininho-ai-veja-video-rv1-1-23668287.html.

NOTES

1. For an account of this incident, see Zarur et al.'s 2019 article and accompanying video featured online in *Globo Extra*.
2. As historian Rogério Dezem points out in Arcanjo and Tavares's 2020 article in *Folha de São Paulo*, Bolsonaro's stereotypical views of Japanese Brazilians are not only commonplace throughout Brazil; they are also likely amplified by the president's having spent a significant amount of his childhood and adolescence in Vale do Ribeira, São Paulo, a region that played a historically important role in Japanese immigration to Brazil.
3. Note, however, that this is far from the only time Bolsonaro has directed pejorative remarks toward people of East Asian appearance. See, for example, his racist imitation of "Chinese eyes" during a live stream on Facebook with Hélio Lopes (*Istoé* 2019) or his racist rebuke of journalist Thaís Oyama, a third-generation Japanese Brazilian, following the publication of her book *Tormenta* (Storm), about the first year of Bolsonaro's presidency (Arcanjo and Tavares 2020).
4. See, for example, "Japão" (2018) and "Bolsonaro vence em Nagoia e Oizumi com mais de 90% dos votos válidos" (2018).
5. For more information on the 2014 election results of Brazilians voting from Japan, see *IPC Digital* (2014) and *Alternativa* (2017), and for the 2010 election results, see Sarmento (2010).
6. Figure compiled by the author using data drawn from Japan's Immigration Bureau and Ministry of Justice websites.
7. According to data from Brazil's Superior Electoral Court, or Tribunal Superior Eleitoral (TSE), of the 104,838,753 valid votes counted in all of Brazil for the second term of the 2018 presidential election, 57,797,847 (55.13 percent) went to Jair Bolsonaro and 47,040,906 (44.87 percent) went to Fernando Haddad. Compare this to the 185,401 total valid votes counted among all overseas Brazilians, of which 131,671 (71.02 percent) went to Bolsonaro and only 53,730 (28.98 percent) went to Haddad. Data from the TSE is available at http://divulga.tse.jus.br/oficial/index.html (accessed September 7, 2019).
8. See Mitchell, this volume, for a discussion of corruption as a floating signifier and as a common idiom for discussing politics in Brazil.
9. Petrobras, or the Brazilian Petroleum Corporation, is a semipublic entity that, in 2014, was at the heart of Operação Lava Jato (Operation Car Wash), the largest corruption scandal in the history of Brazil. The Brazilian Development Bank, or Banco Nacional de Desenvolvimento Econômico e Social (BNDES), for its part, has been accused—notably by Bolsonaro and his government—of being in cahoots with the former PT leadership and big business.
10. Bolsa Família is a Brazilian social welfare program characterized by conditional cash transfers that then-president Lula initiated in the early 2000s. Supporters consider it an important factor in lifting millions of

Brazilians out of poverty, while critics view it as a vehicle for encouraging laziness and buying votes. Prior to Bolsa Família, cash transfer programs known as Bolsa Escola, Bolsa Alimentação, and Auxílio Gás (School, Nutrition, and Cooking Gas Allowances) had existed under the Cardoso administration of the 1990s. Bolsa Família replaced and unified these three previous programs.

11. Under then-presidents Lula and Dilma, credit became widely available for the first time to people of all classes. Government-controlled banks provided many poor and middle-class citizens with loans and credit cards in an attempt to stimulate Brazil's economy, particularly in the wake of the 2008 financial crisis. Credit soared, but so did debt and defaults on loans (see Bevins 2013).

12. See Patricia de Santana Pinho, this volume, and Payne and de Souza Santos (2020) for a related discussion of backlash among Brazil's traditional middle class against PT income redistribution programs and the upward mobility of the poor.

13. See Moisés Kopper, this volume, for a pertinent analysis of aspirations around "material hope" and the struggle to avoid falling back into a condition he calls "negative hope."

PART IV OLD CHALLENGES, NEW ACTIVISM

13 · HOLDING THE WAVE

Black LGBTI+ Feminist Resilience amid the Reactionary Turn in Rio de Janeiro

LASHANDRA SULLIVAN

The public outcry in response to the assassination of Rio de Janeiro's first Black, openly lesbian city councilwoman, Marielle Franco, in March 2018 drew attention to the considerable coalition-building and political activism occurring within social movements in Rio, of which she was an exemplar and central figure. Black feminists and LGBTI+[1] activists constitute critical and formidable voices in city politics. These are politics shaped most recently by the rise of one of Rio's former federal congressmen and now president of Brazil, Jair Bolsonaro—a misogynist, proudly homophobic, and openly nostalgic enthusiast for the country's military dictatorship that lasted from the 1960s through the 1980s. Also in 2018, Wilson Witzell was elected state governor—his governance includes anti-Black "shoot to kill" policing policies.

In this chapter, I explore a seemingly basic, but not to be taken for granted, element in the lives of Black feminists and LGBTI+ activists and nonactivists alike: their ability to hold on despite the crisis. The concept of *segurar* (holding on / staying upright) refers to an embodied social practice, and a challenging one at that. Its degree of difficulty is unevenly distributed across society. As scholars/activists in the Combahee River Collective (2012 [1977]) argued when they coined the terms *intersectionality* and *interlocking oppressions*, we inhabit differently marked bodies that differentially traverse racism, class, and heteronormative patriarchy.[2] It is worth noting that holding on / staying upright implies its counterpoint—that is, the concept of falling. The latter may have underlying causes stemming from the aforementioned intersectional and systemic social challenges. One recurrently finds oneself encountering an obstacle to staying upright. This condition may serve as an impediment not just to staying upright but to proceeding along one's way, to pursuing a path, even a path that one is attempting, despite it all, to envision and forge.

Eduardo Viveiros de Castro (2004) wrote that one could describe walking as "controlled falling." This description neatly captures *segurar* in Rio, even more so now, where going about one's day is an exercise in overcoming whatever one's odds are of staying on one's feet, staying in place, of keeping going. Let us praise this mundane, yet formidable, feat. Controlled falling, when falling is willed by forces beyond you, abuts the sizable counterforce of gravity. The analogy of gravity raises questions about what sorts of physics and metaphysics are in play in this conception of staying upright.

Since January of 2017, I have worked with a cross section of Black feminist and LGBTI+ activists, academics, and artists to query how the political, economic, and cultural transformations of recent decades have translated into activist mobilizations. In Rio de Janeiro, inflection points of the current crisis include a historic economic collapse; the 2016 impeachment of President Dilma Rousseff, which removed the Workers' Party (the PT) from power; state fiscal crises following massive spending in the run-up to the 2014 World Cup and 2016 Olympics; and the extensive graft and subsequent imprisonment of former Rio de Janeiro governor Sergio Cabral in 2017. Additionally, 2018 brought the military takeover of the security of Rio de Janeiro in February (notably not the first intervention of its kind in the city since the end of the aforementioned military dictatorship), the assassination of Marielle Franco in March, and the political imprisonment of former President Luiz Inácio Lula da Silva in April. We may view these events as part of a backlash against the gains made by progressive activism and electoral politics since the early 2000s, itself a product of a longer dureé of politics.[3]

I argue that an aesthetics of governance overarches this right-wing turn—an ultraconservative, neofascist glorification of violence evidenced in explicit rhetoric, gestures, and enactments in state policies and programs. For example, one of Bolsonaro's signature moves performatively mimics shooting a machine gun, all while brandishing a broad grin. This public gesture, often imitated by his supporters, serves as a fitting appurtenance for Bolsonaro's advocacy for extrajudicial killings of "criminals" (Londoño and Andreoni 2018), labeling of social justice activists as terrorists (Fox 2019; Phillips 2018), as well as his grossly homophobic and misogynistic rants (Brum 2018).

As pointed out in the introduction to this book, such aesthetics speak to the centrality of affect in politics. Affective registers operate as the embodied, intimate, and visceral domain of macro-level political transformations. In Rio de Janeiro, the state violence against intersectionally marked racial, classed, and sexualized bodies has accelerated. For example, in the first half of 2019 (between January and June), police in Rio de Janeiro killed 881 people, a 30 percent increase over that time span from the previous year (*Economist* 2019). Even before the 2018 elections, Brazil had one of the world's highest rates of violence (including murder) of LGBTI+ people (Grupo Gay da Bahia 2017), especially against Black lesbian and trans women (Gonçalves 2015).

I focus on the concept of *segurar* or *segurar a onda* (literally to hold the wave), to reference what might be either a physical or moral posturing, as both a metaphor and a tangible challenge. For example, I asked a Brazilian friend of mine about the phrase and its uses. He responded, "evitar um breakdown" (avoid a breakdown), attempting to help me get a sense of things. In practices of daily life, not necessarily stressful even, you find yourself tasked with having to *segurar a onda*.

The sorts of intellectual and experiential theorizing occurring through this practice present possible insights into collective strivings to survive what is happening in Brazil right now, and in reactionary politics unfolding elsewhere (such as the United States) as well, for those similarly embodied and disproportionately subjected to the brunt of this reactionary moment. Friends describe to me how Marielle Franco's murder "messed" (*mexeu*) with them and stirred up something within them. It knocked the wind out of them.

I am deliberately speaking in metaphors as both poetic speech and literal description. These are the terms by which people shared with me what is happening in their bodies. On the one hand, they piece together acts of revolt in the form of explicitly antiracist, antipatriarchal, and antiheterosexist public demonstrations as moments of overt politics. On the other hand, they are carrying on the rather quotidian practices of daily life, going about their days simply managing to not be swept away or brought down (e.g., by the police, stress, or grief). In other words, *segurar* is an effort at well-being, which amid these circumstances is necessarily an act of defiance.

While in other work I explore different aspects of the concept of *segurar*, such as joyful social practices like dancing and erotic longing (Sullivan n.d.), in this chapter I focus on how *segurar* occurs in the entwinement of matter and memory in the aesthetics of the built environment. I argue that what Rancière (2007) calls the "politics of aesthetics" factors into the placemaking and self-making practices of Black feminist and LGBTI+ activists. I argue that *segurar* is a countermanding practice of resilience in the face of the aforementioned reactionary governance. *Segurar* involves conscious and unconscious processes of remembering, which are embodied social practices and reference the intersectional markings of the body—racial, gendered, sexualized, and classed. It consists of efforts to survive violence through tactics of placemaking and self-making in conscious and unconscious invocations of memory (Certeau 1984).

In the remaining sections of this chapter, I (1) explain *segurar* as an embodied practice of remembering and remaking the city of Rio, with a focus on the Lapa neighborhood, and (2) analyze how *segurar* sheds light on politics in intersectional aesthetics.

I begin, however, by clarifying the reactionary nature of the political crisis in Brazil as it concerns the intersections of race, gender, class, and sexuality. It is to this nature of the crisis that I now turn.

CRISIS AS BACKLASH

We must view the rise of right-wing politics like those of Bolsonaro in light of the shifting terms for politics wrought by the multiscalar transformations in Brazilian society since the turn of the twenty-first century. Black feminist and LGBTI+ activists seek to make their lives more livable and visible under current conditions of economic austerity and political retrocession from progressive gains made under the Workers' Party (PT) government, which was in federal power from 2003 to 2016.

The people I work with describe the current crisis as a moment of intensification rather than something new.[4] Brazil consistently ranks as one of the most unequal countries in the world in terms of wealth, education, health, and other social indicators, a situation made worse by the current crisis. For example, the homeless population in Rio has increased 150 percent in the last three years (Vilela 2017). These inequalities are significantly marked by racial disparities in a country that has a majority Afro-descended population. For example, as recently as 2002, only around 2 percent of university students in Rio were Black (Rohter 2001). Additionally, the country has some of the world's highest rates of violence (including murder) against LGBTI+ people, which disproportionately affects Black trans women.

Over the course of the early 2000s, however, life at the aforementioned interstices had begun to change.[5] First, the implementation of quotas in the university system and other public institutions saw poor and Black people entering the higher education system in Brazil in significant numbers for the first time in the country's history. Likewise, public expenditures expanded the university system and public sector. Accordingly, decades-long activist efforts bore fruit and more university-related activists joined these efforts.

Additionally, this period coincided with an expansion of purchasing power by poor and Black Brazilians due to the government's fiscal policies of the era. For example, extension of credit for cars and houses, social policies requiring a higher minimum wage, social programs subsidizing food (e.g., the Bolsa Família), schooling, and health care all put more money into the hands of Black Brazilians. Working-class and Black Brazilians began to circulate in spaces heretofore exclusively occupied by a white middle class, such as airports, universities, and elite shopping malls. These changes, while minimal, were meaningful in a country significantly marked by racism and class stratification.

Also, Black Cariocas (residents of Rio) began to more robustly embrace *negritude* (e.g., through natural hairstyles like Afros and dreadlocks) because of a conjuncture of factors, valorizing *negritude* in complicated ways. While certainly predating this era, such expressions of this type of aesthetic Blackness expanded to include a broader popular mass audience in Rio.

These converging factors significantly impacted the terms for politics, particularly Black politics in its intersections with gender and sexuality. Black activists continue efforts demanding respect for and fulfillment of their citizenship rights, notably calling for an end to exorbitantly high rates of police killings of Black people. Rio's chapters of feminist organizations like Rede Nacional de Feministas Anti-Prohibicionistas (RENFA; National Feminist Network against the War on Drugs) explicitly link the drug war to anti-Black genocide. They utilize Black feminist critiques in public forums and engage in direct actions like the Marcha para Maconha (March for Marijuana), which feature signs such as those reading "Sou feminista e Negra e Não Passo Beque para Machista" (I'm Black and Feminist and I Don't Pass My Joints to Misogynists) to end drug prohibition and its attending violence.

This is also a moment in which an open embrace of Black LGBTI+ identities gained more widespread visibility. Begun in the early 1990s, multiracial LGBT organizations like the Articulação Brasileira de Lesbicas likewise engage in intersectional activism with overlapping and shared public actions with organizations like Associação de Mulheres Felipa de Souza and Complexo G (a collective of LGBTI+ *favela* residents).[6] Recent years have also seen the emergence of Black LGBTI+ events and spaces: *bailes de favela* and *festas negras* (social gatherings for Black LGBTI+ people, as well as Bicha Preta [a conversation group for Black gay men in Rio]).

It is no coincidence then that during the vote on impeachment in 2016, conservative congressmen often cited defense of the family as their reason for impeaching Rousseff for budget maneuvers.[7] Some, such as then-congressman and now president Jair Bolsonaro, explicitly waxed nostalgic about the era of the military dictatorship and its violent, tortuous figures like Colonel Carlos Brilhante Ustra. Among the subsequent postimpeachment conservative government's first actions was the abolishment of the ministries defending the rights of women, Black, and LGBTI+ people.

It is helpful to consider these events in light of a report published by Black lesbian activists Dayana Guzmão and Michele Seixas (2018). Included in an anthology written on and by lesbians in Brazil, their chapter was titled "Dez Anos de Atuação do Movimento de Lésbicas no Complexo da Maré: Reflexões de Sapatões Faveladas" (Ten Years of Activism of the Lesbian Movement in Complexo da Maré: Reflections by Favela Lesbians). They detailed and analyzed some of the intersectional challenges of living and movement building in the Maré *favela*. They note the troubling advance of religious conservatism and the dramatic proliferation of radical Protestant (Evangelical) churches that, often in coalition with drug traffickers in a given *favela*, dictate "social rules" of living in the territories. Guzmão and Seixas recall that over the past five years, they have seen the expulsion of African-based religions from Maré and the spurring of Evangelicalism. They detail the impositions encountered by lesbians, such as rites of exorcism as a way to cure lesbianism. They also include reports of evictions of outed lesbians from their homes. Physical violence persists as well, with messages like "Se essas mulheres querem ser homens vão apanhar como homens" (If these women want to be men they will get beat up like men; 2018, 109).

When I focus on the concept of *segurar*, I am analyzing how activists at the intersections of the backlash survive and insist on their ongoing well-being. They do so against the tide of longstanding asymmetrical material conditions (e.g., wealth inequalities, structural changes in labor, uneven access to land and other forms of property), in which the legacies of slavery and systemic racism, sexism, and homophobia in Brazil weigh heavily.

WALKING WITH SPIRITS

The weight of history referenced above is more than metaphor. Social actors at the intersections of the backlash feel this in their bodies as they move through the cityscape. The aesthetics of the built environment of the city—architecture of buildings, layout of roads—inculcate social actors who indeed make and remake the city in their crossings.

In this chapter, I am in dialogue with Aisha Beliso-De Jesús (2013) who, writing about Cuban Santeria practitioners, reminds us that self-making practices—or habitus—occur in perpetual relations with those who have lived before us—what she calls spirit copresences. We can think of the events that I am describing in Rio as unfolding in what Beliso-De Jesús calls a racial historical matrix. Sensing of spiritual copresences entails self-making through somatic registers whereby what one senses occurs in dialogue with a racialized past. That sensing is with historical actors—enslaved ancestors, deities—with whom one shares ongoing circumstances of shared subjection to (neo)colonial structures. One navigates these places as embodied and enmeshed in social relations with and through things and experienced amid an ongoing reproduction of racialized violence under neocolonial structures. Practices of re-membering (put together or perpetually reconstituting) the self through copresences of varying sorts are rematerializations that transpire through memory, consciously or unconsciously.

Marielle Franco's murder took place a few blocks from the Casa das Pretas (House of Black Women), which is located in the neighborhood of Lapa. She had attended a public forum there titled "Young Black Women Who Are Changing Power Structures" (Ramaswamy 2018). Lapa is famous as a hub of tourist-oriented nightlife. However, along the lines of Casa das Pretas, the neighborhood also features a critical mass of social justice–inspired Black feminist and LGBTI+ activism, as well as coalitional artistic productions like the *Teatro dos Oprimidos* (Theater of the Oppressed) or politicized carnival street bands (*blocos*) like *Bloconcé* (Rubim 2020).

One evening in mid-2018, I was sitting in Lapa with a group of fellow activist friends at a pizza parlor. A Brazilian friend, Graciela,[8] described a moment that she experienced on the bus while traversing the neighborhood. She described that she was on the city bus a few months after Marielle Franco's assassination when she suddenly felt lightheaded and passed out without knowing why. Without realizing, she was traversing the area where Marielle had been murdered. Marielle was a fellow activist and comrade whom she had known personally.

Graciela did not tell me that she had experienced Marielle's ghost or anything along those lines when she passed out. No, she merely described how she had remembered without remembering that the street she was on was the site of Marielle's murder. Memories of Marielle and of what took place there pieced themselves back together for Graciela merely through her passing through. Here an enmeshment of mind, body, and place coalesced and brought her down.

Graciela was passing near the intersection where assassins fired into Marielle Franco's car, killing her and the driver. Graciela passed by that site months later during a routine commute. She had remembered Marielle and the murder without noticing; re-membered without remembering why.

I have visited that part of Rio many times. Located in a border area between Lapa and downtown, I was there one day in 2018 to visit Casa das Pretas for an event about Black feminism. Navigating that part of the city on a weekday around 6:30 p.m., just at dusk, I was struck by that peculiar feeling of how a bustling downtown-adjacent area can yet feel empty, as those who work there depart and those who live there return, or some such feeling of the in-between of presences and absences. Office workers give way to the many patrons of sidewalk bars and restaurants and the interactions of the homeless, the poor, and the sellers of knickknacks or peanuts left on small shards of paper on tabletops in hope of exchange for a *moeda* (coin).

Michel de Certeau (1984) writes that there are no places that are not inhabited by spirits. Fragments of memory lend histories or flashes of the past as spirits haunt a locale. Treating thorny questions of materiality and memory, Collins (2016) similarly ponders the materialization of history in making the built environment of the Pelourinho neighborhood in Salvador de Bahia. He describes how we piece together history in the construction of that built environment, including in its preservation. Far from a mere backdrop, the material objects of our world are active participants in our practices of being/making ourselves. Objects call forth memories. That which has come before has not passed. In Rio, this is a world built by slavery and racialized, gendered, sexualized forms of domination that are no less implicated in Rio's ongoing remaking, as evidenced in Marielle's assassination.

I should state explicitly that practices of *segurar* (staying upright / holding on) are processual. They are nonsequential with other practices, with which they are inseparable. To stay upright implies, requires, and entails the practice of lying down and other moments of rest: necessary complements to staying upright. These processes present transfigurations of dispositions between standing, walking, running, and lying down. All are rematerializations precipitated by muscle memory, conscious recollection, or other physiobiological, emotional, and psychological processes.

This is a central element to my argument. In the concept of *segurar* / *segurar a onda*, I am talking about the procession between the different phases of being and becoming, both interior and exterior planes of being, as one goes about the practical activity of living. They are nonsequential, constantly shifting, and situated always in objective materializations in and through which we live, which are the making of life.

Attention to the mundane workings of the body in motion helps capture how these phases/dispositions are intertwined and animated by memory. Walking, for example, as controlled falling underlines how the aforementioned phases of motion are shared coconstituted conditions/statuses that require recollections. You don't consciously reflect on how to walk; one remembers without remembering. This includes orienting the body as one navigates the city. Such delimited improvisations strike me as iterative of the controlled falling one reenacts with every step in and through the flows of daily life. Prescribed routines unfold through open-ended encounters in countless moments of unconscious choreography that make up a city. One remembers unconsciously, unthinkingly, and in or out of sync, though ever in rhythm. The past remains in your body and in the material landscape, dead matter that is all too lively, structuring the present, determinative but never completely foreclosing.

Practices of making and remaking the area as such underline forms of coping and resilience occurring in the city, as well as enacted through the built matter of areas like Rio in bodily practices of remembering. The latter refers to conscious and unconscious engagements with and through the architecture of buildings, the layout of roads, plazas, and iconic structures like the Arches of Lapa.

Lapa presents striking contrasts as an urban landscape. As a site of residence, working-class life transpires amid more well-to-do residents and newer edifices wrought with gentrification policies of recent decades. Begun in the late 1980s, programs like the Cultural Corridor plan sought to transform Lapa into a rollicking hub of middle-class leisure/nightlife by attracting private capital. This included partnerships between public and private financing for a mix of construction projects and renovation of older buildings from the colonial and turn-of-the-twentieth-century Belle Époque periods. Led by Francisco Pereira Passos, elites during the so-called Belle Époque era (approximately 1898—1914) sought to transform Rio into a sort of Paris in the tropics. Features included Haussmannesque demolitions, construction of thoroughfares, and architecture imitating designs from Georges-Eugène Haussmann's Paris (like the Opera house; Pinheiro 2002).[9]

The Cultural Corridor program likewise consisted of zoning changes and marketing campaigns that reshaped the area from the previously dilapidated state incurred with mid-century, postindustrial decline in the city center and severe economic recession in the 1980s. The latter saw the municipality introduce harsh Shock of Order and later Project Lapa Legal policing policies designed to "clean up" informal economic activities in the streets (Caruso 2015). Such discourses covertly carried all the accompanying anti-Black and antipoor connotations and targets. As such, they echo state and elite rhetoric and aims from the aforementioned colonial and Belle Époque periods, which Needell (1984) describes as explicitly concerned with efforts to "de-Africanize" the city.[10]

As mentioned above, Black feminist and LGBTI+ placemaking and self-making activities in Lapa and larger Rio were previously facilitated by state financial and political support, fruits of organizing from decades past.[11] Though undercut by the recent reactionary turn in politics, such activism nevertheless persists. Prior state support ushered in spaces for headquarters for civil society organizations like the Black-led lesbian activist organization Mulheres Felipa de Souza, though several of such offices have closed as a result of the aforementioned budget cuts.

To return to the vignette, my last visit to the Casa das Pretas was in June 2018. Graciela's recollection of what happened to her there, as well as the events surrounding and following Marielle Franco's murder, stayed with me as I made my way through the neighborhood. I approached the building, whose address is inconspicuous, with no signage on the exterior. The door was locked, no windows to peer in, but there was a smallish opening where I could see light from inside. There was an intercom and a buzzer to ring. I did so and someone answered, though with no invitation to enter. Only a simple, "Oi?" (Hello?). I had the feeling that I was being watched by whoever had answered the buzzer, wherever they were, because of the camera above my head directed toward the entryway. I looked up at the camera. I explained that I had been invited by an elder Black lesbian activist and friend and that I was interested in the event being held to discuss Black feminism that was scheduled to start in an hour. He said that they would open in an hour and that I should come back.

I noted the security and wondered about the aftermaths of the assassination. I had randomly seen trucks of uniformed military personnel in my travels across the city in June 2018 that I had not seen in February earlier that year, nor the year before during fieldwork. I recalled the video of a police operation in Maré the week before, which had been circulated by activist friends and more broadly on WhatsApp and had gone viral. It showed a low hovering military helicopter, in which an officer leaned out and shot an automatic assault rifle into the densely populated neighborhood below. Several people were killed in what was described as an antidrug trafficking operation. People who were bystanders were also brought down, including an eight-year-old boy in his school uniform.

I am reminded of Beliso-De Jesús's (2013) aforementioned concept of a racial historical matrix, in which the somatic registers through which one senses, for example, spiritual copresences, occur in dialogue with a racialized past that is not past. One experiences and navigates places as enmeshed in social relations that are an ongoing reproduction of racialized violence under neocolonial structures. More than mere coping with trauma, such bodily registers and embodied navigations put together or perpetually reconstitute the self, materializations of historical memory, consciously and unconsciously.

The Rua dos Inválidos, running in front of the Casa das Pretas, is a one-way street leading to an intersection. On the intersection sits the Museu da Polícia Civil do Estado do Rio de Janeiro (Museum of the Civil Police of the State of Rio de Janeiro) on one corner; across sits an office supply store. On the last day that I visited in 2018, people were mulling about that area. I got the feeling you get of being in a place after an event has just ended, after a room has mostly emptied. You feel the remnants of vacated presences. Something is left over in that area of Rio. Activity continues, though in a seemingly dimmer light. There is an ambulation of phases, comings and goings, standing up and sitting, and in between. Of motion and rest. Of ceaselessness. Passing by, Graciela described to me that she managed to sit up again on the bus that day, somehow.

SEGURAR AND THE POLITICS OF AESTHETICS

In the remainder of the chapter, I analyze the *segurar* concept as it concerns the relationship between activism and aesthetic life, in the coping and forging ahead required amid these circumstances. The concept references the play of feeling in the experience of the ordering of the world that one experiences in embodied practices of daily life. This has a special significance in the world of media representations that inundate us: the circulation of images and sounds through which we see ourselves and imagine new vistas for living and freedom.

In 2018, I posted the following question to Facebook, "Alguém pode me ajudar com umas dicas? Estou procurando representações das lésbicas negras na mídia brasileira (filme, televisão, música, etc.)."[12] I received various recommendations for musicians: Mart'nalia, Sandra da Sá, Ellen Oleria, Pepe e Nenem, Marília Corrêa, Monique Caetano, Bia Ferreira, Luana Hansen Figueiredo. But I received the most poignant response when I asked specifically about visibility in TV and cinema. A friend in Rio responded, "TV e cinema eu acho que inexistem. Se fosse lésbica OU negra eu conseguiria te ajudar."[13] Thus the rendering of the visibility and invisibility of Black lesbian lives "on screen," so to speak, and the invisibility of Black lesbians project a reality in which one cannot be Black and lesbian and recognized. Black lesbians do not exist, do not matter.

As Jacques Rancière (2007) argues, politics involves the power to determine what can be seen and not seen, the making of the visible and invisible. Therefore, power determines what counts and matters and what counts so little as to not matter and therefore remain invisible, as though it does not exist. This power struggle over what is allowed to be, to exist, and to count as reality entails an ordering of the senses. This is what Rancière (2007) calls the "politics of aesthetics." The determination of what you can perceive constitutes part of the making of the social order. Or as Povinelli (2016) puts it, politics is the "ordering of the sensible," which transpires through a struggle to shape and to define reality and to determine what is as that which should be. Here I would argue, such machinations give form to the contours of what matters—literally the material composition and disposability of bodies in space. Recall the underlying nature of the reactionary backlash, as I described above.

The Grupo de Mulheres Felipa de Sousa (Felipa de Sousa Women's Group) is a Black feminist nonprofit organization that presents counteraesthetics toward coping through such brutalities. Founded on July 29, 2001, the group brings together lesbian, bisexual, and other nonheteronormative women. In coalition with broader networks of feminist and LGBTI+ activists in Rio, Brazil, and internationally, they are forging ways to both survive and turn back the right-wing neofascist wave. Their work focuses on feminist LBTQ sexual education and consciousness-raising activities regarding structural racism, misogyny, and homophobia in Rio's working-class neighborhoods, strategically aimed at engendering and building social resistance across the neighborhoods.

Felipa de Sousa's past and current programs include attempts to reorder and challenge common sense. The traveling exhibit "O Que Eles Levam No Peito" (What They Carry on Their Chests) raises consciousness and facilitates debate regarding violence against women. The exhibit consists of clothesline-shaped displays. On exhibit are T-shirts with sexist imagery and sexist phrases. Activists collect the T-shirts from people encountered in daily life while roaming the city.

Such is the prominence of misogynist slogans and imagery; these shirts fill the exhibit. The showing facilitates debates regarding the pervasiveness and perfunctory frequency of sexism and its contribution to violence against women in society.

Other activities include conversation groups with and for lesbian women, public forums to promote greater lesbian visibility, exhibits, and performances to educate on LGBT+ women's history, as well as to agitate against misogyny, homophobia, and transphobia. Their stated mission is to make society aware of the full rights of lesbians, bisexual women, and other women: "We do this work through programs and activities designed to improve our communities' living conditions, contribute to our community members' transformation into agents of social change, toward full citizenship and political awareness. We also promote exchanges with other related organizations, at [the] national and international level, as well as advocacy groups of other groups and/or human rights organizations; promote women's self-esteem with a view to improving their quality of life; participate, support and disseminate cultural, literary and sporting or any other work of interest to women; provide services and promote cultural awareness and transformations."[14]

Since its founding, Grupo de Mulheres Felipa de Sousa has prepared and executed projects in partnership with government and nonstate funders. They also conduct programs to discuss and disseminate information regarding the changing rights landscape, including the ever-shifting statuses and dismantling of public funding, policies, and programs that were gained in the last decade.

As another example, the performance piece "Madam/Lady History" (Senhora Pasado) is an improvisational performance that discusses the symbols, iconography, and "signaling" in and about the history of the lesbian movement in Brazil. Such symbols and signs—a form of LGBTI+ flagging and "being out"—are a part of an oral history of lesbian life, which the performance chronicles. The show recounts such symbols and performative aspects of lesbian culture in Brazil, chronologically tracing lesbian history in Rio from the 1970s until the present day.

I witnessed a performance of Senhora Pasado while attending an activist conference in Rio in 2018. Beliso-De Jesús's racial historical matrix concept also nicely captures the overlay of memory and afterlives invoked through the performance. While the aesthetic stylings and gestures of Carioca lesbians from that bygone era came to life through the performance, the line between representing them and re-presenting them (i.e., having them present again) felt like more than a metaphor as I moved through the audience trying to capture Senhora Pasado from closer up. I felt that viscerally as I gazed at and heard the interactions between the performer and audience.[15] As an ethnographer, I was learning about the signifying practices of Carioca lesbians of that bygone era for the first time. Yet, in the knowing nods and responses of the audience I was brought into a collective recollection, a resignifying of bodies and the space of the city.

Representation matters in the shaping of our realities and the configuration of what the broader society understands as existing, as mattering, and as possible. Kara Keeling (2007) describes such intersections and convergences of Blackness and lesbianism as countermoments to "hegemonic reality." They exemplify the seemingly impossible horizons for freedom and remaking of the world. In the entwinement of aesthetics and activism and mundane moments of conscious and unconscious remembrance, we see how Black and lesbian Cariocas cope and create resilience referenced as *segurar*.

Black lesbians move through this world with an acute sense of the proverbial non-sense of it, the performative and actual violence enacted against us through state and nonstate apparatuses.[16] Our intersectional identities amount to immense vulnerability and, therefore, to violence in multiple forms, including erasure in representations that pervade the society. Yet the forms of remembering, intentional and unconscious, such as in the earlier ethnographic vignette about

Graciela, point to forms of perseverance and recovery that may be otherwise overlooked as mundanely quotidian. Such resilience occurs through cultivation of embodied wherewithal in forms of re-membering.

It is worth remembering how the term *intersectionality*, which has rightly become famous and widely used, was coined by Black lesbian feminists almost fifty years ago. In "A Black Feminist Statement," members of the Combahee River Collective (2012 [1977])—Barbara Smith, Beverly Smith, and Demita Frazer—declared that as Black lesbian women, their articulations of and fight for feminism necessarily required that they not choose between or prioritize activism based solely on gender or race. In order to gain freedom, we must necessarily always think and act intersectionally. As Keeanga-Yahmatta Taylor (2012) points out, the collective was named after the site of the Combahee River in the state of South Carolina, where Harriet Tubman led a military raid that freed 750 slaves during the American Civil War. So already, we see in the inspiration for the name of the collective a central focus on liberation from bondage and servitude that is led by Black women.

In the traversing and crossings, and in the motions and movements that constitute the remaking of the daily life, the city, and possibilities for being and becoming Black, woman, and Brazilian, we see ongoing activist practices occurring to counter reactionary politics. Black feminist and LGBTI+ activists in Rio seek to hold on / stay upright and yet insist upon more than mere survival. They cope and creatively insist on the remaking of Rio through forms of *segurar*, the complexity of which I have tried to capture in this chapter. I have done so in the spirit of *segurar*, which I am witnessing in Rio and toward which I hope this work contributes.

ACKNOWLEDGMENTS

Foremost, I am grateful for the generous support and spirit of collaboration of the people with whom I work in Brazil. I would also like to thank colleagues and friends in Brazil and the United States for their generous comments and feedback on this work in workshops and writing groups over multiple rounds of drafts and revisions.

REFERENCES

Aguião, Sylvia. 2015. "A produção de identidades e o reconhecimento de sujeitos e direitos: Algumas possibilidades da perspectiva interseccional e da articulação de marcadores sociais da diferença" [The production of identities and the recognition of subjects and rights: Some possibilities of the intersectional perspective and the articulation of social markers of difference]. Paper for specialization course in gender and sexuality—EgeS. Disciplina 3—Sexualidade. Supplementary material. Rio de Janeiro: CLAM/IMS/UERJ, 2015.

Beliso-De Jesús, Aisha. 2013. "Santería Copresence and the Making of African Diaspora Bodies." *Cultural Anthropology* 29 (3): 503–526.

Benjamin, Walter. 1999. *The Arcades Project*. Cambridge, Mass.: Harvard University Press.

Brum, Eliane. 2018. "How a Homophobic, Misogynist, Racist 'Thing' Could Be Brazil's Next President." *Guardian*, October 6, 2018. https://www.theguardian.com/commentisfree/2018/oct/06/homophobic-mismogynist-racist-brazil-jair-bolsonaro.

Caruso, Haydeé. 2015. "A ordem e a desordem de ontem e de hoje: Notas etnográficas sobre a polícia na Lapa carioca" [Order and disorder from past and today: Ethnographic notes about police in Rio de Janeiro's Lapa]. *Civitas—Revista de ciências sociais* 15 (1): 66–83.

Certeau, Michel de. 1984. *The Practice of Everyday Life*. Berkeley: University of California Press.

Cohen, Cathy. 2005. "Punks, Bulldaggers, and Welfare Queens: The Radical Potential of Queer Politics?" In *Black Queer Studies: A Critical Anthology*, edited by E. Patrick Johnson and Sharon Holland, 437–465. Durham, N.C.: Duke University Press.

Collins, John. 2016. *Revolt of the Saints: Memory and Redemption in the Twilight of Brazilian Racial Democracy.* Durham, N.C.: Duke University Press.

Combahee River Collective. (1977) 2012. "A Black Feminist Statement." In *How We Get Free: Black Feminism and the Combahee River Collective,* edited by Keeanga-Yahmatta Taylor, 210–218. Chicago: Haymarket.

Economist. 2019. "Police Killings in the State of Rio de Janeiro Are at a 20-Year High." September 3, 2019. https://www.economist.com/graphic-detail/2019/09/03/police-killings-in-the-state-of-rio-de-janeiro-are-at-a-20-year-high.

Fox, Michael. 2019. "Clampdown on Housing Rights Activists in Bolsonaro's Brazil." *Nation,* August 27, 2019. https://www.thenation.com/article/brazil-bolsonaro-activists-housing-homeless-rights/.

Gonçalves, Juliana. 2015. "Marcha das mulheres negras, a marcha que faz sentido." *Carta Capital,* November 16, 2015. https://www.cartacapital.com.br/sociedade/marcha-das-mulheres-negras-a-marcha-que-faz-sentido-7941.html.

Grupo Gay de Bahia. 2017. *Relatorio 2017: Pessoas LGBT mortas no Brasil.*

Guzmão, Dayana, and Michele Seixas. 2018. "Dez anos de atuação do movimento de lésbicas no Complexo da Maré: Reflexões de Sapatões Faveladas" [Ten years of activism of the lesbian movement in Complexo da Maré: Reflections of Sapatões Faveladas]. In *Nossas histórias, nossas vozes: Resistências históricas de mulheres lésbicas e bissexuais no Brasil,* edited by Diana Raffaella Kalazans Ribeiro, 98–113. Rio de Janeiro: Editora Metanoia.

Keeling, Kara. 2007. *Witch's Flight: The Cinematic, the Black Femme, and the Image of Common Sense.* Durham, N.C.: Duke University Press.

Londoño, Ernesto, and Manuela Andreoni. 2018. "'We'll Dig Graves': Brazil's New Leaders Vow to Kill Criminals." *New York Times,* November 1, 2018. https://www.nytimes.com/2018/11/01/world/americas/bolsonaro-police-kill-criminals.html.

Needell, Jeffrey. 1984. "Making the *Belle Epoque* Concrete: The Urban Reforms of Rio de Janeiro under Pereira Passos." *Journal of Urban History* 10 (4): 383–422.

Phillips, Tom. 2018. "'A Political Rupture': Far Right Ready to Roll in Bolsonaro's Brazil." *Guardian,* November 2, 2018. https://www.theguardian.com/world/2018/nov/03/a-political-rupture-far-right-ready-to-roll-in-bolsonaros-brazil.

Pinheiro, Eloísa Pinheiro. 2002. *Europa, França e Bahia: Difusão e adaptação de modelos urbanos (Paris, Rio e Salvador)* [Europe, France, and Bahia: Diffusion and adaptation of urban models (Paris, Rio, and Salvador)]. Salvador: SciELO da UFBA.

Povinelli, Elizabeth. 2016. *Geontologies: A Requiem on Late Liberalism.* Durham, N.C.: Duke University Press.

Ramaswamy, Chitra. 2018. "Marielle Franco Had to Resist—No Wonder She Didn't Survive." *Guardian,* March 19, 2018. https://www.theguardian.com/lifeandstyle/2018/mar/19/marielle-franco-brazilian-political-activist-black-gay-single-mother-fearless-fighter-murder.

Rancière, Jacques. 2007. *The Politics of Aesthetics.* London: Continuum.

Rohter, Larry. 2001. "Multiracial Brazil Planning Quotas for Blacks." *New York Times,* October 2, 2001. https://www.nytimes.com/2001/10/02/world/multiracial-brazil-planning-quotas-for-blacks.html.

Rubim, Maira. 2020. "Bloconcé: Primeiro bloco do carnaval não official homenageia Beyoncé" [Bloconcé: First street band of nonofficial carnival to pay homage to Beyoncé]. *Yahoo! Notícias,* January 5, 2020. https://br.noticias.yahoo.com/bloconcé-primeiro-bloco-carnaval-não-145147158.html.

Sullivan, LaShandra. n.d. "Black Queer Feminism and the Politics of Revelry in Rio de Janeiro." Paper presented at the conference of the American Anthropological Association, Vancouver, B.C., November 22, 2019.

———. 2020. "Re-thinking the State in Africa through Gabon's Aesthetics of Governance." *Social Dynamics: A Journal of African Studies* 46 (1): 104–131.

Taylor, Keeanga-Yahmatta. 2012. *How We Get Free: Black Feminism and the Combahee River Collective.* Edited by Keeanga-Yahmatta Taylor. Chicago: Haymarket.

Vilela, Flávia. 2017. "Number of Homeless Nearly Triples in Rio." *Agência Brasil,* June 17, 2017. http://agenciabrasil.ebtc.com.br/en/direitos-humanos/noticia/2017-06/number-homeless-nearly-triples-rio. No longer extant.

Viveiros de Castro, Eduardo. 2004. "Perspectival Anthropology and the Method of Controlled Equivocation." *Tipití: Journal of the Society for the Anthropology of Lowland South America* 2 (1): 3–22.

Wheatley, Jonathon. 2019. "Rio de Janeiro's Militias: A Parallel Power in Bolsonaro's Brazil." *Financial Times,* March 24, 2019. https://www.ft.com/content/bdd61718-4b10-11e9-bbc9-6917dce3dc62.

NOTES

1. I use the acronym LGBTI+ (lesbian, gay, bisexual, transgender, and intersex), although I primarily discuss lesbian activists in this chapter. The people with whom I conduct fieldwork in Rio used the term *lesbian* to refer to women who have sexual and/or romantic desires for other women, regardless of whoever else they may desire. In other words, the category *lesbian* includes women who may otherwise also identify as bisexual or heterosexual. The people with whom I work in Rio didn't use the term *queer*. I have heard the term rejected as "white" and "middle class." This echoes some of the important criticisms of the term in its reappropriation by Black feminist scholars like Cohen (2005) in the U.S. context.
2. Taylor (2012) points out that the origin of the term *intersectionality* was created by the Combahee River Collective in its "A Black Feminist Statement."
3. Such gains include a 2018 Supreme Court ruling criminalizing homophobic and transphobic acts.
4. This accords with Perry's (2019) analysis of how a long history of Black feminist mobilizations reminds us of just that longer durée of anti-Black gendered state violence in Brazil. The current moment is both distinct and continuous with this longer history.
5. I would like to thank Everton Rangel and Wescrey Pereira for insights along these lines.
6. For further discussion of LGBTI+ organizations and activism, see, for example, chapters by Henning and Jarrín (both in this volume).
7. See Jarrín (this volume) for more elaborate discussion of Rousseff's impeachment and the conservative backlash against LGBTI+ and feminist gains.
8. I have changed all real names to aliases in order to protect confidentiality.
9. The Cultural Corridor and Belle Époque schemes exemplify what I call an aesthetics of governance. By this I refer to the connection between social organization and spatial organization, which directly implicates political economy and the social production of categories like race, gender, and sexuality in the organization of space. See Sullivan (2020) for more commentary on Benjamin (1999) and aesthetic governance.
10. See Cantero (this volume), for example, for more discussion of the centrality of racial capitalism to the development ideologies in Brazil.
11. Aguião (2015) argues that formal identification with categories like lesbian, gay, and bisexual cannot be understood separately from the civil society formations facilitated by interactions with the state over recent decades.
12. In English, this translates as "Can someone help me with some recommendations? I'm looking for representations of Black lesbians in Brazilian media (film, television, music, etc.)."
13. Translation: "In TV and cinema, this doesn't exist. If you were looking for lesbians *or* Black women, I'd be able to help you."
14. Correspondence with the author in 2019.
15. Smith (2016) brilliantly discusses Black Brazilian performance and activism, specifically the blurring of the real and the staged that the performance embodies and references. For further discussion of Black feminist LGBTI+ activism, see Jarrín (this volume).
16. By nonstate apparatuses, I am referring to such disparate and myriad forces as Evangelical churches (Guzmão and Seixas 2018) and armed private militias (Wheatley 2019) in Rio de Janeiro, for example.

14 · LGBTTI ELDERS IN BRAZIL
Subjectivation and Narratives about Resilience, Resistance, and Vulnerability

CARLOS EDUARDO HENNING

In June of 2018, I attended the XV National LGBT Seminar, which was hosted by progressive National Congress parties in Brasilia, to talk about my research on elderly LGBTTI people.[1] The event theme, coordinated by then-congressman Jean Wyllys, was precisely the health, well-being, and the aging of the LGBTTI community in Brazil.[2] At the conference panels that day, activists and researchers from all over the country shared the shock and mourning over the recent political execution of Marielle Franco, the left-wing, Black, lesbian PSOL councilwoman, who had gained prominence for her feminist, antiracist, pro-LGBTTI social activism and her defense of Rio de Janeiro's poor population.

I recall that several of us, people from many different backgrounds, spoke then about the frightening strengthening of the Brazilian far right after the coup that removed Dilma Rousseff from her presidency in 2016, as well as the possibilities to resist the conservative wave in the country. The conservative coalition known as Bullets, Bulls, and Bibles (BBB) was at the time expanding and further consolidating its power and political influence. Despite all this, few of us were seriously considering the possibility of victory for then-candidate Jair Bolsonaro—a mediocre right-wing politician with a history of apologies for torture, violence against LGBTTI people, as well as notoriously racist and misogynist speeches. Nor did we imagine that less than a year after that seminar, Wyllys—one of Bolsonaro's most notorious critics and opponents—would have to relinquish his political mandate and exile himself from Brazil, after being threatened with death by radical and conservative right-wing groups. It is still difficult to make sense of so many vertiginous events and the affective shift that Brazil has undergone in less than a decade.[3]

In recent years the Brazilian public had been bombarded by a tsunami of fake news about progressive politicians and intellectuals that associated them with the most infamous of crimes and practices. Some of these fake news even influenced the outcome of the presidential election. One of the most notorious examples was the "gay kit," educational material that according to Bolsonaro was aimed to encourage homosexuality among children. His campaign stated that Fernando Haddad, a presidential candidate from the Workers' Party (PT), had authorized the distribution of this "kit" during his time as minister of education. This type of fake news—which has been circulating since 2011 to stop the educational debate about sexual and gender diversity—was shared without end via messages and social networks on the internet. It is clear that these discourses demonized sexual and gender diversity for opportunistic political and electoral purposes.

Amid the dizziness of these events, I was preparing myself for a period of fieldwork in the context of Eternamente Sou, a nongovernmental organization in the city of São Paulo and a pioneer in advocating the "cause of LGBTTI elders" in Brazil. In the following months, I would research more intensively the narratives of volunteers and people assisted by this NGO. My fieldwork took place in the second half of 2018 and was therefore marked by the intense and stressful polarization of that year's political context. Bolsonaro's growing popularity, especially after the September 2018 attack on his life, generated a wave of fear among activists from minority political movements. In the weeks leading up to the election, allegations of physical and verbal abuse, as well as threats of extermination of LGBTTI people by Bolsonaro supporters across the country, had multiplied.

In this sense, I was able to follow and, in many moments, share with my interlocutors, moments of intense apprehension, fear, and anguish regarding the advance of the far right in the polls. Beyond the fear, we also shared many moments of mutual support and hope that ultraconservative projects based on Christian fundamentalisms and radical neoliberal economic projects would not come to power in the country. With polls showing Bolsonaro with a considerable advantage and a strong chance of victory, however, the tension and fear between LGBTTI activists were increasingly palpable. Among these circles it was possible to hear many reports of people having anxiety or panic attacks, planning to flee the country, researching ways to apply for political asylum or refugee status in other countries, and even attempting suicide. In the face of the concerns that a fascist regime could be established in the country, there were joking comments in some activist groups, accompanied by nervous laughter, which questioned which concentration camp we would prefer to be sent to.

Despite this extremely tense climate, I could see that such concerns seemed to affect younger LGBTTI activists in different ways when compared to the perceptions of my older interlocutors. In this chapter, therefore, I analyze the impacts of this recent turbulent political conjuncture from the perspective of three of my older interlocutors: Marcelo, sixty-three years old, a cisgender Black gay man; Esther, sixty-six years old, a cisgender Black lesbian; and Leda, a sixty-seven-year-old "white-but-mixed" travesti. As we will see, for most of them to survive and reach older age seemed somehow a victory and a privilege in itself.

I will address, in particular, what they pointed to as possibilities of survival and political resistance by LGBTTI people in the face of growing conservatism that seemed (and still seems) to threaten democratic freedom. Having lived part of their youth during the last military dictatorship in Brazil (1964–1985), their narratives in general terms highlighted their experiences with previous totalitarian regimes. They also addressed their daily hardships of having to deal with homophobia, lesbophobia, and transphobia, as well as, in some cases, racism and poverty during their entire lives in relation to the new "struggles of the present."[4]

First I will present some brief discussions regarding life course, old age, and LGBT gerontology. Then I will analyze my interlocutors' narratives over how their past "struggles, battles and fights" for the right to exist highlight a consistent commitment to an everyday resistance as their only viable alternative. My argument here is that it is possible to acknowledge some vivid ethics and aesthetics of courage and resilience through the analysis of their narratives, which has a strong generational component. While they used those experiences to mark a generational gap, they also mobilized it to support the younger LGBTTI folks in despair and defend both their right to exist and the maintenance of the democratic regime in the country.

LIFE COURSE, OLD AGE, AND LGBT GERONTOLOGY

The life course and its different moments have been analyzed in recent decades by history and the social sciences, not as universal and unchanging issues, but as plastic, variable, and in historical and cultural transformation (Ariès 1978; Featherstone 1994; Cohen 1998; Debert 1999). In this sense, analyzing aging, gender, and sexual diversity has been especially productive in focusing on current transformations in the life course, particularly in old age. For example, in contrast to conceptions that deny the relevance of sexuality for the elderly, there has emerged in recent decades what Debert and Brigeiro (2012) call a "process of eroticization of old age," which deeply shifts the place of sexuality at this moment in life. However, this new eroticization of old age in mainstream gerontology remains largely confined to heterosexual, cisgender, Caucasian, and monogamous subjectivities, limiting itself to a heteronormative panorama of aging (Henning 2014, 2016), and still promoting an erasure of issues related to sexual and gender diversity.

Having its roots in pioneer publications in the late 1960s, LGBT gerontology is a field that has been questioning both the conception of asexuality in old age and the heteronormative panorama over aging. The term *LGBT gerontology*, though, could be seen as an umbrella and provisional term that would include a set of relatively disparate and multidisciplinary investigations of the aging of LGBTTI people.[5] This field has been promoting a significant investment in the process of biopolitical constitution of this new aging population.[6] In general, these elderly are conceived as having idiosyncratic necessities that need to be known and managed by creating specific social programs, training dedicated professionals, by establishing particular practices and institutions of population management.

If initially this biopolitical process seemed to be confined to North America and some few other European countries, it has spread in recent years beyond those territories in a transnational awakening of the "LGBT elders" issue. In the Brazilian context, we are facing the concomitant development of LGBT gerontology with what I call the birth of an *orgulho grisalho* (a gray pride), which politically associates LGBTTI pride with the positive affirmation of being old.[7] Having that in mind, this gerontological field has decisively contributed to the establishment of biolegitimacy processes (Fassin 2009, 49), regarding the constitution of the LGBTTI elders as new subjects.

This process, however, is obviously not limited to research and publications on the subject but also focuses on the creation of organizations similar to Eternamente Sou, working specifically or primarily on what is claimed to be idiosyncrasies of the aging of LGBTTI people in several countries (Henning, 2016).[8] In São Paulo, Brazil, this emergence has taken place from 2017 onward, causing a growth in the visibility of aging LGBTTI people as a topic.

Although Eternamente Sou is a relatively new organization in the city of São Paulo and does not yet have regular funding sources, it nonetheless gathers an expressive team of volunteers counting with about thirty professionals. These include administrators, gerontologists, geriatricians, psychologists, social workers, social scientists, publicists, musicians, therapists, and dance and theater professionals. Their volunteers are mostly between the ages of twenty and sixty and identify themselves in various ways in terms of racial, gender, and sexual identities, although most identify as cisgender, middle class, and gay or lesbian. In addition, this team of volunteers was active, dynamic, and, despite the short existence of the NGO, had been organizing various events, courses, and lectures on old age and on sexual and gender diversity, as well as having excellent local, regional, and national political articulations. This set of features has ensured rapid visibility of the organization's activities and agenda regarding elderly LGBTTI individuals in Brazil.

Eternamente Sou also serves a few dozen LGBTTI seniors on a weekly basis through social, recreational, and varied programs. During the critical months of my fieldwork, this organization was definitely central in building a sense of community and safety, as well as in ensuring some collective hope among volunteers and those who were assisted by the NGO. I participated intensively in its activities and interviewed twenty-five people, most of whom were volunteers or were assisted by this organization. Most of the older interlocutors were between fifty and seventy years old and identified as lesbian, gay, bisexual, travesti, transsexual, or transgender. In what follows, I analyze interviews with three of my closest interlocutors during my fieldwork.

"ANOTHER BATTLE AMONG MANY OTHERS!": THE OLD WARRIORS AND THE RISE OF BOLSONARO IN BRAZIL

Marcelo—a fictitious name like all the others mentioned here—was one of my first field contacts and became one of the closest. By the time we met and I interviewed him—two weeks before Bolsonaro's victory—he was about to turn sixty-three years old. One thing that struck me from the start was his amazing energy, despite the serious health problems he was facing. He seemed almost always to be vivacious, smart, funny, and agile. He defined himself as a "cisgender man," a term he had recently learned with young volunteers from the nongovernmental organizations he attended. Marcelo was about six feet tall and identified himself racially sometimes as *negro* (Black), sometimes as *mestiço* (mestizo). When asked about sexual identity, he identified himself in different ways at different times; sometimes saying he was gay/homosexual, sometimes that he was bisexual, although sometimes he specified that he preferred not to categorize himself.

Marcelo stated that he was "living with HIV and fighting HIV" since the late 1980s, when he found himself seropositive in Brazil. At the time, he said, that was a "death sentence." He has been an activist in Brazil and Portugal for over twenty years in nongovernmental organizations defending LGBTTI rights as well as the rights of people living with HIV. Considering this set of "struggles" in different forms of activism, and also in terms of dealing with lifelong homophobia and racism, he has more than once declared himself *velho de guerra* (an old warrior) and always "ready to fight." He said he had retired in the mid-1990s and was lower-middle class, earning little over two minimum wage salaries and spending almost everything on his medicine.

In addition to the "battle" against HIV, Marcelo was diagnosed with leukemia around 2012, and in 2015, he discovered he had prostate cancer as well, which he also claimed to be fighting against with all his heart. He reported having an adult son, about thirty-five years old, with whom he had no contact whatsoever. Marcelo also claimed to have little contact with his family of origin, since his parents were deceased and his sisters and brothers lived in Rio de Janeiro. Besides that, most of his relatives seemed to support Bolsonaro, which contributed to the distance between them. However, Marcelo said he had a good relationship with his nieces, who were more "open minded" than the rest of the family. One of his nieces, the only one who lived in São Paulo, helped him with his health problems "when she could, once in a while," he said.

Besides his family of origin, the volunteers from Eternamente Sou, an organization he had discovered a few months before, helped him with everyday matters. One such support he received was in the search for a new home, which became necessary after the owner of the house in which Marcelo resided (and in which he had to share a room with two heterosexual men, also *bolsonaristas*) expelled him in an episode of homophobia and racism. He also reported to me that Eternamente Sou had been assisting him through socializing meetings and eventually guidance on his rights related to health issues. Marcelo stated, however, that most of the time he used to take care of his health issues absolutely by himself, even in situations of great fragility, such as after chemotherapy sessions.

As soon as we started talking, Marcelo addressed Bolsonaro's expressive vote in the first round of the presidential election, putting into perspective his "struggles in life" in front of what he saw as another imminent threat:

I see that younger gay men are panicking over Bozo's victory. But I don't think it's worth all the stress. I know there have been street attacks on gays and travestis, but I think this is just a phase. Sometimes when I see people in a panic, wanting to flee the country I think: guys, I've been living with HIV for over thirty years, I found out in 1987, I've been fighting leukemia since 2012! It's chronic leukemia, I'm going to die with it. Soon after leukemia I discovered that I had to also fight prostate cancer as well. Honestly, Bozo is not my main concern. My life is not defined by what this person says, thinks or does. . . . It's not that I'm not afraid of death, I have my ups and downs, but my life has always been a struggle for survival. It has always been like that. Fighting for life requires tremendous courage. That's why Bozo doesn't scare me. The times I had chemotherapy, I just had some help from one of my nieces. Most of the time I had to deal with it by myself. There were times when I didn't even have the strength to get up from my chair and take a few steps. That, definitely, was a fight for me! Clowns like Bozo come and go. They are not the ones who stay. They sure cause damage, of course, but life goes on and what we do with life is what matters. If we get cornered, they win. They want to make us panic. I'm just afraid that if he wins, he will end the SUS [the Public Health System].

Throughout our conversations, Marcelo made a point of putting into perspective and even neutralizing Bolsonaro's potential threat as just one of his many "struggles for life." In his view, "fighting" and "resisting" have been present throughout his entire life, having to face periods of poverty and daily forms of racism and homophobia since he was a small child. In this regard, Marcelo used to say that he "never had the chance of being carried away by depression, when hard times punched" him in the face. According to him, that was something that only rich people had the privilege to do, and his only alternative was to face the everyday challenges and try with all his forces to find a way to overcome them.

During the last military dictatorship, when he was very young, he was arrested for being part of a youth group at church due to potential "subversive activities." Marcelo said he had to spend a few nights in jail, although luckily he was not tortured. But beyond the military dictatorship, he emphasized above all his "great fight" against HIV/AIDS from the mid-1980s on. For him, those who lived through that time went through their own version of the "Vietnam War." In his view, younger gay men did not go through the "hard times" of yore, the even stronger racism and homophobia from back then, and didn't have the slightest notion of the "battle" at the time. This lack of experience, in his opinion, would make the younger gay folks more easily panic with "Bolsonaro's threat." For Marcelo, these past experiences and his daily "fight" against leukemia and prostate cancer (which he would later inform me was inoperable) were the practical issues that demanded his full attention.

In his narrative, Marcelo often stressed the need to manage and confront fear—as he had done many times in the past and still had to currently do—and saw them as central instruments in the fight against the new conservatism that was emerging in the country. Although he admitted many times that the LGBTTI youth of nowadays was very brave and audacious as well, he also liked to highlight the lack of experience of the youth with the "thicker prejudice," as well as the military dictatorship and the epidemic crisis of HIV/AIDS from the past. As we will see, other of my older interlocutors seemed to share some of these points of view.

Another interlocutor with whom I spent time and interviewed more than once was Esther. She defines herself as a lesbian, was sixty-six years old, has a daughter (who is also a lesbian), and said she was married, when young, to a man for about ten years. Only after her divorce did she come to understand herself as a lesbian. At the time, in the late 1970s, she also became involved with the feminist movement and participated in the founding of the PT (Workers' Party) in São Paulo.

Esther is a very kind woman who says she likes to dress well and is almost always in a good mood. A very easygoing person, wherever she goes, Esther publicly claims to be "a proud old lesbian!" She had a white father of Italian descent and a Black mother, and she racially identified herself as *negra* (Black). She worked most of her life as a teacher in São Paulo state schools and had recently retired. She was middle class and received a pensioner's salary plus a pension for being a widow.

After the divorce with her husband, she had some relationships with women, which, she said, did not make her happy, until finding the partner with whom she had a stable relationship—formalized through a civil union—for thirteen years. With this partner—her second marriage—she claims to have been very happy, but the relationship ended with the death of her wife due to a massive stroke. Since becoming a widow, Esther has faced periods of depression and devastating grief, from which she began to recover only recently. By mid-2018, she was starting a relationship with a new partner and they had plans of living together on the coast of São Paulo. Her partner was still "in the closet" to her children, which Esther disapproved of and put their relationship at risk.

The interview with Esther, in turn, took place between the first and the second round of the presidential elections. Bolsonaro had almost won in the first round, and in this interview, she discussed the elections and her predictions about the country's future. She also addressed her political participation in feminist and lesbian movements in the late 1970s, as well as her involvement in the founding of the PT (Workers' Party), among other issues:

> We have faced so much bad things in this country since the dictatorship. Even if this creature is elected, we will be able to survive. I'm sure of that. In the late 1970s, I became involved in political struggle through the women's movement. I was part of the group of mothers of the Catholic Church. I wanted to mingle after divorcing my ex-husband. At that time, I had many discoveries and new beginnings. I wanted to make new relationships, open myself up. There were lots of important feminists and lesbians, and they opened my head wide. It was a beautiful companionship, real support among very beautiful women. Everything Bozo hates we did at the time and it made us truly happy. [Laughs.] I was really happy to be in love a long time later, when I met my wife, who died four years ago. I met Beatriz, this last partner in 2001, on the UOL chat. Shortly after, we got married and lived together for thirteen years and only separated in death. And I suffered a lot; it was four and a half years ago and I suffered terribly. I thought I couldn't survive. And her death was sudden. She had a hemorrhagic stroke, it happened in front of all the teachers of our school. When I see so many people panicking and afraid of Bolsonaro winning, sometimes I stop and think, but I've been through such terrible situations! I've survived so many situations that I thought I wouldn't be able to handle. And I'm not here? If this guy wins the elections, we will defeat him on the streets. You can't despair, you have to fight, right? And I'm very proud and happy for having being part of it [the feminist and LGBTTI activism in the 1970s and 1980s].

Esther, like many interviewees who lived during the days of the last military dictatorship, or engaged in the political resistance at the time, seemed to carry with them a set of experiences that they claimed to have prepared them to cope with hard situations without giving in to "despair"—something they see as inherent among the youth—especially in regard to the imminent threat of a new authoritarian regime in Brazil.

Such interlocutors claimed to have experienced significant struggles, challenges, and losses in life, politics, the economy, democratic freedoms and made a point of reassuring younger activists, sometimes putting themselves as living proof that it was possible to survive, to resist, and to continue "fighting." Esther, in fact, was one of the interlocutors who made the point of constantly putting her past struggles into perspective as a way to reassure and strengthen the LGBTTI youth for contemporary battles.

Another interlocutor who also highlighted her lifelong struggles and her ability to survive them was Leda, a sixty-seven-year-old travesti who racially defined herself as "branca, mas misturada" (white but mixed) and heterosexual. In a country known for an extremely high murder rate of travestis, transsexuals, and transgender individuals and a very low life expectancy—of about thirty-five years old—for them, Leda used to say that she is truly a survivor, that she never thought she would reach her current age, and that she is very proud of being old.

She started "working the street" very young, at the age of twelve, "when I was still a kid," and remained a sex worker for many years. She currently lives primarily on a minimum wage grant from the São Paulo municipality, as part of a literacy program, as she is illiterate. As the grant she receives is not always enough to survive, Leda says sometimes she still "works the street" (which means to do sex work) and says, "I may be old, but there are definitely those who want me!"

Her interview took place a few weeks after the second round of elections, with the confirmation of Bolsonaro's victory. Leda told me she was born in the state of Ceará, in an arid and, at the time, very poor region and "was given" at the age of five to a family of influential politicians. In this and other homes, she worked intensively on cleaning, shopping, maintaining the house, and as a nanny, mostly without earning any salary at all. Leda claims to have harsh memories of that time, memories of various humiliations and violence, also because she was always "very feminine."

Tired of humiliation and semislave labor, she claims to have escaped the situation and spent a period as a child living homeless on the streets of Fortaleza. According to her:

By the time I ran away from home I was about ten, eleven years old and I had no ID! No birth certificate, nothing. At that time, they said that fags [*viado*] didn't need an ID. How hungry I was, Carlos. [She feels emotional and needs some time to go on.] I do not know how I did not die of hunger, cold, and so many beatings I had to face as a kid. After Fortaleza, I was about seventeen years old when I went to São Paulo, and then I made my career on the streets here. I spent many years without having any news about my family. They never came looking for me. I found a brother on Facebook this year; a friend helped me to find him. He convinced me to go back to Ceará to visit them. Of course I already bought gifts for everyone. I know my brothers are all on Bolsonaro's side, but Valdecir said that a brother is brother and that no politics will interfere in that. Look, I don't care about Bolsonaro, I want him to explode! Honey, I lived at the time of the Maluf's Rota [a very violent police force in the 1970s and 1980s], I lived on the streets during the dictatorship, when they would land batons on our heads. The only way to make them stop beating us was to shout that we had HIV. That's when they stopped, because they were afraid of getting infected. I saw them kill a lot of travestis. Taking them in the van and we never heard of them again. I have baggage with me, dear. There's not that many things that makes me afraid, oh no. . . . But I get a little worried about going back to Ceará, to tell the truth, but I trusted what my brother said over the phone. Blood is bigger than politics.

Pain, courage, and resilience intersect a great deal of Leda's narratives about her life. Although she was not organized politically in traditional terms throughout the military dictatorship, her narrative is not absent from painful memories of the repression and harassment of sex workers, particularly travestis, in the 1970s and 1980s. The murder and disappearance of many of her old travesti friends made her emotional several times.

While Marcelo was concerned about his daily struggle with health and Esther seemed to be dealing with her plans to move and live with her new partner by the beach, Leda, in turn, was very much involved with her long-awaited literacy project and reunion with her family of origin, even though she was afraid of the *bolsonarismo* among her relatives. Although these interlocutors' narratives do not equate to having to deal with the macropolitical conjuncture, the three of them—as well as most of my older interlocutors—claimed to have experienced true hardships throughout their lives and, therefore, feel more prepared and confident about having to deal with an eventual ultraconservative government.

The general tone of their narratives pointed to a notion of empowerment and strength through the existence of a "baggage" of past experiences—as Leda put it—accumulated over a lifetime. It is possible to note in their narratives an ethics and aesthetics of courage and resilience in times of adversity. In a similar manner to Marcelo's statement that he never had the privilege of being depressed or to give up when facing hard times, most of my interlocutors tended to agree, one way or another, with him. Sometimes it seemed to me that their narratives highlighted a metaphor of life as a battlefield with no periods of armistice. All the warlike and conflict expressions, like fights, battles, and struggles, were significantly present through their narratives marking in their view a kind of generational divide.

But at the same time, that "baggage" was used as an accusation against the youth. This ethics and aesthetics of courage and resilience was mobilized as a kind of intergenerational contribution they offered to younger LGBTTI people, albeit through criticism of their inexperience and naive despair. Such narratives, moreover, can be seen as profoundly marked in generational terms with regard to locating not the absence of fear but the continuing need for confronting it as the only path in terms of survival and agency. For my older interlocutors, the "struggle" was permanent, with regard to both everyday micropolitics and broader confrontations. From this perspective, life has always been and will always be a struggle, and such notions are indelibly inseparable in these narratives. So this "life as battlefield" had a sort of pluripotent character: at the same time it was mobilized in order to offer emotional support for the younger LGBTTI folks, it also acted like a rhetoric tool to defend both their right to exist and the maintenance of democracy in the country.

It is important to note that Marcelo, Esther, and Leda's considerations, to some extent, seem to be in line with the crisis competence hypothesis put forward by some LGBT gerontology researchers in the 1970s (Henning, 2016). This hypothesis claimed that addressing homophobia, lesbophobia, and transphobia early on—and I could add racism, poverty, and historical contingencies among my interlocutors—had made many LGBTTI older people feel better prepared and resilient to cope with new challenges and crises throughout their old age when compared with the broader population.

However, even though they claimed to have "baggage" that advantageously prepared them for new eventual "battles," practically all my older interlocutors defended the existence and expansion of organizations such as Eternamente Sou. Despite claiming to be "strong," "resilient" and "experienced" in the battles of life, all of them said that more LGBTTI elder-oriented organizations are needed, particularly in conservative contexts, when entire administrations are trying to erase dissident subjects in terms of gender and sexuality. Interlocutors such as Marcelo and Leda, even though they considered themselves to be strong, showed deep vulnerabilities at various times, even admitting that they needed stronger social support networks to deal with financial crises, the continuous homophobia and transphobia, as well as health care fragilities in their maturity.

It is significant that most of my older interlocutors lived with a variety of chronic diseases such as diabetes and heart and thyroid problems. Only a minority of them stated that they were also HIV positive. Unlike most of the reports gathered in the field, Esther was one of the few who said she was fully satisfied with the support she received from her daughter, as well as from her new partner and other close friends, and was not dealing with financial challenges. Even she, however, claimed that Eternamente Sou had a big contribution in changing her life for the better, securing an expansion in her social support networks and helping her overcome depression and better cope with her grief.

Marcelo, for example, despite the apparent vigor while facing so many "fights," had only the occasional support of his niece. For him, the support he received from Eternamente Sou was crucial for socialization in times of crisis, loneliness, weaknesses in his health, and the search for a new residence. Leda, in turn, claimed to spend long periods completely alone, as she had very few friends left. Her friends, particularly the travestis, were almost all much younger, as her older friends "had all been lost along the way."

Thus although they liked to assert their lives as marked by courage and resilience to adversity, such "old warriors"—as Marcelo liked to assert himself—were also largely impacted by undeniable vulnerabilities that became even more worrisome with Bolsonaro's victory. In this sense, such vulnerabilities could not be ignored in the analysis of their narratives, even if they were strongly marked by a relentless ethics and aesthetics of courage and resilience.

FINAL CONSIDERATIONS

In my current investigation, I have been able to access more complex scenarios than in my previous fieldwork,[9] especially in terms of race, class, gender, and sexuality. Many of my current interlocutors were from the lower middle class and working class and were economically precarious, living in low-income collective housing and even at risk of becoming homeless. The desire to have regular and continuous support from an institution focused primarily on LGBTTI seniors was recurrent and shared. Almost all claimed that such an organization was necessary, especially thinking of a future time when they would become less independent.

Although they displayed an image of resilience through their narratives, carrying with them a "baggage" of past experiences and struggles that prepared them and strengthened them for new battles, all were wary of future prospects. One way or another, they were concerned with the radical neoliberal political-economic proposals of the Bolsonaro government, and in particular the risk of extinction (or privatization) of the public health system in the country.

Moreover, they feared a radical social security reform—which would be eventually approved—that could reduce the value of their pensions (already quite low in some cases), or even extinguish them. Thus even in face of the combative narratives of my interlocutors as "old warriors" ready for new "fights," most of them showed very concrete concerns and vulnerabilities given the growing threats Bolsonaro and his cabinet posed to human rights policies.

Although the Brazilian National Congress has not yet created laws that protect and guarantee equal rights with respect to dissident sexual and gender identities, in recent years the Brazilian LGBTTI movement has achieved important legal victories. The Federal Supreme Court and other legal entities—although they can be seen by some as coresponsible for Brazil's complex political and economic situation—guaranteed the right to same-sex marriage in 2011, the right to rectify civil records by changing the name of travestis, transsexuals, and transgender people without the need for psychiatric reports or gender confirmation surgery in 2018, and the criminalization of homophobia and transphobia was approved throughout the country in June 2019—but in this matter, regulation is still needed. These were certainly crucial achievements at a very adverse time to the basic guarantee of human rights.[10]

It is ironic, however, that just as the process of subjectification of the LGBTTI elderly begins to take shape, as well as the development of LGBT gerontology in Brazil, the country faces one of the worst governments in its history concerning human rights, particularly with regards to gender and sexual diversity. Among other things, this process is complicated by a political conjuncture that not only denies the relevance of any debate on dissident sexual and gender identities but also attempts to completely erase the existence of LGBTTI people from public discourse.

Considering the combative narratives of these "old warriors," as well as the limitations and the potential vulnerabilities they faced, Marcelo's final words are illustrative of the ideas debated here, particularly the notion of "fighting" as sort of a vital commitment, as the only way to keep resisting, and ultimately, as the only way to keep existing: "I will continue to fight, even old and tired, as I have always done! After all, what else can I do? What alternative do I have?"

REFERENCES

Aguião, Silvia. 2018. *Fazer-se no "estado": Uma etnografia sobre o processo de constituição dos 'LGBT' como sujeitos de direitos no Brasil contemporâneo*. Rio de Janeiro: EdUERJ.
Ariès, Philippe. 1978. *História social da criança e da família*. Rio de Janeiro: Zahar Editores.
Cohen, Lawrence. 1998. "Não há velhice na Índia." In *Antropologia e velhice*, edited by G. G. Debert, 73–134. Textos Didáticos 13. Campinas: IFCH/Unicamp.
Debert, Guita Grin. 1999. *A reinvenção da velhice: Socialização e processos de reprivatização do envelhecimento*. São Paulo: EDUSP.
Debert, Guita Grin, and Mauro Brigeiro. 2012. "Fronteiras de gênero e a sexualidade na velhice." *Revista brasileira de ciências sociais* 27, no. 80 (October 2012): 37–55.
Fassin, Didier. 2009. "Another Politics of Life Is Possible." *Theory, Culture and Society* 26 (5): 44–60.
Featherstone, Mike. 1994. "O curso da vida: Corpo, cultura e o imaginário no processo de envelhecimento." In *Antropologia e velhice*, edited by Guita Debert, 49–71. Campinas: IFCH/Unicamp.
Ferreira, Glauco B. 2012. "Arco-íris em disputa: A 'parada da diversidade' de Florianópolis entre políticas, sujeitos e cidadanias." Master's thesis, Programa de Pós-Graduação em Antropologia Social, Universidade Federal de Santa Catarina.
Foucault, Michel. 1988. *História da sexualidade I: A vontade de saber*. Rio de Janeiro: Graal.
Henning, Carlos Eduardo. 2014. "Paizões, tiozões, tias e cacuras: Envelhecimento, meia idade, velhice e homoerotismo masculino na cidade de São Paulo." PhD diss., Programa de Pós-Graduação em Antropologia Social, Unicamp, Campinas.
———. 2016. "Is Old Age Always Already Heterosexual and Cisgender? The LGBT Gerontology and the Formation of the 'LGBT Elders.'" *Vibrant* 13 (1): 132–154.
———. 2020a. "LGBTI Resistance in Contemporary Brazil." *Fieldsights*, January 28, 2020. https://culanth.org/fieldsights/lgbti-resistance-in-contemporary-brazil.
———. 2020b. "O nascimento do orgulho grisalho: Idosos LGBT e as batalhas por futuros viáveis." In *Direitos em Disputa: LGBTI+: Poder e diferença no Brasil contemporâneo*, edited by Regina Facchini and Isadora França, 72–86. Campinas: Editora da Unicamp.
———. Forthcoming. "LGBTTI Elders in Latin America: The Pragmatic Turn on the Recent Expansion of Organizations for LGBTTI Elderly." In *Gender, Sexuality and Life Course: Research and Dialogues over Contemporary Social Transformations*, edited by C. E. Henning, G. G. Debert, and J. A. Simões. Wilmington, Del.: Vernon Press.
Simões, Júlio Assis, and Regina Facchini. 2009. *Na trilha do arco-íris: Do movimento homossexual ao LGBT*. São Paulo: Fundação Perseu Abramo.

NOTES

1. The abbreviation stands for Lesbian, Gay, Bisexual, Travesti, Trans, and Intersex. In general terms, I will use "LGBTTI," since it has been increasingly used in activism that was part of my fieldwork. In any case, I use the acronym conceiving its meaning as open. In the Brazilian case, the "queer" category is not significantly widespread.
2. This chapter is a result of postdoctoral periods at the Department of Anthropology of USP (2018–2019) and the Institute of Latin American Studies at Columbia University in New York (2019). I am particularly grateful to Julio Assis Simões and Richard Parker for their support.
3. For a detailed contextualization of the dramatic social, political, and economical recent transformations in Brazil, particularly the thought-provoking debate over the recent affective shift in the country, see Junge, Jarrín, Cantero, and Mitchell's introduction to this volume.

4. See Jarrín's chapter, in this volume, for a complex analysis of the bold resistance practices of Brazilian gender nonconforming activists and *artivists*, as well as the "visceral politics" used by the opponents of LGBTTI rights in Brazil.

5. In this chapter, I will use *LGBT gerontology* mainly because it is still the most used term in the field today. See Henning (2016) for a detailed review and discussion on the topic.

6. I take biopolitics as a social form that has emerged from the eighteenth century onward, which sought to rationalize the problems faced by government practice regarding specific phenomena of the set of human beings taken as a population, encompassing health, hygiene, rates of birth, longevity, and race (Foucault 1988, 131).

7. See Henning (2020b) for more on the *orgulho grisalho* (gray pride) topic.

8. See Henning (forthcoming) for more on these institutions and this transnational biopolitical process in cities such as London, Paris, Madrid, Mexico City, and Buenos Aires.

9. See Henning (2014).

10. About the Brazilian LGBTTI movement, see Simões and Facchini (2009), Ferreira (2012), Aguião (2018), and Henning (2020a).

15 · DISGUST AND DEFIANCE
The Visceral Politics of Trans and Travesti Activism amid a Heteronormative Backlash

ALVARO JARRÍN

Transclandestina 3020 was not your typical São Paulo runway show. Every single person strutting down the makeshift catwalk was gender-nonconforming in one way or another, and very few of the bodies on display fit normative beauty standards. Most of the models were working class and dark skinned and identified as *travestis*,[1] trans women, trans men, or *bichas* (feminine gay men). The clothes, which were mostly made from recycled textiles, were futuristic and defied gender norms—imagining how fashion and gender would look in the year 3020 but also paying tribute to the clandestine forms of border-crossing that travestis are forced into today. There was a strong theatrical element to the event, because the models entered the space through a doorway that mimicked a church entrance and ceremoniously deposited objects they were carrying onto a central altar, before moving away with exaggerated gestures and dance moves that included vogueing.[2] The designer who had organized the fashion show, herself a trans woman, imagined the purpose of the event as a way "to imagine a future where trans folk are no longer at the margins. Most of the models come from Pentecostal backgrounds and were expelled from home, and have had to sell their bodies on the street to survive. I see the Bible as an instrument of domination" (interview with author, July 1, 2019). She proudly showed me two of the pieces of clothing she considered to be the centerpieces of the fashion show—one a shiny robe for a space-age priestess, the other a dress that had provocative biblical scriptures from the imaginary Gospel of Jezebel and Gospel of *Mateusa* (the feminine version of Matthew).

Transclandestina 3020 exemplifies a new type of trans activism emerging in Brazil that combines political acts with different types of art, including fashion, music, theater, and social media interventions. Known as *artivismo* (artivism), this form of political engagement borrows from a long Brazilian history of using artistic performances such as theater to comment on the loss of democratic freedoms during a dictatorship (Dunn 2016; Moraes 2018), or to criticize Brazil's race and class inequalities (Smith 2016; Alexandre 2017). What is new about this type of activism is the emphasis it puts on (1) making gender-nonconforming bodies visible, (2) imagining a future where gender creativity is celebrated rather than spurned, and (3) directly confronting the transphobia of Brazil's religious right by appropriating Christian symbols and resignifying them through art. When I interviewed the models participating in *Transclandestina 3020*, most of them mentioned the difficult political moment Brazil was going through following the election of Jair Bolsonaro and considered this fashion show to be a response to the hate coming from the political sphere. Nearly all the models were highly engaged in producing political art that in some way celebrates transfeminine and transmasculine subjectivities, including spoken word, poetry, theater, music, and performance art, and some were able to make a living from their art. I also saw many of these gender-nonconforming artists perform at other artistic venues and political rallies across São Paulo, including a public audience on LGBTTI[3] rights in the São Paulo legislature and the Second Annual Trans March (organized as a more political alternative to the yearly São Paulo pride parade).

In this chapter, I will argue that gender-nonconforming activists in São Paulo purposely blur the boundaries between art and politics in order to produce visceral reactions in their audience. Rather than simply attempting to provide logical or legal arguments regarding the value of trans and travesti lives, which can easily fall on deaf ears, what I call "visceral politics" is an effective tactic insofar as it engages the public sphere within the same affective register used by the opponents of LGBTTI rights. There is little logic to the discourse of disgust deployed by the Brazilian religious right to condemn LGBTTI rights, because it operates mostly at the level of emotion, capturing audiences through hyperbolic fears of "slippery slopes" and dire warnings regarding innocent children being seduced or perverted. In the first section of this chapter, I will demonstrate that Jair Bolsonaro's campaign fully embraced a politics of disgust in the effort to delegitimize the Workers' Party and capture the presidency. I will then analyze specific instances of how trans and travesti activists counter this politics of disgust with what Leticia Alvarado (2018) calls "abject performances": artistic events that directly engage with how society produces abjection, and by doing so embrace the destabilizing force of being a minoritarian subject that does not fit into normative ideals. Alvarado (2018) argues that abject performances are utopic insofar as they reject the normative inclusion of respectability politics and imagine a radically different future. While the Brazilian religious right engages in a nostalgic project of recapturing a more normative past, one where "God, Nation, and Family" came before the concerns of minoritarian subjects, events like *Transclandestina 3020* engage in a different temporality—imagining a future where gender is irrelevant and where even the Bible is inclusive of gender-nonconforming bodies. This defiant visibility and appropriation of religious symbols, in a society that seeks to render trans and travesti subjectivities invisible or immoral, creates a mirror that refuses the distancing effect of disgust and demands affective recognition.

More broadly, this chapter seeks to add the literature on social movements by emphasizing the importance of emotion and affect in building, maintaining, and energizing social movements. As Deborah Gould (2009) argues in *Moving Politics*, the "emotional habitus" of a social movement is central to transforming paralyzing feelings of despair into more actionable feelings of passionate anger. Although some of the gender-nonconforming activists I interviewed in São Paulo expressed being depressed or scared after Bolsonaro's victory, I was surprised by how many were energized and moved into action by this setback, putting their anger toward the government into creating new art and proposing new types of activism.[4] Travestis have been engaged in political activism since at least the 1980s, organizing into sex-worker collectives that protested against the constant violence they experienced from clients and from the police (Klein 1998). However, they have been largely marginalized from the more mainstream LGBTTI movement in Brazil, unable to access the respectability politics that gay men engaged in to get access to rights like same-sex marriage. In response, travestis have embraced political tactics that highlight, rather than undermine, their abject status in society, and thus directly defy the difference "between normal, upstanding citizens and low-life, perverse travestis . . . by foregrounding and challenging the generative structures that permit that differentiation to exist in the first place" (Kulick and Klein 2003). As I will show, the visceral politics of artivism is an ideal new venue to challenge the social structures that mark travestis as outsiders, because these performances engage audiences emotionally and are uniquely able to undermine the distance that separates gender-nonconforming subjectivities from cisgender subjectivities. Politically, art can make profound demands from an audience, asking them to not simply recognize the Other as equal, but defying them to question why the chasm between gender identities exists in the first place.

THE POLITICS OF DISGUST

Before I tackle gender-nonconforming activism, I want to give some background on the situation these activists are confronting and the importance of affect within that battle. Homophobia and transphobia—and the politics of disgust they rely on—have been central to Jair Bolsonaro's rising political career for nearly a decade. He was one of the first congressmen to denounce the so-called *gay kit*, a set of antihomophobic sex education videos and pamphlets developed by NGOs for the Ministry of Education in 2011, at the beginning of Dilma Rousseff's presidency. Even though these materials were aimed at middle and high schoolers, Bolsonaro claimed that they targeted children as young as six years old. He denounced the *gay kit* as a nefarious threat to the family because it "incentivized homosexualism and promiscuity" and made children "easy targets for pedophiles" (Huffington Post Editorial Team 2018). By claiming that children were being brainwashed and sexually threatened, Bolsonaro produced an affective reaction of disgust and horror that permeated the news sphere for weeks on end and generated endless debates. Eventually, the Rousseff government backed down and pulled these educational materials, but Bolsonaro realized he had touched a nerve in Brazilian society, and from that moment on, he and his allies began to rally their Evangelical base by using the antihomophobia education kit as a cudgel that allowed them to denounce all LGBTTI advances in Brazilian society. The Christian right has become a true political force in Brazil over the past two decades, and the large Evangelical voting bloc in Congress was absolutely central in the legislative coup that led to the impeachment of Dilma Rousseff in 2016. Many of those Evangelical congressmen mentioned God and family values in their vote against Rousseff (Prandi and Carneiro 2018), portraying her political demise as a victory against what they described as harmful "gender ideology" (Betim 2017).

The specter of "gender ideology" has a long global history that can be traced as far back as the 1990s, when the Vatican began to use the phrase to oppose the inclusion of reproductive and sexual rights in international conferences organized by the United Nations (Corrêa 2018). In Brazil, the phrase "gender ideology" gained popularity in the early 2000s, when Evangelical congressmen began to decry advances in LGBTTI rights as a threat to the family and to the natural order of things (Machado 2018). When Bolsonaro launched his presidential campaign in 2018, he made combatting "gender ideology" a central campaign promise. In one event in front of an Evangelical audience, he affirmed the Christian character of the nation and warned, "They want to put in the head of our children that they can decide if they are a girl or a boy when they are already thirteen or fourteen years old. My daughter will be a woman and my sons will be men" (Freire 2018). Bolsonaro's austere neoliberal economic project, which was unpalatable to the majority of the population, required that he make the campaign not about economic policy but about fear of social change. His campaign mobilized affect by portraying Bolsonaro as an authoritative father-like figure who would eliminate immoral forms of disorder, restore traditional social norms, and return Brazil to its former glory. As Sianne Ngai (2007, 338, 340) argues, disgust "has been and will continue to be instrumentalized in oppressive ways" and has been frequently deployed "by the political right throughout history, as a means of reinforcing the boundaries between self and 'contaminating' others." Bolsonaro's outright embrace of state violence to restore order—symbolized both by his nostalgia for the dictatorship and by his trademark gesture of pointing his hands like a gun—seemed to imply that those disgusting others would once again be rendered disposable if he were elected. (See Kalil, Pinheiro-Machado, and Scalco, this volume.)

One of the most potent aspects of the politics of disgust is the way it circulates, spreading misinformation like a contagion, fueled by the fear and outrage it causes among those receptive to those messages. During the entire 2018 presidential campaign, Bolsonaro claimed repeatedly that his opponent from the Workers' Party, Fernando Haddad, had created the antihomophobia education kit during his tenure as minister of education. He made television appearances and aired ads with a book supposedly used to teach sex to children, which had nothing to do with the original educational material. When the central election authorities in Brazil ordered the removal of these ads due to their demonstrated falsity, the information continued to circulate through social media (Moura 2018). Hundreds of fake news stories that provoked fear and revulsion were easily propelled on WhatsApp, the form of social media communication that has become most widespread in Brazil (Chagas, Modesto, and Magalhães 2019). Some of these instances of fake news were patently absurd, such as the claim that Fernando Haddad had equipped schools with *mamadeiras eróticas*, or "erotic baby bottles" that had penis-shaped teats, yet seemed to go unchecked within online echo chambers (Mont'Alverne and Mitozo 2019). Other false stories claimed that Brazil's most famous drag performer, Pabllo Vittar, would become the new face of the next Brazilian bill for R$50 (Ortega 2018) and would join LGBTTI politicians to tour the country's schools and spread gender ideology among children (Quessada and Pisa 2018).

The reason the drag performer Vittar causes so much anxiety among conservative circles is because she has transcended gay subculture and has gone mainstream, forcing average Brazilians to confront their prejudice or double down on it. The notion that Vittar could have her face stamped on national currency seemed to suggest that the state itself had been captured by pernicious LGBTTI social capital. Even though this notion was fueled by paranoia, the inroads that LGBTTI activists had made into achieving some of their key demands from the state under the Workers' Party was absolutely tangible, from the state recognition of same-sex unions and one's gender identity, to social programs meant to provide employment and education to trans- and travesti-identified Brazilians. Bolsonaro mobilized fears of the Other to his advantage very successfully and evoked a nostalgia for a time when everyone knew their place—the twenty-one years of dictatorship that he has frequently described as great for the country and necessary to eliminate communist influences (Snider 2018). As the historian Benjamin Cowan (2016) has argued, the Brazilian dictatorship repeatedly portrayed alternative sexualities and nonnormative genders as a threat to the nation, so Bolsonaro simply echoed that political tactic to great effect.

REMEMBERING ABJECTION, RETHINKING THE FUTURE

The theater piece *As 3 Uiaras de SP City* [The Three Sirens of São Paulo City] makes the connection between the dictatorship and present-day Brazil very explicitly. The play retells and critiques a series of violent police operations led by José Wilson Richetti that occurred in the 1970s and 1980s, which sought to "clean up" São Paulo by rounding up and torturing gay men and travestis. Starring two gender-nonconforming actresses who play the part of sex workers, as well as a cisgender actress who plays the part of a feminist activist, the play is a chilling portrait of the dehumanizing tactics used by police, who portrayed travestis as dangerous criminals and AIDS vectors that needed to be contained and eliminated from public spaces. When I watched the play in June of 2019, I found it highly effective in moving the audience to rethink the politics of disgust deployed by the state. One particular scene reenacted protesters in front of the police station, demanding the release of travestis who have been arrested, and two of the actresses urged members of the audience to join the protest. About half the audience joined the actresses on stage, and we were quickly provided with protest signs and encouraged to echo the protest chants. The effervescence of the protest was cruelly interrupted, however, as the police suddenly entered the scene, hurled insults and threats at us, and then pointed guns at us to force us to take our seats again. By allowing audience members to experience both the thrill of activism and the fear caused by police violence, the play was able to employ affect to help us experience the abjection suffered by minoritarian subjects and what it feels like to have one's demands for citizenship be violently silenced. The play also chronicles the ways in which detained travestis would cut their own bodies as a protest tactic, using the disgust toward HIV-positive bodies to their own advantage. The disgust of the state is thus revealed as paranoid and self-defeating.

Despite its focus on the past, *As 3 Uiaras de SP City* also imagines a different future. The play begins with one of the actresses addressing the audience directly, and declaring, "We are tired of [prostitution], now we want to invest in poetry, invest in culture. We will leave the gutter to become stars." By starting in this manner, the play challenges the stereotype that all travestis are destined for sex work and could never envision a different occupation for themselves. Without moralizing sex work, the push for "artivism" is also a way to expand the opportunities available for travestis, and the audience is encouraged to see themselves as part of this transformation by supporting this new type of art. Additionally, the play seeks to create alliances between trans and cis women in the effort to transform society, symbolized by the friendship between the two travesti characters and the cis feminist character. As one of the characters explicitly says, "The revolution will take longer, but it will happen, built by us women, whether we are trans, cis, lesbian, heterosexual, bisexual, Black, white, Indigenous, disabled, fat, thin, mothers, HIV-positive, old or young." In the preface to the published version of the play, the author (a trans woman named Ave Terrena) makes a concrete connection between the past and the present, arguing that violence has not disappeared but has only become modernized, and she dedicates the play to Marielle Franco and Dandara dos Santos, a lesbian woman and a travesti who were violently murdered this decade. (See chapter by Sullivan, this volume.) Remembering both past and present forms of gendered violence, the play challenges the continuous forms of abjection suffered by LGBTTI individuals in Brazil. This "abject performance" (Alvarado 2018), nonetheless, insists that a different future is possible. Toward the end of the play, one of the travesti characters defiantly declares, "Memory is resistance, so that other women become stronger in the future."

The activism evident in performance pieces created and starred by gender-nonconforming Brazilians is in constant dialogue with more traditional political activism engaged with policy and human rights. On June 26, 2019, Ave Terrena, the author of *As 3 Uiaras de SP City*, spoke during a public audience in the São Paulo legislature on LGBTTI rights, urging those present to not forget the genocide suffered by travestis during the dictatorship. She and others present highlighted the historical memory embodied by older gender-nonconforming activists like Neon Cunha, who collaborated in the creation of the play and was now being publicly honored for her years of dedication to the cause. As Neon Cunha approached the stage to speak, however, a member of the audience shouted, "She is the future!" highlighting the ways in which this remembrance of the past does not simply look back but simultaneously beckons a new future. Without naming Bolsonaro, Neon Cunha pointed out how nostalgia for the dictatorship is impossible for those subjects in abject positions, describing how the state back then and today refuse to recognize travesti and trans identities. Gesturing toward more global concerns, Neon Cunha also critiqued the ways in which the mainstream LGBTTI movement silences the contributions of trans women of color, including the work of Marsha P. Johnson and Sylvia Rivera in the United States. This particular public audience, which was organized by Erika Hilton, one of two Black gender-nonconforming women elected to the São

Paulo legislature, was particularly critical of the mainstream gay movement in Brazil, which one speaker described as "racist" and another said "does not represent us." As the LGBTTI movement in Brazil begins to center Black gender-nonconforming experiences in its activism, the movement is abandoning a politics of respectability in favor of more radical racial and economic justice. When activists claim figures like Neon Cunha as "the future" of Brazil, they are also rethinking what political demands are more urgent and what bodies should matter most in that fight.

THE CONTACT ZONE OF VISIBILITY

Sara Ahmed (2004, 87–88) reminds us that disgust "operates as a contact zone. . . . [An] object becomes disgusting, in a way that allows the subject to recoil, only after an intimate contact that is felt on the surface of the skin." Although disgust usually culminates in an imperative to expel the offending object from the body politic, there is a moment of possibility in that brief intimate encounter, where the Other thought of as disgusting becomes confused with the self, and the fear or revulsion toward the Other can be lessened through continuous exposure, becoming something akin to mutual understanding. Much of the "artivism" being created and promoted by gender-nonconforming activists in Brazil seeks to render trans bodies visible and familiar, thus confronting the revulsion toward trans bodies that is promoted by the religious right. They seek to push the boundaries of what is acceptable, however, rather than strive for easier forms of normative inclusion. As the editors of the collection on trans cultural production, *Trap Door*, argue, the doors opened by the heightened visibility of trans bodies offer the possibility of recognition and understanding but can also work as a trap, "accommodating trans bodies, histories and culture only insofar as they can be forced to hew to hegemonic modalities" (Gossett, Stanley, and Burton 2017, xxiii). For example, the trans bodies that are deemed acceptable or even celebrated by mainstream society, whether it be in the United States or Brazil, are those that fit the gendered and racial standards of beauty and whose appearance reaffirms the gender binary rather than undermine it. The visceral politics of gender-nonconforming activism seeks to push back against these bodily standards altogether, in order to expand the conditions of possibility under which trans bodies are recognized.

For example, activists from the Brazilian Institute of Transmasculinities (IBRAT) created an image for the Day of Transgender Visibility that showcased a trans male torso with very visible scars from a mastectomy, with the caption, "This is not controversial, we just want to be happy! We are proud of our bodies, proud of our history." Instead of showcasing a trans man who passes as a cisgender male, or even a torso with faded scars, this image celebrates the bodily difference that marks this body as transgender. An activist who posted this image on Instagram, and who is one of my interlocutors, added some thoughts on the image, saying,

> When we look closely, we perceive how much society has forgotten about itself and never remembered us. Affection is now one of our demands. Affecting others and being affected is one of our objectives. We are studying how we can re-learn how to see, how to listen, and how to speak. We perceive that the lack of human connection has sometimes caused our brothers to escape through our fingers, getting lost in so much discrimination and injustice (and we use the word BROTHERS to refer to all trans men and nonbinary transmasculine individuals). Lack of affection is a very cruel attempt against our lives, and that is why we feel the necessity to make this campaign.

The campaign thus beckons the viewer to reevaluate their stance in relation to transmasculine identities, calling out the violence inherent in disgust and rejection, since it leads to elevated rates of suicide among trans men. The campaign also goes beyond a simple call for tolerance, asking the viewer to unlearn their discriminatory attitude and learn to love trans bodies. The picture of the visibly trans male torso signals a refusal to "pass" as cisgender, while the call for affection humanizes trans bodies and asks the audience to empathize with the vulnerability experienced by trans men in Brazil. At the Trans March in 2019, I was surprised by how many trans men were parading shirtless, whether they had undergone a mastectomy or not. Their visible difference, rather than their ability to pass, was how they opted to showcase their pride in who they were.

Another activist tactic regarding visibility is celebrating the existence of trans bodies through their perceived sexual deviancy. The travesti artist and musician Linn da Quebrada, who describes herself as a "gender terrorist," wrote a song titled "BlasFêmea/Mulher" (BlasFemme/Woman) that celebrates travestis for making a living through sex work. The song lyrics confront head-on the ways in which sex work and gender nonconformity generate "disgust" in Brazilian society, and it challenges the listener to let go of those stereotypes. By using words like *diva of the gutter*, the song rethinks the terms of recognition under which travestis are understood and valued. A travesti's association with "sewage" or with "favelas" suddenly becomes an asset, an aspect of her ability to "deconstruct" and resignify her body, which is described as a revolutionary act akin to an occupation of private property. The song's title and the use of feminine pronouns assert the feminine personhood of travestis, even as the song asserts the bodily differences of travestis that complicate the gender binary. This is not a sanitized body that passes as feminine but rather a body that confronts the listener with its female penis, demanding recognition despite this difference. Travesti femininity is compared in the title to blasphemy, hinting at the moral condemnation suffered by travestis but also refusing respectability as a path to social acceptance.

Urias, who identifies as a trans woman, released a song with a similar message titled "Diaba" (Female Devil). The song directly confronts the perception of gender-nonconforming women as devilish or immoral, embracing the term *diaba* as a symbol of an empowered femininity that refuses respectability. The lyrics chastise the listener for calling the singer "dirty, crazy and immoral" and point out that it is society's norms and laws that render her "evil" in their eyes. The lyrics emphasize the defiant existence of gender-nonconforming subjects despite the lack of legal recognition of their gender identity and despite the religious condemnation coming from the Brazilian Christian right. This is an "abject performance" (Alvarado 2018) insofar as it embraces the destabilizing properties of a minoritarian identity. Claiming that trans women are the real "pillar" of the Brazilian family, the song appropriates and decenters patriarchal religious discourse that describes men as pillars of the family.

In the music videos for both songs, sex work is reimagined as a powerful source of dignity. Set in the darkness of nighttime streets, the imagery in both videos oscillates between eroticism and violence, provoking visceral reactions in the viewer. In the video for "BlasFêmea/Mulher," Linn da Quebrada is initially shown praying to a Black saint or orixa, and the wax from a candle falls on her body in an erotic manner that resembles semen. Sex is thus compared to a transcendent religious experience rather than a source of shame. In the rest of the video, Linn da Quebrada plays a travesti sex worker walking the streets of São Paulo and sharing moments of camaraderie with other travestis. When she is physically assaulted by a group of men, the travestis band together and stop the men. This both reflects and reverses the daily forms of violence suffered by gender-nonconforming individuals in Brazil, imagining a collective speaking back that privileges survival and resilience. Similarly, the music video for "Diaba" shows Urias playing a sex worker who walks into a bar (based on the sexualized clothing she is wearing), where she telekinetically moves around furniture without touching it to make space for her entrance, showcasing her supernatural nature. The men at the bar gesture toward attacking her, but they seem unable to touch her and end up brutally fighting each other in a circle around her. The specter of physical violence is deflected onto those who want to enact it, reminding the viewer that this violence exists but it ultimately betrays the insecurities and toxic masculinity of the men who want to carry it out. The viewer is also captivated by the power and presence of Urias, who looks directly at the camera, unbothered by the fight around her. At the end of the video, she walks away from the empty bar, now wearing a red snakeskin outfit and a snake pendant that emphasizes her sensuality and symbolizes her devilish qualities. Neither of the videos asks for acceptance from the viewers or for normative inclusion in society—rather, they celebrate the perceived sexual deviancy of trans and travesti women, demanding inclusion on their own terms.

FAITH AND BLASPHEMY

When Urias embraces the stereotype of being a female devil and provocatively exclaims, "Fuck your beliefs," she is speaking back to the Christian right's tactic of shaming LGBTTI subjectivities as un-Brazilian, immoral, and harmful. Many of my interlocutors understand this moralistic discourse as one of the main impediments to the advancement of LGBTTI rights in Brazil, and they feel compelled to respond to it through their art and their activism. By reclaiming and appropriating Christian religious symbols in ways that expand the definition of what is just, trans and travesti activists seek to redefine Christian morality and include their own stories and subjectivities within religiosity. Linn da Quebrada, for example, routinely inserts herself in religious imagery as part of her artistic production. On her Instagram page, she posts pictures that photoshop her face onto the body of the Virgin Mary and drawings that portray her as Jesus during the Last Supper. By associating her travesti subjectivity with these religious figures, Linn da Quebrada suggests that travesti suffering due to discrimination and other forms of hate resemble the martyrdom of Christian religious figures. Linn da Quebrada has also tattooed a crown of thorns on her forehead, along with the pronoun *she*, permanently marking her body the association between her gender identity and religious sacrifice. Although Christians might consider these images and tattoos to be blasphemous, Linn da Quebrada crafts an intimate connection between the religious figures that Christians love and the gender-nonconforming bodies they condemn, creating a cognitive dissonance that is not easily resolved.

This dissonance is part of the lived experience for many gender-nonconforming Brazilians raised in religious households or who still practice a religion. During the First Conference on LGBTTI Churches and Communities that took place in São Paulo in 2019, most of the speakers (all of whom identified as trans men, trans women, or travestis) remarked on transphobia within religious communities and the difficulties of reconciling their identities and their faith. Their experiences of abjection, however, did not prevent them from asserting their relationship to the divine. One trans man testified that he had to leave the church he grew up in due to the conservative attitude of his pastor toward gender-nonconforming identities: "A homeless travesti came asking for help at the Evangelical church I frequented. It was an upper-middle-class church, and they gave her housing, saying she was definitely welcome. But they would keep referring to her with masculine pronouns and would keep offering masculine clothes to her. She cut her hair, she let her beard grow, but one day she disappeared, leaving those masculine clothes behind. People that want God in their lives are sometimes able to stay in Christian churches but have to withstand the oppressions they suffer daily." The speaker said he eventually "broke with man but not with God," still felt inspired by the Bible, and firmly believed that Jesus Christ would never delegitimize a person's identity. He also said he felt God's presence in that conference space. A pastor at the conference who identifies as a trans woman went even further, claiming that "a Church that does not welcome a travesti has blood on its hands," and describing God as also experiencing a "transition" the moment he transmuted from his divine fatherly form into a human form. Jesus was the first trans person, she explained, and the first to be rejected for speaking a language of love rather than hate. By describing Jesus as trans, she was able to claim the moral high ground in the discussion about the morality of trans identities.

At the conference, many speakers also referenced performance pieces that associate the suffering of Jesus with the suffering of gender-nonconforming Brazilians. People fondly remembered the 2015 performance during the yearly São Paulo Pride Parade by a trans woman called Viviany Beleboni, who appeared at the parade crucified, covered in blood, and wearing a crown of thorns, with a sign above her head that condemned homophobia. This performance, a travesti activist explained during the conference, symbolized the suffering that trans individuals and travestis experience in their everyday lives. The outcry that this performance caused among the religious right, she said, was a clear sign of their hypocrisy, because they had no problem with other reinterpretations of the story of Jesus, but "when a travesti portrays herself as Jesus she cannot do it, because she is considered impure." This "abject performance," therefore, made a literal connection between Jesus and gender-nonconforming identities that resonates with trans and travesti activists even years later.

Some of the presenters at the conference expressed even more admiration for a recent theater piece titled "The Gospel according to Jesus, Queen of Heaven," which imagines Jesus coming back to Earth as a travesti. This one-person show, performed by the travesti actress Renata de Carvalho, has been met with protests and has been censored and canceled without previous notice in several Brazilian cities. Carvalho has even received death threats for her role in the show. She nonetheless has persisted with her performances, sometimes putting on the piece even as the set was being removed. As she explained in a newspaper interview, "Jesus has been played by a Black woman, by a child, but the problem here is Jesus being played by a travesti. Jesus can be anyone except LGBT, except travesti. The trans body is seen as dirty, as possessed by a demon, it causes discomfort" (Oliveira 2018). For Carvalho, the play is important precisely because it confronts the viewer's discomfort with gender-nonconforming identities, challenges the presumption that these identities are somehow dirty or polluting, and reclaims the humanity of travestis through the figure of Jesus. After one of her performances, Carvalho declared:

> There is only one way to humanize and naturalize trans bodies, and that is to have them be present in different spaces, which can only be achieved through real representation. Visibility is not enough to avoid marginalization. If trans bodies are included in all collectives, this country will no longer be the country that most kills travestis worldwide, the second cause of death will not be suicide. We need to humanize and naturalize the trans body, and we can only accomplish that if we become familiar with it, in order to erase all the labels, stigmas and criminalization it suffers. (*Teatro em Cena* 2018)

Note Carvalho's dismissal of visibility as a form of inclusion that does not fundamentally transform the social relationship to gender-nonconforming bodies more widely, because it merely tolerates them. Instead, she is asking for a more radical transformation of Brazilian society to truly transform disgust and rejection into love and acceptance, at all levels and in all spaces, and is using the visceral reaction of audiences to familiar religious narratives to achieve that.

CONCLUSION: DEFIANCE AGAINST ALL ODDS

Brazilian trans and travesti activists envision a shared political project that stares in the face of the Bolsonaro regime and does not despair, because in many ways they always expected disgust to operate in the way it does. As many of my interlocutors pointed out to me, Brazil already had one the highest murder rates for gender-nonconforming individuals in the world, and the violence against trans and travesti bodies did not begin with the election of Bolsonaro. What Bolsonaro does is to render the politics of disgust so obvious and so hyperbolic that it almost becomes a parody of itself, even if it also emboldens those who hate LGBTTI folks. For example, when Bolsonaro tweeted a video of a golden shower in order to criticize the presence of queer acts and subjectivities in a Carnival parade, he was widely condemned and ridiculed, and he was forced to retreat and delete the video. He seemed to be contaminated by the very sexual act he was denouncing, betraying the ways that disgust can collapse the distance between object and subject. The work of the artists and activists I have described in this chapter use the fungibility of disgust to their advantage and create daring performances and audiovisual media to produce visceral reactions in their audiences, thus challenging our perception of gender-nonconforming bodies as deviant, dirty, or immoral. What emerges from that work is a vision of a different future that widens the political, religious, erotic, and professional possibilities for gender-nonconforming individuals in Brazil.

In some ways, the election of Bolsonaro can be interpreted as the dying gasps of an old order that is becoming untenable. It is easy to forget that the same election that brought us Bolsonaro also brought a record number of women to the Brazilian congress (*Folha de São Paulo* 2018), including the first three Black trans congresswomen (Antunes 2018). As Erika Hilton, one of those three women, told me during an interview, "One of the most potent revolutions we are undergoing is intersectionality, so that no body is left behind. We women are stronger together, and with Black women being elected, we can take the population out of poverty. We are a wave that has risen and cannot be tamed." A similar thought was put forward by Linn da Quebrada, who wrote the following on her Instagram the day after Bolsonaro's victory:

> Now is not the moment to be fearful, much less to retreat. They are the ones who are fearful in the face of all our victories and advances. I would also be afraid if I were in their place, and that is why I cannot let go of all that we have achieved until now, and I ask that you join me in this battle. Now is the moment to join together, to sharpen our dialogue, to have our voices echo, to make our bodies present, to build and elaborate new strategies, to build intersectional politics, understanding our common demands. Even though we are all different we have so much in common. It's our difference that protects us, that joins us, that moves us and helps us move as a collective. In our particularities, whether we are Black, trans, lesbians, women, and/or workers, this was never about them. This is about us. So let's come together to break loose.

The transfeminism embraced by trans and travesti activists is fully intersectional, and it seeks to build bridges across difference to accomplish its goals. These activists are perfectly aware that their lives are at risk by being so vocal and visible, but they nonetheless remain hopeful and defiant, confident they can use their brand of visceral politics to recruit us to their cause.

REFERENCES

Alexandre, Marcos Antônio. 2017. *O teatro negro em perspectiva: Dramaturgia e cena negra no Brasil e em Cuba*. Rio de Janeiro: Editora Malê.

Alvarado, Leticia. 2018. *Abject Performances: Aesthetic Strategies in Latino Cultural Production*. Durham, N.C.: Duke University Press.

Antunes, Leda. 2018. "Erika Malunginho, Erika Hilton e Robeyoncé Lima: As mulheres trans eleitas em 2018." *HuffPost* (Brasil), November 17, 2018. https://www.huffpostbrasil.com/2018/11/17/erica-malunguinho-erika-hilton-e-robeyonce-lima-as-mulheres-trans-eleitas-em-2018_a_23590733/.

Betim, Felipe. 2017. "Se Deus derrubou Dilma, fé na melhora da economia segura Temer." *El País Brasil*, August 20, 2017. https://brasil.elpais.com/brasil/2017/08/03/politica/1501715251_361448.html.

Chagas, Viktor, Michelle Modesto, and Dandara Magalhães. 2019. "O Brasil vai virar Venezuela: Medo, memes e enquadramentos emocionais no WhatsApp pró-Bolsonaro." *Esferas* 14:1–17.

Corrêa, Sonia. 2018. "A 'política de gênero': Um comentário genealógico." *Cadernos pagu*, no. 53. https://doi.org/10.1590/18094449201800530001.

Cowan, Benjamin A. 2016. *Securing Sex: Morality and Repression in the Making of Cold War Brazil*. Chapel Hill: University of North Carolina Press.

Dunn, Christopher. 2016. *Contracultura: Alternative Arts and Social Transformation in Authoritarian Brazil*. Chapel Hill: University of North Carolina Press.

Folha de São Paulo. 2018. "Percentual de mulheres eleitas para a Câmara cresce de 10% para 15%." October 8, 2018. https://www1.folha.uol.com.br/poder/2018/10/percentual-de-mulheres-eleitas-para-a-camara-cresce-de-10-para-15.shtml.

Freire, Sabrina. 2018. "Em evento evangélico, Bolsonaro se posiciona contra ideologia de gênero." *Poder360*, April 29, 2018. https://www.poder360.com.br/eleicoes/em-evento-evangelico-bolsonaro-se-posiciona-contra-ideologia-de-genero/.

Gossett, Reina, Eric Stanley, and Johanna Burton. 2017. *Trap Door: Trans Cultural Production and the Politics of Visibility*. Cambridge, Mass.: MIT Press.

Gould, Deborah B. 2009. *Moving Politics: Emotion and ACT UP's Fight against AIDS*. Chicago: University of Chicago Press.

HuffPost (Brasil). 2018. "'Kit Gay': A verdade sobre o programa alvo de críticas e fake news de Bolsonaro." October 24, 2018. https://www.huffpostbrasil.com/2018/10/24/kit-gay-a-verdade-sobre-o-programa-alvo-de-criticas-e-fake-news-de-bolsonaro_a_23565210/.

Jarrín, Alvaro. 2016. "Untranslatable Subjects: Travesti Access to Public Health Care in Brazil." *Transgender Studies Quarterly* 3 (3–4): 357–375.

Klein, Charles. 1998. "From One 'Battle' to Another: The Making of a 'Travesti' Political Movement in a Brazilian City." *Sexualities* 1 (3): 327–342.

Kulick, Don. 1998. *Travesti: Sex, Gender and Culture among Brazilian Transgendered Prostitutes*. Chicago: University of Chicago Press.

Kulick, Don, and Charles Klein. 2003. "Scandalous Acts: The Politics of Shame among Brazilian Travesti Prostitutes." In *Recognition Struggles and Social Movements: Contested Identities, Agency and Power*, edited by Barbara Hobson, 215–238. Cambridge, UK: Cambridge University Press.

Machado, Maria das Dores Campo. 2018. "O discurso cristão sobre a 'ideologia de gênero.'" *Revista de estudos feministas* 26 (2). https://www.scielo.br/scielo.php?pid=S0104-026X2018000200212&script=sci_arttext&tlng=pt.

Mont'Alverne, Camila, and Isabele Mitozo. 2019. "Muito além da mamadeira erótica: As notícias compartilhadas nas redes de apoio a presidenciáveis em grupos de WhatsApp." *Anais do 8º Compolítica* 15. http://ctpol.unb.br/compolitica2019/GT4/gt4_Montalverne_Mitozo.pdf.

Moraes, A. P. Quartim de. 2018. *Anos de chumbo: O teatro Brasileiro na cena de 1968*. São Paulo: Edições SESC.

Moura, Rafael Moraes. 2018. "TSE determina remoção de vídeos de Bolsonaro sobre 'kit gay' no Facebook." *Estadão*, October 10, 2018. https://politica.estadao.com.br/noticias/eleicoes,tse-determina-remocao-de-videos-em-que-bolsonaro-cita-kit-gay,70002548946.

Ngai, Sianne. 2007. *Ugly Feelings*. Boston: Harvard University Press.

Oliveira, Joana. 2018. "Jesus pode ser tudo, menos travesti." *El País Brasil*, July 23, 2018. https://brasil.elpais.com/brasil/2018/07/23/cultura/1532371217_501094.html.

Ortega, Rodrigo. 2018. "Pabllo Vittar fala sobre ser alvo de 'fake news': 'Antes me incomodava, hoje dou risada.'" *G1*, April 18, 2018. https://g1.globo.com/pop-arte/musica/noticia/pabllo-vittar-fala-sobre-ser-alvo-de-fake-news-antes-me-incomodava-mas-hoje-dou-risada-veja-video.ghtml.

Prandi, Reginaldo, and João Luiz Carneiro. 2018. "Em nome do Pai: Justificativas do voto dos deputados federais evangélicos e não evangélicos na abertura do impeachment de Dilma Rousseff." *Revista brasileira de ciências sociais* 33 (96). https://www.scielo.br/scielo.php?pid=S0102-69092018000100501&script=sci_abstract&tlng=pt.

Quessada, Miguel, and Licia Frezza Pisa. 2018. "Fake News versus MIL: A difícil tarefa de desmentir Goebbels." Paper presented at the XXIII Congresso de Ciências da Comunicação na Região Sudeste, Belo Horizonte, 2018.

Smith, Christen A. 2016. *Afro-Paradise: Blackness, Violence and Performance in Brazil*. Urbana: University of Illinois Press.
Snider, Colin M. 2018. "'The Perfection of Democracy Cannot Dispense with Dealing with the Past:' Dictatorship, Memory, and the Politics of the Present in Brazil." *Latin Americanist* 62 (1): 55–79.
Teatro em Cena. 2018. "Renata Carvalho comenta atos de censura à 'O evangelho segundo Jesus, Rainha do Céu' (2018)." YouTube video. https://www.youtube.com/watch?v=gud8qAIV1to.
Vartabedian, Julieta. 2018. *Brazilian Travesti Migrations: Gender, Sexualities and Embodiment Experiences*. London: Palgrave Macmillan.

NOTES

1. The subjectivity of *travestis* differs in key ways from transgender identities elsewhere, insofar as many travestis feel that their gender identity is a crystallization of their homosexual desire (Kulick 1998), and they engage in unique rituals of migration, beautification, and bodily transformation (Kulick 1998; Vartabedian 2018). In this chapter, I use the term *travesti* instead of *trans* in order to avoid the erasure that happens when we assume Anglophone categories can be applied everywhere (Jarrín 2016).
2. Vogueing is a dance developed in the New York City ballroom queer scene of the 1980s, which has recently gained a lot popularity in Brazil, particularly among gender-nonconforming folks.
3. LGBTTI stands for Lesbian, Gay, Bisexual, Travesti, Trans, and Intersex, and is a common acronym used in Brazil within the context of queer and trans rights.
4. See the chapters by Sullivan and Henning in this volume for other similar examples of LGBTTI perseverance in Brazil.

16 · "BARBIE E KEN CIDADÃOS DE BEM"
Memes and Political Participation among College Students in Brazil

MELANIE A. MEDEIROS, PATRICK MCCORMICK, ERIKA SCHMITT, AND JAMES KALE

In September 2018, two months after far-right politician Jair Bolsonaro announced his candidacy for president of Brazil, the Facebook page "Barbie e Ken Cidadãos de Bem" (Barbie and Ken Good Citizens) shared a meme. The meme depicts a blonde Barbie doll in its packaging wearing a T-shirt with a picture of Bolsonaro and the words "Bolsonaro Presidente." The package labels Barbie as a "Bolsominion" (Bolsonaro's minion) and a speech bubble extending from Barbie states, "I am not obligated to be a feminist." Throughout 2018, memes featuring Barbie and Ken dolls, or similar, were circulated widely on social media, with new memes cropping up as political events unfolded. How can we characterize the role of such memes as part of political participation in Brazil leading up to the 2018 election? And how did engagement with political memes influence the political subjectivity of young adults in Brazil? In this chapter, we take an anthropological approach to these questions, seeking to understand Brazilian college students' ideas about the Barbie and Ken memes and what they felt the memes could accomplish.

New media have transformed the ways individuals engage with politics, creating contemporary forms of political participation and activism (Shifman 2014; Stalcup 2016). Anthropologists investigate social mediascapes (Jin and Yoon 2016) as sites of political protest and resistance, exploring their roles in social movements (Juris 2012), and examining the strengths and weaknesses of digital protest (Bonilla and Rosa 2015). During Brazil's 2018 presidential race, "hashtag activism" (Bonilla and Rosa 2015) in the form of *#elenão* (#nothim) or *#elenunca* (#neverhim) dominated the social media networks of Brazilians and even foreigners who protested Bolsonaro. These hashtags were often coupled with satirical memes featuring images of Barbie and Ken and text that mirrored Bolsonaro's rhetoric and the discourses of some of his supporters. The images of Barbie and Ken were employed to represent and mock white, cisgender, and middle- and upper-class Brazilians who supported Bolsonaro's campaign.[1] Media scholars assert that memes bolster and frame contemporary politics, bringing awareness to social justice issues, and enabling people to affirm their beliefs and identities, while asserting their viewpoints within their social networks (Denisova 2019; Mina 2019; Shifman 2014; Stalcup 2016).

In this chapter, we build on Shifman's (2014) argument that the creation and sharing of political memes represent a new form of political participation, as well as Kunreuther's (2018, 1) assertion that using one's "voice," including on social media, "serves as a metaphor for political participation." We argue that for some Brazilian college students, the creation and sharing of the Barbie and Ken memes were ways to voice opposition to Bolsonaro's politics and rhetoric as well as to the social injustices reflected in the discourses of some of his supporters. We examine the relationship between voice and sense of self (Kunreuther 2018), discussing how, for college students whose intersecting social identities shaped their political consciousness, using memes to voice their viewpoints was a political activity that formed part of their political subjectivity—their "understandings of themselves as political subjects" (Junge 2018, 5). We also discuss the content and interpretations of the memes, examining how, for many Brazilian college students, the Barbie and Ken memes offered timely and critical commentaries on sexism, racism, class inequality, meritocracy, homophobia, power, and privilege.

Anthropologists have noted that ethnographies of social media, social movements, and social media activism should include data from both virtual and physical field sites (Bonilla and Rosa 2015; Juris 2012; Postill and Pink 2012). Accordingly, our virtual field site was the Barbie e Ken Cidadãos de Bem Facebook page, where we analyzed the page's content, including the comments posted by page visitors between September 2018 and January 2019. Additionally, we conducted in-depth semistructured interviews with thirty-four college students and one 2018 graduate (eighteen to thirty-five years old).[2] We asked life history questions, followed by questions about the use of social media in general and for political activism. During the interviews, we showed the students images of the Barbie and Ken memes and asked them to describe and explain the memes. We then asked students to share their perspectives on the sharing of memes as a form of political participation. Finally, students reflected on their own political engagement and activism.

We interviewed students in three Brazilian cities that reflect dramatic diversity in geography, population demographics, and wealth—Salvador, Goiânia, and Curitiba. Although the northeast city of Salvador voted for the leftist Workers' Party (Partido dos Trabalhadores; PT) candidate Fernando Haddad in the runoff of the 2018 presidential election (with 68.6 percent of the vote), in Goiânia and Curitiba, Bolsonaro won by a large margin (74.2 percent of the vote in Curitiba and 76.5 percent in Goiânia; TRE-PR 2018). By interviewing college students in these three different cities, we hoped to garner divergent viewpoints on Brazil's political climate and the use of political memes among young adults. In turn, our participants represented diverse political perspectives. Two students were Bolsonaro supporters. Other students voted for Democratic Labor Party (PDL) candidate Ciro Gomes or for Haddad in the first round of the election. In the runoff election, while some students voted for Haddad, others nullified their ballots or left their ballot blank (*branco*).[3] Therefore, while there was some consistency in students' critiques of Bolsonaro, their political views were not uniform. Some wholeheartedly supported the PT, while others criticized it as ineffective or corrupt. In some cases, students expressed ambivalence toward all parties and candidates (cf. Junge et al., this volume).

Students were asked to identify their sex, gender, sexual orientation, religion, and race. Racially, students self-identified with the census color categories of *branco/a* (white) and *pardo/a* (brown/mixed race) or with the noncensus category of *Negro/a* (Black), which denotes a Black subjectivity.[4] The participants represented diverse social identities but were all cisgender. All but one of the students attended federal universities. Many of the students were first-generation college students, and some directly benefited from the federal university quota program instituted under PT governments. Several students also mentioned other positive effects of PT policies on their lives. We recognize that our results may have differed if more of our participants had attended private colleges, and/or if more participants had been Bolsonaro supporters.

BARBIE AND KEN, GOOD CITIZENS

In June 2017, (an) anonymous person(s) created the Facebook page Barbie e Ken Cidadãos de Bem. The page's profile picture featured two blonde Barbie and Ken dolls in what appears to be a "selfie." The page's first public post was a meme with an image of a Ken-like doll. The embedded text reads, "Racism is against ALL the races. I, a white person, suffered a lot of racism. Yes; in school I was called WHITEY [*branquelo*]." All the memes that followed this one of Ken were satirical, commenting on topics of racism, homophobia, sexism, and class inequality. As students explained, memes such as this one are meant to *ironizar* (mock) Brazilians whose various social

FIGURE 16.1. "Racism is against ALL the races. I, a white person, suffered a lot of racism. Yes; in school I was called WHITEY [*branquelo*]."
Source: https://www.facebook.com/pg/barbieekencidadaosdebem/

identities give them privilege and scoff at Bolsonaro supporters from privileged backgrounds. The majority of college students we interviewed identified the 2018 election season as the first time they had encountered these memes. The Barbie and Ken memes, known colloquially as the *Barbie Facista* (Fascist Barbie) or *Barbie Bolsominion* memes, were posted and shared on social media through a variety of platforms, including the Cidadãos de Bem Facebook page; the Instagram account barbieeken17 (Barbie e Ken FACISTA); people's personal Facebook, Instagram, and Twitter accounts; and WhatsApp exchanges. While a semiotic analysis of the interpretation of memes is beyond the scope of this chapter, it is important to note that our interviews with Bolsonaro supporters suggest the "polysemic potential" of the Barbie and Ken memes. In other words, the memes can be interpreted in a number of ways (Shifman 2014, 150). However, we focus on the interpretation of the majority of our participants, who were not Bolsonaro supporters.

When shown images of the Barbie and Ken memes during their interviews, the vast majority of college students in our study were able to quickly identify who Barbie and Ken were meant to represent and why their images were chosen. Lisa, a twenty-nine-year-old bisexual, Black woman studying genetics in Curitiba explained, "Here in Brazil, people who are very rich, very snobby... we call Barbie. They are usually a white person, who has never suffered racism. Generally it's people who have good financial conditions, such as never having to go hungry, living in a good neighborhood and having the privilege of having a good school, a private school. Like, Barbie, white, blonde, thin, pretty, and rich." The discursive practice of referring to elite, white Brazilians as "Barbies" was visually replicated in the Barbie and Ken memes. According to students, Barbie's appearance (clothing, jewelry, hair, etc.) in the memes indexed her social status as a member of Brazil's upper class. The imagery of Barbie and Ken also references middle- and upper-class Brazilians' aspirations for American standards of living and consumption practices. Thus the selection of Barbie and Ken to represent Brazilians whose race and class granted them privilege was a strategic effort not only to index a certain class of Brazilian but to critique their aspirations as well.

Furthermore, the use of the phrase *cidadãos de bem* (good citizens) in the title of the Facebook page juxtaposes Barbie and Ken and the Brazilians they represent against the *vagabundos* (criminals) Bolsonaro promised to protect his supporters from in his campaign rhetoric (Kalil, Pinheiro-Machado, and Salco, this volume). Thus labeling Barbie and Ken as "good citizens" marks them as Bolsonaro supporters, but also, when paired with discriminatory "speech" in the memes, it highlights the disturbing irony in identifying racist, sexist, or homophobic people as "good citizens."

CRITIQUES OF ANTIFEMINISM, HOMOPHOBIA, RACISM, AND MERITOCRACY

Starting in the 1980s after the birth of Brazilian democracy, the Brazilian feminist and Black feminist movements made significant inroads into dismantling Brazil's patriarchal systems of oppression to advance women's rights. Under the PT, Black women's rights in particular were the focus of policies extending employment rights and benefits to domestic workers (Sullivan, this volume). Scholars argue that Bolsonaro's misogynistic campaign rhetoric, and the support it garnered, was a direct response to feminist advances and to a dynamic younger generation of feminists (Pinho, this volume), as well as to the perceived threat to normative masculinity (Kalil, Pinheiro-Machado, and Scalco, this volume).

However, antifeminist views were not exclusive to Bolsonaro's male supporters, and one meme we showed students focused on these female supporters. The meme's text reads, "I am not a feminist, I am FEMININE. A woman's place is where she wants to be as long as she respects herself. She doesn't need to show her body." Many of the students labeled the Barbie in this meme as "antifeminist." Several felt that Barbie was ignorant of the fact that the freedoms she enjoys were a product of the feminist movement. Arya, a twenty-three-year-old straight, Black woman studying dentistry in Goiânia, asserted, "Her statement is so wrong and many women these days are reproducing it. They were only able to get where they are because of the feminist movement, which allowed women to enter into the job market, although many women still receive less than men for the same work." Joana, an eighteen-year-old pansexual, white woman studying literature in Goiânia argued that there was a connection between the viewpoint voiced by Barbie and the "conservative movement." Joana expressed, "This is the conservative movement in Brazil that, in truth, is the patriarchy wanting to convince women that they don't need feminism. They want to introduce very *machista* [chauvinist] values, such as how to respect oneself, no need to show the body. They are wanting to disqualify feminist discourse." Joana, Arya, and other students viewed Barbie's statement as antifeminist, rather than expressing an alternative form of feminism, and a reflection of sexism among Bolsonaro's supporters.

Similarly, Bolsonaro's campaign articulated homophobic and transphobic views that moralized heteronormativity, promising to reinstate "family values," which, according to his campaign, the PT had dismantled. The campaign deplored recent advances in the rights of LGBTQ+ individuals and their mainstream visibility. It vilified LGBTQ+ people through what Jarrín (this volume) calls the "politics of disgust," manipulating the moral anxiety experienced by Brazilians living under precarity.[5] In response to Bolsonaro's rhetoric and the influx of homophobic and transphobic messages circulating through social and mass media, memes emerged that mocked individuals who denied their homophobia yet still supported Bolsonaro (cf. Junge, this volume).

In one meme, Barbie declares, "Me, homophobic? I have several gay friends." Discussing this meme, students noted that true allies of the LGBTQ+ community did not need to clarify that they were not homophobic and that the clarification actually revealed their homophobia. In another meme, a Barbie doll holding a blond baby doll states, "I love the gays but I prefer that my son be macho!!! #*Prontofalei* #*ptnuncamais* #*elesim* #*b17*." This meme also mocks the Bolsonaro supporter as a hypocrite who claims to love gay people but is actually homophobic. The inclusion of the hashtags #*prontofalei* (#thereIsaidit), #*ptnuncamais* (#PTnevermore), and #*elesim* (#yeshim), index this Barbie's support of Bolsonaro on many levels, both in her critique of the PT and in the use of #*elesim* (#yeshim) as a reply to the widespread #*elenão* (#nothim) movement against Bolsonaro. The meme serves as both a critique of homophobic discourse and a rebuke of Bolsonaro and his supporters for being homophobic.

A third element the Barbie and Ken memes commented on was racism in Brazil. The racial fluidity prevalent in Brazil contributed to a national ideology of a racial democracy, which allowed middle- and upper-class Brazilians exhibiting traits associated with whiteness to deny the existence of racism while simultaneously benefiting from it. As the PT enacted policies to address racial inequality, resentment grew among middle- and upper-class Brazilians whose white privilege was challenged by the upward mobilization of the majority Black and brown Brazilian working class, leading to what Pinho (in this volume) calls "injured whiteness."[6] In the period leading up to Bolsonaro's election, as middle- and upper-class Brazilians became more comfortable vocalizing racist sentiments, liberal activists used the Barbie and Ken memes, among other methods, to highlight racism in Brazil. The meme in which Ken claims to be the victim of racism after being called "whitey" (*branquelo*) is one example of a meme mocking injured whiteness.

In another meme we showed our participants, Barbie exclaims, "Me, racist? I even have Black friends." The students we interviewed felt that the "I have Black friends" discourse was very common and often used to justify everyday forms of racism. After viewing this meme, Mattos, a thirty-two-year-old, straight, parda woman studying psychology in Salvador, spoke passionately

FIGURE 16.2. "Me, racist? I even have black friends."
Source: https://www.facebook.com/pg/barbieekencidadaosdebem/

about Brazil's racial climate: "This is bullshit . . . because [people say] 'I can have friends—Black friends—but I don't want my son to marry a Black girl, you know?' I think that it is a veiled form of racism. It's like, someone says, 'I am not racist, but I know somebody who is.' And so, everyone knows someone who is racist, but [they] don't think they, themselves, are racist. It doesn't add up." Leading up to Bolsonaro's election, Brazilians could no longer feign ignorance of Brazil's racial realities (Pinho, this volume), and the Barbie and Ken memes were a vehicle for critiquing Brazilians who were racist and/or were in denial of their racist beliefs and racial bias.

A fourth element the memes critiqued is Brazilian meritocracy. Despite strong evidence to the contrary, in 2018 many Brazilians believed economic and social mobility were earned through hard work and enterprise based on a system of meritocracy.[7] Meritocratic discourses were used to criticize programs addressing social inequality, and the people who directly benefited from them were often racialized (Pinho, this book). Bolsonaro often employed rhetoric around meritocracy when discussing the economic crisis and, in response, memes also mocked the notion of meritocracy in Brazil. One meme featuring Ken states, "These days, those who don't move up in life are those who don't want to. I myself am twenty-three years old and I'm already the foreign trade manager in my father's business." Pablo, a twenty-two-year-old gay white man studying anthropology in Salvador explained the image as "mocking the Brazilian meritocracy, in which white people who have many opportunities say that for you to ascend, you only need to want it, but it is not the truth." As Pablo asserts, memes such as this one portray young middle- and upper-class Brazilians as ignorant of their privilege and the obstacles facing the upward mobility of many Brazilians. This and many other memes direct their criticism toward younger generations of the Brazilian elite, rather than their parents. Although we do not have data specifically on why young, elite Brazilians are the focus of the memes, we speculate that the meme creators are commenting on discourses existing among their peers, as well as among wealthy, white celebrities and in the popular media.

In addition to tackling themes of privilege, discrimination, and inequality, memes speaking directly to political discourse in Brazil emerged in 2018. One meme depicts Barbie stating, "The PT almost destroyed my life." Flavia, a twenty-two-year-old straight, Black woman from Salvador

FIGURE 16.3. "The PT almost destroyed my life."
Source: https://www.facebook.com/pg/barbieekencidadaosdebem/

studying English, echoed the majority of students we interviewed when she discussed this meme: "There was a discourse during the elections that the PT destroyed people's lives and that's why it has to get out of power. These people who say that are usually people who have never been [negatively] affected by the government because they were in a very comfortable social class. So I really do not know where they get this from." This meme mocks the views of the members of Brazil's middle and upper classes who resented the upward mobilization of the working class under the PT and whose criticisms of PT's policies intensified with the 2014 economic crisis. Even students who criticized the PT and argued it was a corrupt political party were supportive of meme content that chastised elite Brazilians over their failure to recognize their privilege and their dramatic statements of suffering.

In another meme, Barbie states, "Dictatorship? Torture? Ustra?[8] This isn't anything close to the communist dictatorship of these 13 years that PT was in power." As Apolo, a nineteen-year-old gay, white man studying English in Curitiba explained, "These people . . . who are the Barbies,

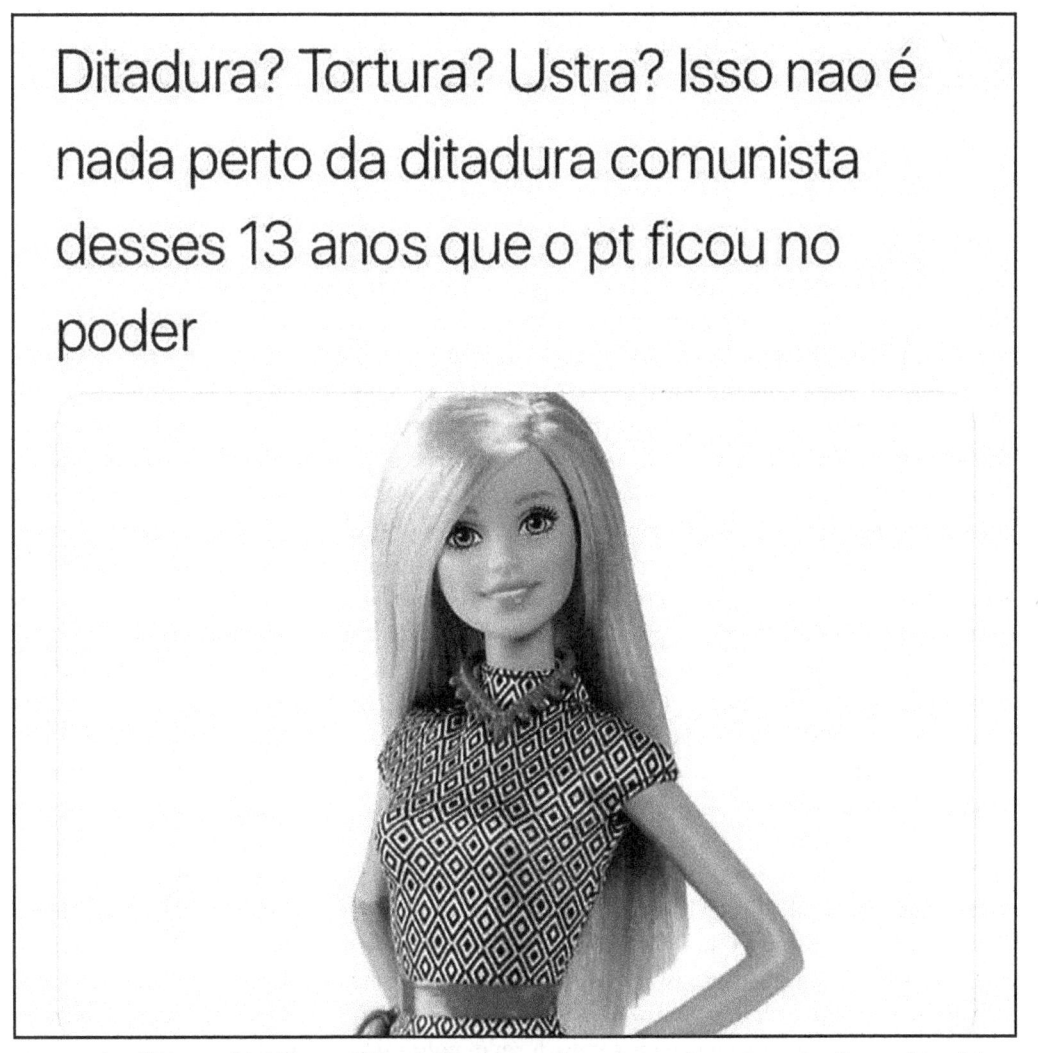

FIGURE 16.4. "Dictatorship? Torture? Ustra? This isn't anything close to the communist dictatorship of these 13 years that PT was in power."
Source: https://www.facebook.com/pg/barbieekencidadaosdebem/

because they are white people, heterosexual, with high purchasing power who talk about issues that do not necessarily influence them much . . . are people who are very lacking in awareness of society. Her social class and conditions allow her to remain unaffected directly by the dictatorship, particularly to the point her life is at risk because of the dictatorial regime, which would be the case of a poorer person, a Black person, a transsexual person, a homosexual person, a person who is part of some minority group in society." This meme prompted several students to give detailed accounts of Brazil's history of authoritarian rule.[9] Notably, though this particular meme does not mention Bolsonaro directly, students drew connections between the statement made in the meme and Bolsonaro's campaign rhetoric, which defended Ustra, torture, and the dictatorship. Students who supported the PT also used this meme to challenge the notion that the PT was a communist party, stating that they were more centrist than Bolsonaro supporters claimed. Thus this meme prompted students to develop their own interpretation of political history, contemporary politics, and political discourse.

The students' interpretations of all the memes also revealed the social and political salience of the memes for college students and foregrounded some students' perceptions that sharing the memes was a form of political participation. For these students, the creation and sharing of the Barbie and Ken memes was an opportunity to voice concerns over social issues and Bolsonaro's run for president, and indexed them as political subjects.

BEYOND EFFICACY: SHARING MEMES AS VOICING AND POLITICAL PARTICIPATION

Today, social media is increasingly used as a tool of social activism, with platforms such as Facebook and Twitter becoming popular spaces for encouraging social change. However, as Bonilla and Rosa (2015, 10) have noted, "The long-lasting effects of digital modes of activism remain hotly debated. For some, these acts represent fleeting moments of awareness, quickly replaced by the customary innocuousness of social media pleasantries." Some scholars and activists have denounced social media activism as having a short-lived impact, arguing it cannot replace in-person activism (Wasik 2009). While our purpose was not to measure the efficacy of the Barbie and Ken memes as a form of activism, we were interested in students' perceptions of the role and impact of the memes. Students' perspectives on sharing memes as an impactful form of political activism were largely informed by their understanding of what constitutes activism, and their own political subjectivity. Although some students felt that sharing the Barbie and Ken memes was ineffective, we discovered that many students viewed the memes as a powerful and necessary response to Bolsonaro's campaign rhetoric. These students argued that the memes granted them the means to voice their opposition to Bolsonaro and mock the discourses of his supporters.

Although students recognized the memes as a product of the political climate and a form of social and political activism, their opinions differed as to whether the memes had a tangible impact on politics or social injustice. Lua, a twenty-four-year-old bisexual, white woman studying English in Curitiba, felt that the creation and sharing of memes was a form of activism but that it was ineffective. She measured efficacy by the ability to make change—in particular changing the minds of Bolsonaro's supporters—and did not believe the memes had the power to change opinions. However, while Lua argued against the political impact of the memes, she described the sharing of Barbie and Ken memes as an opportunity for voicing one's political perspectives: "For people who are against Bolsonaro, [the memes] became a form of political activism. But in truth, I don't think it's activism that makes a difference, because posting a meme on the internet is not going to make a difference. In that way, a person posts so that other people know what their political position is.

It ends up creating unity. The people who think alike unite to laugh and joke together."[10] Although the Barbie and Ken memes could be viewed as contributing to the polarization of Brazilian society, Lua presented an alternative viewpoint: that a strength of the Barbie and Ken memes was that they created a sense of solidarity among Brazilians who were against Bolsonaro and social injustice. Therefore, for Lua and other students, the memes were a valuable opportunity to connect with like-minded individuals and vent their frustrations.[11]

Other students agreed that the memes were not necessarily effective in swaying the views of Bolsonaro supporters, partially because they would not appear in the social media feeds of all Brazilians. Elena, a twenty-three-year-old straight, parda woman studying English in Salvador, asserted, "Change is very difficult. It takes a lot of time. I think [the memes] might be a spark for the person . . . represented by Barbie . . . to begin to reflect. However . . . the chances of a person being represented here seeing a meme like this on the internet are minimal because they do not follow certain pages that would publish those memes, you see? Perhaps, if these people who create these memes discussed these memes in spaces other than just social networks." Elena believed that while the Barbie and Ken memes may make some Brazilians reflect on their own beliefs, in many cases they are not even exposed to the memes as a result of their own social media curation.

However, Elena also argued that concrete results were not a measure of the efficacy of the memes as a form of protest. She explained that for many Brazilians, social media in general, and the Barbie and Ken memes more specifically, enabled Brazilians to share their "*voz*" (voice) and speak out against multiple levels of social inequality and oppression. A meme featuring Barbie stating, "Racism doesn't exist, my great-grandmother was Black, I also have Black blood," prompted Elena to discuss the myth of the racial democracy in Brazil. She highlighted the way in which widespread social media use had created a new avenue to express long-held criticism surrounding the notion of racial democracy in Brazilian culture: "To [be able to] say that this is an illusion, that this is a constructed discourse that, in fact, racism still exists. With social networks, people started to have a voice they did not have before. It gives voice to certain people who didn't have a voice." Bonilla and Rosa (2015, 10) argue that while the act of sharing a meme or a tweet may be "fleeting by nature," it is a product of and response to "accumulated frustrations" over oppression and marginalization, and for some, a lifetime of injustice. For individuals with marginalized social identities, social media is a relatively safe place for sharing one's views and for speaking out against injustice. Therefore, for Elena and other students, sharing memes that mocked marginalizing discourses was a way to challenge these discourses and also a political act that influenced their sense of self.

Other students argued that the Barbie and Ken memes were an effective form of resistance against Bolsonaro's rhetoric. Theo, a twenty-two-year-old gay, white man studying English in Curitiba, described the Barbie and Ken memes as a "demonstration of resistance. We take this discourse and we subvert their discourse; that racist, meritocratic, homophobic, sexist discourse. We make these people feel ashamed for spreading these discourses." Theo felt strongly that creating and sharing these memes directly challenged discriminatory discourses. For Theo, being a politically active Brazilian citizen was not limited to participating in traditional "street" protests but also consisted of "reflection," "thinking," "receiving information and knowledge," "questioning," and "trying to inform others." Theo argued that posting memes was a way for people to demonstrate their political positions and invite discussions among fellow nonsupporters of Bolsonaro but also other people in his social network, such as family members who were supporters. He also explained that his working-class background informed his activism: "I was denied a lot of things and it is important for me to position myself politically in favor of people having access [to social benefits] I did not have access to." Likewise, his identity as a member of the LGBTQ+ community also inspired his activism. Although for Theo sharing memes was not the only form of political activism, he believed that by using memes to challenge the discourses spread by Bolsonaro, he was opening up a dialogue that could encourage others to reconsider their privilege and their political views. The sharing of memes was a key component of Theo's sense of himself as an activist and his political subjectivity.

Like Theo, Vicente, a twenty-seven-year-old gay, Black man studying French in Curitiba, also saw the memes as a form of resistance against Bolsonaro and Brazilian elites. He explained, "Now I see that these people represented in these memes of Ken and Barbie are returning to positions of power and their discourse has been getting stronger, but I see that there is a movement of resistance as well. I think the very existence of these memes is a resistance movement. I think that just the fact that one can perceive the historical moment in which we live and manage to create a meme, making fun through an image, that is a resistance." Vicente stated that as a Black, gay man, these movements spoke directly to him. However, Vicente also recognized the ways in which he had privilege as a cisgender man, saying his activism was directed at "giving space" for people with less privilege to have a voice and share their experiences, whether virtually or in person. For Vicente, the Barbie and Ken memes afforded him the opportunity to speak out against various forms of injustice and contribute to social movements that were important to him as a result of his social identities.

POLITICAL PARTICIPATION ON SOCIAL MEDIA VERSUS THE "STREET"

Several students felt that through sharing the memes within diverse social networks—particularly through Facebook, which was largely used to stay in touch with family and friends—there was the chance of reaching people whose views the memes reflected. Levi, a twenty-five-year-old bisexual, pardo man studying business in Goiânia, argued, "The dissemination of memes is a political act of making people reflect on what is set in society; the forms of oppression in that society." He explained the challenges he faced during and after the presidential campaign when it became clear that his family members, especially those from older generations, supported Bolsonaro's candidacy and did not find his rhetoric problematic. Levi lauded the memes and actively posted memes to his Facebook account in an effort to encourage his family members and others to reflect on social issues: "I think that for those who did not participate in debates around gender, race, and class and politics, I think they [the memes] helped them to reflect. [People would say] 'I did not understand [this meme] here. Explain it to me.' . . . and [I'd] explain it." Levi believed that by sharing memes, family members with differing social and political beliefs were being exposed to social justice issues. Notably, other students reported decreased engagement with certain social media forms, such as Facebook, to avoid interactions with family members whose views they did not share or to avoid feeling overwhelmed and sad.[12]

Recognizing his privilege as a cisgender, and pardo, rather than Black, man, Levi felt that he had a responsibility to "fight against oppression." He described the intersection of multiple forms of oppression in Brazil, explaining that they were all connected and therefore one cannot speak out against one form and not another. He argued that "it has to do with my *lugar de fala*" (literally "speaking place," but functionally, social position). While Levi spoke out against racism, gender discrimination, and homophobia, the issue most present for him was that of class, "on my Instagram, I also post reflections on class . . . because I don't come from a rich family." For Levi, the sharing of the memes was a form of communicating one's views to friends and family members and was also a political act against discrimination and inequality. His sense of self as someone who was politically engaged was informed by his belief that sharing these memes could have an impact on the social and political views of his friends and family.

Students expressed that posting the Barbie and Ken memes was a way of taking a political stance by voicing one's social and political views to one's social network. Iara, a twenty-six-year-old straight, white woman studying English in Curitiba, explained, "I think from the moment that someone creates this content and is sharing it, [they are] already doing a political act, because it is . . . showing a position . . . that they do not accept [something] and thinks this government is pathetic. So who shares [the memes] . . . is politically positioning themselves." For her, and other students, the sharing of memes allowed them to construct a political stance that contributed to the formation of their political subjectivity. However, for many students like Iara, their sense of themselves as political agents was also informed by their perceptions that in-person or "street" activism was more effective than social media activism. While Iara recognized the value of using social media, and the Barbie and Ken memes specifically, to make a political statement, she went on to lament that many people, herself included, limited their political involvement to social media. She believed that people should "go to the street to really protest, you know? Organize themselves; do effective things in effective ways. There's really a lack of people protesting the right way for what we want, for the changes we want, or against what we don't agree with." For Iara, activism was effective if it resulted in social or legislative change, and she believed that street activism had greater potential for encouraging change than social media activism.

For students such as Cesar, a twenty-year-old straight, pardo man and electrical engineering student from Goiânia, the Barbie and Ken memes were a key "part of the political movement in Brazil." Cesar said that he participated in protests against Bolsonaro "through social media, conversing with other people. In the street itself, I never went to protest. I'd go. I don't know why I never went." Cesar expressed a sense of guilt that he was not active in street protests, stating that sharing memes was only a "small form" of activism. Cesar's concern that his activism was limited to social media was echoed in the narratives of other students who felt that "street" activism was a more effective form of activism.

Benjamin, a thirty-one-year-old recent economics master's program graduate and straight, white man from Curitiba, referenced social media activism as "sofa activism." He argued, "The political activists in the past . . . were organized. In Brazil there exists the UNE, União Nacional dos Estudantes [National Student Union]. When someone joins, they stop being passive and merely sharing their ideas. They are actually acting so that things happen. A person who really raises the banner at the university and goes to defend the university, I think this is an activist . . . a person who simply says, 'I am against the university [budget] cuts,' but continues living their lives, they are not an activist." Benjamin articulates a notion of political activism tied to civil society, or what Alvarez and colleagues (2017, 3) refer to as the "civil society agenda" and the belief that "'civic' civil society participation in governmental and intergovernmental institutions enhances or expands" democracy. Alvarez and colleagues assert that the civil society agenda does not always benefit democratic processes, and other forms of political engagement can also be effective. Yet Benjamin and a few others argued that people's lack of engagement with political institutions and activism outside of social media prevented change from occurring. As Iara, Cesar, and Benjamin indicated, the varied views of the efficacy of social media activism strongly impacted how students evaluated their own political participation.

Shifman (2014) argues that for younger adults who are less likely to engage in formal political activities, political memes are an accessible and attractive form of political participation. For Shifman (2014, 123), political memes serve three overlapping purposes: (1) political persuasion or advocacy, (2) coordinated grassroots activism among social networks of people rather than organizations, and (3) "modes of expression and public discussion . . . an accessible, cheap, and enjoyable route for voicing one's political opinions." Many students we interviewed did view the memes as a valid form of political participation, arguing that the memes were powerful opportunities to voice their beliefs and views publicly and engage in discussions with like-minded individuals, and/or, in some instances, with family and friends with opposing views. The narratives of students with marginalized social identities also demonstrate an important relationship between their social identities, the social and political issues they rallied around, and the methods of activism in which they chose to engage. For these students, the Barbie and Ken memes were a unique mechanism for voicing their opposition to social injustice, which granted the memes meaning and value as a form of political participation (Bonilla and Rosa 2015; Junge 2018).

Stalcup (2016, 146) argues that "new media technologies" are "a kind of equipment that could generate new relationships and subjectivities . . . shaping new political subjects and collectives." For Brazilian college students, voicing their opposition to Bolsonaro and the discourses of his supporters was an important form of political participation and key to their sense of selves as politically engaged Brazilians. Their political subjectivity emerged as a direct response to marginalizing discourses circulating during the campaign and the aggravated threat of discrimination, violence, and inequality his election could bring.

CONCLUSION

The year 2018 was a critical moment in Brazilian history during which advances in human rights and social benefits for marginalized groups were under attack by a presidential campaign that, among other tactics, weaponized the fragility of elite Brazilians. Brazilians from both ends of the ideological spectrum employed social media to voice their thoughts on the campaign and what it represented for Brazilian society. The Barbie and Ken memes emerged as creative and well-constructed, critical responses to Bolsonaro's rhetoric and discourses spread by his supporters. These political memes are representative of new genres of social media activism that bring into question the extent to which these forms of media constitute an emerging form of political participation in democratic societies (cf. Shifman 2014). We argue that during the 2018 presidential race in Brazil, social media and political memes were vehicles through which young adults, even those whose political participation had previously been minimal, could engage with the political and social issues facing Brazil during this precarious time.

Voicing one's views and concerns is a symbol of political participation and is a critical component of a liberal democracy (Kunreuther 2018). During the 2018 election, when populist discourses hailed a return to authoritarianism and threatened Brazil's already precarious democracy, the ability to partake in democratic practice assumed an even deeper meaning for Brazilians. For Brazilian college students, sharing the memes was an opportunity to take a symbolic stand against Bolsonaro's racist, sexist, homophobic, and classist rhetoric and the social discourses circulating alongside it. For students who felt personally targeted by this rhetoric, the memes and the act of sharing them were especially salient. Thus we also argue that the use of memes to voice their social and political views contributed to students' understanding of themselves as activists and political agents, or in other words, their political subjectivity. Our findings indicate that political memes and other forms of new media are emerging as important new forms of political participation that also contribute to the political subjectivity of young people and merit further investigation across cultural, political, and social contexts.

REFERENCES

Alvarez, Sonia E., Gianpaolo Baiocchi, Agustín Laó-Montes, Jeffrey W. Rubin, and Millie Thayer. 2017. Introduction to *Beyond Civil Society: Activism, Participation, and Protest in Latin America*, edited by Sonia E. Alvarez,

Jeffrey W. Rubin, Millie Thayer Gianpaolo Baiocchi, Agustín Laó-Montes, 1–24. Durham, N.C.: Duke University Press.

Bonilla, Yarimar, and Jonathan Rosa. 2015. "#Ferguson: Digital Protest, Hashtag Ethnography, and the Racial Politics of Social Media in the United States." *American Ethnologist* 42 (1): 4–17.

Denisova, Anastasia. 2019. *Internet Memes and Society: Social, Cultural, and Political Contexts*. London: Routledge.

Goldstein, Donna. 2013. *Laughter Out of Place: Race, Class, Violence, and Sexuality in a Rio Shantytown*. Reprinted with a new preface. Berkeley: University of California Press.

Hart, Marjolein't, and Dennis Bos, eds. 2007. *Humour and Social Protest*. Cambridge: Cambridge University Press.

Jin, Dal Yong, and Kyong Yoon. 2016. "The Social Mediascape of Transnational Korean Pop Culture: Hallyu 2.0 as Spreadable Media Practice." *New Media and Society* 18 (7): 1277–1292.

Junge, Benjamin. 2018. *Cynical Citizenship: Gender, Regionalism, and Political Subjectivity in Porto Alegre, Brazil*. Albuquerque: University of New Mexico Press.

Juris, Jeffrey. 2012. "Reflections on #Occupy Everywhere: Social Media, Public Space, and Emerging Logics of Aggregation." *American Ethnologist* 39 (2): 259–279.

Kunreuther, Laura. 2018. "Sounds of Democracy: Performance, Protest, and Political Subjectivity." *Cultural Anthropology* 33 (1): 1–31.

Mina, An Xiao. 2019. *Memes to Movements: How the World's Most Viral Media Is Changing Social Protest and Power*. Boston: Beacon.

Postill, John, and Sarah Pink. 2012. "Social Media Ethnography: The Digital Researcher in a Messy Web." *Media International Australia* 145:123–134.

Shifman, Limor. 2014. *Memes in Digital Culture*. Cambridge, Mass.: MIT Press.

Stalcup, Meg. 2016. "The Aesthetic Politics of Unfinished Media: New Media Activism in Brazil." *Visual Anthropology Review* 32 (2): 144–156.

Tribunal Regional Eleitoral (TRE-PR). 2018. "Eleições 2018." Accessed April 29, 2019. http://www.tre-pr.jus.br/eleicoes/eleicoes-2018.

Wasik, Bill. 2009. *And Then There's This: How Stories Live and Die in Viral Culture*. New York: Penguin.

NOTES

1. Excluded from the memes' commentary, usually, are Bolsonaro's other supporters, such as working-class Brazilians, including individuals who had previously supported the Workers' Party (Kopper; Mitchell; and Rojas, Olival, and Spexoto Olival, this volume).
2. Students were selected for participation using convenience sampling.
3. A ballot can be nullified with a mark on a paper ballot or by digitally entering a number that does not correspond with a candidate on an electronic ballot.
4. The Brazilian census uses five color or race (*cor ou raça*) categories: white (*branca*), black (*preta*), brown (*parda*), indigenous (*indígena*), or yellow (*amarela*). Brazilians informally use over one hundred terms to describe themselves. Since the 1970s, the Black movement in Brazil has advocated for the adoption of a *Negro* (Black, with a capital B) identity that demonstrates racial consciousness.
5. See chapters by Junge, Henning, and Jarrín in this volume.
6. See Sullivan in this volume.
7. See chapters by Jerome and Pinho in this volume.
8. Brazilian army colonel Carlos Alberto Brilhante Ustra was accused of torturing hundreds of activists from 1970 to 1974 during Brazil's military dictatorship.
9. See Junge et al., this volume.
10. The use of humor in social and political movements has a long history (Hart and Bos 2007). Memes can employ humor to garner attention, increase their distribution, entertain, and ease the tension of tense political and social conditions (c.f. Goldstein 2013). While most of the students interpreted the memes as ironic and comical, other students asserted that since they represented real discourses, they were not actually humorous.
11. Memes also play a role in cultivating community, collective identities, and kinship (Denisova 2019).
12. See chapters by Junge, Jerome, and Henning in this volume.

ACKNOWLEDGMENTS

We owe an enormous debt of gratitude to this volume's authors, who revised their chapters many times, diligently answered our constant emails, and in the end, contributed brilliant ethnographic scholarship. We are also grateful to our editor at Rutgers University Press, Kimberly Guinta, who enthusiastically supported this project from the beginning. Thanks also to our two anonymous reviewers, whose insightful feedback strengthened the volume greatly, and to Jason Scott for his translation of Lilia Moritz Schwarcz's critical overview. All four of us are appreciative of support from our home universities, SUNY New Paltz, Rutgers–Newark, College of the Holy Cross, and the University of San Francisco. Finally, we express our deep gratitude to the people whose narratives are shared in these pages.

Ben wishes to thank the Wilson Center for International Scholars, the Fulbright Commission of Brazil, the National Science Foundation/Cultural Anthropology Program, and the School for Advanced Research for institutional support during his research and planning for this volume. Sean is grateful for the institutional support of the National Science Foundation/Cultural Anthropology Program, the School for Advanced Research, The Institute of Social and Political Studies (IESP) of the State University of Rio de Janeiro, and Rutgers Global. Alvaro thanks College of the Holy Cross for funding their research, but above all they want to thank the activists and artists willing to speak to them and share their time for this article. Lucia sends acknowledgements to the Social Science Research Council, and to the generous interlocutors in Rio de Janeiro, for their participation in her research.

NOTES ON CONTRIBUTORS

KARINA BIONDI holds a PhD in social anthropology from Federal University of Sao Carlos (UFSCar). She is currently a professor at the State University of Maranhão (UEMA), where she coordinates the Laboratory of Studies in Political Anthropology (LEAP). Biondi's research interests include prisoners, criminals, and technologies of crime control and punishment. She wrote *Sharing This Walk: An Ethnography of Prison Life and the PCC in Brazil* (winner of the APLA 2017 Book Prize) and *Proibido Roubar na Quebrada: Território, Lei e Hierarquia no PCC* (winner of the LASA Brazil Section Book Prize 2019).

LUCIA CANTERO is an associate professor of international studies at the University of San Francisco. Her areas of research include infrastructures, affect, consumer culture, algorithms, objects, and space. Within this, her work focuses on branding, advertising and markets as sites for the construction of political subjectivity and the ways these "kinaesthetic" processes inflect formations of race, class, and gender/sexuality. She is currently completing *Olympic Afterlives*, a monograph on design tactics and the reconfiguration of public sphere and space after Rio 2016. She has recently begun a project with data scientists on AI, machine learning and bias in Brazil.

JOHN F. COLLINS is a professor of anthropology at Queens College and the CUNY Graduate Center. He is cochair of the Columbia University Brazil Seminar, and from 2011 to 2017 he directed the Program in Latin American and Caribbean Studies at Queens College. In addition to numerous articles, Collins is the author of *Revolt of the Saints: Memory and Redemption in the Twilight of Brazilian Racial Democracy*, which earned the 2016 Anthony Leeds Prize for Urban Ethnography, translator and editor of *Sharing This Walk: An Ethnography of Prison Life and the PCC in Brazil*, and coeditor of *Ethnographies of U.S. Empire*.

FALINA ENRIQUEZ is an assistant professor in the Department of Anthropology at the University of Wisconsin–Madison. Her research examines Brazilian musical practices and their discursive and structural relationships to entrepreneurship, neoliberalism, and multiculturalism.

CARLOS EDUARDO HENNING is an associate professor of anthropology at the Social Sciences College (FCS) and the chair of the Graduate Program in Anthropology (PPGAS) at the Universidade Federal de Goiás (UFG). Henning was a visiting scholar at University of California, Santa Cruz (2011–2012), at Universidade de São Paulo (2018), and at Columbia University (2019). His current research examines activism, institutions, NGOs and discourses on aging and sexual and gender diversity, more specifically regarding LGBTI+ elders in South America. His broader work addresses issues on gender, sexuality, old age, generation, life course, urban studies, LGBTIQ gerontology and queer/cuír anthropology.

ALVARO JARRÍN is an associate professor of anthropology at College of the Holy Cross. Their research explores the imbrication of medicine, the body, and inequality in Brazil, with foci on plastic surgery, genomics, and gender-nonconforming activism. They are the author of *The Biopolitics of Beauty: Cosmetic Citizenship and Affective Capital in Brazil* (University of California Press), which explored the eugenic underpinnings of raciological thought among plastic surgeons and the aesthetic hierarchies of beauty that reinforce racial inequality in Brazil.

JESSICA JEROME is an associate professor in the Department of Health Sciences at DePaul University. She is the author of *A Right to Health: Medicine, Marginality, and Health Care Reform in Northeastern Brazil* (2015). Trained as a medical anthropologist, her research examines the origins of health care inequalities in urban contexts.

BENJAMIN JUNGE is a full professor of anthropology at the State University of New York at New Paltz. He is the author of *Cynical Citizenship: Gender, Regionalism, and Political Subjectivity in Porto Alegre, Brazil* (University of New Mexico Press, 2018). Junge's research examines class mobility, political affinities, gender, sexuality, health, and religion in Brazil. He codirected a three-year investigation of political subjectivities among the demographic sector once known as Brazil's "new middle class," focusing on perceptions of the 2013–2018 crisis, cultural memory of authoritarian pasts, and the rise of popular conservativism.

JAMES KALE is a multilingual researcher, freedom fighter, and educational activist. He is the founder of Kale Solutions, where he partners with organizations, institutions, and schools to elevate their curriculum, programming, design, and services. His work and audiences include a range of nonprofits, charter schools, CEOs, and universities both in the United States and abroad. He is also the founding chief of staff and director of special projects for an urban assembly charter school in New York City. Kale has a BA in applied psychology and human development and sociology as well as an MEd in curriculum and instruction and teacher education from Boston College.

ISABELA KALIL has a PhD in anthropology from the University of São Paulo. She is an associate professor at the São Paulo School of Sociology and Political Science (FESPSP) and coordinator of the NEU—Center for Urban Ethnography at the same institution. Prior to joining FESPSP, she was a visiting scholar at Columbia University (New York City) in the Department of Anthropology.

MOISES KOPPER is a social anthropologist currently working on the technopolitics of Brazil's inequality measures and its powers to fashion images of national futurity. His forthcoming book *Architectures of Hope*, a long-term ethnography of *Minha Casa Minha Vida*, charts the effects of first-time homeownership among once–socially ascendant Brazilians. Kopper holds a Marie Curie Postdoctoral Fellowship at the Laboratoire d'Anthropologie des Mondes Contemporains, Université Libre de Bruxelles. Previously, he was a postdoctoral research associate at the Max Planck Institute for the Study of Societies (Cologne) and the Center for Metropolitan Studies (São Paulo). His research centers on hope and class, subjectivity and affect, (post)neoliberalism and statecraft, policy design and implementation, economic expertise, and algorithmic governance.

PATRICK MCCORMICK is a PhD student in the Department of Political Science at the University of Minnesota. His area of interest, developed while spending time in both Nicaragua and Brazil, is democratic consolidation and democratic back-sliding in Latin America.

MELANIE A. MEDEIROS is an associate professor of anthropology at the State University of New York–Geneseo. She is the author of *Marriage, Divorce and Distress in Northeast Brazil: Black Women's Perspectives on Love, Respect, and Kinship* (Rutgers University Press, 2018). Dr. Medeiros's research examines social media and youth political and social justice activism in Brazil. She is also an engaged, critical medical anthropologist who studies health disparities facing Black communities in Brazil and the United States, and im/migrant communities in the United States.

SEAN T. MITCHELL is an associate professor of anthropology at Rutgers University, Newark. His book *Constellations of Inequality: Space, Race, and Utopia in Brazil* (University of Chicago Press, 2017) won the 2018 Social Science Book Prize from the Latin American Studies Association Brazil Section. He is also coeditor of *Anthropology and Global Counterinsurgency* (University of Chicago Press, 2010) and author of many articles. He writes about inequality politics in Brazil and elsewhere. His book in progress traces the rise and fall of Brazil's early twenty-first-century "new middle class," and through it, the nature of the Workers' Party governments' social democratic project and of opposition to it.

ALEXANDRE DE AZEVEDO OLIVAL is a professor at Universidade do Estado de Mato Grosso (Alta Floresta). He has a PhD in veterinary medicine (Universidade de São Paulo). Over the past thirteen years, he has worked in Alta Floresta drawing on his veterinary background to address the larger problems of rural development and the conditions under which peasant agriculture may thrive—in particular, participatory efforts to support the construction of silvopastoral agroecological systems.

ROSANA PINHEIRO-MACHADO is an anthropologist and a lecturer of international development in the Department of Social and Policy Sciences at the University of Bath. Previously, she was a lecturer at the University of Oxford and held visiting positions at the University of São Paulo and Harvard University. She is an award-winning columnist of the *Intercept Brasil* and the author of several books, including *Amanhã Vai Ser Maior* (Planeta, 2019), which discusses the conservative turn and resistance in Brazil.

PATRICIA DE SANTANA PINHO is an associate professor in the Department of Latin American and Latino Studies at the University of California, Santa Cruz. She is the author of several publications on blackness, whiteness, racism, and forms of resistance to racism in Brazil, including *Mama Africa: Reinventing Blackness in Bahia* (Duke University Press, 2010). Her latest book, *Mapping Diaspora: African American Roots Tourism in Brazil* (University of North Carolina Press, 2018), examines the construction of transnational black solidarity within the geopolitical context of the African diaspora. Pinho is a native of Salvador, Bahia, and has a PhD in social sciences from the Universidade Estadual de Campinas—UNICAMP, Brazil.

DAVID ROJAS is an assistant professor at Bucknell University. He has a PhD in anthropology (Cornell University) and since 2009 has pursued a multisited ethnography in Brazilian Amazonia and United Nations environmental forums that focuses on political responses to mass-scale socioecological destruction.

LUCIA MURY SCALCO completed her PhD in social anthropology at the Federal University of Rio Grande do Sul (UFRGS). She is the coordinator of the Division of Policies for Family, Gender and Generation at the Center of International Studies on Government (CEGOV/UFRGS). She is also the president of the NGO Coletivo Autônomo do Morro da Cruz, planning and coordinating educational projects in an impoverished area in the city of Porto Alegre, Brazil.

ERIKA SCHMITT is a PhD student of school psychology in the Department of Educational Psychology at Texas A&M University.

LILIA MORITZ SCHWARCZ is a full professor of anthropology at the University of São Paulo and a global scholar and visiting professor at Princeton. She has published several books, among them four in English: *The Spectacle of the Races* (1999), *The Emperor's Beard* (2004),

Brazil: A Biography with Heloisa Starling (2017), and *The Brazil Reader* with James Green and Victoria Langland (2018). She was a fellow at the Guggenheim Foundation (2006–2007) and at the John Carter Brown Library (2007), and she has been a Tinker Professor at Columbia and a visiting professor at Oxford and Leiden. She received a commendation from the Brazilian Order of Scientific Merit (2010).

ANDREZZA ALVES SPEXOTO OLIVAL is the current coordinator of Instituto Ouro Verde's (IOV) agroecological network. She has an MA in veterinary medicine and postgraduate specialization courses on land reform (Universidade Federal de Lavras) and production cooperativism (Universidade Federal de Viçosa). Since 2004 she has worked in Alta Floresta helping design and put in place the IOV's highly decentralized and participatory structure in close partnership with social movements and peasant organizations.

LASHANDRA SULLIVAN is an anthropology professor at Reed College. She conducts research on the intersections of race, ethnicity, gender, sexuality, and social movements in Rio de Janeiro, as well as in the center-west state of Mato Grosso do Sul, Brazil. Her research in Rio de Janeiro focuses on Black feminism, LGBTQ+ organizing, and Black empowerment. In Mato Grosso do Sul, she has conducted research on roadside protest camps of Guarani land activists and their confrontations with agribusiness plantation owners. She analyzes the emergence of protests with rural economic development—specifically deforestation, mass displacement of people, and the casualization of labor.

SARAH LEBARON VON BAEYER is a lecturer of anthropology at Tufts University and an applied anthropologist. Previously she was a lecturer at Yale University and the University of Heidelberg. Her research focuses on transnational migration, race and ethnicity, and diaspora. Her book *Living Transnationally between Japan and Brazil: Routes beyond Roots* was published by Rowman & Littlefield in 2020.

INDEX

Page numbers followed by *f* and *t* indicate figures and tables, respectively.

abandonment, economy of, 130, 131–134
Abe, Shinzō, 173
abject performances, 207, 210, 212, 214
abstentions in voting, 156
affect, 6–8, 15, 93–94, 184, 208, 210
affirmative action, 63, 67
agroforestry, 135, 137–138, 139
Aguião, Sylvia, 194n11
Ahmed, Sara, 211
Allison, Anne, 7, 144
Alvarado, Leticia, 207
Alvarez, Sonia E., 229
Amazon region, 16, 129–141
Amnesty Law (1979), 8
Amoêdo, João, 176
Amparo Alves, Jaime, 70
Anderson, Perry, 44, 194n2
Ansell, Aaron, 84, 104–105
anticorruption politics/discourse, 71, 79–90. *See also* corruption/corruption investigations
Anti-Crime Packages, 122
antifeminism, 221–222
anti-intellectualism, 99
Anti-Terrorism Law, 122
apathy, 155–168
Appadurai, Arjun, 51, 119
Articulação Brasileira de Lésbicas, 186
artivismo (artivism), 18, 206, 207–208, 210, 211
aspirational consumption, 43–44
aspirational whiteness, 66, 70–72
assentamentos, 129–131
Associação de Mulheres Felipa de Souza and Complexo G, 186
As 3 Uiaras de SP City (The Three Sirens of São Paulo City), 209–210
Auxílio Gás, 180n10

backlands (*sertão*), 103–115, 106*f*
Bahia, 103–115
Bahian Military Police (PMBA), 103
bailes de favela, 186
Bannon, Steve, 100
Barbie Bolsominion memes, 221
"Barbie e Ken Cidadãos de Bem" (Barbie and Ken Good Citizens), 218–231, 220*f*, 223*f*, 225*f*
Barbie Facista (Fascist Barbie) memes, 221
BBB (Bullets, Bulls, and Bibles), 92, 195

BDM (Bonde dos Malucos), 112
Beleboni, Viviany, 214
Beliso-De Jesús, Aisha, 187, 189, 191
Belle Époque era, 188–189
Bento, Maria Aparecida Silva, 64
Berlant, Lauren, 79
Bicha Preta, 186
Biondi, Karina, 95
biopolitics, 197
"Black Feminist Statement, A" (Combahee River Collective), 192
Black LGBT movement, 18, 183–194
"BlasFêmea/Mulher" (BlasFemme/Woman), 212
BNDES (Brazilian Development Bank), 173
Boeing, 87
Bolsa Alimentação, 180n10
Bolsa Escola, 180n10
Bolsa Família, 16, 54, 63, 67, 106–107, 108, 160, 173, 174
bolsonarismo, 63–64
Bolsonaro, Jair: alternative music scene and, 142; Bahia and, 105; Barbie and Ken memes and, 218–231; calls from to dissolve Congress and Supreme Court, 8–9; cruel pessimism and, 85–86; election of, 3, 4, 13, 26, 48, 62, 82; extrajudicial killings and, 184; firearms and, 14, 50, 55–57, 59, 60; first year of administration of, 2; Japanese Brazilians and, 17–18, 169–180, 172*t*; LGBT community and, 19, 183, 186, 195–196, 198–203, 222; Mato Grosso and, 129, 134; memes and, 218–219; meritocracy and, 223; Ministry of Culture and, 146; Morro da Cruz and, 53–55; Northeast and, 38; Pereira family and, 29–32; politics of disgust and, 207, 208–209, 215; press and, 122; prisoners and, 93; religious conversion of, 92; "revolution" and, 99–100; right-wing populism and, 4–5, 14; Rio de Janeiro and, 81; support for, 20, 138–139, 165, 165*f*, 219
Bonde dos Malucos (BDM), 112
Bonilla, Yarimar, 226, 227
Borges, Micheline, 67–68
Braga, Ruy, 64
branquitude (whiteness), 15, 62–75, 222
Brazilian Communist Party (Partido Comunista Brasileiro; PCB), 39–40
Brazilian Democratic Movement Party (Partido do Movimento Democrático Brasileiro; PMDB), 4, 39–40, 131
Brazilian Development Bank (BNDES), 173

239

Brazilian Institute of Transmasculinities (IBRAT), 211
Brazilian Social Democracy Party (PSDB), 22n3, 156, 169–170
Brazilian Socialist Party (PSB), 154n10
Brexit, 5, 82
Brigeiro, Mauro, 197
Brown, Wendy, 59
Bullets, Bulls, and Bibles (BBB), 92, 195

Cabral, Sérgio, 184
Caixa Econômica Federal, 168n1
Campari, 108f
Campbell, Colin, 51
Campos, Eduardo, 145, 154n10
Cantero, Lucia, 7, 104
Carandiru Massacre, 94
Cardoso, Fernando Henrique, 3, 38, 42, 108, 180n10
Cardoso, Leônidas, 118
Carneiro, Sueli, 67, 94
car ownership, 44–45, 57
Carvalho, Olavo de, 100
casa grande (master's home), 15
Castro Rea, Julián, 174
Catarse, 150
categorical imperative, 104–105
Catholic Church, 95
"C class," 45–48
Ceará, 14, 38–49
Certeau, Michel de, 188
Cesarino, Letícia, 93
Chow, Rey, 12n6
Citizen Constitution, 13, 47
civil society agenda, 229
CleanGovBiz, 122
CNP (National Council on Petroleum), 118
Collins, John F., 93, 188
Comaroff, Jean, 166
Comaroff, John, 121, 166
Combahee River Collective, 183, 192
communism, aversion to, 174–175
conservative nostalgia, 2–3, 8
consumerism, inclusionary market, 14
contact zone of visibility, 211–213
Contreiras, Luz, 118
corruption/corruption investigations, 3–4, 84–87, 120–122, 173. *See also* anticorruption politics/discourse
Costa, Dia Da, 79
Costa Vargas, João, 114
COVID-19, 1, 10, 139–140
Cowan, Benjamin, 209
credit, availability of, 180n11
crisis competence hypothesis, 202
crowdfunding, 149–150
cruel optimism, 79
cruel pessimism, 79–90, 167

Cuadros, Alex, 85, 86, 87
Cultural Corridor, 188–189
cultural policies, federal, 145–146
Cunha, Neon, 210–211

Dallagnol, Deltan, 3, 122
da Quebrada, Linn, 212, 213, 215
Darke, Sacha, 94
da Silva, Suzane, 68, 69f, 72
Day of Transgender Visibility, 211
death penalty, 92
Debert, Guita Grin, 197
de Carvalho, Olavo, 34, 100
de Carvalho, Renata, 214
DEM (Democrats Party), 131
Democratic Labor Party (PDL), 219
Democrats party (DEM), 131
Derrida, Jacques, 114
de Sousa, Felipa, 190–191
despairing hope, 129–141
developmental nationalism, 118, 123
Dezem, Rogério, 179n2
"Diaba" (Female Devil), 212–213
Dias, Camila Caldeira Nunes, 95
Dignidade Médica, 68
disgust, politics/discourse of, 207, 208–209, 215, 222
distrust, 163
domestic workers, 67, 221
dos Santos, Dandara, 210
drug trafficking, 52, 53, 112
Duarte, Regina, 62–63

economic inequality, 2
economy of abandonment, 130, 131–134
education, 14, 63, 67
elders, LGBTTI, 195–205
electrification efforts, 132–133
#elenao (#nothim), 218, 222
#elenunca (#neverhim), 218
Embraer, 86–87
emotional habitus, 207
employment brokerage firms, 170
Engelmann, Fabiano, 122–123
entrepreneurialism, 145–146, 151
entrepreneurial monetarism, 99
eroticization of old age, 197
Eternamente Sou, 196, 197–198, 202–203
Evangelical Christian movement: expansion of, 186; growth of, 20; Japanese Brazilians and, 172–173; among poor, 159; prisoners/crime and, 92, 92f, 93–94, 95–100; Rousseff impeachment and, 208. *See also* religious right

family, notion of, 14, 25–37
Faoro, Raymundo, 85, 86, 87
favelas, 129, 130–131

fear, strategic mobilization of, 70–71, 72
Federal Cultural Incentive Law, 145
Felipa de Sousa Women's Group (Grupo de Mulheres Felipa de Sousa), 190–191
Feltran, Gabriel de Santis, 95, 99
feminist activism: Barbie memes and, 221–222; progress of, 221
festas negras, 186
firearms, 14, 50–61
First Command of the Capital (Primeiro Comando da Capital; PCC), 15, 91–102, 103, 112
First Conference on LGBTTI Churches and Communities, 213–214
Flauzina, Ana, 63–64
Fonseca, Claudia, 52
Foreign Corrupt Practices Act (United States), 123
Foucault, Michel, 104
Franco, Marielle: assassination of, 4, 18, 62, 183, 184, 187, 195; dedication of play to, 210
Fraser, Nancy, 59
Frazer, Demita, 192
free pass movement, 120
Freyre, Gilberto, 68
fundamentalism, religious, 64

"gay kit" educational material, 33, 195, 208, 209
"gender ideology," 208–209
gender-nonconformity. *See* LGBT community
generational differences, in Northeast, 38–49
Gershon, Ilana, 149
Girard, René, 12n6
global economic crisis (2007–2008), 3
Globo, 176
Goldstein, Donna M., 50
Gomes, Ciro, 38, 42, 219
Gonçalves, Ana Maria, 67–68
"Gospel according to Jesus, Queen of Heaven, The," 214
Gould, Deborah, 207
Graham, Stephen, 58
gray pride (*orgulho grisalho*), 197
Greenwald, Glenn, 122
Gregg, Melissa, 94
Growth Acceleration Program (PAC), 155
Grupo de Mulheres Felipa de Sousa (Felipa de Sousa Women's Group), 190–191
Guzmão, Dayana, 186

Haddad, Fernando: campaign of, 2; desire for change and, 176; "gay kit" educational material and, 195, 209; nickname for, 174; in Northeast, 38; run-off election and, 26, 81–82; support for, 30, 219; voting results for, 165, 165f
haken gaisha system, 170
Hall, Kira, 50
Halliburton, 123

Han, Clara, 143
Hanley, Eric, 176
hashtag activism, 218, 222
Haussmann, Georges-Eugène, 188
health councils, local, 47
hedonism, imaginative, 51
Helena (owner of smallholding), 129–134, 138–139
Herzfeld, Michael, 105
Hilton, Erika, 210, 215
Hirata, Daniel Veloso, 95
HIV, 198, 202
Hochschild, Arlie, 174
holding on/staying upright (*segurar*), 183–194
Holston, James, 45
Homeless Workers' Movement (MTST), 71
home ownership, 45, 155–168
homicide rates, 70, 94–95, 99, 215
homophobia, 208, 222
homosexuality, 28, 32, 33, 34, 64. *See also* LGBT community
hopeful despair, 129–141
hybrid war, 99

IBRAT (Brazilian Institute of Transmasculinities), 211
ignorance, 68
Ikeuchi, Suma, 172
imaginative hedonism, 51
IMF (International Monetary Fund), 42
inclusionary market consumerism, 14
Ingram, Matthew Bruce, 50
injured whiteness, 66–68, 72, 222
Instituto Ouro Verde (IOV), 130, 135–136, 137, 139
Inter-American Convention against Corruption, 122
Intercept Brazil, 89n3
interlocking oppressions, 183
"internal enemy," fear of, 70–71
International Monetary Fund (IMF), 42
intersectionality, 183–194, 215
IOV (Instituto Ouro Verde), 130, 135–136, 137, 139

Japanese Brazilians, 17–18, 169–180, 171f, 172t
Jarrín, Alvaro, 222
jeitinho, 121–122
Jerome, Jessica, 115n1
Johnson, Marsha P., 210
Junge, Benjamin, 104, 153n5
juridico-extraction, 121

Kalil, Isabela, 51
Kalouv, 142, 148, 150
Kant, Immanuel, 104–105
Katiara, 112
Keeling, Kara, 191
Klein, Charles H., 153n5
Kopper, Moises, 83

Kubischek, Juscelino, 107
Kunreuther, Laura, 218–219

Landless Rural Workers' Movement (MST), 71
lavagem, 109
Lava Jato (Operation Car Wash), 3, 79, 82, 83, 86, 89n3, 117, 120, 122, 174
Law 2004, 118
Law of Fiscal Responsibility, 122
Leão, Danuza, 66
Leirner, Piero, 99
Letter to Getúlio (Lobato), 118
LGBT community: Barbie and Ken memes and, 227–228; Black LGBTI+ feminist movement, 183–194; Bolsonaro and, 222; elders, 195–205; trans and travesti activisim, 206–217. *See also* homosexuality
LGBT gerontology, 197
Light for Everyone (LpT; Luz para Todos), 132–133, 134
Living Transnationally between Japan and Brazil: Routes beyond Roots (von Baeyer), 171
Lobato, Monteiro, 16, 62–63, 118
Lopes, Hélio, 179n3
LpT (Light for Everyone; Luz para Todos), 132–133, 134
Lula da Silva, Luiz Inácio: arrest of, 15, 26; Bahia and, 106; cultural policies and, 145; economy and, 3; imprisonment of, 2, 4, 62, 184; Japanese Brazilians and, 173, 175; Marilda on, 81; new middle class and, 79; Northeast and, 38, 42; Petrobras and, 116–117, 121; the poor and, 41; poverty reduction and, 1, 44; whiteness and, 71
Luz para Todos (Light for Everyone; LpT), 132–133, 134

"Madam/Lady History" (Senhora Pasado), 191
Maduro, Nicolás, 174
Magalhães, Juraci, 39–40
Mais Médicos (More Doctors), 67–68
Malafaia, Silas, 92–93
Malícia Champion, 149
mangue beat, 145
Manso, Bruno Paes, 94
Marasco, Robyn, 130
Marcha para Maconha (March for Marijuana), 186
Marques, Vagner Aparecido, 95
masculinity, firearms and, 50–61
mass communication, affect and, 7–8
Massumi, Brian, 7, 121
material hope, 155–168
Mazzarella, William, 6, 100
media: LGBT community and, 190; overseas voters and, 176. *See also* social media
medicine and medical care, 103–104
MEI (Microempreendedor Individual; Individual Microentrepreneur), 143, 144, 146

Mello, Fernando Collor de, 121
memes, 218–231
Menuzzi, Eduardo de Moura, 122–123
meritocracy, 223–226
mestiçagem, 72, 73
Microempreendedor Individual (MEI; Individual Microentrepreneur), 143, 144, 146
middle class: alternative music scene and, 142–154; emerging, 43–45; new, 15, 79–90
militarization of city life, 57–58
Minha Casa Minha Vida (My House, My Life), 17, 86, 155, 158, 166, 167
Ministerio Público Federal (MPF), 122–123
Ministry of Culture, 146
Miranda, Maria, 118
Miskolci, Richard, 65
misogyny, 64
Mitchell, Sean, 72, 114, 130, 153n5, 167
More Doctors (Mais Médicos), 67–68
Moreno Figueroa, Monica, 72
Moro, Sérgio, 3, 4, 79, 89n3, 121–122, 123, 174
mourning period, 96
Moving Politics (Gould), 207
MPF (Ministerio Público Federal), 122–123
MST (Landless Rural Workers' Movement), 71
MTST (Homeless Workers' Movement), 71
Mulheres Felipa de Souza, 189
multiculturalism, 145
music scene, 16–17, 142–154
mutt complex (*complexo da vira lata*), 89n15
My House, My Life (Minha Casa Minha Vida), 17, 86, 155, 158, 166, 167

Nathalia (owner of smallholding), 135–138, 136f, 138f
National Congress in Brasília, 18, 195, 203
National Council on Petroleum (CNP), 118
National Program for Strengthening Family Agriculture (Programa Nacional de Fortalecimento da Agricultura Familiar; PRONAF), 132, 133–134
National Program for the Dissemination of International Legal Cooperation, 122
National Program for the Strengthening of Family Farming (PRONAF), 16
National Truth Commission, 8
Needell, Jeffrey, 189
negative hope, 157, 160, 167
negritude, 185–186
neo-Pentecostalism, 64, 71
Neves, Aécio, 3, 169–170
"new economy," 144
new middle class, 15, 79–90
New Party (Partido Novo), 176
Ngai, Sianne, 208
nostalgia, conservative, 2–3, 8
Novo Horizonte, 129, 130, 131–134

Nunes, Raul, 57
Nunes Arruda, Inácio, 39–40

Odebrecht, Marcelo, 121, 123
O'Dougherty, Maureen, 143–144
OECD (Organisation for Economic Co-operation and Development), 122
Oil Industry Workers Union (SindPetro), 119
Oil Is Ours, The (Miranda), 118
"Oil Is Ours, The" campaign, 117–120
Olival, Alexandre de Azevedo, 83
Oliveira Lima, Roberto Leonel de, 121
Olivieri, Cristiane Garcia, 154n8
Operation Car Wash (Lava Jato), 3, 79, 82, 83, 86, 89n3, 117, 120, 122, 174
"O Pré-sal é Nosso," 119
"O Que Eles Levam No Peito" (What They Carry on Their Chests) exhibit, 190–191
Organisation for Economic Co-operation and Development (OECD), 122
orgulho grisalho (gray pride), 197
Oyama, Thaís, 179n3

PAC (Growth Acceleration Program), 155
Paes, Eduardo, 1
Partido Comunista Brasileiro (PCB; Brazilian Communist Party), 39–40
Partido do Movimento Democrático Brasileiro (PMDB; Brazilian Democratic Movement Party; Party of the Brazilian Democratic Movement), 4, 39–40, 131
Partido do Movimento Democrático Brasileiro (PMDB; Party of the Brazilian Democratic Movement), 4
Partido dos Trabalhadores (PT; Workers' Party). *See* PT (Partido dos Trabalhadores; Workers' Party)
Partido Novo (New Party), 176
Party of the Brazilian Democratic Movement (Partido do Movimento Democrático Brasileiro; PMDB), 4
Pasieka, Agnieska, 176–177
patron-client structures, 104–105, 111, 113, 115, 130
Paula, Ana, 1
PCB (Partido Comunista Brasileiro; Brazilian Communist Party), 39–40
PCC (Primeiro Comando da Capital; First Command of the Capital), 15, 91–102, 103, 112
PDL (Democratic Labor Party), 219
Pedro Malasartes, 103–104, 109–111, 110f, 112–114
Pereira family, 13–14, 25–37, 27f
Pereira Passos, Francisco, 188
Petrobras, 8, 16, 38, 86, 116–125, 173
petrolao corruption scandal, 120–121
pharmakon, 114
Piaia, Victor, 57
Piketty, Thomas, 84
Pinheiro-Machado, Rosana, 51, 53, 64, 70
Pinho, Patricia de Santana, 222
"pink tide," 4
pistoleiros, 112, 113
Piza, Edith, 64
Plano Real, 42, 107
Plea Bargaining Law, 122
PMBA (Bahian Military Police), 103
PMDB (Partido do Movimento Democrático Brasileiro; Brazilian Democratic Movement Party), 4, 39–40, 131
police militarism, 99
political memes, 19, 218–231
politics of aesthetics, 185, 190
Population Crisis Committee, 145
populism: description of, 5; right-wing, 4–6
Porto Alegre, 14, 17, 50, 51–55, 59, 104
Povinelli, Elizabeth, 130, 132, 190
precarity, 142–154, 222
Pré-Sal Petróleo S.A., 125n3
Primeiro Comando da Capital (First Command of the Capital; PCC), 15, 91–102, 103, 112
prisons, 91
private democracies, 163–166
Programa Nacional de Fortalecimento da Agricultura Familiar (National Program for Strengthening Family Agriculture; PRONAF), 132, 133–134
Project Lapa Legal, 189
PRONAF (Programa Nacional de Fortalecimento da Agricultura Familiar; National Program for Strengthening Family Agriculture), 16, 132, 133–134
prosperity theology, 71
protection of family, 58–59
protests (2013), 2, 3, 83, 120
PROUNI (Programa Universidade Para Todos), 68
PSB (Brazilian Socialist Party), 154n10
PSDB (Brazilian Social Democracy Party), 22n3, 156, 169–170
PSL (Social Liberal Party), 18, 156, 170, 174
PT (Partido dos Trabalhadores; Workers' Party): affect and, 7; in Bahia, 105; Barbie memes and, 224–226, 224f, 225f; corruption investigations and, 8; fall in credibility and popularity of, 3–4, 16, 138–139; generational differences with regard to, 14; Japanese Brazilians and, 169, 173–176; LGBT community and, 185; Minha Casa Minha Vida (My House, My Life) and, 17, 155–156; multiculturalism and, 145; Northeast and, 38–39, 46–48; Petrobras and, 116, 117, 121; poverty reduction and, 1, 2; presidential election and, 26; rural development programs and, 129–134

Quotas Law, 67

racial democracy, 227
racial historical matrix, 187, 189

racism: political memes and, 220–223, 220f, 223f; whiteness and, 62–75
Rádio Frei Caneca, 154n13
Rancière, Jacques, 185, 190
rationalities, 104–105, 112–113, 114
reactionary wave, 62–75
Recife: generational tensions and, 25–37; music scene in, 142–154
reciprocity/economic exchanges, 109
Rede Globo, 3, 8
Rede Nacional de Feministas Anti-Prohibicionistas (RENFA; National Feminist Network against the War on Drugs), 186
Red Label, 108f
religious affects, effects of, 91–102
religious fundamentalism, 64
religious right, 206–207, 213–214. See also Evangelical Christian movement
RENFA (Rede Nacional de Feministas Anti-Prohibicionistas; National Feminist Network against the War on Drugs), 186
Residencial Bento Gonçalves, 155–168, 156f, 164f
revenge killings, 112
Riacho Seco, 16, 103, 106–109, 111–115
Ribeiro Corossacz, Valeria, 63
right-wing populism, spread of, 4–6
Rivera, Sylvia, 210
Rojas, David, 83
Rosa, Jonathan, 226, 227
Roth-Gordon, Jenifer, 70
Rousseff, Dilma: BBB and, 92; da Silva and, 68, 69f; economy and, 1; "gay kit" educational material and, 208; impeachment of, 4, 6, 8, 15, 117, 120, 162, 184, 195; Japanese Brazilians and, 173; LGBT community and, 186; Marilda on, 81; Minha Casa Minha Vida (My House, My Life) and, 158; National Truth Commission and, 8; new middle class and, 79; ouster of, 62; Petrobras and, 16, 38; protests against, 46; reelection of, 3; support for, 53, 83, 165
rural development programs, 129–134

Safatle, Vladimir, 129–130
safety, perceptions of, 163
same-sex marriage, 203
Samet, Robert, 12n3
Santa Catarina, 19–20
Santo André prison, 92f
Santos, Hélio, 63
São Paulo, firearms and, 50, 51, 55–60
São Paulo Pride Parade, 214
Satellite Launch Center, 90n20
Sayan-Cengiz, Feida, 59
Scalco, Lucia Mury, 51, 53, 64, 70
Scharff, Christina, 148
Second Annual Trans March, 207

Sedgwick, Eve, 68
Seeds of the Portal, 135, 137
segurar (holding on/staying upright), 18, 183–194
Seigworth, Gregory J., 94
Seixas, Michele, 186
self-making practices/habitus, 187, 189
senzala (slave quarters), 15
Serra, José, 169–170
sertão (backlands), 103–115, 106f
sexism, 64
Shifman, Limor, 218, 229
Shock of Order, 189
SIC (System of Cultural Incentives), 146
Silveira, Valdir João, 96
SindPetro (Oil Industry Workers Union), 119
Singer, André, 41, 43
Sixth-Floor Collective, 148–149
Size Switch, The (Lobato), 125n4
slavery: abolition of, 19–20, 21f; whiteness and, 65, 68
Smith, Barbara, 192
Smith, Beverly, 192
Smith, Christen A., 194n15
Smith, David Norman, 176
Social Liberal Party (PSL), 18, 156, 170, 174
social media: memes and, 218–231; presidential election and, 25–37
socioeconomic mobility: injured whiteness and, 66; in Northeast, 38–49; Pereira family and, 27–28
Solano Gallego, Esther, 68
Souza, Jessé, 8, 86
Sovik, Liv, 64
Spektor, Matias, 175
Spexoto Olival, Andrezza Alves, 83
spiritual copresences, 187–188, 189
Stalcup, Meg, 99, 100, 230
street activism, 228–230
subproletariat, 39–42
SUDENE (Superintendency for the Development of the Northeast), 107
Summer Olympics (2016), 1, 131, 184
Superintendency for the Development of the Northeast (SUDENE), 107
SUVs, 57–58
System of Cultural Incentives (SIC), 146

Takaki, Raul, 169
Taylor, Keeanga-Yahmatta, 192, 194n2
Tea Party, 174
Tekin, Caner, 59
Temer, Michel, 3, 4, 117
Terrena, Ave, 210
trans and travesti activisim, 18, 206–217. See also LGBT community
Transclandestina 3020, 18, 206, 207
transfemicide, 19

Trans March, 212
transnational labor migration, 169–180
Transparency International, 121, 122
Transparency Law, 122
transphobia, 208, 213
Trap Door (Gossett, Stanley, and Burton), 211
Treze de Maio, Santa Catarina, 19–20, 21*f*
Trump, Donald, 5, 34, 50, 57, 82, 176
Tubman, Harriet, 192

UN Convention against Corruption in International Commercial Transaction, 122
União Nacional dos Estudantes (UNE; National Student Union), 229
United States: corruption investigations and, 3; Foreign Corrupt Practices Act of, 123; Lava Jato (Operation Car Wash) and, 83
Urias, 212–213
Ustra, Carlos Alberto Brilhante, 186, 225*f*, 226, 231n8

vagabundos, 53, 54, 55, 57, 59–60
Vale, 118–119
Vargas, Getúlio, 16, 117–118
veridiction, regime of, 99
vida bandida, 51, 52, 59

visceral politics, 207–208
visibility, contact zone of, 211–213
Vittar, Pabllo, 209
Viveiros de Castro, Eduardo, 183

"weapon play," 56
Weber, Max, 104
What They Carry on Their Chests ("O Que Eles Levam No Peito") exhibit, 190–191
whiteness (*branquitude*), 15, 62–75, 222
Wilson Richetti, José, 209
Witzell, Wilson, 183
women: bolsonarismo and, 64; firearms and, 58–59. *See also* feminist activism
Workers' Party (Partido dos Trabalhadores; PT). *See* PT (Partido dos Trabalhadores; Workers' Party)
worker-versus-bandit dichotomy, 70
working-class politicization, 104
World Bank, 122
World Cup (2014), 1, 83, 131
Wyllys, Jean, 64, 195

XV National LGBT Workshop, 18, 195

Zaluar, Alba, 52